Asset Securitization

Asset Securitization

International Financial and Legal Perspectives

Edited by
Joseph Jude Norton and Paul R. Spellman

BLACKWELL
Finance

Centre For Commercial Law Studies
Queen Mary and Westfield College
University of London

Copyright © Basil Blackwell Limited 1991

First published 1991

Basil Blackwell Ltd
108 Cowley Road, Oxford, OX4 1JF, UK

Basil Blackwell, Inc.
3 Cambridge Center
Cambridge, Massachusetts 02142, USA

British Library Cataloguing in Publication Data

A CIP catalogue record for this book is available from the British Library.

Library of Congress Cataloging in Publication Data

Asset securitization : international financial and legal perspectives
    edited by Joseph Norton and Paul Spellman.
      p.   cm.
    ISBN 0–631–17808–2 :
    1. Asset-backed financing—Law and legislation—United States.
  2. Asset-backed financing—United States. 3. Asset-backed
financing—Law and legislation—Great Britain. 4. Asset-backed
financing—Great Britain. I. Norton, Joseph Jude. II. Spellman,
Paul.
  K1331.A77 1991
  346'.0666—dc20
  [342.6666]
  90–44928 CIP

Typeset in 11 on 13 pt Plantin
by Wyvern Typesetting Ltd, Bristol.
Printed in Great Britain by TJ Press Ltd., Padstow, Cornwall.

Contents

The Editors and Contributors

The Editors

Professor Joseph J. Norton, Cameron Markby Hewitt Professorial Fellow in Banking Law, Centre for Commercial Law Studies (London); Professor of Banking Law, SMU School of Law (Dallas); of Counsel, Winstead Sechcrest & Minick, PC, Dallas and London.

Paul R. Spellman, Partner and Head of Asset Securitization Practice Group, Haynes and Boone, Dallas.

Other Contributors (Alphabetical)

David Barbour, Director and Head of Business Section, Winstead Sechcrest & Minick, PC, Dallas, Texas.

Rupert Beaumont, Partner, Slaughter & May, London.

Andrew A. Bernstein, Associate, Cleary, Gottlieb, Steen & Hamilton, New York City.

David C. Bonsall, Partner, Freshfields, London.

Robert Bordeaux-Groult, Partner, Cleary, Gottlieb, Steen & Hamilton, New York City.

Walid A. Chammah, Managing Director of The First Boston Corporation, New York City.

Mitchell S. Dupler, Partner, Cleary, Gottlieb, Steen & Hamilton, Washington, DC.

Stephen M. Edge, Tax Partner, Slaughter & May, London.

Professor Edward P. M. Gardener, Director, Institute of European Finance, University College of North Wales, Bangor, Wales.

Michael Murphy, Tax Solicitor, Slaughter & May, London.

David Z. Nirenberg, Associate, Cleary, Gottlieb, Steen & Hamilton, New York City.

Barbara A. Nunemaker, Senior Vice President, Standard & Poor's Debt Rating Group, London.

Robert Palache, Partner, Clifford-Chance, London.

Steve Parkinson, Partner, Investment Banking Support Group, Ernst & Young, London.

James M. Peaslee, Partner, Cleary, Gottlieb, Steen & Hamilton, New York City.

Graham Penn, Partner, Cameron Markby Hewitt, London.

Andrew C. Quale Jr, Partner, Sidley & Austin, New York City.

David G. Sabel, Partner, Cleary, Gottlieb, Steen & Hamilton, New York City.

Steven L. Schwarcz, Partner, Kaye, Scholer, Frierman, Hays & Handler, New York City, and Adjunct Professor of Law, Benjamin N. Cardozo School of Law, New York.

Gregory M. Shaw, Partner, Cravath Swaine & Moore, New York City.

Andrew Wilson, Corporate Finance, Goldman Sachs & Co., London.

Editors' Preface

This volume on international dimensions of asset securitization is the first publication in a collection on international banking and finance established by the Centre for Commercial Law Studies at Queen Mary and Westfield College, University of London, in cooperation with Basil Blackwell publishers.

This volume is concerned with securitization, and its broad implications in the international financial world. In a simplistic sense, securitization is the repackaging of cash flows into securities, finding its genesis in the early repackaging of mortgages in the United States and in various domestic and international loan participation arrangements. However, more significantly, asset securitization, both in terms of monetary volume and diversity and sophistication of techniques, has become an increasingly important financial technique and risk diversifier for financial institutions.

Growing in usage in the United States in the mid-1980s, asset securitization has now found its way into the United Kingdom and French financial markets and is entering other European markets.

This volume addresses various financial and legal considerations involved with asset securitization in the United States and United Kingdom. The volume also addresses broader international matters such as the new French securitization law, the future of securitization in the European Community as a result of 1992, and the use of securitization techniques in the repackaging of Third World debt. Also, speculation is made by a group of experts concerning the transplantation of US techniques to UK and other European markets.

The editors believe that this volume should be of unique value to all major financial institutions, corporations and accounting firms in the United States, the United Kingdom and other European countries. Because securitization was first developed in the US, European offerings have incorporated many techniques used in the US. US structures are expected to continue to provide a preview (albeit an imprecise preview in light of the different legal, accounting, tax and regulatory regimes) of non-US structures. From the US perspective, the globalization of offerings of securities backed by both US and non-US assets requires an understanding of European markets and the structural differences among the various asset-backed securities traded in such markets.

In putting together this volume, the editors have been privileged to have worked in conjunction with the Centre for Commercial Law Studies at Queen Mary and Westfield College, University of London. Under the auspices of the Centre and its Director and Dean of the College's Law Faculty, Ross Cranston, the editors have been able to assemble written analyses and views of many of the leading world experts on asset securitization.

In addition to expressing their sincere thanks to the Centre and to Dean Cranston, the editors also express thanks to the cooperating institution of the SMU School of Law and its Dean, C. Paul Rogers III. Further, a special thanks is made to the Dallas law firms of Haynes and Boone and Winstead Sechcrest and Minick, PC, which have provided invaluable support for the production of this volume. In particular, the editors wish to thank Cynthia Freeman and Denise George at the Haynes and Boone law firm for their tireless efforts towards completing this manuscript.

Special thanks are expressed to Tim Goodfellow of Basil Blackwell publishers for his work in commissioning this project.

The editors also extend their appreciation to the *Cardozo Law Review* for permitting use of excerpts from Mr Schwarcz's recent article in that journal and to the *International Lawyer* for portions of Messrs Barbour, Norton and Penn's article.

The Centre for Commercial Law Studies hopes that this is the first of a number of quality publications in the area of international banking and finance.

Joseph J. Norton and Paul R. Spellman
Dallas, Texas

Publisher's Style Note

The publisher's preferred spelling style is the Oxford style. Accordingly, with respect to words that can be spelled with either an 's' or a 'z', such as 'securitization', the preferred spelling for this volume is with the 'z'. The publisher and editors recognize that, in the investment and legal fields in the UK, the 's' version may be more commonly used.

Also, as some authors are American and some English, particular authors for particular chapters have been given the option to utilize standard English citation format or Harvard 'Blue Book' style of citations.

The editors and publisher would like to point out that the use of the masculine pronoun 'he' is not gender specific.

Acknowledgements

The editors wish to express their especial thanks to the following individuals who were instrumental in the formation and execution of the original Centre project from which this book is derived: Dean Ross Cranston, Director of the Centre for Commercial Law Studies (London); Richard Farrant, Senior Manager, Bank of England; Brian Quinn, Executive Director, Bank of England; William A. Ryback, Associate Director, Federal Reserve Board of Governors.

1

An Overview of Securitization

WALID A. CHAMMAH

Although much of this chapter is generally applicable, it is presented from the US perspective and experience.

1.1 Introduction: What Is Securitization?

Securitization, in its most basic form, is the repackaging of asset cash flows into securities. In the typical US asset-backed securities (ABS) transaction, the originator continues to service the sold assets and receives a fee for doing so. Either through subordination of additional assets, future cash flows or direct recourse, the originator is made to bear the first losses on the sold assets. The yield to investors – the 'pass-through rate' – is set at a market level appropriate to the characteristics and the quality of the asset pool.

Asset-backed securities rely on structure and collateral to achieve creditworthiness and therefore marketability. In the US, an ABS utilizes a 'bullet-proof' or 'bankruptcy-proof' structure which effectively insulates it from any misfortunes of the selling company. In addition, the credit risk of a single obligor (for example, the issuing company of a conventional debt issue) is greatly reduced through the diversification provided by the large pool of assets typical of most ABSs.

The ABS issuer, most often in the US a grantor trust or special-purpose company, offers ABSs to investors through an underwritten public offering or a private placement. The asset cash flows are remitted to the trustee, which pays scheduled interest and principal payments to the investors. In the typical ABS transaction, any prepayments on the assets are also paid by the trustee to investors. The aggregate cash flow from the assets is always equal to or greater than the required payments on the ABSs. The difference, if any, is usually paid to the selling company as compensation for its role as servicer. (A portion may also be used for credit enhancement, including payment of any fees or funding required for a reserve account.)

1.2 What Can Be Securitized?

1.2.1 *Cash Flow*

The cash flow of the assets fundamentally determines the structure of an ABS. The most readily securitizable assets are those which display the following characteristics:

- predictable cash flows;

- consistently low delinquency and default experience;
- total amortization of principal at maturity;
- many demographically and geographically diverse obligors; and
- underlying collateral with high liquidation value and utility to the obligors.

1.2.2 Structure

There are different types of ABSs, each utilizing a slightly different structure:

- *Asset-backed certificates* are pass-through certificates issued by a trust representing undivided fractional interests in a pool of receivables such as automobile loans or credit-card receivables. Except for any recourse provision, the assets are sold outright by the selling company to the trust.
- *Asset-backed obligations (ABOs)* are debt securities of a special-purpose corporation, owned either by the selling company or by unaffiliated third parties, and collateralized by a pool of financial assets. They are similar to collateralized mortgage obligations (CMOs) because they often utilize multiple tranches, but, unlike CMOs, they may issue either pay-through or fixed pay securities (that is, prepayment risk is eliminated for investors).
- *Asset-backed preferred stock* is issued by a special-purpose, bankruptcy-proof subsidiary which purchases assets such as trade and consumer receivables or intercompany notes from its parent or affiliates. The assets are often supported by a direct-pay letter of credit or surety bond in favour of the subsidiary issued by a AAA-rated commercial bank with the result that the subsidiary's preferred stock issue is able to obtain the highest credit ratings.
- *Asset-backed commercial paper* involves the sale of financial assets to a special-purpose corporation which, in turn, issues commercial paper. Proceeds from the issuance of the commercial paper finance the purchase of the assets. The commercial paper is supported by the cash flow from the assets, the issuance of new collateralized commercial paper or from borrowings under a liquidity facility.

1.2.3 Credit Enhancement

In order to raise further the quality of the pool of assets, it is usually necessary to add credit enhancement. This can come in different forms. Credit enhancement can be divided into two main types: external (third-party or seller's guarantee) or internal (structural or cash-flow-driven).

- *Pool insurance*: Insurance is provided on 100 per cent of the losses on the pool of assets. The issuer of the insurance looks to an initial premium or other support to cover credit losses.
- *Recourse to seller*: In the US, available only to non-bank issuers, this method utilizes a limited guaranty of the seller covering a specified maximum amount of losses on the pool.
- *Letter of credit*: For issuers with credit ratings below the level sought for the ABS issued, a third party provides a letter of credit either with recourse to the seller for any draws (direct pay) or simply backstopping the issuer's recourse obligation (indirect pay).
- *Letter of credit with reserve fund*: The letter of credit is reimbursed from a reserve fund funded by the yield on the assets in excess of the coupon payable to investors plus a fixed servicing fee.
- *Senior/subordinate or A/B structure*: A second class of securities is created which is subordinated in payment of principal and interest to the senior class of securities. Because the subordinate class bears its proportionate share of losses, the amount of subordinate securities issued must be in percentage terms somewhat larger than the equivalent letter of credit or recourse obligation.
- *Structural credit enhancement*: Various features can be created within the structure to raise the credit quality of the securities issued. Credit-card securities typically contain various 'payout events' that cause early amortization if the credit quality of the assets or the performance of the servicer declines.

1.2.4 *Types of Collateral*

Asset securitization began with residential mortgages in the United States at the end of the 1970s. Mortgages were, and still remain, the ideal candidates for securitization. In addition to displaying the ideal cash-flow characteristics described above, many US mortgages have the added benefit of standardization by government agencies (Federal National Mortgage Association – FNMA; Government National Mortgage Association – GNMA; Federal Mortgage Assistance Corporation – FMAC; and Veterans Administration – VA). It was not

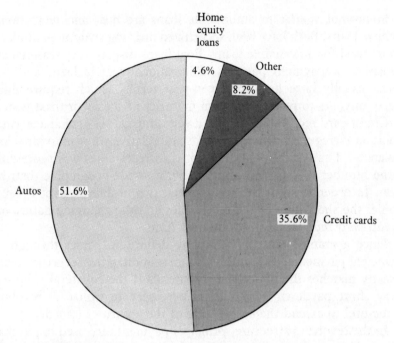

Figure 1.1 Total issuance by collateral, 1985–1989: $58.76 billion (as of 31 December 1989)

until March 1985 that non-mortgage collateral was securitized, with a $192 million offering of lease-backed notes for Sperry Lease Finance Corporation underwritten by First Boston. Since this first issue, the palette of assets securitized has been wide and varied. (See Figure 1.1.)

Automobile loans have represented the majority of the assets securitized. Automobile loans typically exhibit maturities of two to six years, with very stable prepayment patterns. The grantor trust, or 'pass-through' structure, was the first issuing vehicle used and remains the most popular form of automobile loan ABS. In the grantor trust, principal prepayments and regular principal collections are 'passed through' to the investor in their entirety. Interest on the assets is divided between the portion allocable to the investor and that allocable to the servicer and, if a reserve fund structure is used, the credit enhancement. Because they display similar characteristics to automobile loans, light and heavy truck instalment loans have been securitized utilizing structures identical to those used for automobile loans.

Somewhat similar to automobile loans are boat and recreational-vehicle loans. Both have been securitized utilizing structures similar to those used for automobile loans. Boat loans display very seasonal and sensitive prepayment patterns. Recreational-vehicle loans and boat loans usually have five- to fifteen-year terms, which require third-party buyouts to restrict the final maturity of the securitized pools.

Credit-card receivables display a very unusual set of characteristics: short and irregular paydown periods and relatively low individual loan balances. The typical pool of credit-card receivables will represent a large number of different obligors with a wide geographic distribution. In order to securitize such assets, two problems must be overcome: the short lives of the receivables and the changing nature of a credit-card receivables portfolio over time.

Since a grantor trust structure by definition 'passes through' all principal payments, the principal amortization of the securities issued exactly matches the underlying collateral. If the collateral exhibits a very short paydown period, it is necessary to utilize a 'revolving structure' to extend the average life of the securities issued.

In the revolving structure, principal payments are used to purchase new balances, effectively extending the life of the securities issued. At the end of a predetermined period, purchases cease and principal is paid to investors as received. This type of structure can be applied to securitize many types of receivables which display such short average lives such as trade receivables and personal credit lines.

Aggregate balance fluctuations during the life of the transaction are taken care of by the creation of two separate classes of securities. A larger, fixed portion is sold to investors while a smaller, floating portion is kept by the seller.

In order to diminish the impact of the constantly changing characteristics of a pool of credit-card receivables (account attrition, changes in credit profile of obligors), 'payout events' are added to the transaction. If any such events occur, typically a decline in the credit quality of the assets or default by the pool's servicer, the revolving period is terminated and principal amortization begins.

The revolving structure can be applied to securitize many types of receivables which display such short average lives such as trade receivables and personal credit lines.

Home equity loans display characteristics different from the first mortgages, automobile and credit-card loans that make up the bulk of the ABS market. Home equity loans are revolving, floating-rate loans secured by real estate. The structure most appropriate to home equity securitization will depend on the financial objectives of the issuer. Structures originally developed for first mortgages, such as real estate mortgage investment conduits (REMICs), have been utilized and structures similar to credit-cards securitization may make sense for some issuers as well. In most home equity transactions, the certificate rate is floating to eliminate spread risk. Generally, home equity loans have a fifteen-year final maturity with a four- to five-year average life based on expected prepayment rates.

1.3 Why Securitize?

1.3.1 *Sale for Generally Accepted Accounting Principles (GAAP)*

The most important objective of asset securitization is often to qualify as sales of assets. In the United States, such off-balance-sheet transactions fall under the provisions of Statement of Financial Accounting Standards (FAS) No. 77, 'Reporting by Transferors for Transfers of Receivables with Recourse', issued in December 1983. Under FAS No. 77, certain transactions that 'purport to be sales may be treated as such by the selling corporation, even if the seller offers recourse on the sold assets'.

1.3.2 *Sale for RAP*

Entities subject to US Regulatory Accounting Principles (RAP) must conform to more stringent requirements regarding transfers of receivables. In essence, RAP requires that for regulatory reporting purposes, including capital adequacy, commercial banks and bank holding companies must account for sales with recourse as secured financings. The result is contrary to the sale objective of most ABS: the assets remain on the balance sheet and the ABS are considered to be the debt of the selling company. The solution for ABS issuers has been to structure 'non-recourse' ABS, where the yield generated by the collateral which is in excess of the 'fixed costs' of the transaction (investor interest and servicing fee) is retained in a reserve fund to cover credit losses. In general, the reserve fund moves in tandem with the letter of credit, albeit at a much smaller size.

1.3.3 *Sale for Bankruptcy Purposes*

In order to achieve a high rating for the ABS, it is necessary to isolate the sold assets from a bankruptcy of the seller. Most transactions have provided this legal insulation through being structured as sales for bankruptcy purposes. If the assets are truly sold, then there can be no claim on them by the seller's bankruptcy estate. There are several considerations in evaluating a bankruptcy sale: the amount of recourse; tax treatment; the ability to identify the sold assets; and the seller's treatment of the transaction.

The amount of recourse or limited guaranty may affect bankruptcy sale treatment if it is above a level at which legal counsel may opine that the transaction constitutes a sale rather than a secured financing. Second, tax sale treatment reinforces the argument for a bankruptcy sale. The ability to identify the sold assets is a practical as well as principled argument for sale treatment. And finally, the seller's consistent treatment of the transaction is an important element in shaping the overall case for sale treatment.

Most transactions also provide for the trustee for investors to take a perfected security interest in the receivables. A security interest in the receivables provides an additional level of security to investors in the event that the sale treatment is not maintained in bankruptcy. The means of perfecting the security interest varies with the asset type and can require notation on title documents, filing a financing statement under the Uniform Commercial Code, or by possession of the assets themselves.

1.3.4 *Sale for Tax Purposes*

Automobile and other amortizing ABS transactions are typically structured as sales for accounting and tax purposes – in other words, they obtain 'symmetrical' tax and accounting treatment.

In the grantor trust structure, the investor is deemed to earn the entire yield on the receivables but is able to deduct 'reasonable' servicing fees. Another method of accounting for the trust's income is more cumbersome – and therefore less desirable.

This method, 'strip' treatment, deems an interest in the receivables to be retained by the seller, with the net being retained by the investor. 'Strip' treatment may result in an acceleration of taxable income to the seller.

The servicing fee falls under varying accounting and tax treatments. For accounting purposes, the present value of servicing in excess of the basic cost of providing the servicing function – 'excess servicing' – is booked as a gain at the point of sale. This booked asset is then amortized as these excess funds are returned to the seller. For tax purposes, income is recognized as it accrues under each receivable.

For structures in which there is substantial transformation of the cash flow from receivables to investor payments, as in credit-card transactions, symmetrical treatment is more difficult to obtain. Under 'asymmetrical' tax treatment, the seller obtains an accounting sale while at the same time retaining ownership of the assets for tax purposes. The securities are considered debt for both the issuer and the investor.

1.3.5 The Implications of Sale Treatment

Asset securitization liquefies the balance sheet. It allows a reduction in capitalization and loss reserves. More importantly, it increases lending capacity without having to find additional deposits (in the case of depository institutions) or capital infusion.

1.3.6 Ratio Improvement

At the point of sale, FAS No. 77 states that the present value of the excess servicing may be taken as a gain (or loss) on sale.

As shown in Exhibit 1.1, off-balance-sheet treatment has a direct impact on the seller's financial ratios. Scenario A assumes that consumer loans and debt are reduced by the same amount. Scenario B assumes that consumer loans are securitized and replaced by an equivalent amount of consumer loans, thereby leaving debt unchanged. The immediate impact on the income statement is the reduction of consumer loan interest income by the yield on sold assets, and the increase of servicing fee income by an amount equal to the basic servicing fee (for the life of the ABS) and the gain on sale (at the point of sale only). The reduction of interest income, as illustrated in Scenario A, is only partially offset by the increase in servicing fee income. Because interest expense is reduced, the effect on net income is an increase. The combination of the increase in net income and the decrease in assets has a dramatic effect on return-on-assets (ROA) in Scenario A. ROA is not as impacted in Scenario B, because there is no

Exhibit 1.1   Pro-forma effects of securitization

Assumptions:

Consumer assets sold	$200,000,000
Yield on short-term investments	8.00%
Yield on consumer loans	12.00%
Yield on all other loans	10.00%
Pass-through rate	9.00%
Company funding rate	
Deposits	7.00%
Debt	10.00%
Operating expenses	1.00%
Application tax rate	34.00%

Gain on sale taken over a two-year average life

Case scenarios:

A – Sell receivables and use proceeds to reduce debt
B – Sell receivables and invest proceeds in new consumer loans

Balance sheet
($ in millions)

	Base case	Scenario A	Scenario B
Assets			
Cash and due from banks	$ 100.0	$ 100.0	$ 100.0
Short-term investments	120.0	120.0	120.0
Consumer loans	200.0	–	200.0
All other loans	1,580.0	1,580.0	1,580.0
	$2,000.0	$1,800.0	$2,000.0
Liabilities			
Deposits	$1,000.0	$1,000.0	$1,000.0
Debt	600.0	400.0	600.0
Other liabilities	300.0	300.0	300.0
Shareholders' equity	100.0	100.0	100.0
	$2,000.0	$1,800.0	$2,000.0

Income statement
($ in millions)

	Base case	Scenario A	Scenario B
Interest on short term investments	$ 9.6	$ 9.6	$ 9.6
Consumer loan interest	24.0	–	24.0
All other loan interest	158.0	158.0	158.0
Interest expense			
Deposits	70.0	70.0	70.0
Debt	60.0	40.0	60.0
Net interest income	61.6	57.6	61.6
Servicing fee income[a]	–	14.0	14.0
Operating expenses	20.0	20.0	22.0
Other expenses	10.0	10.0	10.0
Income before applicable taxes	31.6	41.6	43.6
Applicable taxes	10.7	14.1	14.8
Net income	$20.9	$27.5	$28.8

	Base case	Scenario A	Scenario B
Ratio analysis			
Equity as a % of assets	5.00%	5.56%	5.00%
Return on assets (ROA)	1.04%	1.53%	1.44%
Return on equity (ROE)	20.86%	27.46%	28.78%

[a]This represents the entire yield spread, a portion of which is allocated as basic servicing and the remainder as a present value gain on sale.

FAS No. 77 permits a gain to be taken on sale, whereas RAP requires income to be recognized as received. A gain results in a further improvement in the ROA and ROE ratios.

net change in assets. Return-on-equity (ROE) is similarly impacted by the increase in net income assets and has a dramatic effect on ROA in Scenario A. ROA is not as impacted in Scenario B, because there is no net change in assets; ROE is similarly impacted by the increase in net income.

1.3.7 *Cost of Capital Reduction*

If equity requirements are conventionally viewed as a function of the balance sheet's debt/equity ratio, then no equity or only a fraction (related to the recourse provided) of that required by conventional debt financing is required to fund assets through an ABS. An ABS issue, structured as a sale, requires no equity support. The effect on the all-in cost of capital, assuming any of a range of balance sheet debt/equity ratios and costs of equity, can be dramatic. In addition, asset sales through the ABS market can be a way to continue to grow without adding new and costly equity.

1.3.8 *Cost of Capital Analysis*

Assuming that assets are funded by a combination of debt and equity, the true cost of capital is the weighted average cost of those two components:

$$[(\text{percentage of equity}) \times (\text{cost of equity})] + [(\text{percentage debt}) \times (\text{cost of debt})]$$
$$= \text{cost of capital}$$

As an example, the cost of an ABS transaction with no recourse can be viewed as the cost of the ABS transaction alone – 9 per cent for instance. If the comparable conventional debt security is 10 basis points less expensive than the ABS (that is, 8.9 per cent for this example), then a break-even cost of equity, assuming a typical bank capitalization of 6 per cent equity, can be computed as follows:

$$[(\text{cost of ABS}) - (\text{percentage debt}) \times (\text{cost of debt})] / (\text{percentage equity})$$
$$= \text{break-even cost of equity}$$
$$[(9.00\%) - (94.00\%) \times (8.90\%)] / (6.00\%)$$
$$= 10.57\%$$

The break-even cost of equity, 10.57 per cent in this example, is the maximum amount of pre-tax equity cost that allows the weighted average cost of capital with conventional funding to break-even with an ABS issue. Any cost of equity above 10.57 per cent makes the cost of capital raised through an ABS issue less expensive than the mix of debt and equity required by conventional funding.

1.3.9 *Rating Agencies' Perspective*

Asset-backed securities incorporate some form of credit enhancement in order to raise the creditworthiness of the assets to investment grade. To obtain a particular rating, both the quantity and the quality of any credit enhancement must be consistent with the sought-after rating category. To establish the quantity of credit enhancement, a rating agency examines the originator's underwriting standards, the concentration and creditworthiness of the underlying obligors, and the portfolio delinquency and net loss history. The rating agency also examines the transaction documents to determine the integrity of the structure. The originator typically prepares a presentation for the rating agencies describing the loan operation and the portfolio. The rating agencies generally seek historical data for five full years. The review of the underwriting and servicing includes analysis of the originator's method of soliciting new business, maximum debt-to-income ratios, appraisal procedures, title insurance requirements and the frequency of credit reviews.

1.3.10 *Alternative Funding Source*

An ABS issue allows the transformation of assets into highly rated securities. An essential characteristic of the transformation is that investors can purchase the securities without detailed knowledge of the underlying assets. For an issuer, this can mean access to an entirely new group of investors who are willing to buy these highly rated securities supported by a seller's assets. These same investors, however, might not be interested in a conventional debt obligation of the same seller. The result is a new funding source for many issuers that, given the broad and growing ABS market, may not be subject to some of the market vagaries of conventional financing.

1.3.11 *Asset/Liability Matching*

Since most of the ABS supported by amortizing assets pay principal to investors as it is received on the underlying assets, the result for a seller is perfect asset/liability matching. Substantial increases or decreases in prepayment behaviour will not cause a mismatch with the asset funding. In addition, the ability to pay interest on a monthly basis, not semi-annually or annually as in conventional securities, provides the issuer with additional protection from reinvestment risk.

1.4 The Future

In 1985, when the first ABS were issued, the dominant transaction was an automobile grantor trust issued by an automobile finance company. Today, the dominant asset-backed issue is a credit-card revolving trust, issued by a money-centre commercial bank. The types of assets securitized have broadened from two in 1985 to well into double-digit figures. This decade will see even further diversification.

The trend in commercial bank issuance will continue. In addition to the benefits of asset securitization outlined above, the new risk-based capital framework developed by the Basle Committee on Bank Regulations and Supervisory Practices offers a special incentive for banks to securitize (see chapter 11). Given the insistence on capital adequacy, off-balance-sheet financing is an effective way to free up equity to expand bank's core businesses.

Commercial banks are extremely well suited to be ABS issuers. Commercial banks hold a significant amount of the raw material of securitization: banks own 47 per cent of all consumer assets. In addition, the increasing securities activities of commercial banks suggest that the ABS market is a natural place for banks to exercise their new powers.

In the future, asset securitization will encompass more types of collateral with uneven cash-flow characteristics, such as high-yield bonds and commercial loans. This diversification of collateral types will be equalled by variation in ABS structures. The third-party buyout found in recreational-vehicle transactions, for instance, may find expanded applications with receivables featuring long maturities. In a twist on history, the ABS market, the child of mortgages, may provide some structural innovations applicable to the older market for securitized mortgages.

Foreign markets present opportunities for both investors and issuers. Since the inception of the ABS market, small but consistent quantities of ABSs have been placed abroad. More recently, large quantities of credit-card-backed securities have been sold in Europe. European investors traditionally did not like or fully understand the concept of 'synthetic' triple-A securities, irregular payments of principal and monthly cash flows of most ABSs. Not surprisingly, the Euromarkets have been very receptive to the ABSs with the most conventional cash-flow characteristics – fixed amortization or bullet maturity transactions with quarterly or semi-annual payments. Over the next few years, foreign investors' acceptance of ABS will grow, as more investors become familiar with the particular characteristics of these securities.

The future is promising for non-dollar ABS issuance as well. The UK mortgage market is the first step in the internationalization of the ABS market. The first non-mortgage ABS was completed in the autumn of 1988 with Hifin Finance's issuance of commercial paper backed by trade receivables originated by Union Carbide Corporation in several European countries. France has recently passed legislation creating vehicles for asset-backed securities. Non-dollar ABSs are likely to be issued during the near future in Deutsche marks and Australian dollars. Yen and Canadian-dollar ABSs will appear eventually as well.

The position of various bank regulators and the common minimum maturity requirements remain hurdles for the issuance of ABS abroad. The Bank of England last year issued guidelines on asset sales which clarify the requirements for regulatory sale treatment for financial institutions. Assuming the trend in favourable regulation continues abroad, non-dollar ABSs should be issued in volume in the next few years.

The ABS market will continue to grow and become a central feature of the world's fixed-income markets. ABS offer numerous benefits to issuers as well as an attractive combination of security and yield to investors. The shared interest of issuers and investors is destined to drive the market far beyond the levels seen to date.

2
Structuring and Legal Issues of Asset Securitization in the United States

STEVEN L. SCHWARCZ

Chapter Outline

2.1 Introduction

2.2 History

2.3 Defining the Source of Repayment

2.4 Separating the Source of Payment from the Originator
    2.4.1 Making the SPV 'Bankruptcy Remote'
    2.4.2 Creating a 'True Sale' of the Receivables
        Recourse
        Retained rights and right to surplus
        Pricing mechanism
        Administration and collection of accounts
        Additional factors
    2.4.3 Additional Steps Under the UCC Required to Protect the Transfer

2.5 Regulatory Requirements
    2.5.1 Investment Company Act of 1940
    2.5.2 Securities Act of 1933 and Securities Exchange Act of 1934
    2.5.3 Other Regulatory Requirements

2.6 Conclusion

The author wishes to thank, for their helpful and insightful comments, his partners Gary Apfel, T. Brent Costello, Eric Marcus, Renee E. Ring, Willys A. Schneider, Arthur Steinberg and Peter H. Weil; Myron

2.1 Introduction

Traditionally a company will raise money by issuing securities that represent equity in the company or, in the case of debt securities, entitle the holders to claims for repayment. Sometimes payment of these claims is secured by a lien on certain of the company's properties. In each case the security-holder looks primarily to the company for repayment. If the company becomes financially troubled, or bankrupt, payment of the securities may be jeopardized, or at least delayed.

Structured finance can change the security-holder's dependence on the company for payment, by separating the source of payment from the company itself. In a typical structured financing, a company that seeks to raise cash may sell certain of its assets to a special-purpose vehicle or trust that is organized in such a way that the likelihood of its bankruptcy is remote. The 'sale' is accomplished in a manner that removes, to the extent practicable, these assets from the estate of the selling company in the event of its bankruptcy. The result is that the assets are no longer owned by the selling company, but by the bankruptcy-remote vehicle or trust. The assets themselves are typically payment obligations, such as accounts or other amounts receivable, owing to the company from creditworthy third parties. (In this chapter, these payment obligations are generically referred to as 'receivables'.)

The special-purpose vehicle or trust (hereinafter called the 'SPV'), and not the selling company, will issue securities to raise cash. These securities are intended to be payable from collections on the receivables purchased by the SPV. A potential buyer of the securities therefore looks to the cash flow from the purchased receivables, and not necessarily to the credit of the selling company, for repayment.

This separation of the selling company (hereinafter called the 'originator', because it usually originates the receivables) from the receivables themselves can enable the originator to raise funds less

Glucksman, Vice President of Citicorp Securities Markets Inc.; and Mark P. Trager, Vice President of Citicorp North America Inc., Corporate Asset Funding. The author further thanks his counsel, Kathleen L. Coles, and his associate, Diana Weaver, for their assistance in preparation of the article.

Exhibit 2.1   Balance sheet impact of securitization assets
(XYZ Company)

Assets	Liabilities	Equity	
Receivables $100	Debt $100	Equity $100	Debt/equity = 1
Equipment $100			

1. If XYZ Company borrows $100, secured by its receivables:

Assets	Liabilities	Equity	Ratios worsen
Cash $100	Debt $200	Equity $100	Debt/equity = 2
Receivables $100			
Equipment $100			

2. But if XYZ Company sells $100 of its receivables:

Assets	Liabilities	Equity	Ratios unchanged
Cash $100	Debt $100	Equity $100	Debt/equity = 1
Equipment $100			

3. And if XYZ Company then uses $90, for example, of the cash
to pay off debt, its ratio of debt to equity dramatically improves:

Assets	Liabilities	Equity	Ratios improve
Cash $10	Debt $10	Equity $100	Debt/equity = 1/10
Equipment $100			

expensively, through securities issued by the SPV, than it would cost
to raise funds through securities issued directly by the originator. In
addition, as illustrated in the chart in Exhibit 2.1, the cash that is
raised will not require an offsetting liability to be shown on the originator's balance sheet; from the standpoint of the originator, the cash
represents proceeds of the sale of receivables to the SPV.

If the originator is a bank or similar financial institution that is
required to maintain risk-based capital under the recent capital
adequacy guidelines,[1] securitization also could permit the originator to
sell assets (for example, loans reflected as assets on the bank's financial
statements) for which it would otherwise be required to maintain
capital. This reduces the bank's effective cost of funds.

Furthermore, an originator may be restricted by its indenture covenants from incurring or securing debt beyond a specified level. A structured financing may enable the originator to raise cash in compliance with such covenants, because the originator may be selling assets and not incurring or securing debt. (Whether a structured financing would violate particular covenants requires a case-by-case inquiry.)

2.2 History

The first structured financings, identified as such, started in the early 1970s with the securitization of pools of mortgages.

Initially, mortgages were originated by savings and loan associations. These institutions depended heavily on core deposit flows for funds to finance local housing demand. When the housing credit market collapsed during the Depression, Congress reacted by passing the National Housing Act of 1934, intended in part to create a secondary market in mortgages. To this end, the Federal National Mortgage Association (Fannie Mae) was established in 1938 to provide liquidity for mortgage investment by purchasing mortgages when funds are in short supply, and selling mortgages when funds are plentiful. As the nation's demand for housing increased after the Second World War, a capital shortage developed, and alternative capital streams were needed to finance the growing housing industry. In 1957, the Federal Home Loan Bank Board created a credit reserve system for savings and loan associations by permitting the purchase and sale of participations in interests in mortgage loans.

The first structured financing came in 1970 when the newly created Government National Mortgage Association (Ginnie Mae) began publicly trading 'pass-through' securities. In a mortgage pass-through security, the investor purchases a fractional undivided interest in a pool of mortgage loans, and is entitled to share in the interest income and principal payments generated by the underlying mortgages. Mortgage lenders originate pools of mortgages with similar characteristics as to quality, term and interest rate. The pool is then placed in a trust. Then, through either a government agency, a private conduit or direct placement, certificates of ownership are sold to investors. Income from the mortgage pool passes through to the investors.

In recent years, many different types of assets have been the subject of securitization. Where the securities issued by the SPV are publicly issued, and where rating agencies – such as Standard & Poor's and Moody's – rate these securities, the assets purchased by the SPV tend to be payment streams that have proven histories of past payment and predictable expectations of future payment. Examples would include pools of mortgage loans, trade receivables and credit-card receivables.

On the other hand, where the securities are privately placed, and in some recent transactions as the rating agencies become more comfortable with the credit issues involved with securitization, the assets purchased by the SPV are becoming more creative. For example, recent deals have included payment streams consisting of franchise fees, leases, subrogation claims and even utility surcharges.

2.3 Defining the Source of Repayment

As can be seen, the common thread is that the receivables purchased consist of a payment stream as to which there is a reasonable predictability of payment. Collections on the receivables would be applied to pay principal and interest on the securities issued by the SPV.

Predictability of payment is affected by the nature and identity of both the obligors on the receivables and the originator, and also by the nature of the receivables themselves. From the standpoint of the obligors, there are two risks: delay in payment (sometimes referred to as 'slow pay'), and default in payment (sometimes referred to as 'no pay').

The 'slow pay' risk is that the obligors on the receivables may delay in making their payments. A holder of securities issued by the SPV would not be pleased to learn that his monthly or quarterly interest payment was not made because an obligor delayed his payment. For this reason, the number of obligors on the receivables should be large enough to maintain statistical assurance that, even if a reasonably expected number of obligors delay in making their payments, the securities issued by the SPV will be paid on time.[2]

The 'no pay' risk is that the obligors on the receivables may default in making their payments. This risk in turn depends upon several factors. The obvious factor is the financial ability of the obligors to pay the receivables; an obligor might not pay because it is bankrupt or otherwise having financial problems. An obligor also may have a defence to payment.[3] Therefore, the number of obligors on the receivables again must be large enough to enable the risk of default to be statistically determined.

There are, however, certain factors that can impair the validity of a statistical analysis. It may be that a relatively small number of the obligors (counting, for this purpose, affiliated obligors as a single obligor, because default by any given obligor may signify financial trouble for the affiliates of that obligor) account for a disproportionately large amount of payments under the receivables. Default by these obligors might impair the ability of the security-holders to be repaid. This risk of high concentrations of payments by a relatively small number of obligors is called, naturally enough, the obligor-concentration risk.

The default risk therefore can be managed by the SPV buying receivables having a statistically large number of obligors, and by analysing the obligor concentrations. The financial ability of the obligors to pay, and the possibility that the obligors may be able to assert defences to payment, would also be considered. The default risk then may be addressed by the originator's adjusting the sale price of the receivables to take into account anticipated defaults.[4] Alternatively, or in addition, the default risk may be addressed by credit enhancement. This can take various forms, such as a guaranty, a letter of credit, an irrevocable credit line or a third party purchasing a tranche of subordinated securities from the SPV.[5] The goal is that a creditworthy third party assures payment of all or a portion of the securities issued by the SPV.[6]

Predictability of payment also depends on the nature and identity of the originator. A financially troubled originator is more likely to go bankrupt, thereby raising the question whether the transfer of its receivables is a sale for bankruptcy purposes. If a court holds the transfer not to be a sale, the ability of the SPV to receive collections on the receivables will be delayed and may be seriously impaired. This is discussed in greater detail in section 2.4.2 below.

Lastly, predictability of payment may depend on the nature of the receivables themselves. For example, where the receivables constitute obligations owing for goods sold or services rendered (the standard trade receivables), there are few defences to payment. Perhaps some of the goods sold will turn out to be defective, or some of the obligors will turn out to be minors. But in general a buyer of the receivables can anticipate the delinquency and default risks based on past collection patterns.

This type of predictability may not be obtained if the receivables represent payment for future performance obligations of the originator. A good example is franchise fees. These are amounts payable from obligors, called franchisees, to a franchisor (the originator) in return for the licence to run a business using a special tradename or trademark and selling designated products or services.[7]

Franchise fees may not be payment obligations at all but merely expectations of payment. These fees may be calculated, for example, by a percentage (or other formula) of the franchisee's monthly or other periodic revenues or profits. If there are no revenues or profits, no franchise fee is payable. Also, if the franchisor (originator) fails to perform the contractually agreed upon franchise services, the franchisee may have a legal defence against payment of franchise fees.

In addition, in the case of bankruptcy of the originator, the originator (or its trustee in bankruptcy) may have the right, under section 365 of the Federal Bankruptcy Code, to reject, or terminate, the franchise agreement as an executory contract. An executory contract is any contract where substantial performance remains due on both sides, such that breach by one party of its performance obligations would excuse the other side's obligation to perform.[8] A franchise agreement may well be this type of a contract.[9] Accordingly, an originator that becomes the subject of a bankruptcy case may be able to terminate the contract if it has business reasons to do so.[10]

The rejection of an executory contract by an originator in bankruptcy would subject the originator to a claim for damages for breach of contract. This damage claim, however, has no priority and ranks on a parity with the originator's general unsecured claims. Presumably the claim would be worth less (perhaps far less) than 100 cents on the dollar.[11]

The foregoing analysis of risks was illustrated by reference to a payment stream represented by a franchise contract. The same legal conclusions would obtain, however, for other types of future payment streams – such as leases, licences, and so on – where a contract breach by the originator could raise a defence to payment by the obligors; or where the contract is an executory contract.[12]

2.4 Separating the Source of Payment from the Originator

We have previously discussed the 'source' of payment. The source of payment must be *separated* from the originator in the event that the originator becomes troubled or bankrupt. It is therefore necessary, first, to ensure that whatever happens to the originator cannot affect the SPV (often referred to as making the SPV 'bankruptcy remote'), and second, to ensure that the transfer of the receivables from the originator to the SPV cannot be interfered with (often referred to as creating a 'true sale' of the receivables).

2.4.1 *Making the SPV 'Bankruptcy Remote'*

The SPV itself must be insulated, to the extent practicable, from a possible bankruptcy of the originator. There are several ways the originator's bankruptcy could affect the SPV, and each must be protected against.

If the SPV is owned or controlled by the originator,[13] the originator may have the power to cause the SPV to file a voluntary petition for bankruptcy under section 303 of the Federal Bankruptcy Code. There are no legal standards that must be met for a voluntary petition to be filed.[14] It is therefore important to limit, by design, the ability of the originator to cause the SPV to file a voluntary bankruptcy.[15]

This limitation is normally accomplished by drafting the SPV's charter or articles of incorporation or other organizational documents to restrict the circumstances under which it may place itself in voluntary bankruptcy. Charters of SPVs sometimes provide that the SPV may not place itself into bankruptcy unless the SPV is insolvent *and* a requisite percentage of *independent* board members votes for bankruptcy. Some SPVs are organized with at least two classes of stock; and both classes must vote affirmatively for bankruptcy in order for the SPV to file a voluntary petition. One class of stock then is pledged to, or otherwise controlled by, the holders of the SPV's securities.[16]

These methods are not infallible. Whether they are enforceable will depend upon the law of the particular jurisdiction of formation of the SPV. Delaware law presently appears to offer flexibility in approaches.[17]

Another approach is for the SPV to be neither owned nor controlled by the originator. The SPV may, for example, be owned by an independent third party, such as a charitable institution. If the SPV continued to collect the receivables and pay on its securities even after the originator went bankrupt, the charity (or other third party) would have no incentive to place the SPV in bankruptcy. The SPV could also be structured as an entity that cannot become the subject of a federal bankruptcy case. One such entity is a trust, although 'business trusts'[18] may be the subject of federal bankruptcy cases.[19]

Once the SPV's power to file a voluntary bankruptcy petition is restricted, the next step is to limit the circumstances under which creditors can force the SPV into involuntary bankruptcy. Unlike voluntary bankruptcy, a creditor may not force an SPV into involuntary bankruptcy unless the SPV meets the criteria required for filing.[20] These criteria are that the SPV is either generally not paying its debts as they become due, or that a custodian, other than a trustee, receiver or agent, appointed or authorized to take charge of less than substantially all of the property of the SPV for the purpose of enforcing a lien against such property, has been appointed or has taken possession.[21] One therefore may attempt to protect against involuntary bankruptcy by limiting both the debt that the SPV can issue and the number of trade creditors. (The number of trade creditors can be effectively limited by limiting the business in which the SPV can engage.) These limitations could be included, for example, in the SPV's charter or other organizational documents. Furthermore, any third parties that deal with the SPV contractually could be required to waive their respective rights to file an involuntary bankruptcy petition against the SPV.

Eliminating creditors does not guarantee that the SPV will be protected from the originator's bankruptcy. An equitable doctrine of law, known as substantive consolidation, may allow a court under appropriate circumstances to consolidate the assets and liabilities of the originator and the SPV. Although substantive consolidation usually arises in the context of a bankruptcy both of the originator and of the SPV, a court could order a substantive consolidation even where the SPV is not in bankruptcy or, in the alternative, place restrictions on the operations of the SPV notwithstanding that the SPV is not in bankruptcy.[22]

Courts do not order substantive consolidation lightly. The determination that two entities should be substantively consolidated must be made on a case-by-case basis, after consideration of the relevant facts of each case. Courts will take into consideration both the nature of the relationship between the entities to be consolidated and the effect of the consolidation on the creditors of each entity. Among the factors to be considered for this purpose, the courts have identified the following:[23]

- the degree of difficulty in segregating and ascertaining individual liabilities and assets;
- the presence or absence of consolidated financial statements;
- the commingling of assets and business functions;
- the unity of ownership and interests between the corporate entities;
- the guaranteeing by the parent of loans of the subsidiary;
- the transfer of assets without formal observance of corporate formalities.

The presence of some or even many of these factors does not, however, necessarily mean that a court will order a substantive consolidation. Recently, courts have held that, because substantive consolidation is an equitable remedy, it should not be used to harm innocent holders of securities of the company (in our case, the SPV) that is the target of consolidation.[24]

It therefore would not appear likely that a court would substantively consolidate the assets and liabilities of an SPV and a bankrupt originator in a typical transaction. Nonetheless, substantive consolidation is an equitable remedy, and is highly dependent on the facts.

The foregoing discussion has focused on limiting the circumstances under which the SPV, or its assets, could become subject to a federal bankruptcy case. Certain types of governmental claims, however, that arise against the originator may also be asserted against the SPV, regardless of whether the SPV is in bankruptcy. Under the United States Internal Revenue Code, for example, a claim can be asserted against any member of a consolidated tax group. If the SPV is a member of the originator's consolidated tax group, as would be likely if the SPV is a subsidiary of the originator, the Internal Revenue Service would be able to assert a claim that it has against the originator directly against the SPV.[25]

Another type of governmental claim that may be asserted in this way is a pension claim. Certain governmental claims relating to defined benefit pension plans can be asserted under the Internal Revenue Code and the Employee Retirement Income Security Act of

1974, as amended (ERISA), against any trade or business under common control with the sponsor of the plan (a 'controlled group').[26] For example, if there are unfunded benefits payable upon the termination of a defined benefit pension plan, the sponsoring employer and each member of its controlled group, which could include the SPV, would be liable to the Pension Benefit Guaranty Corporation (PBGC), the agency responsible for administering the ERISA plan termination rules, for 100 per cent of the unfunded benefits.[27] In addition, the PBGC has a lien for its claim against the property of each member of the group, up to 30 per cent of the collective net worth of the group.[28] The lien generally has the same status as a tax lien.[29] In addition, liability for unpaid contributions to an ongoing defined benefit pension plan extends to all members of the controlled group, and a lien on their property (with the same status as a tax lien) will be imposed in favour of the PBGC if the unpaid contributions exceed a certain level.[30] These governmental claims normally would have priority to claims of general security-holders.

It is possible, however, for the claims of holders of securities of the SPV to gain priority over governmental claims by the SPV's pledging its receivables to secure repayment of the security-holders. Such a pledge would come ahead of the governmental claims in most instances.[31]

2.4.2 Creating a 'True Sale' of the Receivables

Having accomplished a separation of the originator and the SPV, it is important to ensure that ownership of the receivables is effectively transferred to the SPV. This is typically referred to as the transfer constituting a 'true sale'. The term 'true sale' is misleading, however, because a given transfer of receivables may well be a sale for certain purposes but not others. For example, the criteria for establishing an accounting sale under Generally Accepted Accounting Principles (GAAP), governed by Statement of Financial Accounting Standards (SFAS) No. 77, are less stringent[32] than the criteria for establishing a sale under bankruptcy law.

The originator transferring its receivables to the SPV presumably would want the transfer to constitute a sale for accounting purposes. That way the financing is reflected on its balance sheet as a sale of assets and not as a secured loan (which would increase leverage). The originator may also want the transfer to be a sale for purposes of its indenture covenants, if such covenants restrict the originator's ability to incur debt or pledge its assets. In many cases, particularly where the indenture itself states that its interpretation is to be governed by GAAP, it may well be the case that a transfer which is an accounting sale also will be viewed as a sale under the indenture.[33] However, whether a given transfer of receivables violates one or more indenture or other contractual covenants is a legal question that turns closely on the precise contractual language and would usually be best interpreted by the originator's own counsel.

The term 'true sale' is most often used in analysing whether the transfer of receivables has effectively removed the receivables from the originator for bankruptcy purposes. If the originator goes bankrupt, and the receivables are no longer owned by the originator but instead are owned by the SPV, then the SPV would own the collections on the receivables. Assuming the receivables were paid, the SPV would then have sufficient cash to pay its securities without defaulting. But, if the transfer is held not to be a sale for bankruptcy purposes, it will be deemed an advance of funds by the SPV to the originator secured by the receivables.[34] The SPV would have a security interest, but not an ownership interest, in the receivables. In such a case, the originator's bankruptcy would, under section 362 of the Federal Bankruptcy Code, automatically result in a stay of all actions by creditors to foreclose on or otherwise obtain property of the originator.

If the transfer of the receivables from the originator to the SPV is recharacterized by the bankruptcy court as a secured loan rather than as a sale, the SPV may not be able to obtain payments collected on the receivables until the stay is modified.[35] Furthermore, under section 363 of the Federal Bankruptcy Code, a court, after notice to creditors and the opportunity of a hearing, could order the cash collections of the receivables to be used by the originator in its business as working capital if adequate protection of the interest of the SPV in the receivables is provided by the originator or its trustee.[36]

In addition, section 364 of the Federal Bankruptcy Code would also permit the originator, if credit is not otherwise available to it and if adequate protection is given to the SPV, to raise cash by granting to new lenders a lien that either is *pari passu* with that of the SPV or, if a *pari passu* lien cannot attract new financing, has priority over the SPV's lien.[37]

Although various courts have considered whether a given transfer of receivables constitutes a sale or a secured loan for bankruptcy purposes, the facts of the decided cases have not been representative for the most part of modern asset-securitized transactions. Accordingly, the cases are not easily harmonized, and different readers may argue as to which factors are relevant and which are entitled to greater weight. Nonetheless, a cluster of factors can be identified that are relevant in most determinations of whether a given receivables transfer is a sale or a secured loan. Each of these factors is indicative of whether the originator truly has parted with the future economic risks and benefits of ownership of the receivables purported to be sold, and whether the SPV has taken on these risks and benefits.

Recourse The most significant factor appears to be the extent of recourse the transferee of the receivables has against the transferor. As the degree of recourse increases, the likelihood that a court will find a true sale decreases. The existence of some recourse does not by itself preclude characterization of the transaction as a true sale. If recourse is present, the issue is 'whether the nature of the recourse and the true nature of the transaction are such that the legal rights and economic consequences of the agreement bear a greater similarity to a financing transaction (*i.e.*, a secured loan) or to a sale'.[38]

Sometimes the seller represents and warrants that all receivables sold meet certain eligibility criteria; and the seller will provide an indemnity for breach of these representations and warranties. To the extent these representations and warranties are not general representations and warranties of collectability, but rather are limited to the condition of the receivables at the time the receivables are sold, this should be no different from a warranty ordinarily given by a seller of a product.[39] Accordingly, such limited representations and warranties and indemnity should not be inconsistent with sale treatment.

Retained rights and right to surplus Perhaps the second-most important factor indicating a secured transaction is the transferor's right to redeem or repurchase transferred receivables. For example, section 9–506 of the Uniform Commercial Code (UCC) and various state mortgage statutes allow a debtor to redeem property before it is ultimately disposed of by a secured party. The absence of a right of redemption or repurchase would be a factor in favour of characterization of the receivables transaction as a true sale.

Several courts have also considered the existence of a transferor's right to any surplus collections, once the transferee has collected its investment plus an agreed yield, as indicative of a secured loan.[40] The right of the transferee of the receivables to retain all collections of transferred receivables for its own account, even after the transferee has collected its investment plus yield, would therefore be a factor in favour of characterization of the receivables transaction as a true sale.

Pricing mechanism Another important factor is the nature of the pricing mechanism. Pricing based upon a fluctuating interest index of the type found in commercial loan agreements, such as the prime or base rate, may be indicative of a secured loan. The pricing mechanism also may be indicative of a secured loan to the extent the purchase price is retroactively adjusted to reflect actual rather than expected collections on receivables.[41] In the closest approach to a true sale, the SPV would purchase receivables at a discount calculated to cover the SPV's funding cost (as well as risk of loss). The discount would be fixed for each sale, and would not be retroactively adjusted to cover the actual funding cost.

Administration and collection of accounts The administration of and control over the collection of accounts receivable are factors frequently cited by courts in resolving the sale/secured loan issue. To be a true purchase, the transferee should have the authority to control the collection of the accounts.[42] Examples of such authority would include (1) ownership by the transferee of all the books, records and computer tapes relating to the purchased receivables, and (2) the transferee's having the right to (a) control the activities of any collection agent with respect to purchased receivables and at any time to appoint itself or another person as collection agent, (b) establish credit and collection policy with respect to purchased receivables, and (c) notify at any time the obligors of the purchased receivables of the sale.

In practice, the seller is often appointed as the collection agent initially. This is not necessarily inconsistent with sale characterization if (1) the seller, as collection agent, will be acting as an agent for the purchaser pursuant to established standards, much like any other agent, (2) the seller will receive a collection agent fee that represents an arm's-length fee for these services, and (3) the purchaser has the right at any time to appoint itself or another person as collection agent in place of the seller.

Sometimes collections of the purchased receivables are paid to the originator and commingled, or mixed, with the originator's general funds. This frequently occurs where the originator collects the receivables each day, but only remits the collections periodically (such as monthly) to the SPV. Besides raising a potential perfection question under the UCC,[43] commingling would, if permitted by the SPV, appear to be inconsistent with the concept of a sale: the originator would be using collections that belong to the SPV. This inconsistency can often be addressed by the originator's segregating and holding the collections in trust, pending remittance to the SPV.[44]

Additional factors   The courts have identified a variety of other factors that do not fall within the categories discussed above but which may be indicative of a secured loan. Among the more significant of these factors are the following:

- The originator of receivables is a debtor of the SPV on or before the purchase date.
- The SPV's rights in the receivables can be extinguished by payments or repurchases by the originator or by payments from sources other than collections on receivables.
- The originator is obligated to pay the SPV's costs (including attorneys' fees) incurred in collecting delinquent or uncollectable receivables.
- The language of the documentation contains references to the transfer being 'security for' a debt.
- The parties' intent, as evidenced by the documentation and their actions, suggests that the parties view the transaction as a security device. Also of importance is how the parties account for the transaction on their books, records and tax returns.

It is rare in modern commercial transactions for all the factors favouring a true bankruptcy sale to be met. There is inevitably a balance. Some recourse is needed to give a reasonable assurance to holders of the SPV's securities that they will be paid. It may be uneconomic for an originator to agree that the SPV obtains the entire surplus of collections once holders of the SPV's securities are paid. In each case the parties structuring the transaction will have to balance how important it is that the transaction be a bankruptcy sale with the other commercial desires of the investors and the originator. This balance will depend, in large part, on the credit quality of the originator. It may be less important to investors to insist on a true sale where the originator has an investment grade rating than where the originator is troubled or in a workout.[45]

2.4.3 *Additional Steps Under the UCC Required to Protect the Transfer*

Once the SPV has been created and the transaction structured, it will still be necessary to take certain steps to protect the transfer of receivables against claims of third parties and in bankruptcy. The Uniform Commercial Code, adopted (with only minor variation) in every state of the United States,[46] provides in section 9–102 that each transfer of an interest in 'accounts' and 'chattel paper', whether or not intended as a transfer for security or a transfer of actual ownership, must be perfected by one of the procedures set forth in the UCC (usually accomplished by the filing of UCC-1 financing statements).[47] The commentary to this section (Official Comment No. 2) explains that the draftsmen had difficulty trying to set guidelines on whether a given transfer was a sale or a secured loan, and therefore established the same filing requirement in both cases. The purpose of the filing is to place third parties on notice of the transfer of the interest in the receivables, so that they will not be misled when extending credit to or otherwise dealing with the originator.[48]

The failure to perfect, in accordance with the requirement of the UCC, can have serious consequences. The secured party or purchaser may not be able to enforce its rights as against later secured creditors who file financing statements covering the same receivables or as against the originator's trustee in bankruptcy.[49]

Curiously, although section 9–102 of the UCC refers to transfers of 'accounts' and 'chattel paper', it does not refer to, and therefore by its terms does not apply to, sales of other types of payment streams. 'Account' is defined in UCC section 9–106 as 'any right to payment for goods sold or leased or for services rendered which is not evidenced by an instrument or chattel paper, whether or not it has been earned by performance'. 'Chattel paper' is defined in UCC section 9–105(1)(b) as follows:

'Chattel paper' means a writing or writings which evidence both a monetary obligation and a security interest in or a lease of specific goods, but a charter or other contract involving the use or hire of a vessel is not chattel paper. When a transaction is evidenced both by such a security agreement or a lease and by an instrument or a series of instruments, the group of writings taken together constitutes chattel paper.

Many common types of payment streams, such as fees payable under a franchise contract, may not fall into either of these categories. Indeed the UCC has other categories, including a catch-all category of 'general intangibles', into which any payment stream falls that is not included in a specific category.

Does the failure of UCC section 9–102 to refer to the sale of general intangibles mean that the draftsmen intended that no legal steps need be taken under the UCC to perfect such sale, or does this failure mean that the UCC was not intended to vary whatever common law requirements were applicable to sales of intangibles? The UCC offers no clue.

The answer to this question, however, can have practical consequences. Prior to enactment of the UCC, different states had varying requirements as to how to protect the interest of a purchaser of accounts receivable and other intangibles. One line of cases, followed in New York and various other states, provided that a sale is not perfected where the transferor retains 'unfettered dominion' over collections.[50] A minority line of American cases, following the English rule,[51] required notice to be given to the obligors on the receivables in order to perfect.

It is unclear, as a matter of law, whether these pre-UCC perfection requirements continue to apply to sales of intangibles that are neither accounts nor chattel paper under the UCC.[52] Such a result would create commercial confusion because of the varying and conflicting state requirements. Perhaps a better approach is to recognize that it is the universally followed procedure for anyone who extends secured credit or is concerned about collateral to search the UCC records. For example, if a company were merely to pledge, as opposed to selling, its intangibles, there is no question that the UCC, which by its terms covers the granting of a security interest in 'general intangibles', would apply.[53] It would therefore appear illogical and inequitable for a buyer that has filed UCC-1 financing statements to be penalized because it did not also follow common law perfection procedures that may be commercially impracticable in today's world. There are, however, no decided cases offering further guidance.

Sometimes the payment stream sold will be evidenced by a promissory note or other negotiable writing evidencing an obligation to pay money. Under the UCC, these are classified as 'instruments' and, because they are negotiable, can only be perfected by the buyer taking possession.[54]

A further concern arises under the UCC where the collections from the purchased receivables are not paid directly to the SPV but instead are paid to the originator and commingled, or mixed, with the originator's general funds. Section 9–306(4) of the UCC provides that, in the event of the originator's 'insolvency proceeding' (presumably meaning bankruptcy), collections of the receivables that are commingled may lose their perfected status and be subject to claims of other creditors and the trustee-in-bankruptcy.[55] In appropriate cases, particularly with financially weak originators, collections of receivables purchased by the SPV may be required to be paid by obligors directly to lock-boxes at banks that do not contain the originator's general funds or to lockboxes owned by the SPV. The SPV could enter into agreements giving it the right to take over lockboxes under appropriate circumstances. Alternatively, if adequate lockbox arrangements cannot be established, an SPV may obtain the right to notify obligors to make payments directly to the SPV.[56]

2.5 Regulatory Requirements

Structuring an asset-securitized financing frequently impacts on a number of federal and state regulatory schemes. The issuance of securities by the SPV, as well as an originator's transfer of receivables to the SPV, may raise the issue of whether registration under the Securities Act of 1933 (the '1933 Act')[57] and state 'blue sky' laws is required and whether as a result of such issuance and transfer the SPV inadvertently has become an 'investment company' within the meaning of the Investment Company Act of 1940 (the '1940 Act').[58] Moreover, there may be special concerns (discussed below) if the originator is itself a regulated industry or financial institution.

2.5.1 Investment Company Act of 1940

Beginning first with the investment company issue, the 1940 Act provides that any entity principally engaged in owning or holding 'securities' must, subject to certain exemptions, register with the US

Securities and Exchange Commission (SEC) as an investment company.[59] The 1940 Act was promulgated as part of the comprehensive
federal securities legislation enacted in the 1930s to curb a number of
perceived abuses in the US securities markets, to protect the public
from being defrauded and to ensure adequate controls and information. Unlike the 1933 Act and the non-broker/dealer sections of the
Securities Exchange Act of 1934 (the '1934 Act'),[60] which focus
principally on the adequacy of disclosure in connection with the issuance, sale and trading of securities, the 1940 Act is a comprehensive,
substantive regulatory scheme – compliance with which is generally
very costly and burdensome.[61] Accordingly, registration of an SPV as
an investment company is generally considered economically unfea-
sible, and transactions are structured so as to fall within various
statutory exemptions from 1940 Act registration.

Under section 3(a) of the 1940 Act, an investment company is
defined in relevant part as (1) an entity which is 'engaged primarily
. . . in the business of investing, reinvesting, or trading in securities'
or (2) an entity 'engaged' in such business, which 'owns or proposes to
acquire investment securities having a value exceeding 40 per centum
of the value of such [entity's] total assets (exclusive of Government
securities and cash items on an unconsolidated basis)'. The term
'security' is defined broadly under section 2(a)(36) to include notes,
stock, bonds, evidences of indebtedness, transferable shares, investment contracts and 'any interest or instrument commonly known as a
"security". . . .'[62]

Most receivables and payment streams appear to fall within the
definition of the term 'security' under the 1940 Act because they are
'evidences of indebtedness'. Nevertheless, several effective exemptions from registration as an investment company may be available to
an SPV. The most frequently used is section 3(c)(5)(A) of the 1940
Act, which excludes from the definition of 'investment company'
entities that are 'primarily engaged' in acquiring or holding receivables that constitute 'notes, drafts, acceptances, open accounts receivable, and other obligations representing part or all of the sales price of
merchandise, insurance, and services'.[63]

Many, but not all, types of receivables will fall under the section
3(c)(5)(A) exclusion. These will generally include the most commonplace type of receivable – trade accounts receivable – since they clearly
represent the purchase price of merchandise. Other types of receivables may not, however, come clearly within the section 3(c)(5)(A)

exclusion.[64] In some of these instances, however, it may be possible to obtain a 'no-action' letter[65] from the SEC, which will in practice have basically the same effect as an exemption from investment company registration.

In *Days Inns of America, Inc.* (avail. 30 December 1988), for example, the SEC staff stated that it would not recommend enforcement action under section 3(c)(5)(A) if a wholly owned subsidiary of Days Inns acquired certain franchise-fee receivables from Days Inns (through another subsidiary), privately issued and sold notes secured by those receivables and loaned the net proceeds from the note sales to Days Inns to refinance certain indebtedness of the parent company. The receivables were characterized as obligations representing part or all of the sales price of various services rendered by Days Inns to its franchisees and on that basis were found to fall within the scope of section 3(c)(5)(A).[66]

Where section 3(c)(5)(A) does not cover the receivables in question, other exemptions may be available. Under section 3(c)(1) of the 1940 Act, for example, '[a]ny issuer whose outstanding securities (other than short-term paper) are beneficially owned by not more than one hundred persons and which is not making and does not presently propose to make a public offering of its securities' is excluded from the definition of 'investment company'. This so-called 'private investment company' exemption is frequently used in conjunction with the private offering exemption under the 1933 Act (discussed below) to place interests in an SPV with a limited number of institutional investors and other holders.[67]

If no statutory exemption is clearly available, sections 3(b)(2) and 6(c) of the 1940 Act permit an SPV to petition the SEC to issue an order exempting the SPV from registration on the grounds that either (1) the SPV is primarily engaged in a business other than that of investing, owning or trading in securities (section 3(b)(2)), or (2) an exemption is necessary or appropriate in the public interest and is consistent with the protection of investors and the other purposes of the 1940 Act (section 6(c)). Obtaining a decision on such an application may take several months, and certainly there is no guarantee that an exemptive order will ultimately be issued by the SEC. Nevertheless, sometimes there is no alternative if investment company registration is not cost-effective.

2.5.2 Securities Act of 1933 and Securities Exchange Act of 1934

Even if an SPV establishes an exemption from registration under the 1940 Act, it will still be subject to the 1934 Act and the 1933 Act to the extent that it issues non-exempt securities. The 1934 Act imposes standards of disclosure and liability for certain types of fraudulent statements or omissions, as well as registration and ongoing reporting requirements for certain publicly held issuers. The 1933 Act also imposes standards of disclosure and requires the filing of a registration statement with the SEC in connection with any 'public offering' of non-exempt securities.

In weighing methods of compliance with the 1933 Act, an SPV will often choose to file a registration statement with the SEC and issue its securities as part of a public offering. Although such registration may take several months and is therefore somewhat time-consuming, as well as costly, registered securities issued by an SPV have the advantage of being freely issuable to and traded by the public.

If a public market is not necessary or if a public offering would preclude a necessary 'private investment company' exemption under the 1940 Act, the SPV may choose instead to issue its securities in a private placement under section 4(2) of the 1933 Act, which exempts 'transactions by an issuer not involving any public offering'. If the private placement is made to a relatively few large institutional investors, such as pension funds and banks, relatively little in the way of specialized disclosure documents may be required; such investors are generally presumed to have the sophistication and bargaining power to elicit from the issuer and its sponsors the financial and other information necessary to make an informed investment decision.

If the private placement is to a larger number of investors, and particularly if non-institutional investors are involved, the SPV may find it prudent to comply with the 'safe harbour' provisions of Regulation D promulgated by the SEC.[68] Under that rule, the SPV may, in general, sell its securities to up to thirty-five 'non-accredited' investors and an unlimited number of 'accredited' investors.[69] If 'non-accredited' investors are included, it will generally be necessary to prepare and circulate a private offering memorandum setting forth certain financial and other information required to be furnished under Regulation D.

Regardless of whether the Regulation D safe harbour is used, securities issued in a private placement will generally be deemed to be 'restricted securities' and may not be resold except in compliance with the registration requirements of the 1933 Act or an exemption therefrom, such as SEC Rule 144 or SEC Rule 144A.[70] In general, rule 144 imposes a two-year holding period unless the securities are resold in another private transaction (in which case the securities will generally continue to be 'restricted' in the hands of the buyer).[71]

Certain other exemptions may be available under the 1933 Act to an SPV that wishes to issue its securities in the public market but wants to avoid the time and cost of filing a registration statement. If the securities are supported by a bank letter of credit, for example, the securities would be exempt from registration under section 3(a)(2) of the 1933 Act.[72] Under the more frequently used section 3(a)(3) 'commercial paper exemption', securities having a maturity of no longer than nine months (that is, 270 days), the proceeds of which are to be used for 'current transactions', are also free from the registration requirements of the 1933 Act.[73]

The only difficulty with the section 3(a)(3) exemption is that the central requirement of a 'current transaction' is not defined anywhere in the 1933 Act. It is therefore necessary to turn to various SEC no-action letters interpreting what is and is not a current transaction under various circumstances. In general, those letters indicate that a 'current transaction' is a transaction which is undertaken by an issuer in the ordinary course of its business operations and which has a relatively short duration.[74]

It also should be noted that, regardless of whether an SPV issues exempt securities or issues non-exempt securities in an exempt transaction or a registered public offering, the anti-fraud provisions of section 10(b) of the 1934 Act and Rule 10b–5 promulgated by the SEC thereunder will apply. Accordingly, an SPV would be liable if, in connection with the issuance and sale of its securities, it employed 'any device, scheme, or artifice to defraud' or made 'any untrue statement of a material fact or [omitted] to state a material fact necessary in order to make the statements made, in the light of circumstances under which they were made, not misleading'.[75]

2.5.3 Other Regulatory Requirements

If the originator transferring its receivables to the SPV is in a regulated industry or is a financial institution, the laws, rules and regulations applicable to it may also apply. In the case of a bank, for example, transferring its own assets to an SPV, or underwriting asset securitization for a third party, the Glass–Steagall Act[76] may restrict the bank's actions. Indeed, the power of a bank to underwrite the sale of interests in securitized assets has only recently been resolved. The Comptroller of the Currency, in 1987, had determined that the sale by Security Pacific National Bank of mortgage pass-through certificates, representing fractional undivided interests in a pool of Security Pacific's own mortgage loans, was not in violation of the prohibitions on bank underwriting contained in the Glass–Steagall Act. The Glass–Steagall Act was a response to widespread bank failures after the stock market crash of 1929, and was intended to protect banks from the risks of investment banking activities, such as underwriting. The Act applies to all national banks and state banks that are members of the Federal Reserve System. The Comptroller's rationale, however, was that the sale by a bank of its own assets was not 'underwriting' of the type prohibited by Glass–Steagall and represented nothing more than the sale of bank assets. The sale of certificates was simply a new way of performing a permitted bank activity or was authorized as an incidental bank power; and the fact that the assets were being sold through the mechanism of pooling did not change this essential nature.

The Comptroller's determination subsequently was challenged by the Securities Industry Association. In 1988 a federal district court judge rejected the Comptroller's position (*Securities Industries Ass'n* v. *Clarke*).[77] In September 1989, however, the Second Circuit Court of Appeals reversed the district court's decision, and decided in favour of the Comptroller's position.[78] The court reasoned that banking activities that are explicitly authorized by statute, and the exercise of 'all such incidental powers as shall be necessary to carry on the business of banking', are permitted to banks notwithstanding that such activities may constitute underwriting or other investment banking activities.[79] The court followed another circuit court of appeals in including in a bank's 'incidental powers' any activity that is 'convenient [and] useful in connection with the performance of one of the bank's established activities pursuant to its express powers'.[80] The court held that Security Pacific's use of mortgage pass-through certificates was indeed 'convenient [and] useful' in connection with its express power to sell its own mortgage loans.[81]

There had been speculation over how broadly the Second Circuit's opinion could be read and whether it would have application to bank underwriting of pooled assets originated by third parties.[82] The Federal Reserve Board, recently has expanded the ability of a bank to underwrite and deal, through nonbank subsidiaries (known as 'section 20 subsidiaries', because they are created pursuant to powers found in section 20 of the Glass–Steagall Act[83]), in securities of an affiliated bank or nonbank so long as the securities are rated by an unaffiliated nationally recognized rating agency. Thus, the section 20 subsidiary of a bank holding company can underwrite and deal in securities backed by mortgage and consumer receivables.[84] The Federal Reserve Board, however, has imposed an overall 10 per cent limit on the amount of total revenue a section 20 subsidiary may earn from underwriting and dealing in such securities. The Securities Industry Association (SIA) continues to challenge the Federal Reserve Board's authorization of bank affiliates to underwrite and deal in all corporate debt and equity securities, subject to a revenue limitation. In April 1990, the United States Court of Appeals for the District of Columbia Circuit barred the SIA from bringing suit against the Board of Governors of the Federal Reserve System on the basis that collateral estoppel precluded the SIA from relitigating the Glass–Steagall Act claims.[85] And so the saga continues.

2.6 Conclusion

In summary, asset securitization has significant potential for enabling companies to obtain economically advantageous financing without necessarily increasing leverage. Parties wishing to take advantage of asset securitization, however, may encounter many complex legal pitfalls. A well-designed structured financing will minimize and avoid these pitfalls.

Notes

1 See Risk-Based Capital Guidelines, Regulation H, 12 C.F.R. Part 208, Appendix A (state member banks); and Regulation Y, 12 C.F.R. Part 225, Appendix A (bank holding companies). For detailed discussion of capital adequacy regulations see chapter 11 of this volume.
2 Even payment streams that are uncertain as to precise timing of collections may be able to be securitized if a credit facility (referred to as a liquidity facility) is provided to advance funds to the SPV to pay debt service if collections are temporarily delayed. While the security-holders

obtain comfort as to timing of collection, a liquidity facility does not necessarily protect the security-holders in the case of larger-than-anticipated defaults.

3 The rights of a transferee of receivables may be subject to obligor defences. See UCC section 9–318(1).

4 There are various ways to compute the purchase price. The most straightforward is to discount the outstanding balance of the receivables to be purchased, taking into account anticipated defaults and delays in collection. If the discount is too small, however, the SPV's security-holders could suffer a loss. But if the discount is too large, the originator would be under-pricing its receivables. Sometimes the discount is intentionally small, but the SPV has a degree of additional recourse (a 'loss reserve') against the originator or against additional receivables. Other times the discount is intentionally large (sometimes referred to as 'over-collateralization'), but the originator retains a right to certain excess collections if the actual defaults do not turn out to justify the large discount (payment of a 'holdback'). The purchase price could also represent a small discount, with the originator absorbing a portion of the risk by purchasing a tranche of subordinated securities from the SPV. These are merely examples. The method of pricing that is selected will depend on business and credit considerations that are beyond the scope of this chapter. It should be noted, however, that the more straightforward the method of pricing, and the more the SPV bears some risk of loss, the more likely it is that the sale of receivables will be considered a true sale for bankruptcy purposes. See discussion in section 2.4.2 above, under the heading 'Recourse'.

5 See generally Schwarcz and Varges, 'Guaranties and other third party credit supports', published as chapter 16 in *Commercial Loan Documentation Guide* (Matthew Bender, 1989).

6 A rating agency that rates the SPV's securities would want the third party to be at least as creditworthy as the rating on the securities. The third party providing the credit support would want to be comfortable, as a business matter, with the ability to be repaid from the originator or its assets. If the third party has a claim for repayment that is enforceable against the originator or its general assets (as opposed, for example, to a subrogation claim limited to the receivables sold), the transaction may appear to provide a form of indirect recourse against the originator. Cf. note 4 and section 2.4.2 above, under the heading 'Recourse'.

7 See, for example, *Black's Law Dictionary*, 5th edn.

8 See House Rep. No. 95–595, 95th Cong., 1st Sess. 347 (1977). See also *In re Grayson-Robinson Stores, Inc.*, 321 F.2d 500 (2d Cir. 1963); *In re Streets and Beard Farm Partnership*, 882 F.2d 233 (7th Cir. 1989), and *Collier on Bankruptcy*, 365–11.

9 See, for example, *Rosenthal Paper Co.* v. *Nat'l Folding Box & Paper Co.*, 226 N.Y. 313, 123 N.E. 766 (1919); *Isquith* v. *N.Y. State Thruway Authority*, 215 N.Y.S.2d 393, 27 Misc.2d 539 (1961); *Gerry* v. *Johnston*, 85 Id. 226, 378 P.2d 198 (1963). Many contracts have been held to be executory, even where the performance obligation has not been obvious. For example, a lease has been held to be an executory contract because of the lessor's obligation not to interfere with the lessee's right of quiet enjoyment. See, for example, *In re O.P.M. Leasing Services, Inc.*, 23 B.R. 104, 117 (Bankr. S.D.N.Y. 1982).

10 For example, the franchisor may be unable to provide the products or perform the training or other services, if any, required under the franchise contract.

11 See Bankruptcy Code, section 365(g). There is a further question that could arise in bankruptcy. Section 552(a) of the Bankruptcy Code provides, in part, that property acquired by a company after the commencement of a bankruptcy case is not subject to a lien resulting from a pre-bankruptcy security agreement. Section 552(b) provides that proceeds of pre-bankruptcy property may be exempt from this restriction. Where the SPV pays for a future payment stream, such as lease rentals, would the SPV be entitled to rentals paid after the originator goes bankrupt? At least one court has said yes. In *United Virginia Bank* v. *Slab Fork Coal Co.*, No. 85–1228 (4th Cir. 1986), the court held that payments made post-bankruptcy under a coal-supply contract were proceeds subject to a pre-bankruptcy lien, even where the bankrupt company would have to continue to supply the coal in order to be paid. *Accord, In re Sunberg*, 729 F.2d 561 (8th Cir. 1984). However, because section 552(b) allows a court to weigh the equities of each case, there is no assurance that a similar result will be obtained in each case. See, for example, *In re Colonial Investment Corp.*, 516 F.2d 154 (1st Cir. 1975); *In re Photo Promotion Associates, Inc.*, 61 Bank. Rep. 936 (Bankr. S.D.N.Y. 1986).

12 The nature of the receivable also can affect predictability of payment where the receivable is prepayable. If, for example, the receivables consisted of mortgage loans and interest rates declined, the obligors might prepay the loans. Although the collections then should be sufficient to prepay the principal amount of the debt securities issued by the SPV, the holders of these securities may have bargained to have their securities outstanding for a longer period of time at a fixed interest rate. The problems associated with prepayments are beyond the scope of this chapter.

13 Sometimes, for example, the SPV is a limited-purpose subsidiary of the originator.

14 The Federal Bankruptcy Code does not require any special procedures for a company to file a voluntary bankruptcy petition. A company would

make this decision like any other significant decision. Unless restricted in its charter or bylaws, a corporation, for example, normally would make this decision by a vote of its board of directors.

15 It appears to be against public policy to remove entirely a company's power to place itself in voluntary bankruptcy. Cf. *Fallick* v. *Kehr*, 369 F.2d 899 (2d Cir. 1966); *In re Weitzen*, 3 F.Supp. 698 (S.D.N.Y. 1933); *In re Tru Block Concrete Products, Inc.*, 10 B.C.D. 106 (S.D. Cal. 1983).

16 If the holders of the SPV's securities control, by pledge or otherwise, a class of the SPV's voting stock, there is a question whether these holders may be exposed to liability claims for 'controlling' the SPV. See, for example, *In re Sea–Land Corporation Shareholders Litigation*, Civ. A. No. 78453 (1988), *Aronson* v. *Lewis*, 473 A.2d 805 (1984), and *Gilbert*, v. *El Paso Co.*, 490 A.2d 1050 (1984), for a discussion by the Delaware courts of what constitutes shareholder control and the type of liability which might accompany such control. Related to this is the issue of whether the holders of the SPV's securities may vote against a bankruptcy proceeding for the SPV when such proceeding might be in the best interests of the equity owner of the SPV (that is, the originator). Courts have held that when a creditor is able to exercise control of a corporation by voting pledged securities, it has a duty to use reasonable care to maintain the value of the collateral. (See, for example, *Citibank, N.A.* v. *Data Lease Financial Corp.*, 828 F.2d 686 (11th Cir. 1987); *Empire Life Ins. Co. of America* v. *Valdak Corp.*, 468 F.2d 330 (5th Cir. 1972). But the creditor nonetheless has the right to protect its legitimate self-interest and need not fall back upon its debtor's recommendations in order to satisfy the duty of reasonable care. *Bankers Trust Company* v. *J.V. Dowler & Co.*, 417 N.Y.S.2d 47 (Ct of App. 1979).

17 See, for example, Delaware General Corporation Law sections 102(b)(1) and 121.

18 A business trust is a trust that carries on a business for profit, as opposed to a non-business trust which is created to hold and preserve the trust property. See *Hecht* v. *Malley*, 265 U.S. 144 (1924); 15(a) *Fletcher Cyc. Corp.*, section 8267 (1980).

19 See Bankruptcy Code section 101(8)(A)(v). If the originator is an entity, such as a bank, that cannot become the subject of a federal bankruptcy case, the requirements for an SPV may be more lenient. See Bankruptcy Code section 109.

20 Section 303(b) of the Bankruptcy Code also has requirements as to the number of creditors and the types of claims that are necessary for filing an involuntary bankruptcy petition.

21 See Bankruptcy Code section 303(h).

22 See, for example, *Sampsell* v. *Imperial Paper Corp.*, 313 U.S. 215 (1941), and *Collier on Bankruptcy*, para. 1100.06, pp. 1100–44 to 1100–46.

23 See *In re Vecco Construction Industries, Inc.*, 4 B.R. 407, 410 (Bankr. E. Va 1980). See also discussion in 5 *Collier on Bankruptcy*, para. 1100.06 (15th edn, 1987), *Chemical Bank New York Trust Co.* v. *Kheel (In re Seatrade Corp.)*, 369 F.2d 845, 847 (2d Cir. 1966), and *In re Manzey Land & Cattle Co.*, 17 B.R. 332, 338 (Bankr. D.S.D. 1982).

24 See, for example, *In re Snider Bros., Inc.*, 18 B.R. 230 (Bankr. D. Mass. 1982); *In re Augie/Restivo Baking Company, Ltd*, 860 F.2d 515 (2d Cir. 1988).

25 Treas. Reg. section 1.1502–6 states that the common parent corporation and each subsidiary that was a member of the group during any part of the consolidated return year shall be severally liable for the tax for such year unless the subsidiary has ceased to be a part of the group as the result of a bona fide sale or exchange for fair value prior to the date upon which the deficiency was assessed, in which case such liability may be limited. No agreement entered into by one or more members of the group with any other member or other person can eliminate or reduce this liability.

26 In general, a controlled group includes parent–subsidiary and brother–sister groups that are under 80 per cent common ownership, and therefore may include an 80 per cent owned SPV. Code section 414(b), (c); Treas. Reg. section 1.414(b), (c); ERISA section 4001(b).

27 See ERISA section 4062(a), (b).

28 See ERISA section 4068(a). The PBGC generally has great latitude in determining net worth, and ERISA was recently amended specifically to provide that negative net worths of group members are *not* offset against positive net worths for these purposes. ERISA section 4062(d)(1).

29 See ERISA section 4068(c).

30 Code section 412(c)(11), (n); ERISA section 302(f).

31 See, for example, *In re National Financing Alternatives, Inc.*, 96 B.R. 844 (B.C.N.D. Ill. 1989), where the court held that receivables acquired by the debtor after a tax lien filed by the IRS had become effective were nevertheless 'qualified property', that is, property covered by the creditor's prior security interest, so long as they were the identifiable proceeds of a contract right acquired prior to the effective date of the tax lien, and had not been commingled with other monies or expended to acquire other properties after that date. Cf. UCC sections 9–301(4), 9–312. Another issue that should be considered in connection with the establishment of an SPV is the extent to which it may be subject to income tax. Although a detailed discussion of tax issues is beyond the scope of this chapter, a few key points should be noted. If the SPV is a corporation wholly owned by a corporate originator, then it can be consolidated, at least for federal income tax purposes, with the originator, thus eliminating a separate tax at the SPV level. (It may or may not, however, be possible to consolidate or combine for state or local income

tax purposes.) Similarly, if the SPV is a trust with respect to which the originator retains sufficient economic interest or control such that the SPV is treated as a so-called grantor trust, there will be no tax at the SPV level, and any income of the SPV would simply be passed through to the originator as grantor. Alternatively, it may be possible to structure an SPV that is a trust in such a way as to assure that it will be treated as a partnership, in which case it would also generally not be subject to a separate level of tax. In other cases, the SPV may be subject to tax in its own right; however, it may in fact have little taxable income, because of offsetting deductions for interest paid on debt securities issued by it.

32 On 23 February 1989, at a meeting of the Financial Accounting Standard Board's Emerging Issues Task Force (EITF), the SEC observer stated that the SEC is becoming increasingly concerned about certain receivables, leasing and other transactions involving special-purpose vehicles. The SEC observer suggested, for the EITF's consideration, certain requirements that the SEC felt should be met in order for the transfers of receivables to be recognized as sales and to avoid consolidation of the SPV and the originator of the receivables. These requirements included that the majority owner of the SPV be an independent third party who has made a substantive capital investment in the SPV, has control of the SPV, and has substantive risks and rewards of ownership of the receivables or other assets purchased by the SPV (including residuals). Although the SEC staff is said to be considering the issuance of a Staff Accounting Bulletin setting forth guidelines on the accounting for transactions involving SPVs, no such Bulletin has yet been issued. See EITF Issue No. 84–30.

33 For example, the indenture covenant may restrict liens securing debt, although the term 'debt' may not be defined in the indenture. Indentures often state that accounting terms used therein are to be construed in accordance with GAAP. A court therefore may use the GAAP definition of 'debt', which is governed by FAS No. 77.

34 See P. Weil, *Asset-Based Lending* (PLI, 1989), ch. 2. A related issue is whether a true sale of receivables can be avoided as a 'fraudulent conveyance' if the SPV pays a purchase price that is less than the reasonably equivalent value of the receivables. This risk is minimal, however, in the typical structured financing because the purchase price for the receivables will normally be determined on an arm's-length basis (although the fairness of the purchase price may be subject to greater scrutiny if the originator is a troubled company). For a discussion of fraudulent conveyance laws, see Schwarcz and Varges, note 5, and Schwarcz, 'The impact of fraudulent conveyance law on future advances supported by upstream guaranties and security interests', 9 *Cardozo L. Rev.* 729 (1987).

35 Section 362(d) provides criteria for the judge to determine whether or not to lift the stay. Whether the stay will be lifted depends upon the facts of the given case. See, for example, *In re Comcoach Corp.*, 7 C.B.C.2d 1191 (1983); and *In re Springwater*, 11 B.C.D. 1220 (1984).
36 Adequate protection is not defined in the Federal Bankruptcy Code. Instead, Bankruptcy Code section 361 gives several examples of what may constitute adequate protection, such as making periodic cash payments to the creditor (section 361(1)) or giving a lien on other unencumbered property in the debtor's estate (section 361(2)), and leaves it for the courts to decide on a case-by-case basis what constitutes 'adequate protection' in the circumstances. See, for example, *In re O.P. Held, Inc.*, 74 B.R. 777 (1987); *In re AIL Industries, Inc.*, 83 B.R. 774 (1988).

For a thorough discussion of the issue of 'adequate protection', see *In re Timbers of Inwood Forest Associates, Ltd*, 808 F.2d 363 (5th Cir. 1987), aff'd, 484 U.S. 365, 108 S.Ct. 626 (1989).
37 Bankruptcy Code section 364 provides as follows:

(d)(1) The court, after notice and a hearing, may authorize the obtaining of credit or the incurring of debt secured by a senior or equal lien on the property of the estate that is subject to a lien only if –
(A) the trustee is unable to obtain such credit otherwise; and
(B) there is adequate protection of the interest of the holder of the lien on the property of the estate on which such senior or equal lien is proposed to be granted.

In practice, it is common for a secured lender in bankruptcy to work out an arrangement, approved by the court after notice and a hearing, whereby the lender in effect readvances the cash collections it receives as new post-petition loans secured by future receivables of the company. For a discussion of these arrangements, see Schochet and Murphy, 'Financing the debtor-in-possession: section 364 of the Bankruptcy Code', 448 PLI/Comm. 445 (1988), and Schochet, Murphy and Germain, 'Post petition financing: section 364 of the Bankruptcy Code', 487 PLI/Comm. 213 (1989).
38 *Major's Furniture Mart, Inc.* v. *Castle Credit Corp.*, 602 F.2d 538, 544 (3rd Cir. 1979).
39 See UCC sections 2–314, 2–315.
40 See, for example, *In re Evergreen Valley Resort, Inc.*, 23 B.R. 659 (Bankr. D. Maine 1982); *In re Hurricane Elkhorn Coal Corporation*, 19 B.R. 609 (W.D. Ky. 1982); *In re Nixon Machinery Co.*, 6 B.R. 847 (E.D. Tenn. 1980).
41 See *Home Bond Co.* v. *McChesney*, 239 U.S. 568 (1915); *Dorothy* v. *Commonwealth Commercial Co.*, 278 Ill. 629, 116 N.E. 143 (1917). A

conservative approach would be for purchases to be made on a discounted basis. The discount could be negotiated prior to each purchase, in part based on the purchaser's then net current cost of funds and the anticipated collection experience of the receivables then to be purchased. Once a discount has been negotiated for each purchase, it would not thereafter be modified or otherwise adjusted for that purchase, irrespective of differences between the actual versus anticipated cost of funds and collection experience. Such pricing would be a factor in favour of characterization of the receivables transaction as a true sale.

42 *People* v. *The Service Institute, Inc.*, 421 N.Y.S.2d 325 (N.Y. Sup. Ct 1979).

43 See discussion in section 2.4.3 above.

44 Alternatively, the SPV may be able to lend proceeds to the originator, although this approach has limited precedent.

45 A company sometimes may require that the receivables transfer be a loan for tax purposes so as, for example, to avoid recognition of a taxable gain that would be triggered if the transfer is treated as a tax sale. Because the bankruptcy and tax sale criteria, although not identical, are similar – and the bankruptcy cases may apply even closer scrutiny than the IRS – structuring a receivables transfer as a bankruptcy sale may well make it also a tax sale.

46 Louisiana has not adopted the Uniform Commercial Code as such. However, articles 1, 3, 4, 5, 7 and 8 of the UCC have been adopted in substance as title 10, Commercial Laws, of the Louisiana Revised Statutes, chapter 1, 3, 4 and 5 (Act No. 92 of 1974, effective 1 January 1975), Acts No. 164, 165 of 1978 (effective 1 January 1979); Article 9 was adopted by Act No. 528 of 1988, effective 1 July 1989, effective date extended to 1 January 1990 by No. 12 of the 1989 Extraordinary Session. *Uniform Commercial Code Reporting Service – State Correlation Tables*, La Page 1 (1989).

47 Chattel paper, however, can also be perfected by the secured party or buyer taking possession. UCC section 9–305.

48 Any argument that the filing of UCC-1 financing statements indicates the parties' intention that the transaction constitutes a secured loan and not a sale can be obviated by stating on the financing statement that the intention is to create a sale and that the filing is being made because the UCC requires it.

49 See Bankruptcy Code section 544(a); *In re Communications Company of America, Inc.*, 84 B.R. 822 (Bankr. M.D.Fl. 1988); *In re Kambourelis*, 8 B.R. 138, 141 (Bankr. N.D.N.Y. 1981).

50 See *Benedict* v. *Ratner*, 268 U.S. 353, 45 S.Ct 566, 69 L.Ed. 991 (1925).

51 *Dearle* v. *Hall*, 3 Russ. 1, 38 Eng. Rep. 475, 10 Eng. Rul. Cas. 478 (1823, 1827); *Corn Exchange Nat'l Bank* v. *Klauder*, 318 U.S. 434 (1943).

52 The UCC, in section 1–103, states that principles of common law not inconsistent with the UCC will continue to apply. This is the so-called 'Swiss Cheese' principle, because the common law fills the holes in the UCC-cheese.

53 See UCC section 9–102(1)(a).

54 See UCC sections 9–105, 9–305.

55 UCC section 9–306(4).

56 An SPV may be reluctant, however, to give such a notice; and an obligor receiving such a notice may choose to ignore it.

57 15 U.S.C. sections 77a *et seq.*

58 15 U.S.C. sections 80a *et seq.*

59 One can perhaps intuitively understand the purpose behind the 1940 Act if one views a company that is principally engaged in owning or holding securities as a miniature stock exchange, and investors in the company as investors in stock traded on the exchange.

60 15 U.S.C. sections 78a *et seq.*

61 For example, the 1940 Act imposes the following general requirements on registered investment companies: (1) restrictions on capital structure (for example, prohibitions or restrictions on the issuance of debt securities), (2) restrictions on the composition of the Board of Directors or other governing body (for example, limits on the number of 'interested persons' appointed), (3) restrictions on investment activities (for example, limits on investments in other investment companies), (4) regulation of advertising (for example, filing of sales literature with the Securities and Exchange Commission), (5) required shareholder votes on a number of issues (for example, approval of adviser contracts, changes in investment policies and appointment of auditors), (6) ongoing reporting and disclosure requirements, and (7) extensive and complicated controls on pricing of investment company shares.

62 Under section 3(a), the term 'investment securities' is defined to include all securities except government securities, securities issued by employees' securities companies, and securities issued by majority-held subsidiaries (provided the owner is not itself an investment company).

63 Section 3(c)(5) similarly exempts entities primarily engaged in making loans to manufacturers, wholesalers, retailers and prospective purchasers of 'specified merchandise, insurance and services'. Under section 3(c)(5)(C), entities primarily engaged in 'purchasing or otherwise acquiring mortgages and other liens on and interests in real estate' are also excluded from the definition of 'investment company' under the 1940 Act. It is this latter exemptive provision which was originally used in securitizing mortgage loans.

64 The SEC has repeatedly emphasized the legislative history of sections 3(c)(5)(A) and (B), which indicates that those sections were intended to

48 STEVEN L. SCHWARCZ

exclude sales finance companies, factoring companies and similar entities from the scope of the 1940 Act. In the case of section 3(5)(B), the SEC staff has interpreted that exemption somewhat narrowly and has refused, for example, to issue no-action letters to companies engaged in making general working capital loans. See, for example, *Alleco, Inc.* (avail. 14 July 1988) (section 3(c)(5)(B) does not include 'a loan that does not relate to the purchase price of specific goods or services even if the loan is secured by the same kind of collateral that secures a sales financing loan'). The staff has indicated, however, that it is currently reviewing 'the application of section 3(5) to various commercial finance activities to determine whether existing staff interpretations should be refined or modified' (*Alleco, Inc.*).

65 A 'no-action' letter is a non-binding response by the SEC staff to a private inquiry indicating that the staff of the SEC will not recommend to the SEC that any enforcement action be taken if a proposed transaction is carried out in a specified manner.

66 See also *Ambassador Capital Corp.* (avail. 6 October 1986) (purchase of air travel credit-card programme accounts receivable falls within section 3(c)(5)(A)); *Woodside Group* (avail. 14 April 1982) (same result regarding acquisition of equipment/facilities lease purchase and option agreements).

67 In placing interests with institutional investors and other entities under the '100 persons or less' exemption set forth in section 3(c)(1), care must be taken to comply with the rule for determining beneficial ownership under section 3(c)(1)(A). Pursuant to that subsection, beneficial ownership by a company is generally deemed to be ownership by only one person. In an important exception to that general rule, however, it is necessary to look through the investing company and count its ultimate security holders if the company owns 10 per cent or more of the outstanding securities of the SPV unless the value of all securities owned by such company in all issuers exempted under section 3(c)(1), together with all securities in issuers which would be exempt thereunder were it not for the beneficial ownership rules, does not exceed 10 per cent of the investing company's total assets.

68 17 C.F.R. sections 230.501 *et seq.*

69 In addition to banks, insurance companies and other institutional investors, the categories of accredited investors under Regulation D include individuals with a net worth of $1 million or more and partnerships and corporations with total assets in excess of $5 million. 17 C.F.R. section 230.501(a).

70 17 C.F.R. section 230.144.

71 The SEC recently adopted Rule 144A. It generally provides a non-exclusive 'safe harbour' exemption for resales of restricted securities to 'qualified institutional buyers', provided that such buyers had more than

$100 million in the aggregate owned and invested in securities on a discretionary basis (or $10 million in securities with respect to dealers). Securities Act Release No. 6862. It is expected that this rule will increase the efficiency and liquidity of the private placement market.

72 Unlike section 4(2), which is a 'transactional' exemption applicable to all types of securities, section 3 of the 1933 Act exempts entire specified classes of securities from the registration requirements of that act. Section 3(a)(2) includes among those classes 'securities . . . guaranteed by any bank', with the term 'bank' defined to mean 'any national bank, or any banking institution organized under the laws of any State, territory, or the District of Columbia, the business of which is substantially confined to banking and is supervised by the State or territorial banking commission or similar official'. This exemption is not often used in structured financing because the letter of credit typically covers only a portion of the securities.

73 Specifically, section 3(a)(3) exempts '[a]ny note, draft, bill of exchange, or banker's acceptance which arises out of a current transaction or the proceeds of which have been or are to be used for current transactions, and which has a maturity at the time of issuance of not exceeding nine months, exclusive of days of grace, or any renewal thereof the maturity of which is likewise limited'. Commercial paper may also be privately placed without registration under section 4(2) of the 1933 Act (discussed above), but this approach is less common.

74 See, for example, *Westinghouse Credit Corporation* (avail. 5 May 1986) (proceeds used for equipment financing, acquisition of personal property through foreclosure, short-term commercial loans, accounts receivable loans, inventory loans and floor-plan loans all constitute current transactions); *American Fletcher Mortgage Investors* (avail. 1 April 1971) (construction mortgage loans and warehousing loans with commitments for permanent takeouts in three years constitute current transactions, but development mortgage loans maturing in five years or less do not).

75 See 17 C.F.R. section 240.10b–5.

76 Banking Act of 1933, ch. 89, Pub. L. No. 73–66, 48 Stat. 162 (1933), codified as amended in various sections of 12 U.S.C.

77 703 F.Supp 256 (C.S.D.N.Y. 1988).

78 *Securities Industries Ass'n* v. *Clarke*, 885 F.2d 1034 (2d Cir. 1989) cert denied, 110 S. Ct. 1113 (1990).

79 Ibid. at 1043.

80 Ibid. at 1044.

81 Ibid. at 1049.

82 For example, because a bank has explicit power to buy a mortgage loan from a third party and subsequently sell it, could the bank buy mortgage loans with the intention of pooling them for securitization?

83 Glass–Steagall Act section 20, 48 Stat. at 188 (codified as amended at 12 U.S.C. section 377 [1988]).

84 The Federal Reserve Board had originally given section 20 subsidiaries the power to underwrite these types of securities backed by receivables originated by third parties. The recent (September 1989) expansion of these powers allows section 20 subsidiaries to underwrite these types of securities backed by receivables originated by the bank or its affiliates.

85 *Securities Industries Ass'n* v. *Board of Governors, Fed. Reserve Sys.*, 900 F. 2d 360 (D. C. Cir. 1990).

3

Securitization Structures in the United Kingdom (with emphasis on Mortgage-Backed Securities)

RUPERT BEAUMONT

3.1 Introduction

By comparison with the United States, securitization is a relatively
recent phenomenon in the international debt market. The first mortgage securitization issue arranged in London for the international
market was MINI, a £50 million refinancing of certain BankAmerica
Finance Limited UK residential property mortgages, which was
launched in January 1985. Since then there has been quite a large
volume of rated UK mortgage-backed issues, principally tapping the
sterling FRN (floating rate note) market. Repackagings of other types
have also been plentiful throughout the second half of the 1980s,
frequently involving the creation of investment instruments of one
type out of other types of marketable security, such as the conversion
of £ fixed-rate gilts into £ zero-coupon debentures (Zebras), $ FRNs
into $ fixed (Flags), $ FRNs into £ FRNs (Stripes) and ECU fixed into
$ FRNs (Ferraris). Sometimes, the objective has been the avoidance
of local legal or tax difficulties (for example, RAPTs, certain participation certificates), to repackage perpetual notes (for example, Pacific
Securities), to enhance sovereign or Third World debt (for example,
Italex, Continental Bermuda). More recently, there has been activity
in the securitization of UK consumer debt, though it seems doubtful
whether these instruments will be frequent visitors to the market in
current conditions.

In view of the predominance of mortgage-backed issues, the
remainder of this chapter, other than a brief section on off-balance-
sheet considerations (see section 3.3 below), will be devoted
exclusively to mortgage-backed securities.

3.2 Mortgage-Backed Securities

3.2.1 *Commercial Incentives*

The commercial considerations which underlie the mortgage-
securitization market are more fully discussed elsewhere in this
volume (for example, chapters 1 and 6). From the perspective of a
consideration of legal structures, the key commercial factor is often
the mortgage originator's desire to remove the mortgage pool from its
balance sheet. Related to this objective is the question of credit risk,

since the retention of any such risk will inhibit the basic objective. Furthermore, where the mortgage originator is a UK authorized bank, the Bank of England insists that the credit risk must be removed as one of the conditions for accepting that the mortgage pool should be excluded from the calculation of the mortgage originator's risk/asset ratio (see below in this chapter and in chapter 10).

The discussion in this chapter will, therefore, concentrate on structures that remove the mortgage pool and the credit risk from the mortgage originator.

3.2.2 *Mortgage-Backed Structures and Ratings*

The considerations briefly mentioned above all point to a special-purpose issuing vehicle (SPV) interposed between the investor and the mortgage originator. There is another compelling reason for the use of an SPV. The securitization of a mortgage pool or, indeed, any other asset pool has *prima facie* attributes of a collective investment scheme for the purposes of the Financial Services Act 1986 (the FSA). The FSA provisions relating to collective investment schemes are designed to regulate collective participation (for investment purposes) in any kind of asset. Stringent marketing restrictions apply; and the 'manager' of the underlying assets would need to be a person authorized to carry on investment business in the United Kingdom. This would involve substantial time and cost devoted to regulatory compliance.

However, there is an exception from the collective investment scheme requirements (granted partly as a result of representations from those involved in the securitization markets) where the 'rights or interests of the participants [that is, the investors] are represented by [debt instruments] issued by a single body corporate . . .'. An SPV may take advantage of this exception (as may the originator or whoever it is who is to service the mortgage pool). On the other hand, US-style 'pass-through' arrangements would almost certainly constitute a collective investment scheme, as would arrangements that interposed a trust structure between the investors and the mortgage pool.

Reduced to its most basic level, the securitization structure revolves round the SPV and the different methods of making it sufficiently creditworthy for an issue.

The question of creditworthiness raises the issue of rating, a subject more fully discussed in chapter 6. The commercial desirability of obtaining a rating from one or both of Standard & Poor's and Moody's also has a very strong influence on the securitization structure. The highest rating, and the one that is generally aimed for in order to raise funds at an acceptable cost, is AAA/Aaa. Such a rating is a message to the market that the ability of the issuer to repay the notes and to pay interest in full and on time is extremely strong. The rating agency will only award such a rating if it is convinced that the integrity of the issuer and its cash flow is virtually assured, come what may.

As part of the agency's assessment of the issuer's resilience, it will determine a 'worst-case' scenario, in which the issuer will still be expected to perform its obligations under the notes. For this purpose, particularly in the case of two-tier (senior/junior) notes, the agency will require from the issuer and its advisers detailed cash-flow projections drawn up on a so-called 'stressed' basis, to reflect the worst-case assumptions. For example, despite the fact that UK building society loan loss experience from 1970 to 1987 (inclusive) shows that losses each year on total building society loans outstanding were less than 0.01 per cent, the Standard & Poor's stress criterion has on some issues involved a default assumption of 20–25 per cent (depending on average loan-to-value) and a house price decline of 37 per cent, resulting in a loss severity assumption of 6 or 7 per cent. During the last two years, Moody's have taken a relatively pessimistic view of the likely rate of mortgage loan defaults in the current economic and competitive environments and Standard & Poor's have also more recently been sounding cautionary notes. Another example of the severity of the Standard & Poor's criteria is the assumed rate of return on cash held by the issuer: LIBOR (London Inter-bank Offered Rate) less 5 per cent per annum, unless a rated source of interest at an assured rate can be demonstrated.

'Stressing' enables the rating agency to quantify the amount of capital and liquidity 'cover' it will require to ensure that in the worst-case situations the issuer will still be able to pay its way. It follows that whatever capital and other support the issuer may have must be copper-bottomed in legal terms, not so much in a liquidation of the issuer (since that is reckoned to be a remote eventuality) but in a liquidation of the provider of the capital or other support. Thus, the issuer's lawyer is required to give the relevant rating agency a legal opinion in considerable detail, typically running to twenty-five or thirty pages.

Securing a AAA/Aaa rating at the closing of the issue is not, of course, the end of the story. The creditworthiness of the issuer will be kept under constant review by the relevant agency/ies during the life of the issue. The issuer's credit rating is vulnerable to events affecting third parties, especially where it relies on the credit standing of a third party (such as the provider of pool insurance or a committed provider of credit). For example, the highly leveraged bid for BAT Industries in 1988/89 caused doubts to be raised over the credit rating of BAT's insurance subsidiary, Eagle Star. Such doubt in turn impacted on those issues for which Eagle Star had provided pool insurance. More general developments – for example, concerning the economy as a whole, or a particular sector of it – could also adversely affect the rating.

3.2.3 Loss and Liquidity Risk Implications

Issuer's basic assets What assets will the issuer have? Obviously, in the case of a mortgage securitization, the principal assets, which will be acquired with most of the net proceeds of the note issue, will be the initial portfolio of mortgages. Others will include whatever cash the issuer has at the outset, for example through the issue of its share capital and the borrowing of any subordinated debt finance that it needs. Some of this cash will immediately be spent on initial expenses and will thus be replaced by an intangible asset – issue expenses – which is of no use to the noteholders and will be written off over the expected average life of the issue. The balance of such cash will be either invested in qualifying short-dated investments or placed on deposit with qualifying institutions. As the issuer's income comes in – principally interest and MIRAS payments (payments from the UK Inland Revenue representing the amount of mortgage interest relief to which the borrowers, if UK taxpayers, are normally entitled and which they obtain at source by way of withholding from the interest payments they make to the lender) – the cash will be either placed on deposit or invested in qualifying investments. Cash representing principal receipts – mainly on redemption of mortgages – will also be so deposited or invested pending its use in making further advances or purchasing substitute loans, if those options are available, or in purchasing or redeeming notes or, perhaps, in meeting revenue or other expenses not covered by income. The issuer's assets will, therefore, from time to time include cash (that is, debts owing by banks) and marketable securities.

This basic picture – that is, mortgage pool plus qualifying liquid assets – would be the simplest structure. However, it would only be acceptable to the relevant rating agency as providing both the necessary loss protection (both in respect of the mortgage pool and in respect of any income shortfalls resulting from certain risks enlarged upon below) and the necessary liquidity (that is, ready cash) to meet the rating agency's various worst-case assumptions if the amount of capital (including subordinated debt finance) paid into the issuer, or unconditionally available to it from an appropriately rated source, was of such a size as to be, as a practical matter, uneconomically large and therefore unacceptable to the originator or whoever else is capitalizing the issuer. Consequently, a number of alternative techniques have been developed over the years – originating particularly in the US – for enhancing the issuer's basic mortgage pool and such liquid assets as it may have from time to time, so as to reduce the need for capital.

Credit risk   This is the obvious risk of the issuer suffering a loss because of some weakness in the assets it owns. It potentially applies to both mortgages and liquid assets and indeed to any other assets such as the benefit of contracts. It applies to both income and principal; if a mortgage borrower goes into default and a loss is realized on enforcing the security, there is obviously both a loss of principal (and therefore a prospective inability to repay the notes in full) and a loss of interest income in the meantime, leading to a prospective or potential shortfall in funds required by the issuer to pay its note interest and other expenses. A similar risk applies if a bank with which funds are deposited becomes insolvent; this risk is generally thought to be adequately covered by limiting the investment of liquid funds to deposits with banks with the top short-term credit ratings (A1+ or P1) and to certain rated or government money-market instruments, or (sometimes) to the notes themselves, subject in all cases to safeguards. As regards the credit risk on mortgages, there are at present two principal alternative ways of dealing with this in a rated issue – pool policies and two-tier issues.

(1) *Pool policies*.   Under this structure the issuer is issued with a pool insurance policy by an insurance company with, or backed by, the requisite long-term credit rating. This must be a long-term policy,

covering the issuer (normally subject to a cumulative maximum of, say, 8 to 10 per cent of the initial mortgage pool) against any loss of principal, interest (including interest on interest) and costs suffered in the mortgage pool to the extent not covered by any other applicable loss insurance (such as a mortgage indemnity policy applicable to the relevant mortgage). If it only pays that share of principal which is not, under the relevant lending criteria, required to be covered by an applicable mortgage indemnity policy, the insurance company issuing the latter policy must also have – or its payment obligations must be guaranteed or reinsured by an institution which has – the requisite credit rating since its failure to pay will result in a credit loss which is not covered by the pool policy. The pool insurer normally requires the mortgages to conform to certain minimum lending criteria, failing which the relevant mortgages may not be insured, though sometimes cover remains available within a smaller cumulative limit. This risk is passed back to the originator, via warranties to the issuer and a put option in favour of the latter on to the former where there is a breach of warranty. Since the originator may well not be rated to AAA/Aaa standard (or at all), there is a theoretical risk of a substandard credit; thus, the rating agency will, if only for this reason, wish to be satisfied with the consistency of quality and accuracy in the originator's lending procedures. One of the pre-issue procedures that is required by the agency is an audit to a high level of confidence on the securitized pool conforming to key lending criteria.

If any excess or deductible is applicable to claims by the issuer under the pool policy, the rating agency will want the full amount of the excess to be funded in cash or by means of a committed facility granted to the issuer by an adequately rated institution. Alternatively, the pool insurer may be prepared to dispense with an excess on claims by the issuer (that is, provide insurance from the floor up) and instead to rely upon some form of reimbursement obligation on the part of, say, the originator.

All of these differing pool-policy structures for the principal loss risk – and there are other permutations that have not been mentioned – will, of course, give rise to different documentation requirements.

(2) *Two-tier (senior/junior) issues.* This structure is now well known in the UK market. The principle is a variation on the basic theme, that the simplest way of covering the credit risk and also the various other risks that are mentioned below is by having a large enough capital. In

a two-tier issue, the (much smaller) junior class of notes is effectively
another layer of capital for the senior (rated) notes. In the simpler
structures, the junior notes simply defer repaying until after the senior
tranche has been repaid in full; and on an enforcement of the security
for the notes, they rank junior to the senior notes. In the more complex cases, started by Household Mortgage Corporation in early 1988,
there is a system for redeeming the junior notes, after an initial period
where only the senior notes redeem, *pro rata* and concurrently with the
senior notes but only so long as at the relevant time there is no
outstanding principal deficiency – that is, a prospective shortfall in
principal caused generally by a mortgage loss – which has not been
made good by subsequent surplus income earned by the issuer.

In these issues, there is a strict order of payments at and between
interest resetting dates for the notes, designed to ensure that the
interest on the senior notes, as well as all other issuer expenses except
interest on the junior notes and on any subordinated funding, is paid
when it falls due so as to keep the issuer solvent. If necessary, these
payments are made at the cost of deferring, at least in the short term
but possibly for ever, the relevant interest payment on the junior
notes. However, if income and any capital receipts are adequate, such
interest as accrues currently is paid and only then is an assessment
made as to whether and to what extent the senior and, if appropriate,
the junior notes can or must be repaid to reflect receipts of principal
moneys by the issuer, mainly from mortgage redemptions. The order
of payments is also designed to ensure that the full amount potentially
repayable on the senior notes is provided for (if not actually repaid) in
calculating what can be repaid on the junior notes.

The deferral of interest and/or principal on the junior notes is not an
event of default; these events are limited to the usual events in relation
to the senior notes and to insolvency and similar events. On enforcement of the security, the junior notes rank in point of security beneath
the senior notes.

Income risks   Under this heading come risks of permanent depletion
or loss of income rather than simply the risk of delayed receipt of
income; the latter – which is a liquidity risk – is dealt with under the
heading 'Liquidity risk' below.

(1) *Interest mismatch and exceptional expense.*   The most important
income risk is the possibility of the mortgage rate being less than that

required – or deemed by the rating agency to be required – to cover the issuer's quarterly note interest expense plus its other expenses such as agency fees, trustee fees, ordinary management expenses, note purchase or redemption expenses, tax (if any) and so on. This gap is most likely to occur through an increase in LIBOR (and thus the interest rate on the notes) at the rate-fixing date, which is not immediately – or is perhaps never – covered by an increase in the mortgage rate. However, the gap could also occur through an unexpectedly high level of other expenditure, such as expected expenses exceeding budgeted levels (a risk Moody's is particularly concerned about), or the occurrence of unexpected liabilities such as a new form of taxation of the issuer, or the costs of convening a meeting of noteholders or litigation.

This interest-shortfall risk is generally covered by a requirement on the issuer, through the agency of the administrator, to reset the mortgage rate at a level sufficient to cover the shortfall in cash no later than the ensuing interest payment date for the notes. But this may be commercially unacceptable to the originator/administrator, and thus it is normally provided that funds may instead be paid to the issuer to bridge the gap. The risk might instead be covered by a third-party (rated) credit facility. In either case, the documents will have to deal with the terms and conditions relating to the repayment of such funding and the payment of any interest thereon. The degree of subordination tends to vary but the funds should at least be locked into the issuer until the shortfall they were covering has been made good by an increase in the mortgage rate over and above that required to cover a shortfall in subsequent interest periods.

Low-start, stabilized, deferred interest and similar mortgages give rise to a further gap in current cash flow (compared with interest payments on the notes) and are covered either by overfunding through the notes, the overfunding being set aside into a fund which is periodically released to supplement cash flow, or by funding from some other (rated) source on similar repayment terms to those referred to above, or from mortgage redemption moneys.

Fixed-rate mortgages, 'collars', 'caps' and similar products usually give rise to the need for a swap or similar instrument from a rated source for the duration of the fixed-rate feature.

(2) Reinvestment rate.   Another income risk applies where cash is held instead of mortgages, for example cash arising from the redemption of

mortgages. Such cash will earn interest at less than the mortgage rate. This will obviously result in a lower income to the issuer and, if the redemption moneys so invested are sizeable and are not invested in the notes themselves, could actually result in an income shortfall after taking account of expenditure.

This risk is often mitigated by the issuer entering into a deposit agreement with a (rated) bank in which the latter assures to the issuer a fixed rate of return, expressed as a margin by reference to LIBOR, on any liquid funds deposited with it. Although this rate will obviously not be as high as the mortgage rate or even the note rate – it is likely to be around LIBID (London Interbank Bid Rate) – it will, if the bank has an adequate credit rating, at least enable the rating agency to allow a more lenient cash reinvestment rate assumption for the purposes of the stressed cash-flow projections than its normal criterion demands. This arrangement, often called a 'guaranteed investment contract', tends to be based on merely an A1+ or P1 credit rating for the relevant bank, that is, a short-term rating. This means that the issuer needs some form of long-term AAA back-up facility. Alternatively, the rating agency is likely to stick to its stringent investment rate assumption for the stressed cash flows after the first year (which is the horizon for a short-term credit rating).

Another method of covering the reinvestment rate risk, even where a guaranteed investment contract is used, is to have a cash fund available for the purpose.

(3) *Swaps and parallel loans.* Both of the above income risks can, alternatively, be dealt with through a swap or parallel loan mechanism. This can tie in with one of the usual means of extracting profit from the issuer where it is not a subsidiary of, nor able to issue preference shares to, the originator, as would be the case under the Bank of England's requirements and to avoid the originator having a 'participating interest' within the meaning of the Companies Act 1989. If the swap or parallel loan counterparty does not have the requisite long-term rating to enable the issuer to obtain the desired rating for the notes, some form of rated guarantee, reinsurance or similar credit enhancement may be necessary.

Liquidity risk We now move on to the general liquidity risk, that is, the risk of the issuer having inadequate ready cash or credit lines to pay its debts as they fall due. This is likely to be principally of relevance to the interest on the notes and the issuer's other revenue expenses, but there is also a liquidity risk on principal – of particular importance on short-dated issues, which are referred to below.

Whether affecting income or principal, the cause of the delay – for example, borrowers changing their bank accounts and failing to complete new direct debit forms – may not necessarily mean that losses will ensue. But the liquidity risk needs to be covered both to avoid insolvency in the issuer and to achieve a rating.

To the extent that the issuer does not have – or is deemed by the rating agency not to have – adequate free cash representing its locked-in capital funds, it will need access to an appropriately rated committed loan or standby letter of credit facility or to a separate fund held in readiness. There have been cases of such a facility being effected in the form of an interim claims facility under a pool policy where, unlike most interim claims provisions in such policies, drawings can be made immediately rather than only when an actual net loss can be estimated after exercise of the power of sale.

Again, the repayment and interest terms under such a facility will require careful documentation. Normally the lender would expect, as to both interest on and principal of drawings under the facility, to rank ahead of the notes on an enforcement of the security on the basis that the facility is in the nature of an overdraft, intended only for temporary use. Prior to enforcement, it is common for the liquidity provider to receive repayment of his drawings only as and when the defaulted interest payments giving rise to them are recovered, but to receive interest currently, perhaps itself funded by a drawing under the liquidity facility.

In a senior/junior note structure, the need for an outside facility for liquidity purposes will normally be unnecessary as the deferral of interest on the junior tranche will fulfil that role so far as interest on the senior notes (and any other revenue expenses of the issuer) is concerned. Obviously, the 'sizing' of the junior tranche will be done having regard not only to the rating agency's assumed worst-case credit loss exposure, but also to the ability of the junior note interest to bear the assumed interest delays on the underlying mortgages. Deferred junior note interest does not itself bear interest.

Normally, the risk of illiquidity for the repayment of note principal is minimal because, apart from repayments during the life of the notes reflecting actual mortgage redemptions, the final maturity occurs after (normally two years after) the final possible mortgage redemption

date. This has been the consistent picture so far in the UK for FRNs.
However, there have, at the time of writing, been two five-year fixed-
rate note issues on the back of twenty-five-year underlying mortgages.
These issues involved an obvious principal liquidity problem in the
absence of some means for the fixed-rate note issuer to obtain the
requisite funds at year 5. This was provided by the grant to the issuer
by an AAA-rated insurance company of a put option at par exercisable
for value on the maturity date of the notes. And instead of the option
being over the then outstanding mortgage portfolio, it was over a
marketable security held by the fixed-rate note issuer, namely an
equivalent principal amount of conventional underlying long-term
FRNs issued by the company holding the mortgage portfolio and
secured on the portfolio.

Summary of loss and liquidity support documents   The documents
that may typically be required to ensure that the issuer is adequately
equipped, in terms of assets and rights over and above its agreed paid
up share capital, are:

1   if the issuer has any form of capital funds by way of loan, including
    those funds which are used to pay initial expenses, a loan agree-
    ment containing suitable subordination conditions and probably
    including as a party the trustee for the noteholders;
2   to meet the credit risk:
    • a mortgage indemnity policy, or at least an interest in the
      originator's existing policy; and either
    • a pool insurance policy and, possibly, an excess reimbursement
      undertaking between the pool insurer and, for example, the
      originator or administrator or alternatively extra capital or
      unconditional access to a separate fund or a committed facility;
      or
    • a senior/junior note structure;
3   to meet the interest-basis risk and the exceptional-liabilities risk,
    an obligation on the administrator to set the mortgage rate
    adequately, in the absence of *ad hoc* funding, the terms of which
    need at least to some extent to be subordinated;
4   to meet the reinvestment-rate risk, a guaranteed investment con-
    tract, with or without enhancement of the counterparty-credit risk
    (for example, by way of guarantee), and/or a cash fund of some
    kind;

5   possibly (as an alternative to the two preceding items) a swap or
    parallel loan agreement with respect to the issuer's income stream,
    with or without enhancement of the counterparty-credit risk;
6   to deal with the liquidity risk (except in a senior/junior note struc-
    ture), a facility agreement from an external source of funds, with
    or without counterparty credit risk enhancement.

3.2.4 Administration

Provision requires to be made for the administration of the issuer's
assets and liabilities. This often involves the appointment of the originator as the issuer's and the trustee's agent for that purpose, since the
originator is frequently the lender and therefore the institution with
the continuing relationship with the borrowers. However, there are
issuers and lenders which retain professional third-party administra-
tors. The rating agencies are naturally concerned to ensure that the
administrator is properly experienced and has the necessary systems in
place. An audit on the initial mortgage pool to a high degree of
confidence is required at the outset and this will be an important part
of the rating agency's process of reviewing the administrator's
capabilities.

Continuity of administration is obviously of the utmost importance.
The administrator may not resign unless a successor is in place.
Moody's attach particular importance to the existence from the outset
of an agreement with the issuer from a suitable organization to undertake the administration role if the need arises during the life of the
notes; this potential successor administrator will require some form of
commitment fee from the issuer. Whether or not there is a successor
agency agreement, access by the trustee to software and files on
termination of the agency is important. Sometimes duplicate disks are
held in escrow for release to the issuer/trustee if the administrator's
role is terminated.

Other issues that need to be addressed are the level and ranking of
administration fees; liability for acts or omissions; and insurance
against error and employee fraud.

The custody and storage of deeds are of major importance, giving
rise to provisions governing identification, access and inspection,
insurance, and the monitoring and control of removal, whether on
redemptions or for other reasons.

The administration of the mortgage pool includes dealing with the important areas of interest-rate setting and arrears management. Unless the administrator is also the original lender or the issuer is a member of the original lender's group of companies, these two discretions will have to be exercised by the original lender in order to comply with the Department of the Environment's and HM Treasury's November 1989 *Statement of Practice*. This document as presently drafted, and its 'adoption' by lenders, are likely to give rise to greater legal difficulties than its predecessor (the Secondary Mortgage Market Working Group's 1987 *Statement of Practice*), unless (which is very unlikely) specific consent to the sale of the mortgages to the issuer has been obtained from the borrowers, or (which is more likely) the originator's standard documentation adequately qualifies its adoption of the new *Statement of Practice* so that its more troublesome provisions are not regarded as implied mortgage terms.

3.2.5 *Structure Protection Provisions*

Various matters need to be the subject of covenants and remedies in favour of the issuer and the noteholders' trustee. Some are also included to protect the originator.

Mortgage pool   Provision must be made for the protection of, and future developments relating to, the mortgage pool and other assets, which may also, subject to suitable safeguards, give the originator a reasonable degree of flexibility in the light of changing mortgage markets. For example:

1   warranties will be required to be given by the originator at the outset, for example, as to the pool's compliance with the lending criteria described in the offering circular and as to the originator's title;
2   the consequence of a breach of warranty should be provided for, normally by a put option back to the originator in exchange for cash at par;
3   a call option for the originator may be included, which might, for example, be exercised if there were a mortgagor's default which the originator wished to handle at a more lenient pace than that allowed by the pool insurers or the note trustee or the rating agency, or to enable a total refinancing;
4   there may be a mortgage-substitution right, involving the need for

warranties in respect of the new loans and an increasing array of
conditions laid down by the rating agencies, generally to prevent
substitution if there is (or is deemed by their criteria to be) a
deterioration in the quality of the pool;
5 the types of mortgage which may be substituted may be fairly
   broadly defined, but different products bring different risks and
   problems;
6 further advances may be permitted, subject to appropriate warranties, suitable procedures to avoid legal difficulties and again
   various conditions precedent;
7 changes in mortgage and other terms may be permitted, subject to
   appropriate warranties;
8 perfection and/or enforcement of the issuer's and the trustee's
   titles should be covered.

Corporate constraints The second main function of these contractual provisions is to lay down certain constraints and corporate disci-
plines, to the extent not covered by negative pledge and other
restrictive covenants in the terms and conditions of the notes (for
example, as to borrowings, disposal of assets and mergers). For
instance, there will be limits on the use of principal moneys in the
issuer's hands, on the types of marketable securities or deposits which
are available to the issuer in investing its cash resources, on the use
and repayment of loan facilities, and on the use of surplus income to
repay subordinated debt or to pay dividends.

3.2.6 *Issuer's and Trustee's Interests in Mortgages*

So far as the mortgages are concerned, practice has differed as to the
type of interest therein that is vested in the issuer. It is now common
practice for the issuer's interest in registered land not to be the subject
of any form of registration at HM Land Registry or to be notified to
borrowers, life companies and so on, but for this step to be reserved in
case the trustee becomes concerned that the security is in jeopardy or
in case it becomes enforceable. The initial transfer therefore only
confers an equitable title on the issuer. A full legal title to mortgages
over unregistered land can be taken, though this leads to some compli-
cation in the context of further advances and it is now common for
only equitable title to mortgages over unregistered land, as well as to
mortgages over registered land, to be taken.

The trustee's security over the mortgages, which is a subcharge and neither registered nor notified, takes effect in equity only, both for registered and unregistered land, but is buttressed by further assurance provisions and irrevocable powers of attorney. This involves obvious legal risks, which should be pointed out in the offering circular.

The trustee will, however, require instant access to the title deeds, which should be held to its order in a manner permitting immediate identification and access. Sometimes the position is complicated by the deeds being held by a third-party depository rather than the originator itself and in these cases the depository should enter into direct undertakings with the issuer and the trustee.

3.2.7 *Notes and Security Documents*

The notes themselves must (if issued by a UK-resident company, as has been the case hitherto) be in bearer form (as well as listed) in order to ensure that the interest can be paid gross. Sometimes a registered option is built in to cater for US investors, but they have to accept that this interest will be paid net of UK basic rate tax unless treaty relief is available. There is no 'gross up' obligation even for bearer notes. Permanent (in the absence of certain events affecting the clearing systems) global bearer notes, traded only by book-entry at the clearing systems, are commonplace, but give rise to questions as to who exactly the noteholders are *vis-à-vis* the issuer and the trustee.

Practice varies on whether redemptions of notes are by drawings or *pro rata*. The latter requires the notes to be in global form. Where there is a junior tranche of notes, which is designed to absorb losses at the end of the day, the only fair method for them to be redeemed is *pro rata*, so that all of the holders of that class of notes share *pro rata* in any losses. There are a number of single-tranche (pool-policy protected) issues which are in global form, some of which provide for underlying notes being selected for redemption by drawings.

The security provisions include appropriate charges over or assignments (subject to a proviso for reassignment) of all of the issuer's assets, together with a general floating charge. Certain of the charges expressed as fixed charges may in fact be floating charges, for example, over liquid assets managed by or on behalf of the issuer and capable of being sold without the trustee's consent each time. In many cases, notices of assignment will be required. Powers of attorney are also executed.

3.3 Off-Balance-Sheet Considerations

3.3.1 *Introduction*

In any type of securitization, whether of mortgages or otherwise, one of the fundamental commercial objectives of the securitization may be to remove the assets and their financing from the balance sheet of the originator and from the consolidated balance sheet of the group of companies of which it forms part. In the mortgage field, there are some funding organizations which have been set up to make and finance mortgage advances introduced to it by other organizations in exchange for a broking fee with the intention that the relevant mortgages and their funding should never form part of the balance sheet of the broker.

In any of these cases, English (or Scottish or Northern Irish) law and UK accounting practices will be applicable if the originator (the person who wishes to avoid having the assets and their financing on its balance sheet) or any of its parent companies is registered in Great Britain.

3.3.2 *The Companies Acts*

Part I of the Companies Act 1989 extensively amends and restates part VII of the Companies Act 1985. One of these amendments applies the duty to prepare group accounts to a parent company in respect of itself and its 'subsidiary undertakings'. This expression is defined in new section 258 of the 1985 Act as supplemented by new Schedule 10A.

It is necessary to ensure that neither the issuing vehicle for the purposes of the securitization nor its parent company, if any, is a 'subsidiary undertaking' of either the originator or the originator's own parent company. On the assumption that neither the originator nor any parent company of the originator (referred to below collectively as the originator) seeks to hold or control a majority of the voting rights in the issuer or its parent company (referred to below collectively as the issuer) or to control board meetings of the issuer, the only two situations which are likely to be of concern in the context of securitizations are the following:

- if the originator has 'the right to exercise a dominant influence' over the issuer, either by virtue of provisions contained in the issuer's memorandum or articles of association or by virtue of a 'control contract', or
- where the originator has a 'participating interest' in the issuer and either it actually exercises a dominant influence over it or it and the issuer are managed on a 'unified basis'.

It will be noted that where the originator has the right to exercise a dominant influence over the issuer as described above, this alone is enough to make the issuer its 'subsidiary undertaking' without the need for any shareholding. This expression is amplified in paragraph 4 of schedule 10A to the 1985 Act as being a 'right to give directions with respect to the operating and financial policies of [the issuer] which its directors are obliged to comply with whether or not they are for the benefit of [the issuer]'. But, as mentioned above, it must arise either by virtue of provisions contained in the issuer's memorandum or articles or by virtue of a control contract, that is, a contract in writing conferring the right, being a right which is of a kind authorized by the memorandum or articles and is permitted by the issuer's law of establishment. In the context of English companies, it seems unlikely that a control contract will exist, since it contemplates in effect the abdication by the company concerned of its basic business decisions to someone other than its directors, even though those decisions may not be for the benefit of the company.

The second situation referred to above is concerned with the *de facto* exercise of a dominant influence (rather than possession of the right to exercise a dominant influence) or the management of the two companies on a unified basis, but only in either case where the originator has a 'participating interest'. This is defined in new section 260 as meaning shares which are held on a long-term basis for the purpose of securing a contribution to the activities of the company in question, by the exercise of control or influence arising from or related to that interest. 'Shares' are defined in sections 259 and 260(3) and, so long as there is no shareholding link between the originator and the issuer nor any deferred shareholding by means of a convertible loan or an option, neither *de facto* dominant influence nor management on a unified basis should cause the issuer or its parent to be a subsidiary undertaking of the originator or its parent.

3.3.3 *Exposure Draft 49*

In May 1990 the Accounting Standards Committee (ASC) issued its Exposure Draft (ED) 49 entitled 'Reflecting the substance of transactions in assets and liabilities', which followed the ASC's earlier ED42 entitled 'Accounting for special purpose transactions'. The thrust of ED49 is to propose a conceptual approach to accounting for assets and liabilities, rejecting a strict formal analysis of 'ownership' or 'liability' in favour of an analysis which depends on the economic substance. The Exposure Draft develops this new conceptual approach by giving practical assistance in relation to various types of complex transactions affecting assets and liabilities, including securitizations.

In essence, if an asset, although sold to an entity which is not a subsidiary undertaking for Companies Act purposes, involves future benefits and risks which will accrue to or be borne by the originator, that asset is to be treated as controlled by the originator. It is then argued that it would be contrary to the overriding requirement of section 226 of the Companies Act 1985 (that the originator's accounts show a 'true and fair view' of its state of affairs) for the relevant asset (and the liability representing its funding) to be omitted from such accounts, having regard to such expected benefits and risks for the originator.

Thus ED49 requires, depending on the circumstances, either that the sale of the relevant asset be disregarded for purposes of the originator's accounts, and that it thus continue to be reflected therein, or (more likely) that the purchaser be viewed as a 'quasi-subsidiary' of the originator and consolidated in its group accounts as if it were a Companies Act subsidiary undertaking. The legality of the latter approach is questionable – new section 227 of the Companies Act 1985 sets out the legal test for inclusion of undertakings in a consolidation and there is a view that the 'true and fair' requirement cannot override this basic requirement. The same result is achieved, however, under the first approach.

ED49 provides that this result (undesirable from the originator's perspective) may be avoided if, broadly speaking, the future risk element for the originator can be virtually eliminated, so that only the expected future net income benefit to the originator remains in the structure. ED49 contains a detailed set of risk reduction requirements for mortgage securitizations, satisfaction of all of which will (if ED49 becomes a Statement of Standard Accounting Practice (SSAP) in its present form): (1) avoid the need for the originator to recognize in its own accounts either the mortgages (and their funding) or their cash flow; (2) avoid the purchasing vehicle (the issuer) being regarded as a quasi-subsidiary and having to be consolidated; (3) require disclosure of the originator's economic interest to be made by way of note to its own (and its group) accounts, including by giving a summary balance sheet and profit and loss account of the issuer, and (4) require recognition in the originator's accounts of the net present value of the estimated future benefit to it of the sale – which is likely to be the future receipts by it under the sale terms of deferred consideration for the mortgages (see 'Profit Extraction' on p. 71).

The list of risk reduction requirements contained in ED49 is similar to that in the Bank of England's February 1989 *Notice* on its supervisory policy on the treatment of loan transfers involving banks. The scope for funding to be provided to the issuer on a continuing basis by the originator is limited. However, as drafted (subject to a few relatively minor modifications), ED49 should enable a carefully structured and documented mortgage securitization to be off balance sheet for the originator. Nevertheless, it remains to be seen how the definitive SSAP looks when issued.

So far as other securitizations are concerned, the relevant application note forming part of ED49 warns that the securitization of assets other than mortgages generally involves considerations that may prevent off-balance-sheet treatment. For example, if the principal function of the securitization is not to generate cash for its originator but, rather, that the assets be held in other parts of the business, or, if there is more active (*de facto*) control of the assets of the issuer by the originator than typically applies in a mortgage securitization, or, perhaps, if there are potential liabilities which are peculiar to the particular type of asset, off-balance-sheet treatment may not apply. No such problem was envisaged in the case of the CARS deal, involving the securitization of motor vehicle hire purchase receivables.

At the time of writing, ED49 has not yet metamorphosed into an SSAP and it therefore remains to be seen how the Accounting Standards Board (ASB), the ASC's successor, will deal with representations received on ED49. Once an SSAP is issued, material departures from it will now be able to be challenged by the ASB's

Review Board, which has authority to seek a ruling from the court as to whether or not the relevant accounts give a true and fair view.

3.3.4 *Banks, etc.*

Where the originator is a bank, one of the objectives is likely to be to ensure that the mortgages and their funding are disregarded for banking supervisory purposes as well as for accounting purposes. Thus, in addition to ensuring that the issuer is not a 'subsidiary undertaking' of the bank or its parent company and that the assets and liabilities are not required to be reflected on the bank's balance sheet by the accounting standard which is eventually issued following ED49, the Bank of England's conditions on mortgage transfers as contained in its *Notice* dated February 1989 will also have to be satisfied. It is beyond the scope of this chapter to discuss these conditions or indeed those applicable to other regulated entities, such as building societies and insurance companies.

3.3.5 *Profit Extraction*

In the wake of the Companies Act 1989 and given that taking profit out by way of a continuing fee is likely to run into value added tax and/or tax deductibility problems, there are now broadly speaking three ways which may be available to achieve the extraction from the securitization vehicle (or its parent) of most of its profit for the benefit of the originator, without the latter holding any form of share in the former and ignoring the use of off-shore vehicles:

1 splitting the cash flows receivable by the vehicle by, in effect, partially assigning the assets concerned so that only part of the cash flow is beneficially owned by the vehicle; however, this gives rise to problems in the case of mortgages because of the MIRAS system; a variation on this theme is the so-called 'receivables trust';

2 providing a deferred consideration to the originator where the assets are sold by the originator to the vehicle or brokerage to the originator where they are created by the vehicle at the introduction of the originator; this can only work if the vehicle is a trading, rather than investment, company for tax purposes and is in any case subject to other conditions to achieve tax neutrality in the vehicle;

3   establishing a swap or parallel loan between the originator and the
    vehicle; again tax neutrality is essential but is not always easily
    achievable and recently the Inland Revenue has expressed doubts
    about both such methods, in certain circumstances.

In all cases the shares in the vehicle must be held otherwise than by
or for the originator, and charitable or heritage trusts are common.
However, difficult liability questions arise for the directors, and an
unlimited indemnity in their favour by the originator could prejudice
off-balance-sheet status.

3.4 Conclusion

The market is developing rapidly and, by the time this book is
published, certain of the techniques addressed in this chapter will
have been overtaken by innovations. A single chapter covering the
whole spectrum of UK legal implications of securitizations can only
deal with some of the many legal issues, and even then not in depth.
Each new product that is sought to be securitized brings with it new
legal problems and adds several further pages to the formal opinions
delivered by the lawyers.

4
Selected Legal Aspects of Structured US Mortgage Financing (Including Certain Bank and Thrift Regulatory Concerns)

DAVID G. SABEL and ANDREW A. BERNSTEIN

Chapter Outline

4.1 Introduction

4.1.1 *Nature of Structured Mortgage Financings*

Mortgages have both market value and borrowing value. Mortgage-backed securities are securities structured on the basis of the market value or borrowing value of identified mortgages determined, in principle, without regard to the creditworthiness of the seller or borrower.

4.1.2 *Types of Mortgage-Backed Securities*

Mortgage-backed securities typically take the form, for tax, accounting and other purposes, of a sale or secured financing of a pool of identified mortgages. In the case of mortgage-backed securities structured as financings, the borrowing value of the underlying mortgages may be based on either their market value ('market-value securities') or their anticipated cash flows ('cash-flow securities'). Because mortgages are subject to acceleration and prepayment, referred to generally as early payment, cash-flow securities may be further divided into

Since the date of this chapter (autumn 1989), a number of significant regulatory developments affecting thrift institutions, particularly new net worth requirements, have occurred (see chapter 11).

securities as to which the investor bears the risk of early payment ('pay-through securities') and securities as to which the issuer bears that risk ('fixed-payment securities').

4.1.3 *Issuers*

In order to maximize the separation between the creditworthiness of the ultimate beneficiary of a mortgage-backed financing and the credit of the mortgage-backed security, it is sometimes necessary, for rating-agency and marketing purposes, for the mortgage-backed security to be issued by a finance subsidiary limited in purpose to the issuance of such securities and activities incidental thereto.

4.1.4 *Credit Support*

Although mortgage-backed securities are structured, in principle, solely on the basis of the market value or borrowing value of the underlying mortgages, it is often necessary, again for rating-agency and marketing purposes, to provide supplemental credit support to protect against the underlying obligors' payment default. This credit support may take the form of an insurance policy, a guarantee, a repurchase obligation or a similar arrangement.

4.1.5 *Servicing*

Mortgages must be 'serviced' on behalf of their owner either by the originator of the mortgages, by an affiliate of the originator, or by an independent, third-party servicer. The servicer typically collects payments on the mortgages and remits those payments, net of the servicer's fee, to the owner/investor. In the event the obligor fails to make a required payment, the servicer is also typically required to pursue payment and, if necessary, foreclose (or otherwise liquidate) the pledged collateral.

4.1.6 *Examples*

Mortgage-backed securities generally take the form of instruments that purport to be either a sale or a financing of the underlying mortgages.

Securities evidencing the sale of mortgages Mortgage-backed securities evidencing the sale of mortgages ('pass-through securities') generally take the form of an undivided fractional ownership interest in the corpus of a passive trust consisting of mortgages (a 'pass-through certificate') or the form of an assignment of a participation interest in specified financial instruments (a 'participation certificate'). The GNMA's 'fully modified pass-through' mortgage-backed certificates and the FNMA's mortgage-backed securities are examples of pass-through certificates. So-called 'stripped' pass-through certificates represent a hybrid instrument. In the typical 'strip' transaction, a trust issues two classes of pass-through certificates, each representing a different ownership (or participation) interest in the principal and interest payments on the underlying mortgages. For example, one class of pass-through certificates might represent the right to receive all principal payments and 90 per cent of all interest payments, with the other class representing an ownership interest in the remaining 10 per cent of the interest payments. Pass-through securities may also provide for senior and junior ownership interests in the trust's assets, in which event the right of the junior certificate-holders to receive periodic distributions is subordinate to the right of the senior certificate-holders.

Debt securities

(1) *Market-value securities.*   An example of a market-value security is a bond secured by mortgages having at all times a market value at least equal to a specified multiple of either (a) the bond's outstanding principal balance plus accrued interest or (b) a portfolio of US government securities having future cash flows at least equal to the future debt service on the bonds. In the event the market value of the collateral falls below the specified level, the issuer may be required to pledge additional collateral, to pay off a principal amount of bonds such that the remaining collateral satisfies the market value test, or to purchase a portfolio of US government securities sufficient to 'defease' the bonds.

(2) *Cash-flow securities.*   The most common examples of pay-through securities are so-called fast-pay/slow-pay collateralized mortgage obligations (CMOs), which are typically structured as multiple-class financings secured by a pledge of a single pool of mortgages. Principal

payments on each class of bonds are made in the order of their stated maturity, such that no principal payment is made on any class of bonds until each earlier class of bonds has been paid in full. Prepayments on the underlying mortgages are 'paid through' to bondholders such that the remaining principal amount of bonds can be supported by the minimum future payments on the remaining mortgages. As a result, the amount and timing of principal payments on a CMO are determined by reference to the amount and timing of principal payments on the underlying mortgages.

(3) *Fixed-payment securities.*   A fixed-payment security is a bond having a fixed stated instalment of principal and interest due on each payment date. The aggregate amount of the instalment may not exceed the minimum scheduled cash flow on the mortgages pledged as collateral. The issuer of a fixed-payment security is typically required to invest any early payments at a rate at least equal to the rate initially used in determining the future debt service requirement on the bonds. Early payments on the underlying mortgages thus do not affect the amount or timing of principal payments on a fixed-payment security.

4.1.7 *Sale Versus Financing*

The use of thinly capitalized limited-purpose finance subsidiaries and, in the case of cash-flow securities, the close connection between the payment terms of the security and the payments received on the issuer's assets may call into question the proper characterization, for tax, accounting and other purposes, of mortgage-backed securities. This issue is discussed in section 4.2 below.

4.1.8 *Bankruptcy*

The legal issues relevant to the insulation of the financial performance of a mortgage-backed security from the bankruptcy or insolvency of the issuer and its affiliates are discussed in section 4.3 below.

4.1.9 *Investment Company Act*

The assets of an issuer of mortgage-backed securities typically consist primarily of mortgages and instruments backed by mortgages (such as pass-through securities), some of which may be considered 'securities' within the meaning of the Investment Company Act of 1940. Section 4.4 below discusses the application of the Investment Company Act to mortgage-backed securities.

4.1.10 *Regulation of Financial Institutions*

The principal holders of mortgages and other instruments of the type used in mortgage-backed financings are financial institutions (banks and thrifts) whose activities are subject to federal and state regulation. Certain of the regulations relevant to the issuance of mortgage-backed securities by banks and thrifts are discussed in section 4.5 below.

4.2 Sale Versus Financing

A mortgage-backed security may purport to be either a sale of mortgages or a financing secured by a pledge of the underlying mortgages. The intended characterization, as a sale or financing, of the transfer of mortgages to a limited-purpose finance subsidiary and their subsequent transfer in favour of security-holders (or a trustee acting on behalf of security-holders) are each subject to recharacterization for bankruptcy, tax and accounting purposes. The issues relevant to the recharacterization of a transfer for bankruptcy purposes, although less well developed, generally look to the same factors considered relevant for tax and accounting purposes. The existence of other creditors having equitable claims on a bankrupt's estate may, however, result in a bankruptcy court recharacterizing a purported sale as a secured financing, without a corresponding recharacterization for other purposes.

4.2.1 *'True Sales'*

The independence of the market or borrowing value of a pool of mortgages may be affected by the recharacterization (as a secured financing) of their purported sale to a limited-purpose finance subsidiary, or by the recharacterization (as a secured financing) of the subsidiary's subsequent purported sale of the mortgages to investors (or to a trustee acting on their behalf). If the parent company is subsequently declared bankrupt and the purported sale to its limited-purpose finance subsidiary is recharacterized as a secured financing,

80   DAVID G. SABEL AND ANDREW A. BERNSTEIN

the transferred assets will remain the property of the parent's estate, subject to the automatic stay and other provisions of the Bankruptcy Code discussed in section 4.3 below. A similar result will follow if the purported sale to investors by the subsidiary is later recharacterized as a secured financing in the subsidiary's bankruptcy. By contrast, if the initial transfer to the limited-purpose finance subsidiary and the subsequent transfer to investors are 'true sales', the subsequent bankruptcy of the parent company or the limited-purpose subsidiary would not affect the market or borrowing value of the transferred assets (absent a 'substantive consolidation' of the parent's and the subsidiary's assets of the type described in section 4.3 below).

Recourse and control   A variety of factors may affect the characterization of a transfer as a 'true sale' or a financing. The principal factor is the transferee's direct or indirect recourse against the purported seller in the event of non-payment by the underlying obligor, in an amount in excess of historical default rates. Having invested on the basis of the seller's credit, the purported purchaser is likely to be treated in bankruptcy together with the seller's other creditors. Recourse to the seller has traditionally taken the form of a direct call on all of the seller's assets. In the case of junior/senior pass-through securities where the junior interest is retained by the seller, it can be argued that similar recourse is indirectly provided in the form of the seller's guarantee of the senior interest, albeit limited to amounts that would otherwise be received by the seller as the holder of the junior interest. The likelihood that the retention of the junior interest will be treated as a guarantee by the seller obviously increases to the extent the amount of the subordinated interest effectively protects the senior certificate-holders against the risk of defaults on the underlying mortgages.

A second important factor in characterizing a transfer is the purported seller's right, as servicer of the mortgages, to control payments received from the underlying obligors and to commingle those payments with its own funds pending their remittance to investors. Amounts on deposit in a bankrupt's general account, invested for the benefit of the bankrupt and not otherwise identified or segregated, may be made available to the bankrupt's creditors in preference to the ownership claims of investors who failed to insist that payments purportedly purchased by them be at all times invested for their benefit and be identifiable as such.

Other factors Other considerations relevant to the characterization of a transfer include:

- whether the seller/servicer remits a fixed amount to the buyer each month, regardless of the amount actually collected on the underlying mortgages;
- whether the seller/servicer has the right to repurchase the underlying mortgages;
- whether the buyer retains the right unilaterally to alter the terms of the transfer;
- whether the buyer makes an independent evaluation of the creditworthiness of the obligors;
- whether the buyer notifies the obligors of the sale; and
- whether the seller/servicer is entitled to payments in excess of the 'purchase price' and reasonable servicing compensation.

Application to pass-through securities The 'true sale' issue is perhaps of greatest relevance in the case of pass-through securities that are intended to be purchased and/or rated without regard to the subsequent creditworthiness of the seller/servicer. Steps that can be taken to reduce the likelihood of recharacterization of pass-through securities include delivery of the mortgage notes and related mortgages to an independent custodian or trustee, recordation of assignments of mortgage in the name of the independent trustee, and segregation of mortgage payments pending their remittance to investors. The decision to take one or more of these steps, all of which involve administrative and other costs, should reflect the intended use of the pass-through securities. For example, participation certificates intended to be used to facilitate whole-loan trading among sophisticated institutions have not traditionally been documented with the same concern for the recharacterization issue as has been the case with pass-through securities intended to be rated and sold to the public or to be used as collateral for other rated mortgage-backed securities.

Guaranteed pass-through securities A pass-through security guaranteed by the seller or one of its affiliates generally precludes the rendering of a 'true sale' opinion of the type required to obtain a rating without regard to the creditworthiness of the seller/servicer, but also renders such an opinion unnecessary in that the rating of a 100 per cent guaranteed pass-through security should be based on the creditworthiness of the guarantor, rather than that of the underlying mortgages.

Treatment of thrift-sponsored pass-through securities   Prior to the enactment of the Financial Institutions Reform, Recovery and Enforcement Act of 1989 (FIRREA) (discussed in greater detail in sections 4.3 and 4.5 below), rating agencies and counsel drew comfort in transactions involving thrift-sponsored pass-through securities intended to be treated as sales from a letter released by the Office of General Counsel of the Federal Home Loan Bank Board stating that, in its opinion, a typical transaction involving a junior/senior pass-through security in which a thrift sells mortgages to a trust and retains the junior interest in the mortgages would be treated as a sale in the event of the insolvency of the thrift in which the Federal Savings and Loan Insurance Corporation (FSLIC) acted as receiver. Under FIRREA, the FSLIC was dissolved and the Federal Deposit Insurance Corporation (FDIC) (or the Resolution Trust Corporation acting under FDIC management) was designated as the primary receiver for insolvent thrifts. The FDIC has not yet indicated whether it concurs with the views expressed in the letter of the Federal Home Loan Bank Board's General Counsel. Accordingly, at least one rating agency has indicated that it will require junior/senior pass-through securities sponsored by thrifts to satisfy its guidelines for secured financings, regardless of whether the transaction is intended to be treated as a sale.

4.2.2 *Federal Income Tax Considerations*

A mortgage-backed financing may be recharacterized for federal income tax purposes in the following ways:

- a transaction structured as a sale of mortgages might be recharacterized as a financing secured by a pledge of those mortgages;
- in a structured financing involving a trust arrangement, the trust might be recharacterized as an association taxable as a corporation; and
- a transaction structured as a financing secured by a pledge of mortgages might be recharacterized as a sale of those mortgages.[1]

The characterization of a transaction for accounting purposes, although not necessarily dispositive for federal income tax purposes, is likely to be given weight, especially if it is inconsistent with the tax treatment.

Sale recharacterized as a financing   If a transaction structured as a sale is recharacterized as a financing the seller will not recognize gain or loss on the transaction and the purchasers will not be treated as the owners of the underlying obligations. For example, if a sale of mortgages is recharacterized as a financing, purchasers that are thrifts will not be considered to own 'qualifying real property loans' within the meaning of section 593(d) of the Internal Revenue Code of 1986, and purchasers that are real estate investment trusts will not be considered to own 'real estate assets' within the meaning of section 856(c)(5)(A) of the Internal Revenue Code.

(1) *Incidents of ownership.*   To avoid recharacterization as a secured financing, a transaction structured as a sale must result in the purchasers having significant incidents of ownership in the underlying obligations.

■ *Market risk.* Probably the most significant incident of ownership of a debt obligation such as a mortgage is the ability to benefit from, or suffer the consequences of, changes in market value resulting from changes in interest rates. A right in the seller to call, or in the purchasers to put, a pass-through security or the underlying mortgages (other than a 'clean-up call' of the type discussed below) at a fixed price is, in general, a factor suggesting financing treatment, as is a right in the seller to retain any proceeds realized on the subsequent sale of an underlying obligation in excess of its initial sales price. The seller's retention of the risk (or benefit) of early payment by the obligors on the underlying mortgages, which effectively insulates the yield realized by purchasers from the consequences of early payment, achieves a similar result and is thus a factor that would likewise support the recharacterization of a transaction as a secured financing.

■ *Control.* Because it is typically economically inefficient for a group of investors in mortgages to undertake servicing responsibilities, these mortgages are generally sold on a servicing-retained basis. So long as the rights and duties retained by the seller/servicer are consistent with those that might be undertaken by a third-party servicer, this retention of control is not significantly detrimental to obtaining sale treatment. The most important items of control – the ability to change the terms of the obligations (absent default) and the right to sell beneficial

84 DAVID G. SABEL AND ANDREW A. BERNSTEIN

interests therein – should, however, be fully relinquished by the seller. Similarly, the right to substitute different obligations for those originally sold (other than as replacements for obligations that fail to conform to representations and warranties of sale) and the right to commingle payments on the obligations with the seller's other assets would be factors supporting the recharacterization of a sale as a financing.

■ *Credit risk.* Credit risk typically is a substantial incident of ownership of a debt obligation. Default protection in the form, for example, of a payment guarantee by a seller is a factor that would support recharacterization of a sale as a secured financing. The likelihood of default protection leading to recharacterization is reduced in the case of sales of fully secured obligations that have a historically insignificant risk of default.

Trust recharacterized as an association taxable as a corporation
Many sales transactions (for example, pass-through securities) are structured as the sale of beneficial interests in the corpus of a fixed investment trust taxable as a grantor trust. Grantor trusts are pass-through entities: the trust pays no entity-level tax and purchasers holding beneficial interests in the trust are taxed as if they directly held undivided ownership interests in the mortgages owned by the trust. If the trust is recharacterized as an association, the purchasers would be treated as owning equity interests in a corporation that owns the underlying obligations, and not as owners of such obligations. Payments made to the purchasers would accordingly be treated as dividends (to the extent paid out of earnings) and not as interest. In addition, the trust would have to pay corporate income tax on income earned on the mortgages, but would not be allowed a deduction for dividend payments made.

(1) *Grantor trust features.* To avoid recharacterization (except as discussed below with respect to junior/senior pass-through securities), a trust structured as a fixed-investment trust taxable as a grantor trust cannot have more than one class of ownership interest (other than ownership interests in specified rights to receive principal and interest on identified mortgages) and must not carry on a business.

■ *Single class of ownership interests.* Under Regulation 301.7701–4(c)(2) (the so-called 'Sears regulations'), a trust will be recharacterized as an association taxable as a corporation if the investors are divided into two or more classes each having different fractional interests in the same trust asset that can change over time. This would be the case in a fast-pay/slow-pay CMO structured as a fixed-investment trust where, at any given time, principal prepayments on the underlying mortgages are 'paid through' to a single class of bondholders. This segmentation by class of the risk of prepayment requires that holders of later classes of bonds (implicitly) exchange their interest on the prepaid mortgage in return for a like interest in a still outstanding mortgage initially owned by holders of the class of bonds then entitled to receive principal payments. This implicit exchange (investment) process is inconsistent with the passivity required of grantor trusts. This implicit exchange is also present in junior/senior pass-through securities, where a junior class of pass-through securities is issued that is subordinate in right of payment to a senior class of pass-through securities backed by the same pool of mortgages. Junior/senior pass-through securities are expressly exempt from recharacterization under the Sears regulations, so long as the other characteristics of a grantor trust are present and the junior interests are retained by the seller of the mortgages, on the ground that this arrangement is economically equivalent to a guarantee of the senior interests by the seller, limited in recourse to its interest in the junior pass-through certificates.

■ *Servicer discretion.* In order to prevent the trustee (and the seller/servicer acting as agent of the trustee) from carrying on a business, the trustee may only perform ministerial activities and other limited activities necessary to conserve the trust assets. The seller/servicer's determination to exercise due-on-sale, due-on-encumbrance and 'call option' clauses contained in mortgages must therefore be made on the basis of objective standards. The need to provide objective servicing standards restricts the flexibility that a servicer might otherwise desire to retain. This is especially true in the case of commercial mortgages. Because servicing decisions may affect early payment, and thus the yield and maturity realized by investors, the use of objective servicing standards must also carefully balance the interest of investors seeking to maximize yields with those purchasing with a view to matching fixed-term liabilities.

■ *Trust assets must be fixed.* The trust may not reinvest, for the account of purchasers, payments received on the mortgages, except for short-term investments acquired and held pending remittance to investors,[2] and the major terms of the mortgages may not be altered absent actual or imminent default. The restriction on reinvestment does not preclude the trust from exercising discretion in determining when to sell trust assets.

Financing recharacterized as a sale to an association taxable as a corporation   CMOs and other 'pay-through' bonds having payment terms determined by reference to the payment experience of the mortgages pledged to secure them are potentially subject to being recharacterized as a sale of an ownership interest in the underlying mortgages. In the event a fast-pay/slow-pay CMO is recharacterized as a sale of the underlying mortgages, the mortgages held in trust (as a security device) would be treated as an association taxable as a corporation, for the reasons discussed above. As with a purported grantor trust that has been recharacterized as an association, payments made to investors would be treated as dividends and not as the return of principal and interest, investors would not be considered the owners of the underlying mortgages, and the trust would have to pay corporate income tax on income and would not be allowed a deduction for dividend payments made.

(1) *Indicia of financing.*   Recharacterization of a CMO as a sale of the underlying mortgages may be avoided by structuring the CMO such that the issuer is engaged in an economically meaningful business, with the potential to realize a gain (or loss) from activities other than the servicing of the underlying mortgages. The potential for issuer economic gain (or loss) may be achieved by mismatching mortgage and CMO cash flows and by the issuer reserving for itself the right to participate in any potential appreciation in the market value of the underlying mortgages.

■ *Mismatching payment dates/investment income.* CMOs are typically structured so that payments on the CMOs are made quarterly or semi-annually, while the underlying mortgages are payable monthly. The reinvestment income earned on the mortgage payments between CMO payment dates may be either retained by the issuer or partially applied to prepay the CMOs, thereby creating a long-term mismatch between the issuer's cash receipts and debt service.

■ *Market appreciation.* A right in the issuer to realize market appreciation in the underlying mortgages will also favour characterization of a CMO as a financing. This right is typically expressed in the form of the issuer's right to call a CMO prior to maturity and, less frequently, to substitute new mortgages in place of those initially pledged as collateral.

REMICs The Real Estate Mortgage Investment Conduit (or REMIC) provisions of the Internal Revenue Code of 1986 significantly altered the federal income tax treatment of qualifying mortgage-backed securities.

In order to qualify as a REMIC, a pool of mortgages must satisfy both an 'asset' test and an 'interest' test. The 'asset' test will be satisfied, in general, if the REMIC's assets consist of qualifying mortgages (including participation interests), cash-flow investments, qualified reserve funds and foreclosure property (the latter, to the extent held for no more than a specified grace period; generally two years from the date of acquisition). The 'interest' test will be satisfied if the REMIC issues two, and only two, types of 'interest'. One type of interest must be a 'regular' interest, unconditionally entitling the holder to (1) a specified amount of principal and interest on that principal amount at a fixed rate (or, to the extent permitted by regulation, at a variable rate), or (2) a fixed portion of the interest payments due on the underlying mortgage loans. The other type of interest must be a 'residual' interest, representing the right to receive all amounts not paid to holders of the regular interests. A REMIC may have any number of classes of regular interests, but only one class of residual interests.

For federal income tax purposes, regular interests will generally be taxed as if they were debt instruments, regardless of whether they would have been so characterized under the general tax principles discussed above. Residual interests, by contrast, will be taxed on their proportionate share of the taxable income of the REMIC (basically, the excess of the income on the mortgages held by the REMIC over the deductions for interest and amortization of discount on the related regular interests). A REMIC will not itself be subject to federal income tax, except to the extent of income resulting from specified prohibited transactions.

The principal advantage of the REMIC legislation is that it provides significant tax flexibility in structuring mortgage-backed securities to take advantage of favourable legal and accounting rules that would not otherwise have been available. For example, a REMIC may issue multiple-class regular interests (that is, CMOs) without regard to the amount of the REMIC's 'equity'.

Because of the flexibility provided by the REMIC rules, many issuers of mortgage-backed securities elect REMIC status. In the first half of 1989 alone, $43.8 billion of REMIC securities were issued, representing over 90 per cent of all mortgage-backed securities issued during the period.[3] The REMIC legislation does not, however, provide relief for transactions requiring the transfer or pledge of mortgages from time to time (as in the case of market-value securities with mark-to-market requirements), and does not otherwise affect the legal, accounting or state tax treatment of mortgage-backed securities. The REMIC legislation is generally effective by election prior to 1992, and generally mandatory thereafter.

4.2.3 Accounting Considerations

Statement of Financial Accounting Standards (FAS) No. 77, 'Reporting by Transferors for Transfers of Receivables with Recourse', together with FASB Technical Bulletin No. 85–2, specify circumstances under which transactions that 'purport to be' sales of mortgages with recourse to the seller should be accounted for as sales, rather than as financings. Three conditions must be satisfied in order to obtain sale treatment:

- the transferor must surrender its control of the 'future economic benefits' relating to the mortgages;
- the transferor must be able to make a reasonable estimation of its obligations under the recourse provisions; and
- the transferee must not be able to 'put' the mortgages sold to the transferor except pursuant to the recourse provisions.

Sale treatment is unlikely if a seller of mortgages is able, at its option, to repurchase the mortgages at a later date, and thereby retain their future economic benefit. This situation may be distinguished from 'clean-up calls', often granted to seller/servicers of pass-through securities, which permit the seller to repurchase transferred mortgages when their aggregate outstanding balance is minor and 'not significant to the transferor'. FAS No. 77 acknowledges that such 'clean-up calls' should not alone preclude a transfer from being recognized as a sale. Sale treatment is also less likely if the seller is unable to estimate the amount of its contingent obligation pursuant to the recourse provisions. According to the Financial Accounting Standards Board, the inability to estimate reasonably the amount of a contingent recourse obligation results in the postponement of sale recognition not because risk has been retained *per se*, but because of the significant uncertainty associated with the amount of retained risk.

Special application to CMOs   FAS No. 77 does not by its terms apply to CMOs, since CMOs do not 'purport to be sales' and are not structured as sale agreements but rather as collateralized borrowings. As a result of the uncertain application of FAS No. 77 to CMOs, in March 1985 the Financial Accounting Standards Board issued FASB Technical Bulletin (TB) No. 85–2, which establishes a presumption that CMOs are to be accounted for as secured financings. TB No. 85–2 does, however, contemplate that a CMO could be recognized as a sale transaction if all but a nominal portion of the future economic benefits inherent in the collateral have been irrevocably transferred to the investor and no affiliate of the issuer can be required to make future payments on the CMOs. Any CMO structured to qualify as a sale under TB No. 85–2 is, absent a REMIC election, unlikely to qualify as a financing for federal income tax purposes, with the adverse tax consequences discussed above.

4.3 Bankruptcy and Security Interests

4.3.1 *Bankruptcy Code and Non-Bankruptcy Code Debtors*

Limited-purpose finance subsidiaries of thrifts and other issuers of mortgage-backed securities are subject to the Federal Bankruptcy Code of 1978, as amended (the 'Bankruptcy Code'). Insolvent thrifts, by contrast, are subject to conservatorships or receivership proceedings. A conservatorship or receivership will generally be conducted by the FDIC (or the Resolution Trust Corporation (RTC) acting under FDIC management) under FIRREA but in some cases may depend on the thrift's insurer, the thrift's chartering authority (state or federal) and the circumstances under which the receiver was appointed. A thrift may be insured by either the FDIC or a state insurance agency. Since the vast majority of thrifts are FDIC insured, this outline focuses on FDIC (or RTC) conservatorships and receiverships under FIRREA.

90   DAVID G. SABEL AND ANDREW A. BERNSTEIN

4.3.2 *Issuer Bankruptcy*

Sales   In the event of the bankruptcy of a seller/servicer of a mortgage-backed security not recharacterized as a financing, the underlying mortgages would not become property of the issuer's estate under section 541(d) of the Bankruptcy Code. In the case of direct offerings by thrift institutions, regulations proposed by the Federal Home Loan Bank Board prior to the enactment of FIRREA made clear that the same result would obtain in the event of the receivership of a thrift. While these regulations might not bind the FDIC (or the RTC) as conservator or receiver of a thrift, it is not likely that a conservator or receiver would attempt to include purportedly sold mortgages in an insolvent thrift's estate without attempting to recharacterize the transaction as a financing.

Financings   In the case of a mortgage-backed security characterized as a financing (either explicitly or by recharacterization) and issued by a Bankruptcy Code debtor, the collateral securing the mortgage-backed security would remain the property of the debtor's estate and foreclosure would be prohibited by operation of the automatic stay provision contained in section 362 of the Bankruptcy Code. The debtor would also have the right to use the collateral so long as the secured party is afforded 'adequate protection'.

   If the issuer is a thrift institution, there is no explicit provision similar to the Bankruptcy Code's automatic stay. Under FIRREA, the FDIC is granted a substantial amount of discretion in conducting a conservatorship or receivership of an insolvent thrift. One option available to the FDIC is to organize a new thrift to take over the insolvent thrift's assets and to assume some of its liabilities. Prior to the enactment of FIRREA, such a 'purchase and assumption' transaction was the most common method of dealing with thrift insolvency. In such a transaction, secured creditors are generally not entitled to accelerate their claims and proceed against the collateral if the secured obligation is assumed, which is usually the case. In addition, a secured creditor presumably would not be able to liquidate collateral pending a decision by the FDIC as to whether the new thrift will assume the obligation. It is not yet clear whether the FDIC will continue the practice of structuring 'purchase and assumption' transactions under FIRREA.

   Regardless of the method of resolution of an insolvency, FIRREA gives the FDIC (or the RTC), as conservator or receiver of an insolvent thrift, the power to determine claims, including claims of 'security, preference or priority' under routine claims procedures. It is generally thought that these procedures will not be applicable to the liquidation of collateral in the possession of a secured creditor. In addition, FIRREA would generally prohibit the exercise of any rights by a secured creditor without the FDIC's consent if those rights arise 'upon, or solely by reason of', insolvency or appointment of a conservator or receiver. Thus a trustee for mortgage-backed bonds issued by a thrift would not be entitled to accelerate the bonds or liquidate the collateral upon the insolvency of the thrift absent the occurrence of an event of default other than the insolvency event. Assuming no default exists prior to the insolvency, the trustee may be required to wait until the next payment is missed before it can exercise any rights against the collateral.

4.3.3 *Parent Bankruptcy*

The issuance of mortgage-backed securities through a finance subsidiary does not necessarily insulate investors from the subsequent bankruptcy or insolvency of the issuer's parent. In addition to the consequences of a bankruptcy court recharacterizing the parent's transfer of assets to its finance subsidiary as a secured financing, discussed above, under certain circumstances a bankruptcy court may order the 'substantive consolidation' of the assets and liabilities of the subsidiary with those of its parent. Substantive consolidation may occur without regard to the solvency of the subsidiary.

Strictly speaking, substantive consolidation may be ordered only when both parent and subsidiary are in bankruptcy proceedings. The term, however, has come to be used more generally to refer to any court order that disregards the separate legal identity of a subsidiary, either by 'piercing the corporate veil' or by finding that the subsidiary is a 'mere instrumentality' or 'alter ego' of the parent. The following factors support recognition of the 'separateness' of the issuing subsidiary:

• the presence of independent officers and directors;
• a separate business office, even if space is subleased from the parent;
• separate books and records and no commingling of assets; and

- the 'holding out' of the subsidiary as a separate entity and not as a division or branch of the parent.

The consequences of substantive consolidation will differ dramatically depending on whether the securities issued constitute secured debt or equity. In the case of secured debt, the security interest should remain effective as against the parent even though the collateral would remain subject to the automatic stay provisions in the case of a Bankruptcy Code debtor. In the case of an equity security, a securityholder would be a stockholder whose claims might be subordinate to those of all the creditors of the consolidated entity.

4.3.4 *Fraudulent Conveyance*

A trustee in bankruptcy may recover, as a 'fraudulent conveyance', any amount transferred for less than a 'reasonably equivalent value' if the debtor was insolvent or rendered insolvent at the time of transfer.[4] A bankruptcy trustee may also recover any amount transferred in violation of state fraudulent conveyance laws.[5] The various state fraudulent conveyance statutes differ in language, but generally are to the same effect as the Bankruptcy Code provision. A 'transfer' for such purposes includes the sale or a pledge of assets. The concern that a transfer will subsequently be found to have been a fraudulent conveyance is greatest in the case of market-value securities, where the market value of the mortgages transferred to a finance subsidiary and pledged in favour of investors may be on the order of 180 per cent of the proceeds realized on issuance and remitted to the parent company. The issuer's subsequent obligation to 'top up', by transferring additional collateral sufficient to satisfy the specified market-value test, raises the same issue. Under the Bankruptcy Code, the satisfaction of antecedent debt would (and under state fraudulent conveyance laws should) constitute value given for the newly transferred assets.

4.3.5 *Preferences*

A trustee in bankruptcy may recover from a transferee any amount 'transferred' on account of an 'antecedent debt' within one year prior to the filing of a bankruptcy petition in the case of a transfer in favour of any 'insider', and within ninety days in all other cases.[6] Corporate affiliates will generally be 'insiders'. Preference problems typically arise in connection with the pledge of additional collateral ('topping up') or the pledge of substitute collateral having a value in excess of the released collateral. The use of an unsecured demand note as a credit-support mechanism also raises preference problems, if payment is made during the preference period. The pledge of collateral simultaneously with the making of the demand note and the issuance of the mortgage-backed security would, however, be for 'new value', and not on account of an 'antecedent debt'. To the extent that the demand note is not under-collateralized, a subsequent payment thereunder in an amount not in excess of the market value of the collateral securing the demand note should therefore not be deemed to be a transfer on account of an 'antecedent debt'.

4.3.6 *Right of Purchase*

Under a former FSLIC regulation, a FSLIC-insured thrift was required to grant the FSLIC a thirty-day right of first refusal in the event of a foreclosure following an event of default (whether or not insolvency-related) involving 'illiquid' collateral. 'Illiquid' collateral included whole mortgage loans and most privately placed mortgage-backed securities. This right of first refusal could both delay fore-closure and reduce foreclosure proceeds.[7] The continuing applica-bility of this rule is unclear.

4.3.7 *Security Interests*

In the case of mortgage-backed securities characterized as secured financings, appropriate steps must be taken to create and perfect the investors' security interest in the underlying mortgages. Otherwise, in the event of the issuer's bankruptcy, investors would have only an unsecured claim against the bankrupt's estate.

Even in the case of transactions that purport to be sales, it is prudent to take the same steps to protect the interests of investors in the event the transaction is recharacterized as a financing. These pre-cautionary steps, generally of little economic or administrative cost, are not likely to be given great weight by a court in determining whether to recharacterize a purported sale transaction as a secured financing.

Perfected security interests in instruments and chattel paper   A security interest in an obligation constituting an 'instrument' within the meaning of Article 9 of the Uniform Commercial Code (UCC) (for example, a mortgage note, any other negotiable instrument and any certificated security) may be perfected by possession. In light of a recent court decision holding (arguably improperly) that principal and interest distributions on a GNMA certificate (that is, a 'certificated security') are 'general intangibles' for purposes of the UCC, it may be prudent to file a UCC financing statement in the appropriate jurisdiction to ensure perfection of an investor's security interest in the distributions on certificated securities. If the obligation instead constitutes 'chattel paper' within the meaning of Article 9 (for example, a lease or an instalment sales contract relating to equipment or other personal property used as additional collateral for a mortgage loan), the secured party must either file a UCC-1 financing statement against the debtor or take possession of the chattel paper. If possession is not practicable, the chattel paper should be stamped to note that it has been sold or pledged. Absent such notation, a bona-fide purchaser for value who takes possession in a subsequent sale or financing involving the same chattel paper may have priority over the interest of the secured party.

Perfecting security interests in mortgages Although mortgage notes constitute instruments for purposes of Article 9, there is no uniform rule as to whether the provisions of Article 9 are applicable to the related mortgage. The source of this confusion is a conflict between UCC sections 9–102(3) and 9–104(j). Section 9–104(j) excludes from the coverage of Article 9 'the creation or transfer of an interest in or lien on real estate', implying that mortgages would not be covered by Article 9. Section 9–102(3), however, states that Article 9 is applicable to obligations secured by transactions or interests outside the scope of Article 9.[8] Based on Comment 4 to section 9–102(3), the safer answer appears to be that perfection of an interest in a mortgage note is accomplished by possession, while perfection of an interest in the related mortgage is governed by local real property law and may require the filing of an assignment of mortgage executed by the debtor. Because various jurisdictions have adopted different interpretations of sections 9–104(j) and 9–102(3), local case law should be consulted. Unlike most other steps required to perfect a security interest, recordation of an assignment of a mortgage may involve considerable expense and administrative inconvenience.

Perfecting security interests in book-entry securities The issuance of FNMA and FHLMC (Federal Home Loan Mortgage Corporation) securities in book-entry form raises complicated perfection issues. Transfer of these securities is governed by federal regulation. Effective transfer of book-entry securities to a purchaser or pledgee will, in most cases, require at least two transfers: a transfer on the books and records of an eligible Federal Reserve Bank to a depository bank maintaining an account with such Federal Reserve Bank, and a transfer on the books and records of such depository bank in favour of the purchaser or pledgee. The interplay of the federal regulations that expressly govern such transfers and the provisions of the UCC that are invoked by the federal regulations may raise questions with respect to, among other things, the bona-fide purchaser status of a transferee and the correct method of transfer.

Perfecting security interests in securities held through a clearing corporation The GNMA has announced its intention to commence transfer of all newly issued GNMA-guaranteed securities through the MBSCC Depository. Under the proposed plan, newly issued GNMA certificates will be issued only to MBSCC, and MBSCC will, in turn, transfer the interests of its members in the GNMA certificates only on MBSCC's books and records. MBSCC will retain physical possession of the certificates. Transfer of interests in GNMA certificates will therefore be governed by the UCC provisions governing the transfer of 'certificated securities' by clearing corporations.[9]

4.4 The Investment Company Act of 1940

4.4.1 *General Application*

The Investment Company Act of 1940 (the '1940 Act') was originally intended to prevent abuses by investment managers in the administration and investment of large liquid pools of funds, typically mutual funds. The 1940 Act regulates any entity that is an 'investment company', defined as any entity that (1) engages primarily in investing, reinvesting or trading in securities (or holds itself out as doing so); (2) issues face-amount certificates of the instalment type; or (3) engages in investing, reinvesting, owning, holding or trading in securities and owns (or proposes to acquire) investment securities whose value exceeds 40 per cent of the value of the issuer's assets.

4.4.2 *Application to Structured Mortgage Financing*

It can be argued that the protections of the 1940 Act are not required in the case of CMOs (and certain other mortgage-backed securities), since (1) the underlying financial instruments are pledged in favour of a trustee under a Trust Indenture Act qualifying indenture, and thereafter no mortgage is added to or substituted for those initially pledged, and (2) the payment terms of the CMO are fixed on the date of issuance. Nevertheless, structured financings will generally involve an 'investment company', since the SEC staff has ruled that notes (or other instruments) are 'securities' within the meaning of section 3(a) of the 1940 Act.[10] As a result of the costs and administrative inconvenience of registering under the 1940 Act, most issuers of mortgage-backed securities have structured their operations so as to fall within one of the statutory exceptions to the definition of an investment company or have sought individual exemptive orders pursuant to section 6(c) of the 1940 Act.

4.4.3 *Mortgage Exemption: Section 3(c)(5)(C)*

The legislative history of the 1940 Act indicates that Congress was concerned that traditional investment companies were susceptible to insider abuse.[11] Companies whose business is primarily holding mortgages and other interests in real estate were excluded from the definition of investment company under the 1940 Act 'because they do not come within the generally understood concept of a conventional investment company investing in stocks and bonds of corporate issuers'.[12] Section 3(c)(5)(C) specifically exempts from the definition of an investment company (and, consequently, from the operation of the 1940 Act) entities that do not issue 'redeemable securities' and are 'primarily engaged in . . . purchasing or otherwise acquiring mortgages and other liens on and interests in real estate'. The section 3(c)(5)(C) exemption is available only if an issuer is 'primarily engaged' in acquiring or holding 'interests in real estate' within the meaning of section 3(c)(5)(C).

Real estate   If an issuer's assets consist wholly or primarily of whole mortgages, the exemption applies by its terms. It is unclear what interests other than mortgages qualify as 'liens on or interests in real estate'. In *US Home Mortgage Credit Corporation*,[13] the SEC staff took a no-action position where the issuer proposed to invest in assets consisting primarily of all of the GNMA certificates representing several pools of mortgage loans. The theory behind the staff's position was that owning all of the GNMA certificates representing a pool of mortgages is equivalent, for the purposes of the 1940 Act, to owning the mortgages themselves, inasmuch as the holder of 'whole-pool' certificates will have the same investment experience as if he owned the underlying mortgages directly. The SEC staff has taken similar no-action positions with respect to issuers' investment in whole-pool FNMA and FHLMC certificates.[14] In *Premier Mortgage Corporation*,[15] the SEC staff also took a no-action position where the issuer proposed to invest its funds primarily in non-recourse pass-through notes, issued by various savings and loan institutions, backed by conventional mortgage loans. The SEC staff again concluded that the issuer would have 'the same investment experience that it would have were it directly investing in the mortgage loans'. The staff has also pointed to an investor's ability to control foreclosure in the event of default as a defining feature of ownership of an 'interest in real estate'.[16]

'Partial-pool' certificates   If an issuer does not own all the certificates relating to a pool of mortgages, the SEC staff takes the position that such 'partial-pool' certificates do not qualify as mortgages or other 'liens on or interests in real estate' for the purposes of section 3(c)(5)(C), but instead represent 'an interest in the nature of a security in another person engaged in the real estate business'.[17] It might be argued that an issuer holding guaranteed partial-pool certificates holds the same bundle of rights as if it held whole-pool certificates. In either case, the servicer of the certificates is required to advance funds to the certificate-holder even if there is a default on one of the underlying mortgages; if the servicer fails to pay, the guarantor (typically, the GNMA, FNMA or FHLMC) is obligated to pay. Whether or not the certificate represents a whole pool, the holder gets paid in the event of default by the obligor of an underlying mortgage and the certificate-holder is indifferent to the mechanics of foreclosure on the underlying mortgage.

Participation interests   Pass-through certificates representing interests in participations, rather than 'whole' mortgages, raise a similar issue. In *Federal Home Loan Mortgage Corp.*,[18] the SEC staff stated that whole-pool FHLMC participation certificates (which may

represent an interest in participations) constitute interests in real
estate for purposes of section 3(c)(5)(C), because the FHLMC has
'unrestricted control over the enforcement of the whole mortgage,
whether it purchases a whole mortgage or only a participation
therein'. The applicability of this position in other contexts is unclear
and language in the letter suggests that it may be limited to its facts.

'Primarily engaged'   In recent years, the SEC staff has relaxed its
view on the meaning of 'primarily engaged' for purposes of section
3(c)(5)(C). Prior to late 1983, the staff had required that at least 65 per
cent of an issuer's assets consist of mortgages or other qualifying real
estate investments. In *Salomon Brothers Mortgage Securities, Inc.*,[19] the
staff modified its no-action position to require only that at least 55 per
cent of an issuer's assets consist of mortgages or other qualifying real
estate interests.

The proportion of an issuer's assets that may be composed of
partial-pool certificates without requiring registration under the 1940
Act has significant consequences for both originators of mortgage
loans and issuers of mortgage-backed securities. The requirement that
an issuer's assets be composed 'primarily' of whole-pool certificates (or
other qualifying interests) has increased the cost of whole-pool certificates. Indeed, at times, the cost of whole-pool certificates has
exceeded the cost of partial-pool certificates, which have traditionally
enjoyed a price advantage as a result of their greater diversity of
prepayment experience. These additional costs are presumably passed
on to investors, an ironic result in light of the SEC's more general
commitment to market principles.

Issuers of mortgage-backed securities have accordingly sought to
eliminate or reduce the whole-pool requirement, while mortgage
bankers, a principal source of current coupon whole-pool certificates,
have opposed such moves. In a letter to the SEC dated 19 January
1984, the Mortgage Bankers' Association opposed the expansion of
qualifying real estate interests to include partial-pool certficates, on
the ground that partial-pool certificates were likely to be backed by
discount mortgages whose use would not result in additional funds
being made available to the primary mortgage market. The Mortgage
Bankers' Association's position overlooks the fact that a substantial
number of discount mortgages are held as whole mortgages by thrifts
and can be readily swapped for whole-pool FNMAs and FHLMCs.
The suggestion that the use of discount mortgages does not benefit the

primary mortgage market is also probably incorrect in that there are significant administrative, regulatory and tax reasons for a thrift to reinvest the proceeds of a CMO issuance in new mortgage originations.

In *Landmark Funding Corp.*[20] and *CMO Mortgage Corp.*,[21] the SEC staff imposed the further requirement that the 45 per cent of an issuer's assets not required to be invested in qualifying interests in real estate be 'primarily invested in real estate-type assets'. The statutory support for this position is unclear, as is its application to an issuer whose non-real estate type assets are not 'primarily' invested in non-real estate assets as a result of prepayments on the underlying mortgages.

The 1940 Act staff appears, more generally, to be taking a conservative view of the availability of the section 3(c)(5) exemption. In *Salomon Brothers Inc.*,[22] the staff stated, in effect, that it would not move beyond its existing no-action positions under section 3(c)(5) in the case of limited-purpose finance subsidiaries. According to the staff, limited-purpose finance subsidiaries should instead seek relief under rule 3a-5 (exempting qualifying finance subsidiaries) or request an exemptive order under section 6(c).

4.4.4 *SEC Exemptive Orders*

Section 6(c) of the 1940 Act authorizes the SEC to exempt any person, transaction or security (or class thereof) from any of the 1940 Act's provisions to the extent that such exemption 'is necessary or appropriate in the public interest and consistent with the protection of investors and the purposes [of the 1940 Act]'. Although section 6(c) orders have been issued, generally in the context of CMO conduit programmes and in relaxation of the whole-pool requirement, the process involves delay and uncertainty of result, as well as a public review process. The need to obtain a section 6(c) exemptive order may cause an issuer to miss a favourable market opportunity, and can also force disclosure of innovative financing structures prior to their use. Since section 6(c) allows the SEC to grant an exemption conditionally, the SEC's imposition of conditions on an exemption may cause expense and delay.

4.4.5 *Banks and Thrifts*

Banks, thrifts and insurance companies are exempted from the definition of an investment company. Mortgage-backed securities issued directly by any of such institutions (as opposed to their subsidiaries) are thus exempt from the 1940 Act, provided that the securities are issued 'with recourse' to the issuing institution. For example, a pass-through security not otherwise exempt under the 1940 Act would not be exempt solely because it was nominally issued by a bank or thrift, if the bank or thrift is not obligated on the security. Indeed, a security issued by an exempt institution, but which is likely to be of limited recourse as an economic matter, may also need to be analysed as a separate entity for the purposes of the 1940 Act.[23]

4.5 Bank and Thrift Regulatory Issues

4.5.1 *Regulated Issuers*

The issuance of mortgage-backed securities by thrifts and commercial banks is subject to the regulatory schemes applicable to these institutions. Thrift institutions may be federally or state chartered, and may be insured by the FDIC or, in some cases, state authorities. Thrifts include savings and loan associations, savings banks and cooperative banks. Under FIRREA the primary responsibility for regulation of federally insured thrifts rests with the Director of the Office of Thrift Supervision (DOTS), as well as the FDIC.

Commercial banks may be either federally or state chartered. The Office of the Comptroller of the Currency (OCC) is the primary regulator of national banks. State-chartered institutions are subject to regulation by state and federal banking authorities. The primary federal regulator of state-chartered banks is the Board of Governors of the Federal Reserve System (the FRB), in the case of banks that are members of the Federal Reserve System ('member banks'), and the FDIC, in the case of FDIC-insured, non-member banks. All banks and thrifts are subject to reserve requirements under Regulation D of the FRB; more generally, the FDIC, in the case of FDIC-insured banks, and the FRB, in the case of member banks, may for certain purposes assert regulatory authority over banks for which they are not the primary federal regulator.

Risk-based capital rules   New risk-based capital rules have recently been adopted for commercial banks and proposed for thrifts.[24] FIRREA requires thrifts to satisfy a risk-based capital standard that is no less stringent than that applicable to commercial banks, and requires substantial restrictions on growth for thrifts that are not in compliance with these and other capital requirements by 1 January 1991. Although differing in detail, both sets of rules require depository institutions to maintain regulatory capital in proportion to their risk-weighted assets. (The proposed thrift rules also require that capital be established in respect of a thrift's interest-rate sensitivity and its collateralized borrowings.) The rules adopted for commercial banks and the rules proposed for thrifts assign significantly lower risk-weightings to obligations issued or guaranteed by the US government or its agencies or instrumentalities (including the GNMA, FNMA and FHLMC), to qualifying one- to four-family residential mortgages, and to securities backed by any of the foregoing. As a result, many depository institutions may have an increased incentive to securitize and sell higher risk-weighted assets (including commercial mortgages and residential mortgages that do not qualify for favourable capital treatment) and to purchase mortgage-backed securities having lower assigned risk-weightings. The risk-based capital rules proposed for thrifts, if adopted, would prohibitively increase the regulatory cost of issuing junior/senior pass-through securities, unless the junior pass-through securities are sold by the thrift.

Qualified thrift lender test   Under FIRREA, a thrift that is not a 'qualified thrift lender' (QTL) faces sanctions, including the imposition of regulation that would otherwise be applicable only to commercial banks and restrictions on the ability of the thrift to engage in new business. Among other factors used to determine QTL status is the proportion of the assets of the thrift that constitute residential mortgage loans and securities backed by residential mortgage loans. Because of the QTL standards, thrifts will have an increased incentive to sell commercial mortgage loans and to purchase additional residential mortgage loans and securities backed by residential mortgage loans.

4.5.2 *Finance Subsidiaries*

For marketing and rating-agency reasons, many mortgage-backed securities can be most effectively issued through limited-purpose finance subsidiaries.

Thrift finance subsidiaries   Federal (and most state) thrifts are strictly limited as to both the nature of their subsidiaries' activities and the amount of parent thrift investment. Federal Home Loan Bank Board finance subsidiary regulations, which will remain in effect under the FIRRE Act unless the DOTS issues a contrary regulation, provide general authority for federal thrifts to establish wholly owned subsidiaries whose sole purpose is to issue debt or equity securities the proceeds of which are made available to the parent thrift. FIRREA generally requires thirty days' advance notice to the FDIC and the DOTS before a thrift can establish a subsidiary, and the DOTS has the power to prohibit the thrift from establishing the subsidiary if he determines that the thrift's ownership of the subsidiary constitutes a serious risk to the safety of the thrift or is inconsistent with sound banking principles or the purposes of FIRREA. FIRREA generally subjects state thrifts to the same investment restrictions applicable to federal thrifts.

Limitations   Thrift finance subsidiaries must have as their sole purpose the issuance of debt or equity securities that the parent thrift would be authorized to issue directly (or, if the parent is a mutual institution, would be authorized to issue if it converted to stock form), and all proceeds from the issuance of securities by finance subsidiaries, net of reasonable costs of issuance, must be remitted to the parent. The aggregate book value of assets transferred to a thrift's finance subsidiaries is limited to 30 per cent of the book value of the parent thrift's total assets as of the date of transfer, and the aggregate fair-market value of the assets transferred is limited to the lesser of (1) 250 per cent of the gross proceeds from the offering or (2) the amount necessary and customary for the securities to be issued. Parent guarantees of finance subsidiary obligations are permitted with certain limitations. The parent thrift must, in any event, own 100 per cent of the voting common stock of its finance subsidiaries, though preferred stock may be issued to third parties.

A parent thrift institution must include in its total liabilities, for purposes of its net worth and capital requirements, the net proceeds of any financing effected through a subsidiary. Excepted from application of this provision are proceeds from the issuance of securities collateralized by assets that have substantially the same duration as the securities issued, both at initial issuance and throughout the life of the securities, 'without active management'. A subsidiary's duration-matched securities offerings must also be collateralized by assets having a market value less than 110 per cent of the gross proceeds of the offering to avoid non-consolidation with liabilities of its parent. The proposed thrift risk-weighted capital rules discussed above would eliminate this duration-matching exception and would instead require that a thrift's capital be computed on a consolidated basis. In addition, FIRREA requires all assets and liabilities of a thrift's subsidiaries to be shown on the books of the thrift unless all investments in and loans to the subsidiary are deducted from capital. Investments in and loans to finance subsidiaries generally would not be required to be deducted from capital under FIRREA.

4.5.3 *Commercial Bank Finance Subsidiaries*

National banks are permitted to establish finance subsidiaries under their general authority to establish 'operating subsidiaries'. Under OCC regulations, operating subsidiaries may be established to carry out any activity that a bank could carry out directly, including borrowings.

The authority of a state-chartered bank to establish a finance subsidiary is, in the first instance, a matter of state law. Most states probably would permit state-chartered banks to effect borrowings through an operating subsidiary. The FRB, as primary federal regulator of state-chartered banks that are members of the Federal Reserve System, evidently does not restrict a state-chartered bank's ability to organize such a subsidiary, so long as the subsidiary engages only in banking activities that the parent could conduct directly.

In April 1986, the FDIC requested comment on proposed guidelines for FDIC-supervised banks that wish to restructure assets and raise funds by setting up special finance subsidiaries to issue equity and debt securities backed by mortgages, including CMOs. As part of the proposal: (1) finance subsidiaries would have been required to be wholly owned by parent banks and parents would have been permitted to transfer no more than 10 per cent of total assets to such subsidiaries; (2) all proceeds and expenses of the security sales would have been required to have been remitted immediately to the parent; (3) the securities sold would not have been permitted to be over-collateralized by more than 200 per cent; and (4) finance subsidiaries would have been consolidated with parents for purposes of regulatory reporting.[25]

In December 1986, the FDIC withdrew its proposed guidelines, concluding that '[a]lthough inappropriate uses of finance subsidiaries are possible, the FDIC believes that such situations should be handled on a case-by-case basis by using existing supervisory powers rather than by trying to address potential problems through the issuance of specific guidelines'.[26]

Establishment of a finance subsidiary would not, under current interpretations, require prior notice to or approval of the FRB under the Bank Holding Company Act in the case of a bank that is a subsidiary of a holding company.

4.5.4 Reserve Requirements

Federal reserve requirements are prescribed by the FRB in its Regulation D. This regulation applies to virtually all US chartered depository institutions, including commercial banks (whether or not member banks), savings banks, savings and loan associations and credit unions. With certain limited exceptions, any borrowing by a depository institution is a 'deposit' for the purposes of Regulation D, potentially subject to a reserve requirement, whether or not the borrowing is designated as a deposit or treated as a deposit for other regulatory purposes.

Sale of assets with recourse   For the purposes of Regulation D, an obligation of a depository institution to repurchase assets sold by the institution constitutes a reservable deposit, except if the assets sold are obligations issued or fully guaranteed as to principal and interest by the United States government or an agency thereof. The FRB has taken the position that, as a result of this rule, a contingent obligation of a depository institution to repurchase assets sold by the institution is also a reservable obligation. Accordingly, with certain limited exceptions, an obligation of an institution to repurchase, or assure payment of, assets sold by the institution constitutes a reservable obligation. The obligation of a depository institution arising from the retention of an interest in (or guaranty of) no more than 10 per cent of a pool of conventional one- to four-family residential mortgage loans sold by the institution is expressly exempt from reserve requirements. This exemption arguably should be available to exempt from reserves a CMO secured by a pool of qualifying mortgage loans so long as the equity of the CMO issuer is limited to no more than 10 per cent of the market value of the pool.

Obligations of subsidiaries and other affiliates Under Regulation D, obligations of a subsidiary of a depository institution are treated as obligations of the parent institution, and as such are subject to the same reserve requirements applicable to obligations issued directly by the parent.

In addition, under the so-called 'affiliate paper' rule, any obligation of an affiliate of a depository institution the proceeds of which are made available to the depository institution is generally treated as an obligation of the depository institution. For purposes of this rule, an entity is an affiliate of a depository institution if either one is a subsidiary of the other or if they are subsidiaries of a common parent. The affiliate paper rule applies, for example, if an affiliate of a depository institution issues obligations and uses the proceeds to purchase assets from or extend credit to the depository institution. The FRB staff has apparently taken the position that a trust or corporate entity established in connection with a financing programme for a particular depository institution will not be regarded as an affiliate of such institution so long as the trust or entity has independent trustees or shareholders and directors.

Applicable reserve percentages The reserve requirement applicable to a deposit obligation depends upon its maturity. At present, non-personal time deposits (which include deposits issued in the form of negotiable instruments or held by non-natural persons) with an original maturity or notice period of seven days or more but less than one and a half years are subject to a 3 per cent reserve requirement, and non-personal time deposits with an original maturity or notice period of one and a half years or more are subject to a 0 per cent reserve requirement.

Regulation D does not expressly address the treatment of deposit obligations which by their terms are subject to prepayment (by acceleration or otherwise) prior to their stated maturity. In the past, the staff of the FRB has informally taken the position that the maturity of obligations subject to acceleration or prepayment upon certain contingencies (other than bankruptcy of the issuer and, possibly, a default in a payment obligation of the issuer) should be determined by reference to the time the obligation would be payable if any such contingency occurred. The staff of the FRB is now informally taking the position that the maturity of a mortgage-based security the amortization of which depends on the amortization of the underlying assets may be determined on the basis of any reasonable amortization assumption made at the time the securities are issued, such as the amortization assumption used in pricing the securities. The 3 per cent reserve requirement would, as a result, apply only to that portion of the principal amount of the securities that would be payable seven days or more and less than one and a half years from the issue date, based on the amortization assumption. Under the informal staff view, an institution might be required to amend its amortization assumption if actual amortization differs greatly from that initially assumed in determining reserve requirements. It also appears that the staff is tacitly taking the position that events of default typically applicable to mortgage-based securities may be disregarded in determining the maturity of the securities.

Proposed changes of Regulation D In May 1986, the FRB approved for public comment proposed amendments of Regulation D.[27] These amendments would, among other things, confirm the general rule that a sale of assets with recourse or retained interest is a reservable obligation (subject to the exceptions mentioned above). The proposals would, however, codify a staff opinion given in at least one case that a sale of assets is not subject to reserves even though the selling institution indemnifies a third party which provides a guarantee of the assets for the benefit of investors, provided that the selling institution has no liability to investors. The proposed amendments would also revise the affiliate paper rule so as not to require any reserves for obligations of an affiliate used to purchase assets without recourse from the affiliated depository institution. On the other hand, the proposals would expand the affiliate paper rule to include obligations of an affiliate that are 'supported' by an obligation of the affiliated depository institution, whether or not the proceeds of the affiliate's obligations flow back to the supporting institution. The proposed rules would also amend the definition of 'affiliate' to include any entity that a depository institution 'effectively manages or controls' or which is 'formed for the purpose of engaging primarily in transactions with the depository institution or its customers . . .'. If these two provisions are adopted as proposed, they would arguably extend reserve requirements to many types of transactions using a special-purpose issuer whose obligations are supported by a depository institution.

4.5.5 Prohibition Against Collateralization of Deposits

National banks are not permitted to pledge assets to secure 'deposits' (with certain limited exceptions) but may pledge assets to secure 'borrowings'. Under OCC regulations, an operating subsidiary of a national bank is generally subject to all federal banking laws and regulations applicable to the parent bank. It is nonetheless reasonably clear that borrowings by a finance subsidiary of a bank, secured by assets purchased from the bank, would not be treated as 'deposits' for the purposes of this prohibition.[28]

In the case of a state-chartered bank, the bank's authority to pledge assets would be governed by state law and, potentially, the FRB or the FDIC. Neither of those two agencies has in any reported action restricted banks subject to their jurisdiction from pledging assets or taken the position that a pledge of assets constitutes an unsafe or unsound banking practice.

A thrift institution's ability to collateralize deposits depends on the regulations of its chartering authority. In the case of state-chartered institutions, applicable state law must be consulted. Federally chartered thrifts have been granted broad power to collateralize deposits pursuant to regulations promulgated under the Garn–St Germain Depository Institutions Act of 1982. These regulations preempt provisions of state law to the extent such provisions purport to govern collateralization of deposits by federal associations. Many states are following suit in permitting collateralization of deposits by thrifts.

4.5.6 Glass–Steagall Act Prohibitions

The Glass–Steagall Act (officially, the Banking Act of 1933) was adopted to separate the activities of investment and commercial banking.[29] Sections 16 and 21 prohibit national banks and other deposit-taking institutions from engaging in the business of issuing, underwriting, selling or distributing securities, except for certain state, municipal and federal securities and other securities which national banks are permitted to issue, underwrite and deal in under section 16. Section 20 of the Glass–Steagall Act prohibits any member bank from being 'affiliated' with an organization 'engaged principally' in the issuance, underwriting, public sale or distribution of non-exempt securities. Section 32 of the Act prohibits certain personnel interlocks between member banks and entities 'primarily engaged' in such a securities business, except as provided by FRB rule. Section 21 contains a proviso that its prohibitions do not affect any right a depository institution may otherwise have 'to sell, without recourse or agreement to repurchase, obligations evidencing loans or real estate'.

The direct sale of participation interests in mortgage loans is generally not prohibited under Glass–Steagall, since such transactions may be regarded as sales of the bank's assets rather than sales effected on behalf of a third-party issuer. Similarly, the sale of mortgages to a trust and the subsequent issuance by the trust of interests in these obligations probably do not violate the Glass–Steagall Act, provided that the trust remains a separate, non-deposit-taking legal entity.

The OCC has taken the position that a bank may sell mortgage-related securities based on the bank's own assets without violating the Glass–Steagall Act. In May 1986, the OCC issued a no-objection letter to the effect that a national bank may, directly or through a subsidiary, issue, underwrite and deal in CMOs secured by GNMAs, FNMAs, FHLMCs or conventional residential mortgage loans.[30] The analysis underlying this letter is set forth at greater length in an 18 June 1986 letter of the Comptroller of the Currency to Senator D'Amato. The Comptroller's letter makes clear that the OCC relied on the theory that a CMO may be treated for the purposes of the Glass–Steagall Act as a surrogate for the underlying collateral, which consists of either obligations issued or guaranteed by an agency or instrumentality of the US government, which a bank may underwrite and deal in, or mortgage loans, which a bank may originate, buy and sell. More recently, national banks have participated in the underwriting of securities that are 90 per cent guaranteed by the US government and 10 per cent collateralized by US government securities, based in part on the SEC's view that these securities qualify as government obligations for the purposes of the federal securities laws.

The OCC broadened the scope of its analysis of the permissibility of banks selling securities based on their own assets in a series of 1987 letters. In a January letter to the Federal Reserve Board, the OCC took the position that securities backed by a bank's own assets should not be regarded as subject to Glass–Steagall's underwriting prohibition. Such securities, reasoned the OCC, merely reflect an interest in the bank's assets. Therefore, since a bank has the power to sell its assets and to borrow money, it also has the power to sell pass-through securities and to sell CMOs so long as those securities are backed by the bank's own assets. In a March letter, the OCC reiterated this view and stated that its analysis would apply to securities backed by commercial mortgage loans as well as residential mortgage loans.

Several banks have named themselves as 'underwriters' of pass-through securities, CMOs and other mortgage-related securities registered with the SEC and sold to the public. In each case the securities were backed by the 'underwriting' bank's own assets. In response to a letter from the Securities Industry Association (SIA) challenging a transaction in which a division of Security Pacific National Bank publicly sold pass-through securities based on the bank's own assets, the Comptroller issued an interpretive letter[31] reaffirming its view that such activities do not violate Glass–Steagall. The Court of Appeals for the Second Circuit recently upheld the interpretation of the Comptroller, reasoning that the sale of mortgage pass-through certificates backed by a bank's assets was a 'convenient and useful' method of accomplishing a permitted sale of mortgage loans and thus incidental to the business of banking and within the powers of the bank.[32] The Securities Industry Association has announced that it will not appeal the decision.

It is clear from informal conversations with the staff of the OCC, and from the Second Circuit's opinion, that the letters discussed above should not be read as an authorization for a national bank or its subsidiary to underwrite or deal in CMOs or pass-through securities issued by another entity or to purchase mortgages from other institutions (other than as incidental to traditional mortgage banking activities) for the purpose of issuing CMOs or pass-through securities.

The ability of depository institutions to issue certain types of mortgage-backed securities consistent with Glass–Steagall is based as much on past issuances not having been challenged as on the opinions issued by the OCC. Possible challenge on Glass–Steagall grounds by a regulator or the SIA is, in any event, significantly increased to the

110   DAVID G. SABEL AND ANDREW A. BERNSTEIN

extent the issuing bank also participates in the underwriting or distribution of the mortgage-backed security.

In several orders beginning 30 April 1987, the Federal Reserve Board has held that an affiliate of a bank may underwrite and deal in mortgage-related securities so long as the affiliate derives no more than 5 per cent of its gross revenues from such activities. The Board's analysis is that this does not violate Glass–Steagall, because the affiliate would not be 'engaged principally' in prohibited underwriting if these 5 per cent limitations were met. The Board's orders granting limited securities underwriting powers to bank affiliates were upheld in two 1988 Circuit Court decisions.[33] The Supreme Court denied certiorari on the Second Circuit's decision.[34] Significantly, and in sharp contrast with the view of the OCC, the Board prohibits a bank's affiliate from underwriting or dealing in securities backed by assets originated by the bank.

Notes

1 See generally James M. Peaslee and David Z. Nirenberg, *Federal Income Taxation of Mortgage-Backed Securities* (1989).
2 See Revenue Ruling 75–192, 1975–1 C.B. 384 (1975).
3 *National Thrift and Mortgage News*, 11 September 1989, p. 21.
4 Bankruptcy Code section 548.
5 Bankruptcy Code section 544(b).
6 Bankruptcy Code section 547.
7 12 C.F.R. section 563–8.2 (1984).
8 See also Comment 4, as amended, to section 9–102(3).
9 UCC section 8–320.
10 See, for example, *Mortgage Backed Income Fund* (pub. avail. 31 July 1979).
11 Sen. Rep. No. 1775, 76th Cong., 3d Sess. (1940).
12 Sen. Rep. No. 184, 91st Cong. 2nd Sess. 37 (1970).
13 *US Home Mortgage Credit Corporation* (pub. avail. 22 June 1983).
14 *Landmark Funding Corp.* (pub. avail. 20 September 1984).
15 *Premier Mortgage Corporation* (pub. avail. 14 March 1983).
16 See *Baton Rouge Building and Construction Industry Foundation* (pub. avail. 1 August 1984).
17 See *Arlington Investment Company* (pub. avail. 31 August 1974).
18 *Federal Home Loan Mortgage Corp.* (pub. avail. 14 June 1985).
19 *Salomon Brothers Mortgage Securities, Inc.* (pub. avail. 8 November 1983).
20 *Landmark Funding Corp.* (pub. avail. 20 September 1984).

21 *CMO Mortgage Corp.* (pub. avail. 22 July 1985).
22 *Salomon Brothers Inc.* (pub. avail. 22 July 1985).
23 See *Prudential Insurance Co.* v. *SEC*, 326 F.2d 383 (3rd Cir. 1964), *cert. den.*, 377 U.S. 953 (1964).
24 See 54 Fed. Reg. 4186 (27 January 1989) (commercial banks); 53 Fed. Reg. 51809 (23 December 1988) (thrifts). Subsequent to the date of this article, new net worth rules for thrifts have been enacted. See chapter 11 for further discussion of capital adequacy rules.
25 51 Fed. Reg. 12561 (11 April 1986).
26 51 Fed. Reg. 45812 (22 December 1986).
27 51 Fed. Reg. 16833 (7 May 1986).
28 See Comptroller Interpretive Letter No. 378 (24 March 1987).
29 On Glass–Steagall Act, see, *inter alia*, Norton, 'Up against "the Wall": Glass–Steagall and the dilemma of a deregulated banking environments', 42 *Bus. Lawyer* 327 (1987).
30 Staff Letter No. 86–9, 22 May 1986.
31 Interpretive Letter No. 388 (16 June 1987).
32 *SIA* v. *Clarke*, slip op., No. 89–6027, 89–6029 (2d. Cir. 8 Sept. 1989). Also see discussion by Steven L. Schwarcz in chapter 2 of this volume.
33 *SIA* v. *FRB*, 839 F.2d 47 (2d Cir. 1988); *SIA* v. *FRB*, 847 F.2d 890 (D.C. Cir. 1988).
34 108 S. Ct. 2830 (1988).

5

Securitization of US Non-Mortgage Receivables

PAUL R. SPELLMAN

Chapter Outline

5.1 Introduction: Revolving Credit Receivables
    5.1.1 Delayed Pass-Through Trust Structure
    5.1.2 Secured Debt Structure
    5.1.3 Special-Purpose Vehicle Commercial Paper Structure
    5.1.4 US Federal Income Tax Status
        Economic risk
        Opportunity for gain
        Other factors

5.2 Instalment Loan and Instalment Sales Contract Obligations
    5.2.1 Factors Favouring or Disfavouring Securitization
        Uniformity of documentation
        Seasoning and payment history
        Interest rates
        Payment terms
        Quality of servicing
        Other factors
    5.2.2 Pass-Through Structures
    5.2.3 Debt Structures
    5.2.4 Federal Income Tax Status
        Fixed investment
        No trade or business
        Single class of ownership interests

5.3 Lease Obligations

5.1 Introduction: Revolving Credit Receivables

The first publicly offered securities backed by US revolving credit obligations were issued in 1987.[1] During 1988, eighteen public offerings of such securities were made, aggregating $7,400 million.[2] In addition, financial institutions accelerated the use of special-purpose entities that acquire credit-card receivables and issue commercial paper backed by the receivables. As of 31 December 1988, in excess of $3,000 million of such credit-card-backed commercial paper had been issued.[3]

Typical bank portfolios of consumer credit-card accounts include a substantial percentage of 'convenience users' who repay their entire outstanding balance each month (in many cases avoiding the payment of any finance charges or interest), a substantial percentage of cardholders who pay only the minimum payment (generally 3 to 5 per cent of the outstanding balance) each month and a substantial percentage who repay their balances at rates between the minimum and maximum. The receivables in such a portfolio at any point in time, exclusive of reborrowings after such time, will be characterized by a short average life (for example, eight months) but a very long final payment (for example, ten years). A credit-card-backed security that is intended to provide the investor with a more stable rate of principal repayment cannot, then, be based on a simple pass-through of payments received on the underlying obligations. Securities that have been issued to date have achieved more stable rates through (1) allocation to investors of a portion of receivables created by new borrowings in the accounts, (2) commitments to add new accounts in the event of rapid paydowns of the original accounts or (3) third-party funding commitments or maturity guarantees. A summary of the structures employed follows.

5.1.1 *Delayed Pass-Through Trust Structure*

This structure is sometimes referred to as a 'pass-through' structure, a 'trust structure' or a 'securitization' structure. The term 'delayed pass-through trust' structure has been invented for the purposes of this writing and is more descriptive. In any event, this structure has been the structure most frequently employed in the US.

The seller of the receivables (the 'sponsor') transfers, as settlor of a newly created trust (the 'trust'), all of its interest in all accounts receivable, whether then existing or thereafter created, in specified accounts. The trust issues certificates ('investor certificates') representing ownership of undivided interests in the trust in an aggregate amount (the 'investor interest') equal to the aggregate face amount of the investor certificates, which is less than the aggregate outstanding balance of the receivables. The investor certificates are sold to the public. In exchange for the receivables, the sponsor receives (1) the net proceeds of the offering of the investor certificates and (2) an ownership interest in the trust representing the remaining undivided interest in excess of the investor interest.

Interest payments are made on the investor certificates in arrears with respect to the outstanding investor amount at the rate and frequency specified in the investor certificates. In the absence of specified unexpected events (sometimes referred to as 'payout events', 'amortization events' or 'liquidation events' and referred to herein as 'early principal payment events'), no principal payments are made on the investor certificates during a preset 'interest-only period'. Early principal payment events generally include, among other things, high portfolio loss rates, yield reduction and other events that may indicate an impaired ability to service principal and interest on the securities. If the investor certificates are supported by a third-party facility to guarantee payment of the outstanding investor interest (a 'maturity facility'), the interest-only period may continue until final maturity of the investor certificates. Otherwise, principal payments are made in instalments, based on collections on the receivables.

The *raison d'être* of the delayed pass-through trust structure is sale treatment on the books of the sponsor. One of the necessary conditions for sale treatment is that the certificates not be characterized as debt instruments; otherwise the sponsor's retained interest in the trust would constitute 100 per cent of the 'equity interest' in the trust and, on a consolidated basis, the transfer to the trust would be ignored. To avoid such a result, the investor certificates generally have the following equity characteristics.

- Receivables are classified as consisting of 'principal receivables' which generally relate to amounts charged by the obligor for purchases of goods or services ('cardholder purchases') or cash advances and 'finance charge receivables' comprising the remainder, including periodic interest or finance charges and various fees. (The revolving credit agreements may not provide for such an allocation, in which case the allocation may be made in the trust instrument.) The investors' ownership interest with respect to principal receivables corresponds to the investor interest.
- During the interest-only period, amounts allocable to the investors' share of collections of principal receivables are paid to the sponsor in exchange for a corresponding amount of principal receivables that would otherwise be allocated to the sponsor, thus maintaining the investor amount at its original level, less any write-offs of principal receivables that are not covered by credit enhancement.
- Collections with respect to the sponsor's share of the receivables are paid to the sponsor. No recourse may be had to such collections to cover shortfalls in payments on the investor certificates.
- Collections with respect to the investors' share of principal receivables are not to be used to pay interest on the investor certificates.
- Instalments of principal, if any, paid on the investor certificates are related to collections of principal receivables corresponding to the investor interest. The percentage used to determine the principal payments allocated to the investors should not be preset at a percentage higher than the investors' expected participation ownership interest in the receivables in the trust at the end of the interest-only period.

In order to protect investors against shortfalls of payments caused by defaults in payment on the underlying receivables, credit support is necessary to indemnify investors with respect to such defaults. The amount of credit support ('credit enhancement') that is necessary depends on, among other things, the following factors:

- The credit rating desired. The higher the required rating, the higher the level of required credit enhancement.
- The estimated rate of defaults. The structure must withstand a

'worst-case scenario' in which defaults occur at a level that greatly exceeds historical levels. The greater the bank's historical level of charge-offs, the greater the required credit enhancement. Other factors may be considered in the estimation process including the level of geographic diversity (a significant factor in the US) and subjective evaluations of the sponsor's origination and collection procedures.

- The estimated portfolio yield. Collections of finance charge receivables in excess of the amount necessary to pay interest on the investor certificates are usually available to cover defaults. The lower the estimated portfolio yield, the greater the required credit enhancement.

Forms of credit enhancement may include third-party guarantees or standby letters of credit, cash reserve funds or subordination of the sponsor's interest in the receivables. Because of accounting and regulatory considerations, credit enhancements of publicly offered delayed pass-through trust issues sponsored by US banks have been limited to use of third-party letters of credit. Maturity facilities may consist of the same types of guaranty or of third-party funding commitments to refinance the investor certificates.

5.1.2 *Secured Debt Structure*

In a secured debt offering, investors purchase debt instruments that are secured by a pledge of all balances, including after-acquired balances, arising from time to time in specified revolving credit accounts. As in the delayed pass-through trust structure, the securities have an initial interest-only period that may be terminated by an early principal payment event. During the interest-only period, all collections on the receivables in excess of the debt service requirement and servicing fees, if any, are retained by the sponsor. Thereafter, all collections on the receivables in excess of any servicing fees are available for debt service. It is generally unnecessary to provide for any allocation between principal receivables and finance charge receivables when this structure is used. Protection against net reduction in outstanding balances, as well as credit support, may be provided by overcollateralizing the issue. Additional credit enhancement may be provided through a cash reserve fund, a letter of credit or another form of third-party guarantee.

The secured debt structure offers certain advantages over the delayed pass-through trust structure. Because no allocations are made between principal receivables and finance charge receivables or between the sponsor's interest and the investors' interest, more cash flow would be available for debt service in a secured debt offering than in a delayed pass-through offering backed by the same pool of accounts. Because the security is classified as a 'debt instrument' and not an 'equity security', qualification of the instrument as a legal investment for certain classes of institutional investors, including pension funds subject to the Employee Retirement Income Security Act of 1974, as amended (ERISA),[4] is less difficult than is the case with the delayed pass-through security. However, the secured debt structure does not permit sale treatment for accounting purposes. For this reason, the structure has not been widely employed.[5]

5.1.3 Special-Purpose Vehicle Commercial Paper Structure

Revolving credit receivables have been securitized through 'special purpose vehicles' (SPVs), that is, corporations not formally affiliated with sponsors whose business is limited to acquisition of assets to be securitized and the issuance of commercial paper or other debt instruments backed by such assets.[6] The normal expectation is that maturing commercial paper will be retired through the issuance of new commercial paper. In order to assure that sufficient funds will be available to retire maturing commercial paper in the event of disruption in the commercial paper market, the commercial paper is supported by a maturity facility, generally a refunding loan commitment from a bank consortium. In addition, credit enhancement must be provided to cover defaults.

The SPV commercial paper structure enables the sponsor to obtain a funding source that may be funded from time to time in varying amounts according to the outstanding balances in the underlying credit-card accounts. The overall financing cost may be attractive, depending on commercial paper rates and other factors. However, as of the date of this writing, uncertainty exists regarding the ability of the sponsor to avoid having to include the SPV in its consolidated financial statements, which avoidance is necessary in order to achieve sale treatment for accounting purposes.[7]

5.1.4 US Federal Income Tax Status

Securities issued as debt instruments of the sponsor will normally be treated as indebtedness of the sponsor for US federal income tax purposes. The tax classification of the delayed pass-through trust structure is more complex. Most offerings of this type have included disclosure that tax counsel has rendered its opinion to the effect that the investor certificates should be treated as indebtedness of the sponsor.

Although the issuance of asset-backed securities through the delayed pass-through trust structure is normally treated as a sale in form and for accounting purposes, the form of the transaction, although an important factor, is not conclusive of its classification for US federal income tax purposes.[8] A transfer of property constitutes, for such purposes, a sale of the property when the owner has relinquished substantial incidents of ownership, especially when the transferee has assumed the burdens of ownership by bearing the risk of loss of the property, and has acquired the benefits of ownership by having the opportunity to realize gain on the property.[9] If, however, holders of the investor certificates bear no significant risk of economic loss and the sponsor retains the opportunity to realize gain on the credit-card accounts, the form of the transaction is not dispositive. Similar considerations apply in determining the classification of a transfer of receivables to an SPV in the commercial paper structure.

Economic risk　Rating agencies generally require that the amount of credit enhancement be sufficient to protect investors against any shortfall of principal or interest payments under 'worst-case scenarios'[10] or 'stressful economic environments'.[11] Unless actual conditions are worse than the worst-case scenarios or the stressful economic environments, it is expected that investors will suffer no loss. Instead, the risk of loss from defaults on the investor interest receivables will be borne by the sponsor or the credit enhancer.

Opportunity for gain　The interest payable on the investor certificates is in the nature of compensation for the time value of the funds that investors have advanced to the sponsor, that is, interest. Thus, such interest is not in the nature of profit from the difference in market interest rates and the rate of finance charges on the accounts.[12] Gain on the receivables resulting from appreciation in their fair market value (for example, as a result of declining market interest rates) is not available to investors. Because the terms of the investor certificates and the underlying receivables differ so significantly, any gain that could be realized by an investor with respect to its ownership interest in the receivables is gain from the investor certificate as a separate instrument and not from the underlying receivables. Further, because the sponsor generally retains entitlement to all amounts payable with respect to the investor interest in excess of amounts payable to investors, amounts payable to the credit enhancer and other fees and expenses, the sponsor, in effect, retains the opportunity for gain resulting from decreases in defaults or increases in yield on the credit-card accounts.

Other factors   Other factors to be addressed in determining whether a delayed pass-through trust transaction may be treated as a debt for US federal income tax purposes include the following.

(1) *Control and possession.*   Retention of possession and control of the property by the transferor is more consistent with a loan than with a sale.[13]

(2) *Differences in terms of obligations.*   When receivables are assigned to an assignee, if the terms of the instrument under which the assignee is paid, including the interest rate, amount due, dates of payment and maturity date, are not related to the terms of the payment on the underlying receivables, the transaction is more likely to be viewed as a mere pledge of the receivables and not as a sale.[14] Conversely, the greater the similarity in terms of the underlying receivables and the instrument under which the assignee is paid, the greater the likelihood of the characterization of the assignment as a sale of the receivables.[15]

(3) *Other incidents of ownership.*   Giving notice to the obligors on the receivables or otherwise making them aware of the transfer of the receivables suggests a sale characterization. Typically, such notice is not given. Placement of responsibility for collection of the accounts and the bearing of the expenses thereof on the transferee of the receivables suggest a sale characterization of the transaction. Typically, servicing responsibilities remain with the transferor. Placement of liability for all property, excise, sales or similar taxes that may arise with respect to the receivables on a transferee suggests sale charac-

terization.[16] An agreement that provides for the transferor to hold the transferee harmless from any action brought against the transferee arising out of the transferor's continued responsibility to make collections will suggest a characterization of the transaction as a loan.[17]

5.2 Instalment Loan and Instalment Sales Contract Obligations

Instalment obligations that have been securitized in the US include unsecured loans and consumer loans and instalment sales contracts backed by motor vehicles, manufactured housing, boats and other collateral. Although incentives exist for securitization of commercial and industrial loans, financial institutions have encountered difficulties in securitizing these assets.

5.2.1 *Factors Favouring or Disfavouring Securitization*

The following factors are among those that govern the degree of difficulty and expense that may be encountered in attempting to securitize a particular type of asset.

Uniformity of documentation The use of uniform documents by the originator of the assets facilitates due diligence document review by the parties and enables the issuer to disclose to investors the terms of the documents governing their rights within a reasonable space. Uniform documentation also facilitates the process of transfer of servicing of the obligations, if necessary. The use of non-standard documents increases the risk that the terms of the obligations may not conform to the disclosure document or to the assumptions used in structuring the transaction.

Seasoning and payment history The level of credit enhancement required is generally based on an estimate of the performance of the asset pool under worst-case scenarios or stressful economic conditions.[18] Although the performance of a pool will depend on a variety of factors that have nothing to do with historical performance, the level of uncertainty is reduced if the originator of the assets has originated similar obligations in a consistent manner over a long period of time and has maintained accurate records of payment history and loss history on such obligations. Experience has shown that delinquency and loss levels are generally highest during the early years of instalment obligations;[19] the greater the 'seasoning', or average age, of the obligations, the lower the expected delinquency rate. For the foregoing reasons, enterprises that are new entrants in the market for origination of particular types of assets encounter greater difficulty in securitizing those assets.

Interest rates   Assets with a constant yield are generally easier to securitize than variable-rate instruments. Market conditions favour securities bearing a fixed rate of interest or a variable rate that fluctuates in tandem with a well-recognized index such as LIBOR, prime lending rates, and so on. If the underlying asset is variable-rate and the security is fixed-rate, then credit enhancement, interest-rate floors or other structural features must be implemented to assure that the cash flow from the underlying assets will be sufficient to service the securities. If both the underlying assets and the security bear interest at a variable rate, but the indices are different, the 'basis risk' of non-parallel index changes must be covered. Even if the same index is used for the assets and the securities, basis risk will nevertheless exist unless the interest rates on all of the underlying assets as well as on the securities are reset at the same periodic times according to a common index. None of these problems are insurmountable, but they do increase complexity. Most securities backed by variable-rate instruments have been 'pass-through' securities for which the yield is, in effect, a blended rate based on the weighted average interest rates of the underlying assets.

Wide variations in interest rates (whether fixed or variable) within a pool are undesirable. If the obligors on the assets have the right to prepay the obligations, consideration must be given to the effect on pool performance if the higher-yielding obligations are prepaid and the lower-yielding obligations are not. As a general rule, the prepayment rate is higher for higher-yielding assets.

Payment terms   Fully amortizing level payment obligations are the most easily securitized. Balloon payments and other non-level payments lead to non-uniform cash flows to investors. Furthermore, obligations with balloon payments are thought to be more likely to default.

Fully amortizing level payment obligations in the US generally fall within one of three categories: 'actuarial', 'simple interest' or 'rule of 78s'.

(1) *Actuarial loans.* Each scheduled periodic payment on an actuarial loan consists of an amount of interest equal to the remaining principal balance multiplied by the per-annum stated interest rate divided by the number of scheduled payment periods within each year. The remaining portion of each payment is applied to reduction of the principal balance. With certain exceptions, payments that are made early or late by a few days do not alter the allocation of a payment between principal and interest. Actuarial loans resemble most US home mortgage loans and present the fewest problems in securitization.

(2) *Simple-interest loans.* Each payment on a simple-interest loan consists of an amount of interest equal to the remaining principal balance multiplied by the per-annum stated interest rate multiplied by the fraction of a year that has elapsed since the prior payment. The remaining portion of each payment is applied to reduction of the principal balance. The amount of each scheduled payment is the amount that would retire the loan on its stated maturity if each scheduled payment were made on its due date. Early payments reduce the principal by more than the scheduled amount and vice versa. Therefore early payments will result in a reduction of the final payment at maturity or an acceleration of maturity while late payments will result in a balloon payment at maturity. Because payments on securities are generally made on fixed payment dates regardless of when payments occur on the underlying obligations, early payments on simple-interest loans result in a potential yield loss to investors that must be covered by credit enhancement or otherwise.

(3) *Rule of 78s loans.* Rule of 78s loans are non-level yield instruments. The portion of each payment that is allocated to earned interest is computed based on the 'rule of 78s'. The yield during the beginning period of such a loan is greater than the actuarial yield and the yield at the end of the loan is lower than the actuarial yield. At any time after the first periodic payment, the amount of principal that must be paid to prepay a rule of 78s loan in full is greater than the amount that would be required to prepay in full an actuarial loan with the same initial principal amount and the same periodic payments. Publicly

offered securities backed by rule of 78s loans have generally been structured by converting the payments to an actuarial basis using an imputed principal balance. Because the imputed principal balance of a seasoned loan is less than the rule of 78s balance, securitization of such a loan may result in a slight loss, depending on the accounting treatment of future excess yield.

Quality of servicing   Servicing of assets includes making collections from obligors, record-keeping, reporting and enforcement of the terms of the obligation, including, for example, policing insurance of the collateral. Investors have a greater level of security if the servicer is financially strong and is experienced in servicing similar assets for its own account. The servicing agreements with investors generally require that the same policies and procedures be applied with respect to the securitized obligations as those applied to the servicer's own portfolio.

Other factors   Other factors that may impede securitization include (1) contractual rights of the obligors to vary the payment terms, (2) a small number of assets in the pool, (3) a high ratio of the largest asset in the pool to the average asset size, (4) infrequent payment dates and (5) failure to meet the exemption requirements set forth in section 3(c)(5)(A) of the Investment Company Act of 1940.[20]

5.2.2 Pass-Through Structures

In a pass-through securitization of instalment obligations investors purchase certificates representing fractional undivided beneficial ownership of the underlying receivables. In public offerings, the receivables, together with any related security interests in collateral securing the receivables, are normally transferred to a trust and investors purchase fractional interests in the trust. The trustee of the trust acts on behalf of investors in dealing with other parties to the transaction, including the seller, the servicer and credit enhancers. In private offerings to a limited number of sophisticated investors, the investors may have the capability to deal directly with other parties and to enforce their rights, in which case the intermediate trust can be eliminated and the securities issued in the form of participation certificates representing direct ownership of fractional undivided interests in the underlying assets.

Payments on a traditional pass-through security on each periodic payment date consist of (1) scheduled principal payments due during the related collection period (for example, a pass-through on the fifteenth day of each month of scheduled principal due during the prior calendar month, in which case the 'payment dates' are the fifteenth day of each month and the 'collection periods' are the respective preceding calendar months), (2) unscheduled principal payments received during the related collection period and (3) interest at a stated rate (the 'pass-through rate') on the remaining principal balance of the pass-through securities.[21] Shortfalls in collections of interest and scheduled principal are covered by credit enhancement. The 'remaining principal balance' of the pass-through security is the initial face amount reduced by all amounts passed through with respect to principal, whether from collections on the underlying obligations, payments from credit enhancement or otherwise. Thus, if defaults occur on the underlying obligations that are covered by credit enhancement, the remaining principal balance of the underlying obligations will exceed the remaining principal balance of the securities.

In a traditional pass-through structure, the aggregate interest payable on the underlying obligations exceeds the aggregate interest at the pass-through rate on the securities during each collection period. The excess is available to pay servicing fees, amounts due to credit enhancers and other parties. Amounts remaining after such payments may be retained by the seller.

Pass-through structures offer the opportunity to qualify for sale treatment for accounting purposes provided that the appropriate limitations on recourse and control are respected. One significant limitation is that the right of the sponsor to redeem or repurchase the underlying obligations is severely limited.

5.2.3 Debt Structures

In an instalment loan-backed debt offering, the securities consist of debt instruments secured by a pledge of the underlying receivables. If the debt instrument is commercial paper, the structure is similar to the revolving credit-backed structure discussed in section 5.1.3 above. If the security represents long-term or medium-term debt, the payment terms must be structured so that, irrespective of the rate of prepayment of principal on the instalment obligations, the cash flow from the instalment obligations will be sufficient to pay debt service on the securities on each payment date and to retire them in full at maturity. As a practical matter, this usually means that the securities are 'pay-through' instruments, that is, the aggregate principal payments on the securities on each payment date are proportional to the aggregate principal payments on the instalment obligations during the related collection period. One reason is that an accumulation of cash for an extended period of time creates reinvestment risk, that is, the risk that funds cannot be invested at a yield as high as the yield on the instalment obligations. One significant offering included a multi-class sequential payment structure similar to the CMO structure used for mortgage-backed securities offerings.[22]

Debt structures offer more flexibility than pass-through structures with respect to payment terms, redemption features and other terms. However, sale treatment of the transaction is unavailable unless the receivables are first transferred to an unconsolidated entity.

5.2.4 *US Federal Income Tax Status*

Pass-through transactions are normally treated as 'grantor trusts' for US federal income tax purposes.[23] If the arrangement qualifies for this treatment then, provided that the transfer of the receivables qualifies as a sale rather than a financing (see section 5.1.4 above for a discussion of some of the relevant factors), the trust will not be taxed and the investors will be taxed as if they directly owned their *pro rata* shares of the underlying receivables. If, however, the transaction is treated as a sale for tax purposes but the arrangement fails to qualify as a grantor trust, the pass-through trust may be treated as an association taxable as a corporation. In the latter event, payments to investors would be treated as taxable dividends and additional income tax would be imposed upon the income of the trust itself, with no deduction for distributions to investors.

In order to qualify as a grantor trust, the arrangement must satisfy, among others, the following conditions:[24] (1) the trust must not engage in the conduct of a business for profit, (2) the trust must be a 'fixed investment trust' with no ability to vary the terms of the investments and (3) the trust must have a single class of ownership interest.

Fixed investment Asset-backed securities structures typically include representations and warranties as to factual matters regarding each receivable. Upon discovery of a breach of a warranty concerning a receivable that cannot be cured, the sponsor is required to repurchase the receivable. In other asset-backed structures, such as the revolving credit delayed pass-through trust structure, the sponsor may be given an additional option to substitute a new receivable for the defective receivable. However, with certain exceptions, a general right to substitute receivables would violate the fixed investment requirement for grantor trusts and, therefore, is not seen (except under narrow restrictions) in pass-through arrangements classified as grantor trusts.[25]

Custom and practice in certain instalment lending businesses include periodic granting, on a discretionary basis, of 'skip a payment' offerings whereby the borrower is allowed to omit one or more periodic payments and to accrue interest during the interim. It is feared that the granting of such options by the sponsor with respect to obligations that are securitized in a pass-through structure would violate the fixed-investment requirement. However, prohibitions against such programmes need not extend to extensions that are granted for credit-related reasons to enhance, in the servicer's judgement, probability of ultimate payment.

No trade or business   If grantor-trust treatment is sought, the servicer must not be given unfettered discretion with respect to servicing of the receivables. For example, the disposition of collateral following foreclosure should be based on standard procedures that do not involve protracted intentional delays based on speculation in the markets for such goods. Otherwise the trust might be viewed as carrying on the business of dealing in such goods.

Single class of ownership interests   US Department of Treasury regulations[26] preclude grantor-trust treatment for trusts with multiple classes of ownership interest. The regulations allow for exceptions wherein the existence of multiple classes is incidental to the purpose of facilitating direct investment.[27]

Debt transactions do not present the same degree of complexity as grantor-trust structures. The principal pitfall to be avoided is the recharacterization of the transaction as a sale, in which case the arrangement potentially could be treated as a trust that does not qualify as a grantor trust and, therefore, results in double taxation, as described above. A discussion of some of the principal factors differentiating between sale and debt characterization for US federal income tax purposes is set forth at section 5.1.4 above.

5.3 Lease Obligations

Lease obligations are payable in instalments and closely resemble instalment loan and instalment sale obligations in many other respects. 'Financing leases' are treated for accounting purposes as loans. The securitization of operating leases, that is, leases not economically equivalent to loans, presents structuring issues not common to other instalment obligations.

The present value of future lease payments of an operating lease is normally less than the value of the leased property. If the sponsor wishes to obtain proceeds from the securities offering based on the value of the leased property, the structure will include a balloon payment at maturity of each obligation based on the residual value from disposition of the leased property. Since the residual value depends on future market conditions, additional credit enhancement may be required in order to assure timely return of principal to investors. Additional principal repayment risk is presented if the lessee has the right to terminate the lease prior to its scheduled expiration. Even if the lessee is required, upon early payment, to pay an amount equal to the present value of the remaining payments, the risk that funds cannot be reinvested at a rate equal to the yield on the securities will jeopardize timely repayment of principal.

If less than the full value of the leased property is being securitized, the seller will wish to retain title to the leased property (and may, for administrative and other reasons, be compelled to retain title in any event). If the sponsor or its subsidiary retains title to the leased property, the transaction may be required to be treated as a borrowing for accounting purposes.[28] Accordingly, securitizations of this type of lease are more frequently structured as debt offerings (or pass-throughs of lease-backed debt instruments) rather than pass-through transactions.

5.4 Collateral Protection

One of the essential elements of a securitization transaction is the creation of a security whose credit quality is based on the performance of the underlying pool of receivables and related credit enhancement and whose credit quality is independent of the financial strength or weakness of the sponsor (or any other third party other than credit enhancers). The cash flow from the securitized assets must not be subject to interruption from adverse claims against the securitized assets or from the insolvency of the sponsor.

5.4.1 *Perfection of the Asset Transfer*

In many securitization transactions, the sale or pledge or the transfer of assets to investors or their trustee is subject to Article 9 of the Uniform Commercial Code (UCC). Table 5.1 indicates generally the classification of various commonly securitized assets under the UCC. Variances from the table may occur, depending on specific circumstances.

Pledges of accounts and general intangibles are perfected under the UCC by filing a financing statement in a central office in the appropriate jurisdiction that, among other things, 'contains a statement indicating the types, or describing the items, of collateral'.[29] Sales of accounts are treated, for such purpose, in the same way as a pledge of accounts.[30] However, a sale of general intangibles is not subject to Article 9 of the UCC and perfection is governed by applicable local law. Because credit-card portfolios generally include both accounts and general intangibles, the delayed pass-through trust structure requires both UCC filing and compliance with the perfection requirements of applicable local law. By contrast, a credit-card-backed debt offering generally requires only a UCC filing.

Both pledges and sales of chattel paper may be perfected either by a

Table 5.1

Type of asset	UCC classification
Credit-card receivables arising from purchase of goods or services	Accounts
Credit-card receivables arising from cash advances	General intangibles
Vehicle loans, leases, or instalment sales contracts	Chattel paper
Trade receivables	Accounts
Unsecured consumer loans	Instruments

UCC filing or by delivery of possession of the documents constituting the chattel paper to the transferee or its bailee.[31] If perfection is solely by filing, the transferee's interest is subordinate to rights of a purchaser for value without notice[32] who takes possession of the chattel paper in the ordinary course of business. With respect to securitization of automobile loans, the standard practice has evolved of perfecting only by filing and disclosing to investors the risk that, through fraud or negligence of the servicer, their rights in the collateral could become subordinate to third parties.

Although the transferee of chattel paper acquires a perfected interest in the chattel paper, the transfer does not in all cases automatically perfect a security interest in the underlying goods in favour of the transferee. For example, in many states, perfection of a security interest in a motor vehicle is effected by notation of the lien on a certificate of title. In some states, a transfer of the lien may be ineffective unless the transferee's name is noted on the certificate of title.

Perfection of a security interest in an instrument can, with certain limited exceptions, be effected only by delivery of possession of the instrument.[33]

Article 9 of the UCC provides that an unperfected security interest (including an unperfected sale of accounts or chattel paper) is subordinate to the rights of, among others, lien creditors, certain innocent purchasers, bankruptcy trustees and receivers in equity.[34] In addition, non-UCC law may impose significant restrictions on transfer or alter priority of the transferee's interest.[35]

A concern exists that a partial assignment of a receivable may compromise its enforceability on behalf of investors. At common law, a partial assignee cannot enforce a debt without the debtor's consent.[36] In equity, at the discretion of the court, a partial assignment is enforceable without the debtor's consent if all parties can be joined in one suit,[37] but in some jurisdictions a partial assignment without the debtor's consent may be invalid even in equity.[38] Even if the equitable doctrine applies, additional delays in collection may occur in the event of the transferor's insolvency because of the necessity of joining the receiver, or the entity to whom the receiver has distributed the unassigned interest, as a party in any suit to enforce a claim. As a general rule, the assignment of receivables by the sponsor should be free of participations and other fractional interests.

5.4.2 *Insolvency Considerations*

If the timely payment of principal or interest on an asset-backed security could be interrupted by the insolvency of the sponsor, then the security cannot be rated materially higher than the credit rating of the sponsor. If the sponsor is an entity subject to the US Bankruptcy Code,[39] certain procedural elements of that Code create a significant risk of impairment of timely payment in the event that the securitized assets are included in an estate subject to a proceeding under that Code.[40] In such offerings, assurance is needed that ownership of the assets has been completely disposed of by the sponsor and that such disposition is not subject to avoidance by the bankruptcy court through characterization of the transfer as a preference,[41] a fraudulent conveyance[42] or a pledge rather than a sale[43] or by 'substantive consolidation' of the assets of the sponsor and the assets of the transferee.[44]

Banks, thrifts and certain other institutions are ineligible to be debtors under the US Bankruptcy Code.[45] If the sponsor is such an institution, the sponsor may retain an ownership interest in the securitized assets, provided that the transfer of the investors' interest is properly perfected and is not subject to avoidance (for example, as a fraudulent conveyance) by a receiver of the institution in a potential insolvency proceeding.

Notes

1 RepublicBank Delaware, 7.15% Credit Card Backed Notes, Series A, Offering Circular dated 16 January 1987, California Credit Card Trust 1987-A, 6.90% Asset-Backed Certificates, Prospectus dated 25 February 1987, California Credit Card Trust 1987-B, 8.20% Receivable Backed Certificates, Prospectus dated 19 June 1987.

2 Compiled from New Issue Guide, *Asset Sales Report* (9 January 1989).

3 Compiled from Moody's Investors Service, 'Index of structured finance issues', *Structured Finance* (May 1989) and Standard & Poor's, 'Asset backed securitization', *Credit Review* (March 1989).

4 29 U.S.C. sections 1001 *et seq.* (1982).

5 To the author's knowledge only two US offerings of revolving credit-backed securities have utilized a secured debt structure other than commercial paper. See RepublicBank Delaware, $200,000,000 7.15% Credit Card Backed Notes, Series A, Offering Circular dated 16 January 1987, and Lomas Bank USA, $250,000,000 9.15% Credit Card Backed Notes,

Series 1988-A, Prospectus and Prospectus Supplement dated 21 October 1988.

6 The term 'commercial paper', as used in US parlance, is normally confined to instruments satisfying the exemption from registration pursuant to section 3(a)(3) of the Securities Act of 1933, as amended, 15 U.S.C. section 77c(a)(3)(1982), which, among other things, must have maturities of not more than nine months at the time of issuance.

7 See 'SEC talks with accountants; trust rules may soon follow', *Asset Sales Report* (22 May 1989).

8 See *Helvering* v. *Lazarus & Co.*, 308 U.S. 252 (1939); *Stein* v. *Director of Internal Revenue*, 135 F.Supp. 356 (E.D.N.Y. 1955).

9 See, for example, *United Surgical Steel Co.* v. *Commissioner*, 54 T.C. 1215 (1970), *acq.* 1971–2 C.B. 3; *Town & Country Food Co.* v. *Commissioner*, 51 T.C. 1049 (1969), *acq.* 1969–2 C.B. xxv.

10 Standard & Poor's Corporation, *S&P's Structured Finance Criteria* (1988), p. 75.

11 Moody's Investors Service, Inc., 'Credit card receivables: Moody's examines the risks', *Structured Finance* (July 1987), p. 5.

12 Cf. G.C.M. 39584.

13 *United Surgical Steel Co.* v. *Commissioner*, 54 T.C. 1215, 1229–30 (1970), *acq.* 1971–2 C.B. 3; *Town & Country Food Co.* v. *Commissioner*, 51 T.C. 1049, 1057 (1969), *acq.* 1969–2 C.B. xxv; *Mathers* v. *Commissioner*, 57 T.C. 666 (1972), *acq.* 1973–1 C.B. 1.

14 *Town & Country Food Co.*, at 1057; *United Surgical Steel Co.*, at 1228; *Schaeffer* v. *Commissioner*, 41 T.C.M. (CCH) 752, 756 (1981).

15 *Bogatin* v. *U.S.*, 78–2 U.S.T.C. para. 9733 (W.D. Tenn. 1978); Rev. Rul. 65–185, 1965–2 C.B. 153.

16 See *Illinois Power Co.* v. *Commissioner*, 87 T.C. 1417, 1439 (1986) (burden of paying taxes and other governmental charges weighed in balancing burdens and benefits of ownership for federal income tax purposes). See also *Yancey Bros.*, 319 F.Supp. at 445–6 (taxpayer's treatment of intangibles tax on transferred notes was evidence of taxpayer's ownership of such notes), and *Schaeffer*, 41 T.C.M. (CCH) at 757 (taxpayer's payment of state income tax on interest received on a transferred note was evidence of pledge of the note, not a sale).

17 G.C.M. 39584.

18 See notes 10 and 11 above.

19 Standard & Poor's Corporation, *S&P's Structured Finance Criteria* (1988), p. 72.

20 15 U.S.C. section 80a-3(c)(5)(A)(1982).

21 US mortgage-backed securities have been issued in pass-through formats that vary from the 'traditional structure' described in the text, for example, interest-only and principal-only 'strips' and multiple-class sequential

payment structures. To date, such pass-through structures have not been extended to non-mortgage assets. Such structures are facilitated by the REMIC provisions of Internal Revenue Code of 1986 sections 860A–G, which are currently applicable only to mortgage assets.

22 Asset Backed Securities Corporation, $4,000,000,000 Asset Backed Obligations, Series 1, Prospectus dated 8 October 1986 and Prospectus Supplement dated 14 October 1986.

23 But see, for example, Chrysler Auto Receivables Company, $250,000,000 Certificates for Automobile Receivables CARCO Series 1986–1, Preliminary Prospectus dated 17 July 1986, at p. 30 (debt treatment for US federal income tax purposes).

24 US Dept of Treasury Regulations section 301.7701–4.

25 US Dept of Treasury Regulations section 301.7701–4(c)(1). The Internal Revenue Service has ruled that, under certain circumstances, the right to transfer assets to a trust for a period of ninety days after its creation does not constitute a power to vary the investment, Rev. Rul. 86–92, 1986–2 C.B. 214, and the right to substitute a new mortgage for a mortgage that has been found to be defective within the first two years of the pool is consistent with grantor-trust treatment, Rev. Rul. 71–399, 1971–2 C.B. 433.

26 US Dept of Treasury Regulations section 301.7701–4(c)(1).

27 The regulations, at section 301.7701–4(c)(2), provide examples of multiple-class structures that qualify for trust treatment including (1) a two-class senior/subordinated structure in which the subordinate piece is retained by the sponsor as credit enhancement and (2) a stripped coupon structure in which each certificate represents the right to receive a particular payment with respect to a specific bond.

28 FASB *Statement of Financial Accounting Standards* No. 13, 'Accounting for leases', as amended through May 1980, para. 22.

29 UCC section 9–402(1).

30 UCC sections 1–201(37), 9–102(1)(b).

31 UCC sections 9–304(1), 9–305.

32 UCC section 9–308(1).

33 UCC section 9–304(1).

34 UCC section 9–301.

35 For example, US federal income tax law provides for a lien in favour of the US government that, with certain exceptions, has priority over other property rights. Internal Revenue Code of 1986, as amended, sections 6321 *et seq.* The assignability of certain health-care receivables under federal programmes is limited. 42 U.S.C. section 1396g(c)(1982), 42 U.S.C.A. section 1396a(a)(32)(West Supp. 1989).

36 *First National Bank of Wayne* v. *Gross Real Estate Co.*, 162 Neb. 343, 75 N.W.2d 704 (1956); 6 *Am.Jur.*2d 'Assignments' section 76 (1963).

37 See generally 80 A.L.R. 413; 6 *Am.Jur.*2d 'Assignments' section 77 (1963); *Restatement (Second) of Contracts* section 326, Comments b and c and Reporter's Note; 3 *Williston on Contracts* section 441–4 (3rd edn 1960).

38 See *Burnett* v. *Crandall*, 63 Mo. 410 (1876); *Citizens & Southern National Bank* v. *Bruce*, 420 F.Supp. 795, 798 (E.D.Mo. – E.Div. 1976), *aff'd* 562 F.2d 590 (8th Cir. 1977); *Skobis* v. *Ferge*, 102 Wis. 122, 78 N.W. 426 (1899); 80 A.L.R. 428–30; 6 *Am.Jur.*2d 'Assignments' section 77, n. 11.

39 11 U.S.C.A. sections 101 *et seq.* (1979 and 1989 West Supp.).

40 Such procedural elements include the automatic stay (section 362), the ability of the trustee to use, sell or lease property of the estate (section 363), the ability of the trustee to obtain credit secured by a junior lien on the property of the estate (section 364), the requirement to turn over property of the estate (section 542), the avoidance of preferential transfers (section 547), and limits on the post-petition effect of security interests (section 552).

41 11 U.S.C.A. section 547 (1979 and 1989 West Supp.).

42 11 U.S.C.A. section 548 (1979 and 1989 West Supp.).

43 See, for example, *Major's Furniture Mart, Inc.* v. *Castle Credit Corporation, Inc.*, 602 F.2d 538 (3rd Cir.1979).

44 See, for example, *In re 1438 Meridian Place, N.W., Inc.*, 15 B.R. 89 (Bankr. D.D.C. 1981), 5 *Collier on Bankruptcy*, para. 1100.06 (1988).

45 11 U.S.C.A. para 109 (1979 and 1989 West Supp.).

6

Credit Ratings on International Asset-Backed Securities

BARBARA A. NUNEMAKER

Chapter Outline

6.1 Introduction

6.2 The Role of Rating Agencies in Financial Markets

6.3 What Does a Credit Rating Address?

6.4 Do Ratings Matter?

6.5 Universal Rating Scales in Heterogeneous Mortgage Markets
  6.5.1 Are Ratings Comparable Across Borders?
  6.5.2 S&P's Approach to Mortgage Markets

6.6 Comparative Mortgage Analysis: A Case Study

6.7 Implications for Other Assets

6.1 Introduction

The intention of this chapter is to provide an overview of uses of credit ratings in international markets and how the process of assigning a rating works for asset-backed securities. First, the definition and uses of credit ratings will be addressed. This leads to an explanation of how credit ratings can evaluate comparable levels of risk when domestic market characteristics and practice vary. Rating criteria for mortgage-backed bonds are then explained using instruments and practices in the United Kingdom as an example. The methodology used in the UK will then be contrasted with what Standard & Poor's (S&P) has found in the French market. Finally, application of these criteria to non-mortgage assets will be considered.

6.2 The Role of Rating Agencies in Financial Markets

To set the stage, think of the example of an intricate game of 'cat and mouse'. The banking and securities industries are relatively highly regulated worldwide, with regulation in the United States posing well-known hurdles to everyone involved. The 'cat and mouse' game has evolved to the stage where financial institutions search increasingly for profitable opportunities that run along the edge of the regulatory envelope. The regulators work full time to keep no more than a few steps behind the bankers. Likewise, on the other side, borrowers are playing 'cat and mouse', striving constantly to find financing opportunities at the finest possible terms while generating the best possible service from their bankers. The pressures on banks on all sides – regulation, profitability and customer service – have encouraged the development of instruments which enhance profitability, reduce risk and funding exposure, while at the same time playing within the rules of the regulators.

As there are some who call Standard & Poor's (S&P) the 'private sector regulator', it is important to understand a rating agency's position in this game. It is useful to remember that S&P's primary and only responsibility is to give an appreciation of credit risk to investors or bondholders. This is defined as being part of the outer circle along with investors and the general public. Issuers, underwriters, solicitors and accountants would form the inner circle. This is because S&P is not party to the transaction, nor a signatory to it. Its views on the structure of the transaction can affect the rating assigned, and S&P works closely with issuers to understand the transactions, but changes to the issues to satisfy the rating conditions are up to the issuer, not S&P.

Obviously, in any new area of the securities market, the rating agency finds itself treading that fine rim between the inner circle and the outer, as it comes to terms with the features that ensure investor protection.

As S&P rates both secured and unsecured debt, it remains conscious of the effect of securitization on the bank's or selling institution's own creditworthiness. Again S&P finds itself treading a fine line between conditions and regulations which would enhance the volume of these securities in the market, and hoping for sufficiently conservative regulation and prudence of and for banks to underpin their creditworthiness. To reiterate S&P's position with respect to the investing public, credibility with them is the only thing that keeps any rating agency in business, and provides a potent incentive to keep criteria at the highest common denominator and not the lowest.

6.3 What Does a Credit Rating Address?

What is S&P saying with its credit rating? S&P's intention is to tell investors the likelihood with which they will be repaid principal and interest on time and in full in accordance with the terms of the indenture for the issue. The rating says nothing about the foreign-exchange or interest-rate risks, or the appropriateness of a security for any investor's portfolio. Most of all, it is *not* a buy or sell recommendation.

Ratings should give the investor a basis for comparison among instruments in the market, a yardstick for comparing credit quality among debt instruments. In a world where risk–return trade-offs spun only around the axis of credit, all AAA bonds or all AA bonds or all BBB bonds would trade at the same price.

From the definition, it follows in principle that a AAA rating implies one is holding debt of unimpeachable quality whether one buys UK government securities, World Bank securities, Marks & Spencer debt or AAA-rated UK mortgage-backed bonds. Are there differences? There can be. While timely payment should be equally likely for each of these instruments, there are significant differences between secured and unsecured ratings. These differences occur in both the rating process and investor perception.

First of all, unsecured debt is based purely on the issuer's promise to pay. An evaluation of the likelihood of payment hinges on past performance, management and strategy. Management can adapt strategy to respond to market developments. Management can also be bought out, potentially changing a company's rating overnight. Issuers of secured or collateralized transactions have no ability to go in and tinker, for good or for ill, with the rated transaction. This means that it is less adaptable to changing circumstances, and protections to cope with all conceivable problems must be in place from the outset. Therefore, in principle, collateralized ratings are less volatile or susceptible to what is called 'event risk' than unsecured ratings.

However, collateralized ratings rely on a variety of third parties who play a role in the transaction. These ratings are called supporting ratings. Changes in the unsecured rating of a supporting party in a secured transaction can affect the rating on the collateralized issue's rating.

The other key difference, of course, is that a structured transaction is secured by the assets in the vehicle company set up to issue the debt. In this way an investor knows exactly what is available to him to reimburse his debt. In the UK, the investors' interest in the collateral is overseen by the trustee. In other countries, such as the US and France, the investor may actually have a direct ownership interest in the vehicle, and hence the collateral, if trust certificates are issued instead of debt instruments.

The utility of a rating service hinges on serving the public's need for knowledge, a not insignificant part of any investor's decision-making process. However, given the volume of securities on offer, the need for concise information is the key. Hence rating symbols. S&P uses the symbols shown to differentiate among securities according to their credit quality. Those above BB are considered investment grade, that is, an investor's principal is not considered to be at risk, while those below BB are considered speculative grade, implying that a higher return should be anticipated since principal may be at risk.

Table 6.1 lists these rating symbols. Once upon a time most rated debt in the Euromarket was AAA or AA, and investors here were considered extremely 'risk averse'. Over time, interest has grown in the whole gamut of rated debt. Likewise with asset-backed securities. In their early days, these complex transactions only sold with a AA or AAA rating. As these markets have become more sophisticated, some investors have traded a degree of credit quality for yield. As examples the unrated subordinated B bonds of UK mortgage-backed senior/junior structures, as well as Grant Street National Bank debt which owns Mellon Bank's non-performing loans, and Frends BV which contains Continental Illinois' leveraged buy-out participations, represent such debt issues.

Table 6.1   Standard & Poor's Rating Symbols for investment grade issuers

Long-term	Short-term
AAA	
AA+	
AA	A−1+
AA−	
A+	A−1
A	
A−	A−2
BBB+	
BBB	A−3
BBB−	

6.4 Do Ratings Matter?

Theories of financial markets suggest that greater information leads to better-informed investment decisions and greater financial market efficiency. Does this translate into each investor wanting to read all the documents to which he is entitled? Does it mean an investor will read the prospectus from cover to cover?

It does not. Rather the use of ratings on asset-backed securities, or any securities, aims to take the complex and simplify it in a way the investor can readily grasp, at the same time giving him adequate information to make an informed investment decision. An investor takes comfort from a rating for many reasons. The foremost among these are:

- it simplifies his investment decisions,
- it means an investor knows an objective third party has examined the transaction, and
- it gives him a benchmark from which to determine an acceptable level of yield for his portfolio.

An issuer has different concerns, but may also find a rating useful. In this case ratings:

- help an issuer to know where his debt should be priced,

- may help him decrease his cost of funds,
- may enhance the liquidity of his securities in the secondary market, and
- helps him get his story across to potential investors.

6.5 Universal Rating Scales in Heterogeneous Mortgage Markets

6.5.1 *Are Ratings Comparable Across Borders?*

Returning to the definition of a rating and Standard & Poor's stated intention to serve investors, the implications for these functions in the increasingly borderless markets about which investors must make decision these days must be evident. An investor needs a benchmark by which to be able to compare the instruments available in different markets. For this reason, ratings must be comparable across borders. It is relatively easy to compare ICI with DuPont or BP and Shell with Exxon, but how can one compare the relative performance of heterogeneous markets such as mortgages or credit cards or automobile loans in different countries? Here, lending conditions, national practices, levels of consumer indebtedness, accounting and regulatory treatment, and legal procedures vary tremendously from country to country. Is it possible to say that a pool of French mortgages is as sound as a pool of English, Swedish or Japanese ones?

S&P's ability to say this hinges on the approach it takes to rating these transactions, while harking back to the definition of a rating as a measure of relative or comparative risk. This means that while conditions and criteria may differ from country to country, S&P should be saying with its rating that an investor is buying comparable risk, not identical securities. Think of it as a means by which to compare apples and pears.

This will become clearer below as S&P's approach is explained. Using mortgage markets as an example, the text will demonstrate how risk varies among countries, and how S&P adjusts for such variations.

6.5.2 *S&P's Approach to Mortgage Markets*

Much time is spent discussing the quality of the collateral in these transactions. While the quality of the collateral backing the transaction is key to the quality of the bond issue and its safety, it is not the only factor which must be examined. S&P takes a three-pronged approach to the analysis of these transactions. Aside from the collateral quality of the assets backing the issue, S&P wants to be certain that under all circumstances, including the insolvency of any party to the transaction, the bondholder gets paid in full and on time. This means inspecting the liquidity of the transaction and all parties which handle the funds transfer or in any way affect the distribution of moneys. In addition, the legal viability of the transaction is critical. S&P and its counsel must be comfortable that there are no legal issues which could interrupt the flow of funds or cause a third party to get access to the collateral.

A deficiency in the collateral can be remedied with additional protections or, alternatively, result in the assignment of a lower rating, but problems in the structural or legal mechanisms may mean that the transaction cannot be rated at all. Structured issues can be thought of as 'go-or-no-go' transactions. They either work or they do not. Working under most circumstances is not good enough.

The quality of third parties playing a role in the transaction is important to the final rating assigned to the transaction. These could be insurers, banks and so on. They must, as a general rule, be rated as high as the rating desired on the bond issue. S&P calls this the 'weak-link concept'. It means that if any party to the transaction cannot perform to the level required by the rating, then the whole transaction must be rated lower.

Still, the primary emphasis in any discussion of mortgage-backed bonds must be on the quality of the collateral. Below is an extremely simplified model of how S&P evaluates collateral quality for UK mortgages. Following that is an explanation of how adaptations are made to these criteria to suit lending practice in other countries.

Before S&P could even enter this line of business, it was necessary to do some very basic research on the nature of mortgage borrowing in the UK. That included such factors as:

- characteristics of the UK housing industry:
  - price performance
  - importance of home ownership
  - tax relief
- characteristics of UK mortgages:
  - usual term

- method of charging interest
- method of amortization of principal
- common characteristics of mortgage underwriting:
- loan-to-value ratios
- income multiples
- minimum and maximum house values
- performance of mortgages over time:
- arrears, defaults and repossession statistics
- legal procedures.

The past performance of lenders and mortgage insurers in the UK was also examined. The data collected formed the basis for drawing some conclusions on the general credit risk inherent in UK mortgages. Remember that if the bondholder is to be repaid on a timely basis it is not only the *ultimate* recovery of the debt, it is the *timely* recovery of the debt that matters, so arrears that are ultimately recovered by repossession could throw a transaction into default if not funded. This is a somewhat different approach from that which a building society or other mortgage lender would take.

Based on this research, S&P drew up its parameters for what is called a benchmark pool. Table 6.2 lists the components of S&P's benchmark for England and Wales. It must be stressed that these benchmark-pool characteristics are not dictating underwriting standards for the housing industry in the UK or any other country. The benchmark pool is a statistical, hypothetical yardstick by which the risk in any given mortgage pool is measured. It is simply demonstrating that statistically S&P would expect a pool that looks like the benchmark to sustain losses of X per cent under a worst-case scenario – not under current mortgage conditions, but under a worst-case scenario during the life of the pool of mortgages. In order to achieve a AAA rating, coverage for this percentage of losses must be available through either insurance or over-collateralization.

Any UK mortgage-backed bond issue rated by S&P will be evaluated against this benchmark. A statistical analysis of the mortgages in any given transaction will be examined to size the expected credit loss relative to the model. It could be higher or lower than the benchmark pool credit loss, which is 7.2 per cent for a AAA rating. But this is a statistical exercise and by no means a science. A qualitative assessment of the originator and servicer of the mortgages, as well as of the quality and reliability of the data, is also brought to bear on the final level of

Table 6.2 Benchmark pool underwriting guidelines for England and Wales

	Guidelines
Mortgage types	Endowment and repayment
Security	First charge on residential property in England or Wales
Property characteristics	Detached and semi-detached
	Purpose-built and converted flats
	Bungalows, maisonettes, and terraced housing
	Freeholds and leaseholds (30 years remaining life beyond mortgage term)
	Vacant possession
	Deed or letter of consent from non-borrower adult residents
Loan-to-value	Up to 80% LTV
Loan size	£15,000–£150,000
Income limits	2.5 times main salary plus 1.0 times secondary salary or equivalent; two times joint income
Credit check	Infolink or CCN and income verification
Geographic dispersion	Maximum 50% pool in the south-east; maximum 25% elsewhere
Regional dispersion	Maximum 0.5% of pool from any primary postal-code designation
Pool size	Minimum 300 loans
Valuers	Royal Institute of Chartered Surveyors or equivalent
Homeowners' insurance	Index linked to annual index and coverage of subsidence
Unrated endowment policy provider	No more than 25% of the policies from any one provider; maturities of the mortgages and policies are to precede the bonds by at least two years
Term insurance	100% level term with policy assignable to lender

Table 6.3 Credit loss calculations for a benchmark pool in
England and Wales

Rating	Reposition frequency (%)	×	Loss severity (%)	=	Credit loss (%)
AAA	15.0		47.8		7.2
AA	10.0		41.5		4.2
A	8.0		36.5		3.0
BBB	6.0		31.5		1.0

credit enhancement required. S&P's credit-enhancement levels for
UK mortgage-backed securities by rating category are shown in table
6.3.

6.6 Comparative Mortgage Analysis: A Case Study

Having sketched S&P's methodology in the UK, France provides a
good comparison, as only recently the French government passed a
law enabling institutions to issue asset-backed bonds (see chapter 13).
This highlights the first key difference between the UK and French
markets for these securities. In the UK, the market developed in
response to issuer and investor demand, and the features of the
financial instruments sold were left to the players in the market to
decide. The Bank of England only came out with its view on these
transactions as regards bank accounting and risk two years after the
first transaction had been sold.

In France, a codified legal system requires the specific authorization
of new types of financial instruments. Market regulators and government supervisors had a role from the beginning in developing both the
framework and the application of the law, albeit with the cooperation
of potential market participants. While this makes the legal issues
clearer, the structure promulgated leaves less room for innovation
among issuers, or for designing instruments tailored to investors'
needs.

De facto, this means that the instruments sold in France will differ
from those sold in the UK or the US. For example, all instruments
will be ownership certificates in the vehicle. Also, vehicle companies
will not be permitted to borrow money for liquidity purposes, which

will in turn require cash up front to be put in the vehicle, increasing the costs of issuance.

Many of the differences between French asset-backed securities and their English or American counterparts are due to the inherent differences in the assets. While English mortgages are predominantly at floating rates of interest, French mortgages are largely fixed-rate contracts. This alone has a strong impact on the ultimate nature of securities issued. Second, French borrowers move house much less frequently than their English counterparts, and mortgages can theoretically be transferred to subsequent purchasers of the house, giving mortgages a longer average life in France than in England. Third, most of the sellers of assets in France are likely to be regulated financial institutions, while banks and building societies in the UK have been slower to securitize assets than their non-bank counterparts.

Standard & Poor's visited with most of the major consumer lenders in France in order to arrive at the same kind of benchmark pool that was developed in England. A brief summary of this research highlights some of the fundamental differences in lending practice between the two countries.

First, the French consumer is generally less indebted than his 'cross Channel' counterpart, though consumer debt is growing rapidly in France. Second, most financial institutions, barring the finance companies, see the extension of personal credit as an integral part of their long-term relationship with their clientele, and weigh their lending decisions more heavily on the client's track record and ability to repay than on any collateral he offers, such as a home.

This may be a function of the fact that the purchase price of a property is used as the measure of its value in France. Few lenders look for specific independent valuations on properties there, unlike in the UK where all property lending requires a valuation.

In order to arrive at securitization criteria in France, it was necessary for S&P to adapt to local practices. Two examples are the ratios used for a benchmark pool. In France it will be necessary to look at a loan-to-price ratio, albeit discounted for the possible inflation of the price over the real value of the property, rather than a loan-to-value ratio. Likewise, S&P will use the ratio of debt service to monthly income, versus the English method of an income multiple (the sum borrowed divided by the borrower's total annual income), since the former is the practice in France.

S&P believes that a different method of analysing geographic concentrations will be required in France than in England. In England the market is differentiated by two zones, the South-East and the rest of the country. In France, property prices vary in three zones: the Paris region, the major cities, and the countryside, where property changes hands only infrequently.

Using appropriate national characteristics, S&P can arrive at a benchmark pool which is representative of mortgage performance in France. To derive overall credit loss assumptions, S&P must also take into account the relatively longer time required to repossess a property in France than in England, and the consequent cost of interest arrears. As mentioned above, legal issues, both in property transfer law and in securities law, will have to be treated as appropriate to France.

With respect to analysing the transaction itself, S&P procedures will be consistent with those applied in other markets. A review of the servicer of the assets will be conducted to ensure that it is capable of the duties required in the transaction. In France, this will also hold for the manager of the transaction and the depository. The documents will be scrutinized to ensure that the mechanisms of the transaction work as expected. Cash-flow programmes will be required as appropriate for the structure of the transactions, and worst-case tests for these cash flows will be tailored to specific interest-rate, prepayment and recovery scenarios in France.

In summary, a buyer of French asset-backed securities will be able to be as confident of the repayment capabilities of a AAA-rated French instrument as they are of a AAA-rated US or English debt security.

6.7 Implications for Other Assets

Other chapters of this book discuss the potential for the application of securitization techniques to other, particularly European, markets. What, if any, role may S&P play in these potential markets? S&P is anxious to take what it has learned in the existing markets in the United States, the United Kingdom, Canada and Australia and apply it elsewhere. However, we are intentionally reactive not proactive in new markets for our services. It is important that S&P begins research at an early stage to be able to react to nascent demand; yet it is clearly not our role to search out new markets for structured financings.

Rather, as believers in the concept that investors drive the business,

S&P must always be convinced that there is a demand for its services before it approaches any new market. It invites any participants in these other European markets to speak to S&P about the potential markets there and how S&P can begin to work with market participants to develop appropriate criteria.

While S&P's original experience with mortgage-backed securities came from the United States, it is important to emphasize that, using the framework of experience in the US, S&P builds criteria locally that suit domestic market conditions and lending parameters, regardless of the asset under scrutiny. It is not a direct imposition of US methodology on foreign markets.

Rather, S&P jargon would say that it works with what are often referred to as 'S&P eyes'. This implies that its accumulated knowledge of securities can be used, when faced with a new instrument, to ask 'What could possibly go wrong?' Then, upon investigation of the strength of the collateral, the experience of the players in the market, and the legal mechanisms involved, it can compare criteria across borders in order to ensure that the investor, in whatever market, is adequately protected.

This can sometimes work contrary to common practice in a country, if traditionally the investor has been asked to take on good faith the performance of certain conventions, or unrated parties considered 'beyond reproach' in those countries. This can include jurisdictions where investors place great faith in the moral responsibility of the originating institution or any of the parties to the transaction to fulfil their obligations. Nevertheless, where such convictions are justified, S&P will often come to accept them, and perhaps feel even safer than in the US, where markets have become increasingly mindful of contractual rather than moral obligations about market practice.

It is important to remember that S&P's ratings are intended to be comparable worldwide, and therefore it must be comfortable that a buyer of a AAA UK mortgage-backed security is as well protected as a buyer of a AAA-rated French automobile-backed transaction or a AAA-rated German mortgage-backed bond. The company's reputation in the bond market rests on this, and on this it cannot compromise. By ensuring this comparability among instruments, S&P is helping the investor to make an informed decision when faced with the myriad of investment possibilities open to him.

7

UK Tax Considerations

STEPHEN M. EDGE and MICHAEL MURPHY

7.1 Introduction

The principal tax issues that arise in relation to an asset securitization are as follows:

- the need to avoid withholding tax on the various flows of income;
- the need to obtain relief for funding costs and front-end costs;
- the need to extract the profit element implicit in the true value of the assets in a tax-efficient manner;
- the need to minimize the impact of irrecoverable value added tax (VAT); and
- the need to avoid asymmetrical tax treatment on currency losses and gains.

This chapter will consider the above issues as they apply to securitizations involving mortgages and HP receivables and also sub-participation in debt receivables, which in many respects is very similar to securitization. The various issues that arise will, at least in the case of mortgages and HP receivables, be considered within a basic framework of a sale of the assets to a special-purpose vehicle which finances the purchase by issuing bonds secured on the assets.

7.2 Mortgages

An initial point to note is that it is preferable to use a corporate vehicle rather than a trust in a securitization; where a trust is used, difficulties may be encountered regarding tax relief for interest paid.

7.2.1 *Withholding Tax*

The income flow from the borrower will be affected by whether the mortgages have been taken out for domestic purposes, in which case the MIRAS scheme will apply, or whether they are commercial, including those which have been taken out by companies, and are thus outside the scope of the scheme. MIRAS, which stands for mortgage interest relief at source, is the statutory mechanism for enabling individual borrowers to obtain tax relief, at source, at the basic rate of income tax (25 per cent for the 1989/90 tax year) up to a specified borrowings limit, on their interest payments.[1] The borrower pays over to the mortgagee the interest net of tax and thereby obtains tax relief on that amount. The mortgagee then recovers its shortfall in interest by claiming the tax which has been withheld directly from the Inland Revenue. Claims can be made on a monthly or quarterly basis in advance and so can be done with little or no cash flow disadvantage provided that interest payments on the securities issued to fund the purchase or the mortgage portfolio are timed accordingly. On the other hand, if the mortgage advances were made to commercial borrowers, the MIRAS scheme will not apply and the more serious withholding tax issues discussed below will need to be considered. The recovery of the interest withheld under the MIRAS scheme can only be made by MIRAS-registered vehicles. However, the Inland Revenue have been very cooperative in allowing vehicles to be registered well in advance of any securitization.

Interest on loans which have been taken out by borrowers which are companies, or partnerships of which a company is a member, and thus fall outside the scope of the MIRAS scheme, must be paid net of tax at the basic rate unless the lender is a bank recognized as such by the UK Inland Revenue.[2] Where corporate borrowers are involved then assignment of the loans by a UK bank to a special-purpose vehicle (SPV) will give rise to a further withholding obligation where, because of the banking exemption, none existed before. Therefore, portfolios of commercial mortgages will not prove attractive assets for securitization purposes as UK tax law currently stands. This is discussed further in section 7.4 on debt participation.

The payments of interest by the issuing vehicle on the mortgage-backed securities will also need to be made without any requirement to withhold tax. This can be done either by structuring the instrument as a Eurobond and thus taking advantage of the exemption from withholding tax afforded to quoted Eurobonds[3] or alternatively by paying the return on the notes as original-issue discount, which does not attract any UK withholding tax.

7.2.2 Relief for Funding and Front-End Costs

Different considerations will be relevant depending on whether the SPV is a trading company or an investment company for UK tax purposes. A trading company, as the name implies, must carry on some kind of dynamic ongoing trading activity. Thus a company which originates mortgages on its own behalf as well as purchasing them is more likely to be given trading status. On the other hand, a company which buys a pool of mortgages and then issues securities on the strength of them without doing anything further is more likely to be an investment company.

The above distinction ought not to be material for the purposes of deductibility for funding costs provided that the mortgage-backed instruments have a maturity of more than a year. However, a trading company is taxed on an accruals basis, whereas an investment company is taxed on a cash basis. This means that a payment of interest by an investment company should be made to coincide as closely as possible with the end of the company's accounting period for tax purposes to avoid deferring the tax relief until the following accounting period. If the SPV issues short-dated securities (less than one-year maturity) then the interest payable on them would be short interest for UK tax purposes. A trading company may only deduct short interest if it is paid wholly and exclusively for the purposes of its trade or to a UK recognized bank, a member of the stock exchange or a discount house. On the other hand an investment company will only obtain a deduction for short interest if it is paid to one of the restricted categories of lender previously mentioned since it is not, by definition, carrying on a trade.[4] In practice short-dated securities can be issued at an original-issue discount, in which case the difficulties mentioned above do not arise. The discount will then generally be deductible by either a trading company or an investment company.

Consideration needs to be given to the question of where the front-end costs should be borne. One problem may arise where front-end costs are borne in the SPV from the fact that these costs must be amortized for accounting purposes. This amortization may give rise to a different level of profit for accounting and tax purposes. If the profit is to be extracted from the SPV by way of dividend then a reduced accounting profit would mean that less profit can be paid by way of dividend to the parent and then ultimately to the originators by way of a broking (brokerage) fee. It is likely that the intention would be to obtain a deduction in the parent company which can be used by way of group relief to offset the profits in the vehicle.[5]

For the reasons mentioned above there may be a mismatch between profits for tax purposes on the one hand and accounting purposes on the other, thereby leading to an insufficiency of group relief. It should also be remembered that group relief can only be utilized on a current-year basis.[6] This can give rise to locked-in losses in the parent company which although available for use by the SPV in earlier years are not used, because the vehicle itself had carried forward losses owing to the fact that the front-end costs were born in the SPV.[7]

Where the assets which are the subject of the securitization are property mortgages then the credit-rating agency requirements may stipulate that they are supported by insurance policies to deal with defaulting borrowers. There is some doubt as to whether these premiums are deductible by an investment company, and so if possible they should be carried by a trading company within the group.

Other front-end costs, such as legal and accounting fees, rating-agency fees, printing expenses and the remuneration of the trustees are deductible by virtue of a specific statutory provision[8] as the incidental costs of obtaining loan finance.

Some FRN ('floating rate note') issues have featured two classes of notes, namely senior and junior notes. The senior notes have a lower rate of return but have preferred security. The junior notes on the other hand will have a higher rate of return but will be the first to bear any losses incurred. This structure may mean that the return payable on the junior notes is dependent in some way on the results of the vehicle company's business. The notes should be carefully structured to ensure that the return on the junior notes cannot be held to be a deemed distribution that would give rise to an obligation to account for advance corporation tax.[9]

7.2.3 *Profit Extraction*

The extraction of the profit element implicit in the true value of the mortgages being securitized represents the most difficult area from a tax viewpoint.

A straightforward solution would be partial assignment of the receipts from the mortgages to the vehicle company whereby only so much as is required to service the debt on the bonds together with running costs is assigned to the vehicle company. Thus the profit element would simply remain in the hands of the originator. A problem arises with this route when domestic mortgages subject to the MIRAS system mentioned above are being securitized. The Inland Revenue take the view that if both the originator and the vehicle company were to be qualifying lenders for MIRAS purposes this would lead to excessive complications and therefore they will not permit two companies to be registered. This means that other methods of profit extraction must be considered.

A further problem may arise if the profit is to be paid out by way of a broking fee, which might on the face of it be considered a suitable method of profit extraction because such a fee should not attract a liability to VAT (see below). The problem will arise where the paying company is an investment company, because there is some doubt whether the broking fee will be deductible for tax purposes in its hands.[10] It may be possible for the vehicle company to pay the profit to its trading parent company by way of dividend, which would be tax neutral between the two companies, and then for the parent company to pay the broking fee to the originators by way of a trading expense which would be deductible. The trading parent would then use the loss it has incurred to relieve the profit in the vehicle company by way of group relief, thus leading to tax neutrality. As mentioned in section 7.2.2 above, careful consideration must be given to the question of front-end costs and the problem which arises where the amortization of front-end costs may lead to a mismatch between group relief and taxable profit in the vehicle company. This problem will not arise if the vehicle company itself has trading status, because for example it too is carrying on the business of originating mortgages on an ongoing basis.

Where the vehicle company has trading status then the profit can be extracted by way of deferred consideration. The mortgages would be purchased at par and then further payments of deferred purchase consideration linked to the funding margin on the mortgages would be made. If the paying vehicle company has trading status then the tax treatment will be symmetrical. As in the previous case, problems arise however where the vehicle is an investment company. This is because the further payments will be in consideration for the acquisition of a capital asset for investment purposes and thus, as a capital rather than a revenue payment, not deductible for tax purposes, although still taxable in the hands of the recipient. This would lead to the profit element being taxed twice.

Alternatively, the profit can be paid out by way of a management or administration fee in respect of the originator's ongoing functions of managing and administering the mortgages. Once again, the fee could be calculated by reference to the interest-rate margin on the mortgages. Such a fee would be deductible by an investment company vehicle but would bear VAT at the rate of 15 per cent, which, because the originator would usually be fully exempt for VAT purposes, would not be recoverable and would therefore represent a direct cost to the transaction. For a fuller discussion of the mechanics of VAT, see section 7.2.4 below.

A further option would be for the vehicle company and the originator to write an interest-rate swap between themselves. Thus the originator would agree to pay to the vehicle company an amount equivalent to the interest rate on the bonds while the vehicle would pay to the originator an amount equal to the interest received from the borrowers. The running expenses incurred by the vehicle company would need to be considered. The law regarding the tax treatment of swaps is in a state of uncertainty in the UK at the moment.[11] Although the payments made under a swap are calculated by reference to interest rates there is no underlying principal indebtedness. Therefore, doubt arises as to whether they are actually interest and therefore as to their deductibility, although in practice the Inland Revenue regard the payments as annual payments which are deductible for tax purposes. Payments under interest-rate swaps are subject to withholding tax (in practice this only applies to the net differential actually paid) unless one party is a bank, in which case payments can be made gross. It may therefore be necessary to use a UK bank as an intermediary.

7.2.4 *Value Added Tax and Stamp Duty*

Value added tax is levied on supplies of goods and services at the rate of 15 per cent. Supplies of goods and services that are subject to tax at this rate are known as standard-rated supplies. The legislation provides for various exceptions from tax at this rate; these supplies are either zero-rated supplies or exempt supplies. Value added tax is a type of purchase tax which is intended to be borne by the final consumer.[12] Thus payments of VAT by a business on supplies made to it which can be attributed to a standard-rated or zero-rated supply on supplies made by it can be recovered by direct reclaim from HM Customs and Excise. Value added tax in these circumstances will therefore only represent a cash-flow cost to the business concerned. Problems arise where the VAT is attributable to an exempt supply. Exempt supplies are conceptually different to zero-rated supplies; although in both cases the purchaser of the goods or services does not pay tax, in the former case there is no VAT on the outward supplies made by the business (output tax) whereas in the latter tax is chargeable but is levied at a nil rate. Unfortunately many supplies in the financial sector are exempt and this leads to VAT irrecoverability problems.

If a broking fee is payable, then this will be an exempt supply for VAT purposes. The company which pays the broking fee therefore will not incur a VAT cost although the company which supplies the broking services, the originator, may incur some irrecoverable VAT on supplies made to it which are directly attributable to making the supply of broking services. On the other hand, if administration and management fees are payable, then these will be subject to VAT at the standard rate. As this VAT will be attributable to the supply of the loan finance in the form of the mortgages, which is exempt for VAT purposes, the VAT will prove to be irrecoverable.

Similarly, VAT that is charged on the supplies of legal and accountancy services, printing costs, rating-agency fees and so on mentioned above will be irrecoverable and so will represent a further direct cost to the transaction.

If the maker and recipient of the supply are part of the same group for VAT purposes (which requires 51 per cent common ownership), then supplies which would normally attract value added tax can be made free of the tax.[13]

Stamp duty is a documentary tax payable on transactions in the UK.[14] It is payable at various rates but most commonly at 1 or $\frac{1}{2}$ per cent depending on the nature of the transaction. However, various transactions are subject to specific exemptions. Stamp duty on the transfer of mortgages was abolished in 1971.[15] In addition the transfer of the bonds is subject to a specific exemption in favour of the transfer of loan instruments.[16]

7.2.5 Currency Losses and Gains

The market practice to date has been to denominate the bonds issued on a mortgage securitization in sterling because UK mortgages are sterling denominated assets. If it was decided to issue notes in a non-sterling currency, then it would be necessary to enter into a currency swap in order to match the underlying obligation on the bonds.

Where sterling depreciates against the currency in question, then a loss will arise; but the loss will be matched by a corresponding gain on the swap. Equally, the converse is true where sterling appreciates against the chosen currency.

In a situation where the issuing vehicle is treated as an investment company a tax mismatch will arise because the loss or gain on the bonds will not be allowable or taxable for tax purposes. On the other hand, the gain or loss on the swap will be taxable or allowable as the case may be. Clearly this asymmetrical tax treatment may work for or against the issuer depending on the way the two currencies move in relation to each other during the life of the bonds.

The gain or loss on the bonds will only be taxable or allowable, and, thus, tax treatment will be symmetrical, where the issuer is a trading company and either the funds are being raised to meet working capital needs or to meet short-term borrowing requirements. A bank or other similarly taxed financial institution should in most cases be able to justify the loans as a working capital requirement provided they have a maturity of preferably five and certainly no more than seven years.

7.3 HP Receivables

Whereas the securitization of domestic mortgages is well established in the UK, the securitization of different types of receivables is a market which has only recently begun to evolve. In this section it is intended to look at the various tax issues which arises on the securitization of a typical type of debt receivable, namely hire-purchase receivables. Many of the issues that arise have already been considered in the previous section and only brief attention will be paid to them. However, there are also some different issues which arise and these will be considered in greater detail.

7.3.1 *Withholding Tax*

Payments made by either individuals or corporates under HP contracts for the purpose of acquiring motor vehicles, plant and machinery and so on can be dissected into payments of capital and payments of hire charges for the use of the asset.[17] Since the obligation to withhold basic rate tax only arises in respect of payments of interest by a corporate borrower and not to payments of rental, the problems connected with the securitization of mortgages in the names of companies discussed above do not arise.

As before, the need to withhold tax on the notes that are issued can be avoided by making use of the Eurobond exemption or alternatively by issuing paper at an original-issue discount.

7.3.2 *Relief for Funding and Front-End Costs*

The issues that arise are the trading/investment company distinction and the accruals/cash basis of taxation, where front-end costs should be borne, the deductibility of the incidental costs of obtaining the loan finance and of the interest payable on the bonds. All these issues have been considered in the above section on mortgage securitization.

7.3.3 *Profit Extraction*

The securitization of HP receivables does not involve the MIRAS scheme nor any similar scheme for obtaining tax relief by reclaiming from the Inland Revenue the amounts in question. Therefore, it is possible to adopt the partial equitable assignment method of profit extraction. This involves the assignment by the originator to the vehicle company of enough of the receivables to meet the funding and running costs of the vehicle company with the originator retaining beneficial ownership of the super-profit. The availability of this alternative method of profit extraction means that the problems discussed in the previous section regarding deductibility of broking fees and the payment of deferred consideration by investment companies should not arise. Where the vehicle company is continuing to write its own HP contracts and has trading status, then the other methods of profit extraction can be considered.

7.3.4 *Value Added Tax and Stamp Duty*

The irrecoverability of VAT once again presents an incremental cost to securitization. To the extent that VAT borne on supplies made to the vehicle company such as legal and accountancy services is directly attributable to exempt supplies within the vehicle, then it will not be possible to recover the VAT. HP receivables by their nature require a higher level of administration, including in particular debt collection services; these services are therefore more expensive to perform. Where the partial assignment method is used then it may be possible to avoid the payment of VAT on management and administration fees by factoring these costs into the partial assignment mechanism. For a charge to VAT to arise, it must be in respect of a supply done for a consideration.[18] It is arguable, therefore, that there is no supply by the originator to the vehicle where the vehicle is merely purchasing part of a pre-administered receivables portfolio from the originator. It may, however, be a rating-agency requirement that if it became necessary to appoint a third-party administrator for whatever reason at a later date then a fee would become payable on which VAT would be chargeable in the normal way.

It is rumoured that HM Customs and Excise are to produce a new explanatory leaflet clarifying their practice in this area and conceivably giving exempt status to this type of supply.

The transfer of the underlying assets would be chargeable to VAT. It therefore may be preferable to transfer only the receivables contracts and not the underlying motor vehicles. The transfer of the receivables, however, should be exempt for VAT purposes.[19] This will have the effect of worsening the originator's liability to VAT since it will increase the proportion of exempt supplies which it is making and therefore reduce the proportion of unallocated expenses on which it can recover the tax paid.[20]

Stamp duty would, *prima facie*, be payable on the transfer of the underlying assets, at the rate of 1 per cent *ad valorem*. It was possible to avoid this by effecting the transfer by delivery. This could be symbolic, through for example in the case of motor vehicles the handing over of the log books rather than through physical delivery of the vehicles themselves. However, as described previously, for VAT reasons it may be advisable not to assign the actual motor vehicles.

The assignment of the receivables would be subject to stamp duty at the rate of 1 per cent *ad valorem*. However, this charge can be deferred by executing the assignment off shore[21] and only bringing it into the UK if enforcement before a UK court is necessary.[22] Alternatively the receivables can be transferred by a written offer with acceptance by performance (for example, by payment) in order to avoid stamp duty, since, as described above, stamp duty is a tax on documents. It is intended that legislation will be introduced to abolish at some time during the course of 1991/2 the charge to stamp duty on the transfer of United Kingdom securities. It is not expected that this legislation will extend to transfers of receivables, but rather that it will be confined to transfers of equity shares in companies.[23]

7.3.5 *Currency Losses and Gains*

If the bonds are issued in a non-sterling currency then, since the underlying asset would be a sterling asset, the same issues as outlined in the previous section will be relevant.

7.4 Debt Participation

Sub-participation in existing debt is conceptually similar to asset securitization and is reasonably common in the UK. Again the issues that arise are often similar to those which are relevant to the securitization of domestic mortgages. As under the previous heading, more attention will be paid in this section to those areas where there are differences.

7.4.1 *Withholding Tax*

The identity of the debtor is of fundamental importance to the question of withholding tax. There is, as previously mentioned, an obligation on a corporate borrower to withhold basic rate income tax on payments of interest.[24] There is no corresponding obligation where the debtor is an individual who is thus able to make payments of interest gross. Therefore, unless the lender is a UK bank (in which case the withholding obligation does not apply), portfolios of loans made to corporate borrowers will not be suitable for sub-participation.

In a situation where loans made to corporates are assigned by one UK bank to another UK bank then it is arguable that the withholding exemption would not apply to payments made to the assignee bank since these payments would not, as the section requires, be on an advance from a bank carrying on a bona-fide banking business in the UK because the original advance will have been made by a different bank. However, it is understood that it is not Inland Revenue practice to adopt this approach and that therefore the withholding tax exemption will apply. Similarly, where the loan is assigned by a UK bank to a non-UK bank, then the Inland Revenue will not contend that income tax should have been deducted if the borrower is unaware of the assignment. On the other hand, if the debt is assigned by a non-UK bank to a UK bank, then the concessionary practice of the Inland Revenue may not apply.

If the sub-participator is an overseas bank operating through a London branch, then the issue of withholding tax may again arise. A withholding obligation arises where payments are made to a person whose usual place of abode is outside the UK.[25] This may be considered to be the case when a non-UK bank is involved in the sub-participation. However, the Inland Revenue do not take this line and do not seek to impose a withholding obligation; to do so would unfairly discriminate against non-UK banks and thus introduce a degree of distortion in the market. The profits of an overseas bank operating through a London branch will be within the charge to corporation tax in any event.[26]

In the banking sector debt participations are more likely to be funded through the inter-bank market than by the issue of notes. If paper is to be issued and the issuer is a non-banking corporate, then the withholding tax obligation may be overcome by virtue of Eurobond exemption or original-issue discount as above.

7.4.2 Relief for Funding and Front-End Costs

The sub-participation in debt receivables by banking concerns or finance houses will be part of their everyday trading activities. Thus, front-end costs should be deductible as a trading expense on an accruals basis.[27]

7.4.3 Profit Extraction

The question of profit-extraction depends in the first instance on the basis of the sub-participation. If, on the one hand, the reason for the sub-participation is the reduction of the original lender's risk then the sub-participator will be entitled to the super-profit that arises from the intrinsic value of the debt. On the other hand, if the aim of the sub-participation is to free capacity on the original lender's balance sheet from a regulatory viewpoint, then the profit element may be for the account of the original lender with the sub-participator receiving a margin over its funding rate.

Once again, the MIRAS problem does not arise, which means that the partial assignment route may be considered appropriate. Alternatively, the profit can be extracted by payment of deferred consideration over the life of the sub-participation equal to the true value of the loans. Management and/or administration fees can also be considered. If management and administration fees are used then the commercial justification of their size may be seen as a problem. However, on the assumption that the parties are acting in a bona-fide manner at arm's length then any level of fee agreed between them should be, by implication, commercially justifiable.

7.4.4 *Value Added Tax and Stamp Duty*

Once again, the irrecoverability of VAT on fees paid raises a problem. The ability of the payer (that is, the sub-participator) to recover these fees is dependent on its partial recovery position for VAT purposes.[28] This is a function of the proportion which the number of standard-rated supplies made bears to the number of exempt supplies made. In the banking sector the recovery of VAT is likely to be low.

The incidence of stamp duty depends on the nature of the debt in which a sub-participation is being offered. If the debt is in the form of commercial mortgages then there will be no stamp duty.[29]

Similarly if loan capital is being assigned then there will be no stamp duty.[30] If, however, loan receivables are being assigned then stamp duty is payable at the rate of 1 per cent of the value of the consideration. In such a situation execution off shore might be considered advisable.[31]

7.4.5 *Currency Gains and Losses*

A banking participator would be likely to match any currency exposure in the normal course of its business. This would mean that gains or losses will be on its trading account, and, therefore, taxable or allowable as the case may be in the normal way as a trading receipt or a trading expense.[32]

Notes

1 Sections 369ff. of the Income and Corporation Taxes Act 1988.
2 Section 349 of the Income and Corporation Taxes Act 1988.
3 Section 349(3)(c) of the Income and Corporation Taxes Act 1988.
4 Section 338(3) of the Income and Corporation Taxes Act 1988.
5 Section 402 of the Income and Corporation Taxes Act 1988.
6 Section 408 of the Income and Corporation Taxes Act 1988.
7 This structure is considered further below.
8 Section 77 of the Income and Corporation Taxes Act 1988.
9 Section 209(2)(e)(iii) of the Income and Corporation Taxes Act 1988.
10 See *Capital and National Trust Ltd* v. *Colder*, (1949) 31 TC 265.
11 See Inland Revenue consultative document on the 'Tax treatment of swap fees' (undated).
12 See generally the Value Added Tax Act 1983.
13 Section 29 of the Value Added Tax Act 1983.

14 See note 23 below, and accompanying text.
15 Section 64 of the Finance Act 1971.
16 Section 79 of the Finance Act 1986.
17 See *Darngavil Coal Co. v. Francis*, 7 TC 1.
18 Section 3(2)(a) of the Value Added Tax Act 1983.
19 Item 1, Group 5, Schedule 6 of the Value Added Tax Act 1983.
20 Section 15 of the Value Added Tax Act 1983, Regulations 29–37 of the Value Added Tax (General) Regulations 1985.
21 Section 15(4) of the Stamp Act 1891.
22 Section 14(4) of the Stamp Act 1891.
23 *Inland Revenue Press Release*, 20 March 1990.
24 Section 349(2) of the Income and Corporation Taxes Act 1988.
25 Section 349(2)(c) of the Income and Corporation Taxes Act 1988.
26 Section 11 of the Income and Corporation Taxes Act 1988.
27 Section 74(a) of the Income and Corporation Taxes Act 1988.
28 Section 15 of the Value Added Tax Act 1983, Regulations 29–37 of the Value Added Tax (General) Regulations 1985.
29 Section 64 of the Finance Act 1971.
30 Section 79 of the Finance Act 1986.
31 Section 15(4) of the Stamp Act 1891.
32 Section 74(a) of the Income and Corporation Taxes Act 1988.

8

US Federal Income Tax Treatment of Mortgage-Backed Securities

JAMES M. PEASLEE and DAVID Z. NIRENBERG

Chapter Outline

8.1 Introduction

8.2 Types of Mortgage-Backed Securities
    8.2.1 Pass-Through Certificates
        General
        Stripped pass-through certificates
        Senior/subordinated pass-through certificates
    8.2.2 Pay-Through Bonds
    8.2.3 Equity Interests in Issuers of Pay-Through Bonds
    8.2.4 REMICs
        General
        REMIC qualification tests
        Exclusivity of REMIC rules/taxable mortgage pools

8.3 Taxation of Holders
    8.3.1 Mortgage-Backed Securities Taxable as Debt Instruments
        Overview
        Treatment of discount and premium
    8.3.2 Equity Interests in Owner Trusts and REMIC Residual Interests
        Introduction
        Common tax characteristics
        Special considerations applicable to owner trusts
        Special considerations applicable to REMICs
        Phantom income

8.1 Introduction

This chapter surveys the principal US federal income tax rules governing mortgage-backed securities.[1] The law in this area was significantly revised by the Tax Reform Act of 1986 (TRA 1986). TRA 1986 gave birth to a new scheme for taxing pools of mortgages that qualify as 'real estate mortgage investment conduits' (REMICs), and the holders of REMIC securities. The legislation also changed the treatment of discount on non-REMIC mortgage-backed securities to take account of the unusual payment characteristics of those securities.

The mortgage-backed securities considered in this chapter are those which are supported exclusively (or almost so) by (1) payments made on a fixed pool of mortgages, or (2) payments made on a fixed pool of mortgages together with earnings from the reinvestment of those payments over a limited period (generally, not more than six months).[2] Typically, these securities have two payment features that distinguish them from conventional publicly held debt obligations: their principal amount (if any) is payable in instalments, and they are subject to mandatory calls to the extent the mortgages which fund them are prepaid. Recently, mortgage-backed securities have begun to be offered to the public that are further distinguishable from conventional, callable bonds by the fact that their value is attributable largely or entirely to rights to interest on mortgages or reinvestment earnings. These securities are issued at a very high premium over their principal amount (which may be zero). Because the unamortized premium is forfeited if the securities are prepaid, holders of such securities may experience a zero or negative rate of return, even in the absence of defaults.

In terms of tax attributes, mortgage-backed securities may differ from conventional, publicly offered debt instruments in two other respects. First, in the hands of institutional investors, certain types of mortgage-backed securities may qualify for certain tax benefits associated with investments in real property mortgages. Second, certain types of mortgage-backed securities are treated for tax purposes as ownership interests in the underlying mortgages rather than as equity or debt of the issuing entity. This 'look-through' feature raises a host of tax issues.

The federal income tax questions peculiar to mortgage-backed securities relate to the features described above, the legal structures that are used in transforming pools of whole mortgages into non-REMIC mortgage-backed securities, and the REMIC rules.

Although this chapter focuses primarily on mortgage-backed securities, the same principles (other than the REMIC rules) will generally apply to securities backed by other types of financial assets.

8.2 Types of Mortgage-Backed Securities

The principal types of mortgage-backed securities that are currently available are pass-through certificates, pay-through bonds, equity interests in owner trusts that are issuers of pay-through bonds and REMIC interests. REMIC interests are either 'regular interests' (which from a tax perspective resemble pay-through bonds) or 'residual interests' (which from a tax perspective resemble equity interests in owner trusts). These securities have two common features: first, they can be used, alone or in combination, to repackage whole mortgages in a manner that increases their attractiveness as investments; and second, the issuers of the securities are not subject to tax on the income from the underlying mortgages as it passes through their hands to investors. If it were not possible to eliminate all material taxes on issuers of mortgage-backed securities – for example, if such securities were required to take the form of stock in a business corporation that was taxable at current corporate tax rates of up to 34 per cent on the gross income from the mortgages it held without offsetting deductions for dividends paid on the securities – such securities would never have seen the light of day.

The various types of mortgage-backed securities that are currently available address the problem of issuer-level taxes in different ways. Pass-through certificates are generally issued by a 'grantor trust' that is not considered to be a taxable entity; indeed, for almost all federal income tax purposes, the trust is simply ignored. Issuers of pay-through bonds (or the owners of such issuers) are generally subject to income tax on the taxable income from the mortgages supporting the bonds, but the burden of that tax is largely eliminated through interest deductions allowed with respect to the bonds. Pay-through bonds are generally issued by owner trusts. An owner trust is classified for federal income tax purposes as either a grantor trust or a partnership, and in either case is not itself subject to tax. Instead, its taxable income is allocated among its equity owners. A REMIC is exempt from tax by statute (except for certain penalty taxes).

The sections which follow describe more fully pass-through certificates, pay-through bonds, equity interests in owner trusts and REMIC interests. Although REMIC interests may take the form of pass-through certificates, pay-through bonds or equity interests in owner trusts, except where otherwise indicated these terms will be used in this chapter to refer only to securities that are not subject to the REMIC rules.

8.2.1 *Pass-Through Certificates*

General In their most common form, pass-through certificates are issued by a trust that holds a fixed pool of mortgages. The arrangement is brought into being by a sponsor, who transfers the mortgages to the trust against receipt of the certificates, and then sells all or a portion of the certificates to investors. The certificates evidence ownership by the holders of specified interests in the assets of the trust. Often, each certificate represents a *pro rata* interest in the mortgage pool. Thus, if 1,000 such certificates are issued, each would represent a right to 1/1,000th of each payment of principal and interest on each mortgage in the pool.[3] The mortgage payments passed through to certificate-holders are reduced by fees for mortgage servicing, pool administration and any applicable guarantees or pool insurance. These fees are fixed in advance over the life of the pool so that certificate-holders can be guaranteed a fixed 'pass-through rate' of interest on the principal balance of the certificates, representing the earnings on the mortgages net of such fees.[4] The power of the trustee to reinvest mortgage payments received by the trust, or proceeds of the sale of mortgages held by the trust, is severely limited in order to avoid possible classification of the trust as an association taxable as a corporation[5] under the Treasury's entity classification regulations.[6] As a result, payments to certificate-holders are usually made monthly in parallel with the receipt of mortgage payments by the trust.

A trust used in any commercially available pass-through arrangement will not have investment powers that risk classification of the trust as an association. Instead, it will qualify as a trust for tax purposes, and, in particular, will be a grantor trust taxable under section 671.[7] Consequently, for federal income tax purposes, the trust will effectively be ignored and certificate-holders will be recognized to be the owners of the mortgages held by the trust.

One consequence of disregarding the separate existence of a pass-through trust is that certificate-holders who report income for tax purposes under a cash method of accounting (which would be true of virtually all holders who are individuals) must report income based on the timing of receipts of mortgage payments by the trust and not on the timing of distributions made to them by the trust.[8] The trustee is viewed as an agent collecting mortgage payments on the certificate-holders' behalf. While certificate-holders are obliged to include in income the gross amount of interest on the mortgages, they are allowed deductions for mortgage servicing and other expenses paid out of such interest, again, on the theory that those amounts are paid on their behalf.[9]

Public rulings have been issued by the Internal Revenue Service which confirm the consequences described above in the case of pass-through certificates guaranteed by the Government National Mortgage Association (GNMA),[10] the Federal Home Loan Mortgage Corporation (FHLMC)[11] and the Federal National Mortgage Association (FNMA)[12] and certificates representing interests in pools of conventional mortgages that are supported by private mortgage insurance.[13]

Because the holders of pass-through certificates are treated as the owners of the assets of the issuing trust, to the extent those assets include mortgages on personal residences that are loans to individuals the holders are subject to a special rule, described below, regarding the character of discount income that is realized as principal is paid.[14] For the same reason, institutional investors that derive tax advantages from the direct ownership of real property loans benefit equally from the ownership of pass-through certificates evidencing interests in those loans.[15]

Stripped pass-through certificates Pass-through certificates may also be issued that represent, instead of a *pro rata* share of all payments on the underlying mortgages, a right to one fixed percentage of the principal payments on the mortgages and a different fixed percentage of the interest payments on the mortgages.[16] Such pass-through certificates are often referred to as 'stripped' mortgage-backed securities or 'stripped' pass-through certificates. They are generally sold when there is a divergence of views regarding prepayment rates. The principal component of a mortgage viewed in isolation without interest is more valuable the earlier it is repaid. On the other hand, interest ceases when principal is repaid, so that the interest component of a mortgage, standing alone without principal, is more valuable the later the date on which principal is repaid. Thus, by varying the mix between principal and interest, the effect of prepayments on a class of pass-through certificates can be changed.

The earliest stripped pass-through certificates that were publicly available were structured to *reduce* the risk to investors of changes in prepayment speeds by transforming discount or premium mortgages into par securities. To illustrate this type of transaction, suppose that a thrift institution holds a pool of mortgages bearing interest at a rate of 10 per cent (net of servicing) at a time when the current market rate of interest for pass-through certificates is 8 per cent. If the thrift believes that investors will assume a higher prepayment rate, and thus are willing to pay a smaller premium for a 100 per cent interest in the mortgages than the thrift thinks is reasonable, the thrift could insulate investors from the risk of a reduction in yield resulting from prepayments by retaining a right to one-fifth of each interest payment on the mortgages and selling the pass-through certificates at par with an 8 per cent pass-through rate.[17] Similarly, if the thrift held discount mortgages and wishes to sell pass-through certificates at par based on those mortgages, it could accomplish its objective by allocating to the certificates all of the interest payments but only a fraction of the principal payments.[18]

More recently, stripped pass-through certificates have been created that are intended to *increase* the risk to all investors of variations in prepayment speeds by creating securities that have greater discounts and premiums than are inherent in the underlying mortgages. The most extreme case is one in which there is a complete separation in the ownership of rights to interest and principal. In a typical transaction, mortgages are transferred to a trust in exchange for two classes of certificates. One class (which may be referred to as 'PO strips') represents the right to receive 100 per cent of each principal payment on the mortgages and the other class ('IO strips') represents the right to receive 100 per cent of each interest payment. PO strips, which are similar to zero-coupon bonds payable in instalments, are issued at a substantial discount and are purchased by investors who, as compared to the market generally, expect a high rate of prepayments, or who wish to hedge against a risk of loss from declining interest rates. (Declining interest rates would generally increase prepayments and thus increase the value of PO strips.) IO strips, which are issued with what amounts to an infinite premium, are purchased by investors who expect a low rate of prepayments or who wish to hedge against a risk of loss from rising interest rates.

Senior/subordinated pass-through certificates   Pass-through certificates typically provide for some type of credit support that protects investors from defaults or delinquencies in payments on the underlying mortgages. Most often, the credit support takes the form of a guarantee, insurance policy or other agreement by the sponsor or a third party to replace defaulted or delinquent payments. However, in many private (non-agency) transactions credit support has been provided by creating senior and subordinated classes of pass-through certificates. Mortgage defaults or delinquencies are charged first against distributions that otherwise would be made on the subordinated class until they are exhausted, thereby protecting the senior class. Additional credit support may be provided through a reserve fund that is funded either with cash provided by the sponsor or with moneys diverted from the subordinated class during the early years of the pool. Under current law, it may be necessary to hold any such reserve fund outside of the pass-through trust as security for a limited recourse guarantee of the mortgages, and to restrict the transfer of the subordinated certificates by the pool sponsor, in order to avoid classification of the trust as an association taxable as a corporation.[19]

Holders of senior or subordinated pass-through certificates are taxed generally in the same manner as if the subordination feature did not exist. The subordination feature is analysed as if the holders of the subordinated certificates wrote a guarantee of the underlying mortgages in favour of the holders of the senior certificates that was secured solely by the subordinated certificates.[20] Payments received by the senior certificate-holders as a result of the subordination feature are treated in the same manner as other payments under a guarantee, namely, as if they were the corresponding payments of principal or interest on the defaulted or delinquent mortgages. The holder of the subordinated certificates is required to report income as if such holder was entitled to receive such holder's full share of the payments on the mortgages, even if some of those payments are diverted to the holders of the senior certificates or are retained in a reserve fund. The subordinated holder is treated as if such holder had purchased the senior holders' share of the payments on the mortgages that are delinquent or in default and generally is allowed a bad debt deduction when the rights to those payments become wholly or partially worthless.

8.2.2 Pay-Through Bonds

Unlike pass-through certificates, which represent an ownership interest in mortgages, a pay-through bond is a debt obligation of a legal entity (typically an owner trust or a corporation) which is collateralized by mortgages. A holder is considered to own the bond, but not an interest in the underlying mortgages, in the same way that the holder of a public utility bond, for example, would be considered the owner of the bond but not of the power-generating station that secures it. Although the payment terms of a pay-through bond and of the underlying mortgage collateral are not identical, the relationship between them may be quite close. In most cases, the mortgages and earnings from the reinvestment of mortgage payments over a short period are expected to be the sole funding source for payments on the bonds, and mortgage prepayments are 'paid-through', in whole or in part, to bondholders in the form of mandatory calls on the bonds.

A collateralized mortgage obligation (CMO) is a type of pay-through bond which is divided into classes typically having different maturities and payment priorities. Most often, CMOs are issued by an owner trust, or special-purpose corporation, organized by a sponsor.[21] As explained below, an owner trust generally is used rather than a corporation when the sponsor wishes to sell the equity interest in the CMO issuer to other investors.

An owner trust is established pursuant to a trust agreement between the sponsor and an independent trustee, acting as owner trustee. The owner trustee is usually a commercial bank. In most transactions the sponsor initially contributes a nominal amount of cash to the owner trustee against the receipt of certificates representing the equity or ownership interest in the owner trust. Upon issuance of the CMOs, the mortgage collateral is transferred to the owner trustee in exchange for the proceeds of the CMOs plus any additional cash equity contribution that may be made to the owner trust, either by the sponsor or by other investors in exchange for certificates. The sponsor may retain its certificates or sell all or a portion of them to others. Pursuant to a bond indenture, the owner trustee pledges the mortgage collateral to another commercial bank acting as the bond trustee.[22] Over the life of the CMOs, the bond trustee collects payments on the collateral, reinvests those payments over a short period, makes payments on the CMOs, pays expenses, and remits any excess to the owner trustee, which distributes such excess to the owner trust equity owners. Equity interests in owner trusts are further discussed in the next section. If the issuer of CMOs is a corporation rather than an owner trust, the structure is substantially the same except that the corporation is substituted for the owner trust. Thus, the issuing corporation pledges the mortgage collateral to the bond trustee which remits any excess cash flow directly to the corporation. The corporation may in turn distribute the cash to its shareholders. The federal income tax treatment of the holders of CMOs is not affected by whether the issuer is an owner trust or a corporation.

CMOs are a more recent innovation than pass-through certificates. They are similar to pass-through certificates in that they are funded primarily out of payments received on a fixed pool of mortgages or interests in mortgages and, as a group, closely resemble those mortgages or interests in terms of the timing and amounts of payments.

Unlike pass-through certificates, CMOs are typically divided into classes that have different priorities as to the receipt of principal and in some cases interest. More often there are 'fast-pay' and 'slow-pay' classes. Thus, all principal payments (including prepayments) are made first to the class having the earliest stated maturity date until it is retired, and then to the class with the next earliest maturity date until it is retired, and so on. Alternatively, principal payments can be allocated among classes to ensure to the extent possible that a designated class receives principal payments according to a fixed schedule. Under that arrangement, the greater stability in the timing of payments on the designated class is balanced by greater variability in the timing of payments on the remaining classes. Another common feature of CMOs is an 'interest accrual' or 'compound interest' class that receives no payments of interest or principal until all prior classes have been fully retired. Until that time, the interest that accrues on such a class is added to its principal balance and a corresponding amount is paid as additional principal on prior classes. In a typical issue of CMOs, there is only one interest-accrual class which is the class with the latest stated maturity. However, an interest-accrual class can also be inserted between classes with shorter and longer terms.

Three other differences between CMOs and pass-through certificates are worth noting. First, CMOs may bear interest at a floating rate (a rate that varies directly or inversely with an index of market rates of interest, such as LIBOR), even though interest is paid on the mortgage collateral at a fixed rate. Second, CMOs generally provide for quarterly payments, with the issuer being responsible for reinvesting monthly receipts on the mortgages until the next CMO payment date. Finally, CMOs are usually callable at the option of the issuer when a more than *de minimis* amount of the CMOs remains outstanding, so that the issuer can potentially benefit from increases in the value of the collateral by selling the collateral and retiring the CMOs.[23]

Tax considerations dictated the original choice of pay-through bonds over pass-through certificates as the vehicle for creating mortgage-backed securities with different payment priorities or a floating interest rate not related to the mortgage collateral. If a non-REMIC pass-through trust issued multiple classes of pass-through certificates having these features, the pass-through trust would be classified as an association taxable as a corporation under the so-called 'Sears regulations' and the certificates would be treated as stock.[24] As a result, the trust would be subject to corporate income tax on the gross income from the mortgages it holds without being allowed a deduction for 'dividends' paid to certificate-holders. Although an issuer of pay-through bonds, or its owners, may be subject to corporate tax on the taxable income of the issuer, deductions are allowed, in determining such income, for interest on the bonds because they are recognized for tax purposes to be indebtedness of the issuer.

Another consequence of the status of pay-through bonds as debt obligations of the issuer (rather than ownership interests in the underlying mortgages) is that holders are taxed based on the payments they are entitled to receive on the bonds rather than on the payments received by the issuer on the underlying mortgages. For the same reason, pay-through bonds are not treated as obligations of individuals or real property mortgages for tax purposes.

8.2.3 Equity Interests in Issuers of Pay-Through Bonds

Typically, a portion of the cash received on the collateral for pay-through bonds (which portion may be small in proportion to the value of the collateral, but significant in absolute terms) is not needed to make payments on the bonds. This surplus cash may be attributable to the spread between the rates of interest on the mortgages and on one or more classes of the bonds, the excess of the reinvestment income actually realized over the amounts assumed in sizing the issue of bonds, profit resulting from the exercise of rights to call the bonds, and any excess mortgages or reserves that are available to protect against mortgage defaults or delinquencies but are not in fact fully needed for those purposes.[25] If the issuer of the bonds is an owner trust, the rights to this surplus cash would be represented by the equity interest in the trust. If the issuer is a corporation, those rights would be represented by stock.

Owner trusts are often chosen over corporations as issuers of CMOs because they permit effective consolidation of the issuer with its owners for tax purposes, without the disadvantage of consolidation for financial accounting purposes, where equity ownership is divided in such a manner that no owner has as much as a 50 per cent interest.[26] Effective consolidation is achieved because owner trusts are classified for federal income tax purposes either as grantor trusts or partnerships. In either case, an owner trust is not itself subject to tax; rather, taxable income or loss of the owner trust (in general terms, the excess of the entire income from the mortgage collateral plus reinvestment income over the deductions allowed for interest paid on the bonds and expenses) is allocated to the equity-holders in accordance with their respective interests.

Because the taxable income of the equity owners is computed based on the net income from the collateral and bonds, it is possible that in any given period the taxable income allocated to an owner will differ significantly from the income such holder would have reported in that period if such holder were taxed based solely on cash distributions from the owner trust. Taxable income that exceeds an owner's income calculated based on cash distributions is often referred to as 'phantom income'. The possible sources of phantom income are discussed in detail below in section 8.3.2 under the heading 'Phantom income'.

8.2.4 REMICs

General As the prior discussion indicates, a grantor trust cannot issue pass-through certificates that are divided into multiple classes with staggered maturities. Also, pay-through bonds cannot be created that provide for payments, in the aggregate, that precisely mirror the payments on a fixed pool of mortgage collateral. Thus, certain securities may be attractive economically but cannot be issued as either pass-through certificates or pay-through bonds, because they have a class structure inconsistent with the grantor-trust rules or match the underlying mortgages too closely to be recognized for tax purposes as debt. Moreover, even if a security could be issued as a pay-through bond, compared with an ownership interest in mortgages, debt often has financial accounting disadvantages (the need to show the debt on someone's balance sheet) and tax disadvantages for certain institutional investors (the debt is not considered a real property loan). Finally, holders of equity interests in issuers of pay-through bonds may realize phantom income.

To address some of these concerns, TRA 1986 enacted the REMIC rules (sections 860A through 860G). These rules treat a pool of mortgages that meets certain requirements as a REMIC if an appropriate election is made, and state how the REMIC and the holders of interests therein will be taxed.

The REMIC rules are applied to a pool of mortgages and related securities based on their functional characteristics, without regard to legal form. Thus, a REMIC may be a state law trust, corporation or partnership, or simply a segregated pool of mortgages that is not a separate legal entity. Similarly, REMIC interests may be evidenced by ownership certificates, debt instruments, stock, partnership interests or a contractual right to receive payments. The functional approach of the REMIC rules allows the state law legal form of a REMIC and the interests therein to be structured to best achieve financial accounting and other non-tax objectives.

By statute, a REMIC is not subject to an entity-level tax (except for certain penalty taxes).[27] Instead, the income from its assets is allocated among the holders of REMIC interests. All of the interests in a REMIC must be either 'regular interests' or 'residual interests', as those terms are defined in the REMIC rules. There is no required number of classes of regular interests. By contrast, a REMIC must have one (and only one) class of residual interests. In general, regular interests resemble conventional debt. There is no similar limitation on the economic characteristics of residual interests.

The income of a REMIC is allocated among the different classes of interests as follows. The income of holders of each class of regular interests is determined as if those interests were debt of the REMIC. The holders of the residual interest are allocated all income of the REMIC, determined as if it were a taxable entity but reduced by the interest deductions that would be allowed to the REMIC if the regular interests were debt.

The allocation of income among REMIC interests is similar to the allocation that would be made if the REMIC were an owner trust and the regular interests and residual interests were pay-through bonds and equity interests in the trust, respectively. However, there are important differences between REMICs and owner trusts. First, as previously noted, there is no requirement that a REMIC or REMIC interests take any particular legal form. Second, the characterization of regular interests as debt of a REMIC follows directly from the statute, and there is no requirement that a REMIC have any minimum equity value or that the payments on regular interests and the underlying mortgages be mismatched. In addition, for purposes of determining the taxation of the sponsor of a REMIC and the status of regular interests as real property loans in the hands of institutional holders, regular interests are treated as ownership interests in the underlying mortgages rather than as debt.

While the REMIC rules represent a significant step forward in the tax law governing mortgage-backed securities, they are not the answer to every prayer. The REMIC rules were created primarily to permit the issuance of multiple-class pass-through certificates. While they achieve that goal, they do little more. The REMIC rules do not, for example, offer much relief from the restrictions on management powers that apply to grantor trusts. The permitted activities of a REMIC are limited, in much the same manner as a grantor trust, to holding a fixed pool of mortgages and distributing payments currently to investors. Indeed, in some respects, a REMIC has even less freedom of action than a grantor trust. Another significant problem with the taxation of non-REMIC mortgage-backed securities – the phantom income that is recognized by issuers, or the owners of issuers, of certain pay-through bonds – is also not resolved by the REMIC rules. Indeed, they make it worse. Where a REMIC issues multiple classes of regular interests with staggered maturities, phantom income is realized by residual interest holders in much the same manner as if they held equity interests in an owner trust and the regular interests were pay-through bonds. However, the REMIC residual holders must contend with certain anti-tax-avoidance rules that do not apply to owner trusts.

REMIC qualification tests To qualify as a REMIC, an entity must elect to be a REMIC and must (1) meet a test relating to the interests in the entity (interests test), (2) meet a test relating to the assets of the entity (assets test), and (3) adopt arrangements designed to ensure that 'disqualified organizations' will not hold residual interests.

As indicated above, the interests test requires all interests in a REMIC to be either regular interests or residual interests.

In general, a regular interest is an interest that is designated as a regular interest and provides for principal payments (or, if the interest is not in the form of debt, similar amounts) fixed as to amount, and interest (or similar amounts) on the outstanding principal amount at a fixed rate (or, to the extent permitted in regulations, a variable rate).[28] The Internal Revenue Service has announced that regulations will be issued allowing interest to be paid on regular interests at a variable rate that is based on an objective interest index or a weighted average of the rates of interest on the mortgages held by the REMIC.[29] However, the fixed or variable rate of interest may not be disproportionately high (that is, an interest will not qualify as a regular interest if it is issued at a substantial premium above its principal amount).[30]

Under legislation enacted in 1988, an interest may also qualify as a regular interest if it provides for a fixed principal amount and interest that consists of interest on a specified portion of the interest on the mortgages held by the REMIC, and such portion does not vary over the life of the regular interest. There is no requirement that the interest on these types of regular interests not be 'disproportionately high' compared with their principal amounts. The purpose of the expansion of the definition was to allow securities similar to IO strips to be issued as regular interests.

An interest will not fail to be a regular interest because it is subordinated to other regular interests in the event of defaults or delinquencies on the underlying mortgages.[31]

A residual interest in a REMIC is any interest that is designated as a residual interest and is not a regular interest. As noted above, there is no requirement that a REMIC residual interest have any minimum value.[32]

There are no requirements as to the number of holders or concentration of ownership of either regular or residual interests.

The assets test requires that substantially all of the assets of a REMIC be 'qualified mortgages' or 'permitted investments'.[33] A qualified mortgage is defined as any obligation (including any participation or certificate of beneficial ownership therein) which is principally secured by an interest in real property (whether residential or commercial), any REMIC regular interest or any 'qualified replacement mortgage'.[34] Thus, qualified mortgages include IO and PO strips and other pass-through certificates (including senior and subordinated pass-through certificates) to the extent the underlying mortgages are qualified mortgages.[35] Qualified mortgages also include loans principally secured by stock owned by a tenant-stockholder of a cooperative housing corporation, as well as loans secured by manufactured housing that meets certain minimum size requirements (including mobile homes but not recreational vehicles).[36] The only permitted investments are (1) 'cash-flow investments' – in general, short-term investments of the cash flow from qualified mortgages held pending distribution on the interests in the REMIC on the next distribution date; (2) 'qualified reserve funds' – in general, investments held in a reasonably required reserve fund to provide for full payment of the expenses of the REMIC, or payments due on the regular interest in the event of default on qualified mortgages or lower than expected earnings on cash-flow investments;[37] and (3) foreclosure property, in general, real property acquired by the REMIC in connection with the default of a qualified mortgage provided the property is not held longer than a specified grace period.

Finally, a REMIC must adopt arrangements designed to ensure that residual interests are not transferred to a 'disqualified organization'. A disqualified organization is generally a governmental entity that would not be subject to tax on income from any residual interest that it held. The reason for limiting transfers to disqualified organizations is to prevent the avoidance of tax on such income. If, despite the arrangements adopted by a REMIC, a residual interest is transferred to a disqualified organization, a penalty tax is imposed on the transferor that is intended to compensate for the tax that would otherwise be imposed on the disqualified organization.

Exclusivity of REMIC rules/taxable mortgage pools   Beginning in 1992,[38] any entity (or any portion of an entity) that is not a REMIC or a thrift institution and otherwise meets the definition of a 'taxable mortgage pool' will be classified as a corporation and will not be permitted to file a consolidated federal income tax return with any other corporation.[39] Thus, such an entity generally will be subject to an entity-level tax. Any entity (or any portion of an entity) will qualify as a taxable mortgage pool if (1) substantially all of its assets consist of debt obligations (or interests therein), more than 50 per cent of which consist of real estate mortgages (or interests therein), (2) the entity is the issuer of debt obligations with two or more maturities and (3) payments on the debt obligations issued by the entity bear a relationship to payments on the debt obligations (or interests therein) held by the entity. Thus an owner trust that issues sequential-pay CMOs after 1991 would be a taxable mortgage pool and could not generally avoid an entity level tax except by electing to be a REMIC.

The general purpose of the taxable mortgage pool rules is to force REMIC elections, so that, among other consequences, the owners of the equity interests in the pool would become subject to the 'excess inclusion' rules (discussed in section 8.3.2 below under the heading 'Phantom income') that apply to REMIC residual interests.

8.3 Taxation of Holders

This section addresses the taxation of mortgage-backed securities in the hands of investors. As the discussion above indicates, the mortgage-backed securities that are currently available are divided into two groups: those that are taxable as debt instruments, and REMIC residual interests and equity interests in owner trusts which are taxed based on an allocation of the taxable income of the REMIC or trust, respectively. The two groups of mortgage-backed securities are considered separately below, beginning with those that are taxable as debt instruments.

8.3.1 *Mortgage-Backed Securities Taxable as Debt Instruments*

Overview Mortgage-backed securities that are treated as debt instruments for tax purposes consist of (1) pass-through certificates, which are considered ownership interests in the underlying mortgages, (2) CMOs and other pay-through bonds, which are debt obligations of the entity that issues them, and (3) REMIC regular interests, which the Code deems to be debt obligations of the issuing REMIC, regardless of their legal form. References in this section (8.3.1) to mortgage-backed securities should be understood to be limited to one of these three types of securities.

In applying the tax rules for debt instruments to a pass-through certificate, it should be kept in mind that such a certificate is not generally considered a single security for tax purposes, but instead represents an ownership interest in each of the mortgages held by the issuing trust. Technically, the holder of a pass-through certificate should calculate income or loss with respect to each mortgage separately by allocating among the mortgages, in proportion to their respective fair-market values, the price paid for the certificate and the price received on resale. Such an allocation is rarely necessary in practice, however, because in most instances the tax results obtained by viewing the mortgages alternatively, in isolation or as a group, would be the same.[40] For convenience, and except where otherwise noted, the discussion below of the tax treatment of mortgage-backed securities will proceed as if the security in question was in all cases a debt obligation of one debtor (either an interest in a single mortgage or a single pay-through bond).

The mortgage-backed securities considered in this section (8.3.1) are generally subject to the Code rules governing conventional debt instruments. Thus, for example, interest on such a security is taxable as ordinary income when such interest accrues, in the case of an accrual-method taxpayer, or when it is received, in the case of a cash-method taxpayer. Assuming the security is purchased at its principal amount, principal payments represent a non-taxable return of the investor's capital regardless of when principal is paid (discount and premium are discussed below). Upon sale of the security, gain or loss is recognized in an amount equal to the difference between the net proceeds of such sale and the seller's 'adjusted basis' in the security (generally, the seller's cost for the security, with adjustments for principal payments and the amortization of discount or premium). Any such gain that is not characterized as interest income under the market discount rules, and any loss, is treated as capital gain or loss, respectively, if the security is held as a 'capital asset', which would be the case unless the holder is a dealer in securities.[41] Capital gain is long term if the security has been held at the time of sale for more than one year. However, as a result of TRA 1986, long-term capital gain is generally taxable at the same rate as ordinary income; however, the Revenue Reconciliation Act of 1990 (RRA 1990) does provide for limited preferential treatment of long-term capital gains for certain individuals.[42] An amount paid as accrued interest upon the sale of a mortgage-backed security between interest payment dates is treated by the seller as an interest payment and may be used by the purchaser to offset the interest received on the next interest-payment date. Two exceptions to the foregoing rules apply to REMIC regular interests, but they are likely to have little, if any, practical significance for most investors.[43]

The tax treatment of a mortgage-backed security is more complex if it was purchased at a price different from its principal amount, that is, at a discount (a price below such amount) or a premium (a price above such amount). If a mortgage-backed security is purchased at a discount, and the holder subsequently receives its full principal amount, the excess of the principal received over the cost of the security will represent additional income. A question then arises as to the proper timing of recognition of that income and as to its character as ordinary income or capital gain. Similar issues exist regarding the use of premium to offset income or increase loss. These questions are addressed in the remainder of this section.

Treatment of discount and premium The traditional approach to the tax treatment of a debt instrument deals separately with three sources of income – stated or coupon interest, original-issue discount and market discount – and one item of expense, which is bond premium. Stated interest was discussed above; discount and premium are considered here.

In general, original-issue discount is discount at which a debt obligation was originally sold to investors by the issuer or, in a public offering, by the underwriters, and market discount is discount that arises from decreases in the market value of a debt obligation following its issuance. The most important difference, in terms of tax consequences, between original-issue discount and market discount is that, in general, original-issue discount is includible in income by the holder of a discount obligation as the discount accrues, whereas market discount is taxable only when principal payments are received or the obligation is sold. The rule requiring the current inclusion in income of original-issue discount has applied to corporate obligations since 1969, but was first extended to obligations of individuals by the Tax Reform Act of 1984 (TRA 1984), effective for obligations issued – which in the case of mortgages means closed – after 1 March 1984.

If a debt obligation has market discount, it must be determined whether the obligation was issued after 18 July 1984, the date of enactment of TRA 1984, or on or before that date. Gain from a sale to a new holder of a mortgage-backed security issued after 18 July 1984 is ordinary interest income to the extent of the market discount that accrued during the period the seller held the security rather than capital gain as was generally true under prior law. The manner in which market discount is allocated among principal payments will also differ depending on whether TRA 1984 applies.

The distinction between original-issue discount and market discount is blurred by the 'bond stripping' rules of section 1286. These rules apply when rights to principal and interest on a debt obligation are sold separately or in different proportions and play a significant role in the taxation of pass-through certificates. If rights to payments on a debt obligation qualify as 'stripped bonds', all income from the holding of those rights (including income attributable to stated interest and all discount) is subject to taxation under the original-issue discount rules.

A further distinction to keep in mind in determining the tax treatment of market or original-issue discount is whether the debtor is an individual or a corporation or other legal entity. Gain realized upon the receipt of a payment of principal on an obligation of an individual (representing market discount, or original-issue discount not previously included in income) is *always* ordinary income, whereas gain from the payment of principal on an obligation of a corporation or other legal entity may be capital gain if the obligation is held as a capital asset.[44] While this distinction has been important in the past, its significance has been eroded by recent legislation. TRA 1984 and TRA 1986 greatly narrowed the circumstances under which gain from a payment of principal will be capital gain in the case of an obligation of a legal entity, and TRA 1986 eliminated the rate advantage of capital gain.

Unlike discount, all premium on a given debt instrument is treated alike. Premium on a debt instrument that is held for investment can be amortized as an offset to interest income if an election is made by the holder under section 171. Before TRA 1986, this election applied only to debt obligations of corporations or governments, and thus was not available for obligations of individuals, such as residential mortgages, or obligations of owner trusts. However, TRA 1986 extended the election to obligations of all types of issuers, effective for obligations issued after 27 September 1985. TRA 1986 also requires the use of a constant-yield method of amortization of premium that is similar to the method, described below, used in calculating accruals of original-issue discount.

In order to understand fully the tax treatment of mortgage-backed securities, it continues to be necessary to distinguish between stated interest, original-issue discount, market discount and premium and to take account of the rules applicable to each. Nonetheless, the law is clearly moving in the direction of taxing all income from the holding of mortgage-backed securities under the rules governing original-issue discount. This trend is evidenced by a number of recent developments.

First, with respect to many common types of mortgage-backed securities, stated interest is treated currently as original-issue discount and is therefore directly subject to the original-issue discount rules. In those instances where stated interest is not now treated as original-issue discount, the consequences for investors of characterizing such interest as original-issue discount would be fairly minor.

Second, many of the pass-through certificates that are now being issued either are or may be subject to the bond-stripping rules of section 1286. As noted above, the effect of those rules is to convert all discount and stated interest into original-issue discount.

Third, TRA 1984 and TRA 1986 have reduced the importance of the distinctions between original-issue discount and market discount, in terms of both the timing of income and the character of income as capital gain or ordinary income.

Fourth, TRA 1986 adopted a new method (referred to below as the PAC method) for calculating accruals of original-issue discount on mortgage-backed securities that takes account of expected prepayments and adjusts for differences between expected and actual prepayments. The legislative history of TRA 1986 generally contemplates that this method will be used in calculating accruals of market discount and premium amortization.

Finally, it has been argued that the Code should be amended to treat market discount in exactly the same manner as original-issue discount, on the ground that the two are economically equivalent from the perspective of investors.[45] Given the Congressional interest in revenue enhancement, it would not be surprising to see this argument prevail some time in the next few years.

In light of these factors, it would be reasonable, if perhaps somewhat premature, to view the rules governing original-issue discount as the basic model for taxing all income from mortgage-backed securities (while recognizing, as the discussion below will indicate, that deviations from that model are required or permitted under current law). For that reason, the discussion below will consider first original-issue discount, including the bond-stripping rules, and then turn to market discount and premium.

The discussion of discount below assumes that the mortgage-backed securities in question have an original term to maturity of more than one year. A different tax regime, which is of little relevance to mortgage-backed securities, applies to discount on short-term obligations.

(1) *Original-issue discount.*   Original-issue discount is defined as the excess of the 'stated redemption price at maturity' of an obligation over its 'issue price'.[46] In the case of an obligation that bears interest at a fixed rate payable at fixed intervals of not more than one year over the entire term of the obligation, the stated redemption price at maturity of the obligation is its principal amount. The issue price of an issue of publicly offered obligations is the initial offering price to the public (excluding bond houses and brokers) at which a substantial amount of the obligations is sold. Thus, neither the price at which the obligations are sold to the underwriters by the issuer, nor the price at which any particular obligation is sold to an investor, determines the issue price.

The definition of original-issue discount applies quite differently in practice to pay-through bonds and REMIC regular interests, on the one hand, and pass-through certificates, on the other hand. Accordingly, these two categories of securities are discussed separately below. The bond-stripping rules are described in the context of pass-through certificates.

■ *Pay-through bonds and REMIC regular interests.* For convenience, the term 'pay-through bonds' will be used to refer to both pay-through bonds and REMIC regular interests.[47]

Pay-through bonds will often have original-issue discount. It is not uncommon for them to be issued at a substantial discount below their principal amount particularly when the mortgages themselves are purchased at a discount. In that event, the pay-through bonds will have original-issue discount, even though the discount mirrors market discount on the underlying mortgages, because the pay-through bonds are new securities distinct from those mortgages.

In addition, a pay-through bond may be considered to have original-issue discount if the rate at which interest is actually paid in each payment period (calculated by dividing the amount of the interest payment by the principal balance of the bond at the beginning of the period) is not the same for all periods and the change in the rate of interest payments is attributable to factors other than changes in an index of market interest rates.[48] In particular, interest on such a bond generally will be treated as original-issue discount to the extent it is paid at a rate that exceeds the lowest rate at which interest is paid during any period over the entire life of the instrument.[49]

One common example of a pay-through bond that provides for interest payments at varying rates is an interest-accrual bond (generally, a bond that bears interest over its entire life at a fixed rate but does not provide for any principal or interest payments until all bonds of the same series with earlier maturity dates have been retired). Because interest on an interest-accrual bond is payable during the initial payment periods at a zero rate, all payments of interest on such a bond are treated as original-issue discount. Thus, such a bond would have original-issue discount equal to the sum of all interest payments thereon, even if it were issued with no discount below its principal amount. Although not entirely clear, for similar reasons, stated interest also may be transformed into original-issue discount in the case of any pay-through bond that has a 'payment-lag' feature (that is, provides for a lag between the end of the period over which interest accrues and the date on which such interest is paid) if the period between the issue date of the bond and the first payment date is longer than the interval between payment dates.

In the case of a pay-through bond that provides for interest at a rate that floats based on changes in the value of an index of market interest rates (for example, LIBOR), the original-issue discount rules should be applied by (1) assuming that interest will be payable in all accrual periods (as defined in note 55 to this chapter) at the rate or rates that would apply if the value of the index remained constant over the life of the instrument at its value on the issue date (this assumption eliminates the floating-rate feature and thus permits the original-issue discount and other tax rules to be applied as if the loan provided for interest at a fixed rate or rates) and then, (2) for each accrual period, adjusting the interest income determined under the first step to reflect the difference between the assumed rate and the actual rate for such period.[50]

An investor who purchases a pay-through bond having original-issue discount at a yield to maturity not less than the yield to maturity at which it was initially offered must include in income in each taxable year that such investor holds the bond the portion of the original-issue discount that is considered to accrue in such year (regardless of whether such investor otherwise reports income under a cash or accrual method of tax accounting). As explained in more detail below, the portion of the original-issue discount on a bond that is considered to accrue in any period generally equals the amount by which the value of the bond would increase during such period if it continued at all times to have a yield to maturity equal to its yield to maturity at the time of issuance calculated based on its issue price. This method of accruing original-issue discount is known as the 'constant yield' or 'scientific' method.[51] It gives effect to the compounding of interest by including accrued but unpaid original-issue discount in the base to which the yield to maturity of the bond is applied in calculating future accruals of such discount.

The yield to an investor of a debt obligation purchased at a discount is greater the shorter the life of the obligation. In the case of most pay-through bonds, it is highly probable that principal will be prepaid to some degree. The possibility of prepayments raises two related questions: first, whether original-issue discount should be accrued based on a yield that is calculated assuming that prepayments will occur at some reasonable rate, and second, how income is to be adjusted to account for differences between the assumed prepayment rate (a zero rate or a reasonable estimate) and the actual prepayment rate. Prior to the enactment of TRA 1986, there were no certain answers to these questions.[52] Because of TRA 1986, it is now clear that, in the case of a pay-through bond issued after 31 December 1986, (1) the yield that is used in calculating accruals of original-issue discount will be determined based on a reasonable assumption ('prepayment assumption') as to the rate at which the underlying mortgages will be prepaid, and, if earnings on temporary investments would affect the timing of payments of the bond, the rate of those earnings, (2) income will be adjusted in each taxable year (whether or not principal payments are made on the bond in that year) to reflect the economic gain or loss for that year (calculated based on changes in present values assuming a constant yield) resulting from past and present differences between actual prepayment experience and the prepayment assumption, but assuming that future prepayments on remaining mortgages will conform to the prepayment assumption, and, (3) in general, those adjustments will increase or decrease interest income and not be treated as capital gain or loss.[53] In general, the prepayment assumption with respect to any issue of bonds will correspond to the prepayment rate assumed in pricing the initial offering of the bonds and will be stated in the offering materials for the bonds.[54] Once determined, the prepayment assumption will not change to reflect changes in prepayment rates occurring after the issuance of the bonds. For convenience, the method for calculating accruals of original-issue discount introduced by TRA 1986 will be referred to as the 'prepayment assumption catch-up method', or 'PAC method' for short.

The following discussion explains in more detail the operation of the PAC method.

A holder of a bond having original-issue discount is required to include in gross income in each taxable year the sum of the 'daily portions' of such discount for each day during the taxable year on which such holder holds the bond. In the case of an investor who purchased the bond in the initial offering at the issue price, two steps are needed to determine the daily portions of original-issue discount. First, a calculation is made of the portion of the original-issue discount that is allocable to each 'accrual period' during the term of the bond. For a bond that provides for payments at fixed intervals over its life except for a short initial or final period, the accrual periods are the periods that end on each payment date and begin on the day after the immediately preceding payment date (or, in the case of the first such period, begin on the issue date).[55] Second, the portion of the original-issue discount attributed to each accrual period is allocated rateably to each day during the period to determine the daily portion of original-issue discount for that day.

Under the PAC method, the amount of original-issue discount on a bond that is attributed to each accrual period is the excess of (1) the sum of (a) the present value, as of the end of the accrual period, of all the payments, if any, to be made on the bond in future periods and (b) the payments made on the bond during the accrual period that are includible in its stated redemption price at maturity, over (2) the adjusted issue price of the bond at the beginning of such period. The present value of the future payments of the bond would be calculated for this purpose by (1) assuming that the mortgages underlying the bond will be prepaid in future periods in accordance with the prepayment assumption (but taking account of the actual prepayments that have occurred to date) and (2) using a discount rate equal to the original yield to maturity of the bond. The original yield to maturity is the discount rate, assuming compounding at the end of each accrual period, that will cause the present value of all future payments on the bond to equal its issue price on the issue date, calculated assuming that the bond will be prepaid in all periods in accordance with the prepayment assumption. The adjusted issue price of a bond at the beginning of an accrual period equals its issue price, increased by the aggregate amount of original-issue discount on the bond attributed to all prior accrual periods, if any, and decreased by the amount of any payments made on the bond in prior periods that were includible in the stated redemption price at maturity of the bond. Thus, it represents the first purchaser's remaining capital investment in the bond adjusted for the amount of the original-issue discount that has been earned and included in income for tax purposes but not yet paid.

It is sometimes necessary, with respect to a particular day that falls within an accrual period, to refer to the sum of the adjusted issue price at the beginning of that accrual period and the daily portions of original-issue discount for all days in the accrual period that are on or before the day in question. That sum is referred to as the 'revised issue price'.[56] The revised issue price at the beginning of an accrual period is the same as the adjusted issue price at the beginning of that period.

The discussion above involves an investor who purchased the original-issue discount bond in the initial offering at the issue price. The daily portions of original-issue discount would be calculated in the same manner for a subsequent holder if such holder purchased the bond at a price not exceeding its revised issue price on the date of purchase. On the other hand, an investor who bought the bond at a price exceeding its revised issue price on the date of purchase (and thus at a yield lower than the bond's initial yield to maturity) would be allowed to offset that excess amount (which will be referred to as an 'acquisition premium') against the daily portions of original-issue discount calculated as described above.[57] In particular, each of those daily portions would be reduced by an amount equal to the product of such daily portion and a fixed fraction, the numerator of which is the acquisition premium and the denominator of which is the daily portions of original-issue discount (determined without regard to any acquisition premium adjustment) for all days after the purchase date through the maturity date of the bond. Thus, if the acquisition premium for any bondholder represents 25 per cent of the aggregate amount of original-issue discount that remains to be accrued after the purchase date, the amount of original-issue discount that would otherwise be required to be included in the holder's income for any day would be reduced by 25 per cent.

▪ *Pass-through certificates.* The degree to which the original-issue discount rules will influence the taxation of a pass-through certificate depends primarily on whether the stripped-bond rules of section 1286 apply. If they do, then the original-issue discount rules will play a central role. On the other hand, original-issue discount is unlikely to be present in pass-through certificates that do not fall within that section, except in cases where interest on the underlying mortgages is scheduled to increase over time. The two types of pass-through certificates are considered below.

As regards pass-through certificates that are subject to the stripped-bond rules, section 1286, which was first enacted in 1982 as section 1232(b), contains special rules governing the taxation of stripped bonds and stripped coupons. A stripped bond is defined as a bond issued with coupons (which, for this purpose, includes any rights to receive stated interest), where there is a separation in ownership between the bond and any coupons that have not yet come due. A stripped coupon is a coupon relating to a stripped bond. The tax treatment of stripped bonds and stripped coupons is generally the same, and the term 'stripped bond' will be used in this discussion to refer to both.

Section 1286 transforms the discount at which a stripped bond is purchased (as well as any stated interest on the stripped bond) into original-issue discount. More specifically, section 1286(a) provides that if a person purchases a stripped bond, then, for purposes of applying the original-issue discount rules of the Code, the stripped bond will be treated, while held by that person, as a bond originally issued on the purchase date having original-issue discount equal to the excess of the face amount of the stripped bond over its purchase price.[58] If a number of stripped bonds are purchased together at one price, which is often the case, the purchase price is allocated among the stripped bonds in proportion to their respective fair-market values.[59]

The classic example of a bond-stripping transaction is a sale by the owner of a whole bond of unmatured interest coupons to one investor and rights to principal to a second investor. (Alternatively, the seller could sell only the coupons or the rights to principal and retain the remaining interests in the bond.) IO and PO strips represent the extension of this transaction pattern to mortgage-backed securities. Because of the extreme sensitivity of the yields of these types of securities to differences in rates of prepayments of the underlying mortgages, they may be thought to resemble equity securities, or possibly options or futures contracts, more than debt. Nonetheless, because the underlying mortgages are debt obligations, and the complete separation of rights to interest and principal on a debt obligation is the clearest possible example of bond stripping, there is little doubt that IO and PO strips fall within the rules of section 1286.

The bond-stripping rules also extend to situations where there is some but not complete separation in the ownership of rights to principal and interest. One common example is the transaction described above (see section 8.2.1 under the heading 'Stripped pass-through certificates') in which a thrift institution holding discount or premium mortgages creates pass-through certificates that can be sold at par by retaining a share of interest payments (in the case of the premium mortgages) or a share of principal payments (in the case of the discount mortgages).

Another example of a pass-through arrangement that may (perhaps inadvertently) be subject to the stripped-bond rules is one in which the underlying mortgages have a range of stated interest rates. In order to be able to quote to investors a single pass-through rate of interest that applies over the life of the pool regardless of prepayment experience, it is common in these circumstances for the pool sponsor or the servicer to receive an 'excess servicing fee'. This fee is payable out of interest received on the higher coupon mortgages and equals the excess of the interest received on those mortgages over the interest that would have been received if those mortgages paid interest at the lowest rate of interest borne by any mortgage in the pool. Although this fee is labelled a servicing fee, it could also be characterized as an ownership interest in a fixed percentage of each interest payment on the higher coupon mortgages. Under that view, the certificate-holders' interests in the higher coupon mortgages would be stripped bonds.

The consequences of recombining all of the stripped interests in a single debt instrument are not clear. It appears, however, that section 1286 would continue to apply to those interests in the hands of any person who had held any of them as a stripped bond, but not apply to a new investor who purchases all of the stripped interests together.

As indicated above, the interest income earned by the holder of a pass-through certificate that is composed of stripped bonds will consist entirely of original-issue discount. This will be true regardless of whether the price paid by the holder equals, or is less or greater than, the principal payments on the underlying mortgages to which the holder is entitled, if any, and regardless of the date of origination of those mortgages. Thus, the rules governing market discount and premium discussed herein will not apply. Under the original-issue discount rules, the holder will report interest income in each taxable year based on the yield to maturity of the stripped bond to such holder. While not entirely clear under current law, such interest income should equal the interest income the holder would have reported if (1) such holder had purchased a single, hypothetical bond, having a single yield to maturity, which provided for payments corresponding to the payments on the underlying mortgages to which such holder is entitled and was issued, on the date on which the stripped bond was purchased by the holder, with an issue price equal to the price paid by such holder and (2) the PAC method applied to such hypothetical bond in his hands. Under the PAC method, such holder's income would depend in part on the prepayment assumption applied to the underlying mortgages.[60] A number of issuers of pass-through certificates that are stripped bonds have stated that they will use the foregoing method (and a prepayment assumption that is consistent with the initial pricing of the certificates) to calculate income reported to investors and to the Internal Revenue Service.

Original-issue discount is not likely to be encountered in a pass-through certificate to which the stripped-bond rules do not apply unless, as discussed below, scheduled interest payments on the underlying mortgages increase over time. The exchange of such pass-through certificates for mortgages is not treated as a creation of a new debt security for tax purposes, so that the existence or lack of original-issue discount is not affected by the price at which the certificates are originally sold. Rather, in testing for the presence of original-issue discount, it is necessary to look to the terms of the original loan between the mortgagor and the mortgage originator, and mortgages are not typically originated at a discount.[61] In any event, the original-issue discount rules of the Code would not apply to whole or *pro rata* interests in mortgages which are obligations of individuals if those mortgages were originated before 2 March 1984.[62] TRA 1984 extended those rules to obligations of individuals for the first time, effective for obligations issued on or after that date. As noted above, a pass-through certificate would not fail to qualify as an interest in obligations of individuals because the mortgages or the certificates are guaranteed by the United States or a US-sponsored agency.

In the case of a fixed-rate residential mortgage originated after 1 March 1984, some portion of the stated interest payments will be included in original-issue discount if the amount unconditionally payable as interest in each month, expressed as a percentage of the outstanding principal balance of the loan, increases over the term of the loan. For example, such a mortgage will be considered to have original-issue discount, even if it was originated at par, if it provides for negative amortization of principal or bears interest payable at fixed rates that are scheduled to increase over the life of the loan. The general effect of applying the original-issue discount rules to loans with these features will be to require holders (1) of a negative amortization loan to include stated interest in income as it accrues, and (2) of a loan that bears interest at increasing rates to take into income interest that accrues based on the yield to maturity of the loan (that is, a yield representing a blend of the stated interest rates).

In the case of an adjustable-rate residential mortgage originated after 1 March 1984, the original-issue discount rules should generally be applied by treating the mortgage as if it provided for fixed-interest payments equal to the interest that would be paid if the value of the index were frozen at its value on the date of origination of the mortgage.[63] Under that approach, stated interest would be included in original-issue discount only if the mortgage provides for a scheduled increase in interest payments not dependent on an increase in the index. Such an increase might occur, for example, because rates are adjusted to market levels following an initial incentive or 'teaser' rate period.

If a mortgage is considered to have been issued with original-issue discount, an investor's interest therein would most likely be taxable under a method similar to the PAC method, except that the prepayment assumption used in calculating yield and present values would be an assumption that no prepayments will occur, and gain from a prepayment would be treated as gain from retirement of the mortgage loan and not as an adjustment to original-issue discount.[64]

(2) *Market discount.*

■ *Overview.* Any discount at which an obligation is purchased below its principal amount (if the obligation has no original-issue discount), or below its revised issue price (if the instrument does have original-issue discount), is considered to be market discount. The treatment of market discount has been significantly altered by TRA 1984 and TRA 1986.

Prior to enactment of TRA 1984, market discount on a mortgage-backed security was generally allocated among all principal payments in proportion to their amounts regardless of when they were due. The discount was included in income as principal payments were received or when the security was sold. Thus, if an obligation having an outstanding principal amount of $1,000 was purchased by an investor for $750, the investor would report 25 per cent of each principal payment as income when the payment was received while he held the obligation. Such income was ordinary income (although not interest income) if the obligation was the debt of an individual; otherwise, it was generally capital gain, assuming the obligation was held as a capital asset.[65] Given the same assumption, gain realized upon sale of the obligation was always capital gain.[66] Such gain would reflect any market discount allocated to the principal of the obligation that remained unpaid at the time of the sale, since the seller's adjusted basis for purposes of computing gain would equal the portion of the initial purchase price, as reduced by the market discount, that was allocated to such unpaid principal.

TRA 1984 and TRA 1986 do not change the rule of prior law that permitted the reporting of market discount on an obligation to be deferred until the obligation is disposed of or principal thereon is paid. However, TRA 1986 introduced a rule for allocating discount among principal payments that can significantly increase the amount of market discount income that is recognized when a principal payment is made. In the case of an obligation that provides for partial principal payments in each accrual period, as is the case with many mortgage-backed securities, this change can have the effect of substantially eliminating the difference between original-issue discount and market discount in terms of the timing of the inclusion of such discount in income.

As to the character of market discount income, as a result of TRA 1984, market discount income reported by the holder of an obligation is treated as ordinary interest income for most tax purposes to the extent of the portion of the discount that accrued while the holder held the obligation. TRA 1984 also provided rules to ensure that accrued market discount will not be exempted from tax under certain non-recognition provisions in the Code. Finally, another TRA 1984 amendment defers deductions for all or a portion of the tax losses that might otherwise be generated by borrowing at market rates to finance low-coupon market discount obligations, claiming current deductions for interest expense on the borrowing and deferring the inclusion in income of the market discount until the obligation is disposed of or repaid. The new market discount rules do not apply to obligations that have an original term of one year or less.[67]

■ *Detailed discussion.* TRA 1984 added to the Code a new section 1276, which applies to obligations issued after 18 July 1984, the date of enactment of the legislation. The section provides that gain from a sale or other disposition of an obligation acquired with market discount[68] will be treated as ordinary income (generally as interest income) to the extent the gain does not exceed the portion of the market discount that is considered to have accrued from the acquisition date to the time of the sale or other disposition. Subject to certain exceptions,[69] such income is recognized notwithstanding other non-recognition rules in the Code. Thus, for example, a holder who makes a donative transfer of a market discount obligation would recognize income up to the amount of accrued market discount even though gifts do not ordinarily trigger the recognition of gain. Similarly, the stripping of a market discount obligation is considered a disposition that triggers the recognition of accrued market discount.[70]

TRA 1986 introduced a new rule for determining the amount of market discount income that is recognized when a partial principal payment is made.[71] The rule, which is found in section 1276(a)(3), states that a partial principal payment on an obligation will be included in gross income as ordinary income to the extent of the accrued market discount on the obligation. In other words, the amount of market discount that must be included in income when a principal payment is received is not, as under prior law, the portion of the remaining market discount that is allocable economically to the principal that is paid (for example, half of such discount if half of the principal balance is paid), but is instead the lesser of the amount of the payment and the amount of market discount that has accrued (and not yet been included in income) on the obligation as a whole. If an obligation provides for principal payments in each year at least equal to the market discount that accrues in that year, then the new rule would effectively require market discount to be included in income as it accrues.

Subject to the discussion in the next paragraph, market discount will be considered to accrue on an obligation under a straight-line method[72] unless the holder elects, on an obligation-by-obligation basis, to use a constant-yield method.[73] If the election is made, accrued market discount for any period will equal the portion of such discount that would have been included in the holder's income during that period as accrued original-issue discount under the rules described above if the obligation had been issued on the date on which it was purchased by the holder and the market discount had been original-issue discount. Most sophisticated investors will make a constant-yield election for all of their market discount bonds because the election will have the effect of slowing the rate at which market discount accrues.

TRA 1986 authorized the Treasury to issue regulations to determine the amount of accrued market discount with respect to an obligation on which principal is payable in instalments. The legislative history[74] states that until these regulations are issued, holders of such obligations may elect to accrue market discount either in the same manner as original-issue discount, or (1) in the case of debt obligations that have original-issue discount, in proportion to the accrual of original-issue discount,[75] or (2) for debt obligations that have no original-issue discount, in proportion to payments of stated interest.[76] In the case of an obligation that would be subject to the PAC method for accruing original-issue discount if the instrument had original-issue discount (which would include any pay-through bond issued after 31 December 1986), the same prepayment assumption that would be used in accruing original-issue discount will be used in accruing market discount, regardless of which of the foregoing methods is used.[77]

As already noted, section 1276 applies only to obligations issued after 18 July 1984. Thus, the section will apply to all pay-through bonds issued after that date. By contrast, it should apply to pass-through certificates issued after 18 July 1984 only to the extent they evidence interests in mortgages originated after that date. In other words, the pass-through certificates should not be viewed as new obligations, distinct from the underlying mortgages for this purpose.

TRA 1984 also added section 1277 to the Code, which requires the deferral of tax losses that would otherwise result from financing an investment in market discount obligations with debt that bears interest at a current market rate. Section 1277 applies to obligations that are acquired after 18 July 1984 (regardless of when those obligations were issued).

(3) *Premium.* In the case of a debt instrument acquired at a premium, section 171 allows the holder (unless the holder is a dealer in securities) to elect to amortize such premium over the life of the instrument. This section was significantly amended by TRA 1986, effective for debt instruments issued after 27 September 1985. Under section 171, as amended, if an election to amortize a premium is made, the premium must be amortized under a constant-yield method. Although the result is not certain, many tax advisers believe that in amortizing premium under the amended section, prepayments should be accounted for under a method similar to the PAC method, at least in the case of a debt instrument issued after 31 December 1986 to which the PAC method would apply if it had been issued at a discount.[78]

In the case of a debt instrument issued on or before 27 September 1985, an investor may elect to amortize premium under section 171 only if the instrument was issued by a corporation or government.[79] If the election is made, bond premium would be amortized under the method of amortizing bond premium that the holder regularly employs, provided such method is reasonable, and otherwise under a straight-line method. In determining whether a premium may be amortized on a pass-through certificate evidencing an interest in residential mortgages, the date of origination of the mortgages would determine whether the new or the old version of section 171 would apply. Thus, an election could be made under section 171 to amortize the premium on a pass-through certificate backed by residential mortgages that are obligations of individuals only to the extent the mortgages were originated after 27 September 1985.[80]

Premium on a debt instrument that is not amortized under section 171 is allocated among the principal payments to be made on the instrument and is allowed as a loss deduction when those payments are made. Such a loss would be an ordinary loss in the case of an obligation of an individual (or a partnership or trust if the obligation was issued prior to 2 July 1982) and otherwise would be a capital loss, provided the obligation is a capital asset.[81]

8.3.2 Equity Interests in Owner Trusts and REMIC Residual Interests

Introduction This section discusses the federal income tax treatment of equity interests in owner trusts and REMIC residual interests. The tax characteristics that are common to both types of securities are discussed first; special considerations applicable to owner trusts are discussed second; special considerations applicable to REMIC residual interests are discussed third; and so-called 'phantom income' is discussed last. Except as otherwise indicated, in the balance of this section 8.3.2, the term 'conduit issuer' means an owner trust or a REMIC, the term 'equity interest' means an equity interest in a conduit issuer, and the terms 'bond' and 'CMO' include REMIC regular interests.

Common tax characteristics As discussed above, conduit issuers are generally not subject to tax.[82] Instead, each holder of an equity interest is required to include in income that holder's share of the net income (or loss) of the related conduit issuer without regard to the distributions made by such issuer. In computing taxable income, the conduit issuer would have gross income consisting principally of interest and discount income from the mortgage collateral, from the reinvestment of mortgage payments and from any reserve funds, and would be allowed deductions for interest (including accruals of original-issue discount) and retirement premiums with respect to the bonds and operating expenses of the issuer.[83] Deductions allowed in any period for bond interest and retirement premiums generally would equal the income that would be reported by original holders of the bonds if they bought the bonds on the issue date at the issue price (in the case of issues of bonds having more than one class, computed on a class-by-class basis), except that in computing accruals of original-issue discount, the one-quarter of 1 per cent *de minimis* rule[84] would not apply.

Special considerations applicable to owner trusts   As discussed above, an owner trust may be classified either as a grantor trust or as a partnership. A major difference between grantor trusts and partnerships is that a grantor trust is essentially ignored for federal income tax purposes, whereas a partnership is recognized as an entity for some tax purposes. Thus, if an owner trust is classified as a grantor trust, each holder of an equity interest therein would be treated as if he purchased and owned directly his share of the assets of the trust, subject to his share of the indebtedness of the trust. Accordingly, such holder would have an initial basis in his share of those assets equal to the cost to him of his equity interest plus his share of the revised issue price of the bonds at the time of purchase of the equity interest.[85] In addition, such holder's income would be computed under his own method of accounting and any elections that may be made, such as to amortize bond premium on the mortgage collateral, would be made separately by each holder. If the holder sold his interest in the owner trust, he would be considered to have sold his interest in the underlying mortgages. Accordingly, if the holder were a thrift institution or bank, any resulting gain or loss would be ordinary income or loss. Distributions from a grantor trust are not taxable.

By contrast, if an owner trust is classified as a partnership, taxable income would be computed, and, in general, elections would be made, at the partnership (or owner trust) level using the partnership's accounting method (which would almost always be an accrual method).[86] Each holder of an equity interest would report the share of the partnership's taxable income allocable to that holder in that holder's taxable year in which the taxable year of the partnership ends. In most cases, the taxable year of the partnership would be the calendar year.[87] Each partner would be considered to own a partnership interest, which would have a basis in the hands of that partner equal to its original cost to the partner (the cash purchase price or the basis of property exchanged for such interest in a tax-free exchange), increased by the share of partnership income and liabilities, and decreased by his share of losses and distributions, allowable to the partner. The amount of the partnership's liabilities in respect to the bonds would equal the bonds' aggregate revised issue price, as described above.

Unlike a grantor trust, a partnership is considered to have its own basis in its assets ('inside basis'). While initially the inside basis of an owner trust that is classified as a partnership would equal the sum of the holders' bases in their equity interests, a discrepancy could develop if equity interests are sold at a gain (or loss). This discrepancy could result in over-taxation (or under-taxation) of a subsequent holder. Such over-taxation (or under-taxation) would be mitigated or eliminated if the partnership makes an election under section 754 to adjust the basis of its assets for purposes of computing the taxable income of such successor partners, or if the sale terminates the partnership under section 708. Under section 708, a partnership is considered to be terminated and reformed if 50 per cent or more of the total interest in partnership income and capital are sold or exchanged within a twelve-month period.[88]

If an owner trust is classified as a partnership, then gain or loss from a sale of an equity interest may be capital gain or loss, even though, in the case of a thrift institution or bank, a sale of a direct ownership interest in the mortgages held by the trust would be ordinary income or loss.[89] Such gain or loss would be computed by comparing the seller's basis in his partnership interest with the amount realized in the sale (which would include the seller's share of the trust's liabilities). Distributions of cash by a partnership to a partner are not taxable unless they exceed the partner's basis in the partnership interest, in which case the excess is treated as gain from sale of that interest. Because such basis could include the partner's share of the trust's liability for the bonds, such gain would be rare in the case of an owner trust.

A pension fund, charity or other tax-exempt investor that is subject to tax on its 'unrelated business taxable income' under section 512 will be taxable on substantially all of its income from an equity interest in an owner trust, regardless of whether it is classified as a grantor trust or partnership.[90]

Special considerations applicable to REMICs The tax treatment of REMICs resembles a partnership more than a grantor trust. Thus, income or loss is computed at the level of the REMIC and is then allocated among the holders of residual interests as ordinary income or loss. In particular, taxable income or loss of the REMIC is computed as of the end of each calendar quarter and each holder of a residual interest is considered to earn, on each day the holder owns such interest, that day's rateable share of the REMIC's taxable income or loss for the quarter.[91] In computing taxable income, regular interests are treated as indebtedness of the REMIC, and all REMICs are required to use an accrual method of accounting.

In order to calculate the taxable income of a REMIC, it is necessary to determine the REMIC's basis in its assets. Generally speaking, a REMIC's aggregate basis in its assets at the time it is formed will equal the aggregate value at that time of all REMIC interests (both regular interests and residual interests).[92] The most significant assets of a REMIC will be the qualified mortgages that it holds. Income from those mortgages will be determined under the rules discussed in section 8.3.1 above, except that a REMIC will be required to include all discount in income as it accrues under the PAC method as if the mortgages had been issued on the date on which they were acquired by the REMIC with an issue price equal to their initial basis to the REMIC.[93]

No Code provision permits or requires adjustments to be made to a REMIC's basis in its assets to reflect subsequent purchases of residual interests at a price greater or less than the seller's adjusted basis. The legislative history of TRA 1986 indicates that it 'may be appropriate' to make such adjustments, but leaves the issue unresolved.[94] Apparently, either Treasury regulations or further legislation will be needed to clarify whether (or how) any such adjustments will be made.

Special rules apply to the portion of the income from a residual interest that is characterized as an 'excess inclusion'. With limited exceptions, excess inclusions are always subject to tax, even in the hands of tax-exempt investors. The excess-inclusion rules were adopted primarily to ensure taxation of 'phantom income' and are discussed further in that context below. Income from residual interests that is not an excess inclusion should be exempt from tax in the hands of pension funds and other tax-exempt investors that are taxable only on unrelated business taxable income to the same extent as, for example, income from a partial-ownership interest in mortgages (that is, the residual interest should not be considered debt-financed income merely because the regular interests are considered debt obligations of the REMIC).

A REMIC will have a net loss for any calendar quarter in which its deductions exceed its gross income. Such a loss may not be carried over or back to other periods by the REMIC but is instead allocated among the current holders of the residual interest in the manner discussed above. However, the portion of such net loss that is allocable to a holder will not be deductible by such holder to the extent it exceeds such holder's adjusted basis in such interest at the end of such quarter (or at the time of disposition of such interest, if earlier), determined before taking account of such loss. Such adjusted basis would generally equal the cost of the interest to such holder, increased by any amount previously included in such holder's income with respect to such interest and decreased by any losses previously allowed to such holder as deductions and by any distributions such holder has previously received. Any loss that is not currently deductible by reason of the basis limitation may be used by such holder to offset his share of the REMIC's taxable income in later periods, but not otherwise.

Gain or loss from the sale of a residual interest will generally be capital gain or loss if the residual interest is held as a capital asset, except that, if the holder is a bank or thrift institution, such gain or loss will always be ordinary.[95] In addition, under section 860F(d) and except as may be provided in Treasury regulations, to the extent that the seller of a REMIC residual interest reacquires such interest, or acquires any residual interest in another REMIC, an equity interest in an owner trust or other interest in a 'taxable mortgage pool' (as defined in section 8.2.4 under the heading 'Exclusivity of REMIC rules/taxable mortgage pools' above without regard to the 1 January 1992 effective date discussed therein) during the period beginning six months before, and ending six months after, the date of such sale, such sale will be treated as if it were a 'wash sale' subject to section 1091.[96] Any loss realized in the 'wash sale' would not be currently deductible, but, instead, would increase the seller's adjusted basis in the newly acquired interest.[97]

Phantom Income

(1) *Overview.* The payments received on the mortgages held by a conduit issuer (net of administrative expenses) will be used for two purposes, to make payments on the bonds and distributions to the equity owners. Thus, it would be possible to view those mortgages as consisting of two separate assets: the 'bond-related assets' consisting of the mortgage payments that will be used to make corresponding payments on the bonds,[98] and the 'equity-related assets' consisting of the mortgage payments that will be used to make distributions on the equity interest.

As discussed above, the equity owners will be taxed based on the taxable income of the conduit issuer calculated by subtracting deductions allowed with respect to the bonds from the issuer's income from *all* of its assets. Thus, it would be possible to express the income reported in any taxable year by the equity owners as the sum of (1) the income of the conduit issuer attributable to the equity-related assets and (2) a net amount of income or loss equal to the income of the conduit issuer attributable to the bond-related assets, less the deductions allowed with respect to the bonds. The net amount (positive or negative) described in clause (2) in the preceding sentence will be referred to herein as 'bond-related income'.

If the yield to maturity of the bond-related assets exceeds the initial weighted average yield to maturity of all of the bonds, then one component of bond-related income would be a net positive amount representing the economic profit resulting from the financing of the bond-related assets with the bonds. However, for reasons discussed below, bond-related income may also be increased in some periods by income that is not economic income, because it necessarily will be matched by losses, reducing bond-related income, in other periods. Such non-economic income or loss is sometimes labelled 'phantom' income or loss. By definition, the phantom income and phantom losses recognized by an equity owner with respect to his equity interest in all taxable years (taking account of gain or loss from the disposition of such interest) must sum to zero.

In a typical offering of multiple-class sequential pay bonds, some phantom income will be realized in the early years after the issuance of the bonds followed by a corresponding amount of phantom losses in subsequent years. The cause is a difference in the distribution over time of the yields that are used in calculating income and deductions.[99] In particular, deductions are calculated separately for each class of bonds, based on the yield to maturity of that class. Thus, the aggregate deductions allowed the conduit issuer in any year will be determined with reference to the weighted average yield of all classes of bonds outstanding in that year. With a rising yield curve, the yield to maturity is lower for earlier-maturing classes of bonds than for later-maturing classes. Thus, the weighted average yield to maturity of outstanding bonds increases over time as bonds are retired. By contrast, the yield to maturity of the mortgages remains constant because they are not divided into sequential pay classes. The effect of using a fixed yield in calculating income and an escalating yield in calculating deductions is to skew deductions toward later years, producing the pattern of phantom income and losses described above.

The creation of phantom income may be illustrated with a simplified example. Consider a conduit issuer that purchases at par a mortgage that bears interest at a rate of 10 per cent, payable annually, and provides for two principal payments of $500, due one year and two years after the date of purchase, respectively. At the time of such purchase, the conduit issuer issues two bonds, each of which provides for a single principal payment of $500 at maturity. The first bond is issued at par, matures at the end of one year and earns interest at a rate of 8 per cent payable at maturity. The second bond bears interest at a rate of 10 per cent payable annually, matures at the end of two years, and is issued at a price of $491.44 to yield 11 per cent. The conduit issuer will be required to make an equity investment of $8.56 to finance the purchase of the mortgage and will receive a cash distribution of $10 at the end of the first year and nothing thereafter, as shown in table 8.1.

Table 8.1 The creation of phantom income

	Years from bond issuance		
	0	1	2
Mortgage payments	($1,000.00)	$600	$550
Bond 1 payments	500.00	(540)	–
Bond 2 payments	491.44	(50)	(550)
Funds available to conduit issuer	(8.56)	10	–

The taxable income of the conduit issuer, economic income and phantom income and loss for the two years that the bonds are outstanding are set out in table 8.2.

Another way to describe the phantom-income problem is that the owner of an equity interest is not permitted to amortize the cost of the interest directly against the cash distributions received – as would be permitted, for example, if the right to those distributions was treated for tax purposes as a debt obligation of the owner trust – but instead recovers the investment in the equity interest over a longer period. Thus, in the example above, although the equity interest in the con-

Table 8.2 Taxable, economic and phantom income

	First bond year	Second bond year
Mortgage income	$100.00	$50.00
(10% of principal balance)		
Deduction on bond 1	(40.00)	
(8% of principal balance)		
Deduction on bond 2	(54.06)	(54.50)
($50 plus original issue discount of $4.06 in first year and $4.50 in second year)		
Taxable income (loss)	5.94	(4.50)
(mortgage income minus bond deductions)		
Economic income	1.44	–
($10 minus $8.56)		
Phantom income (loss)	4.50	(4.50)
(taxable income minus economic income)		

duit issuer becomes worthless following the distribution of the $10 payment at the end of the first year, the equity investor is permitted to treat as a return of capital in that year only $4.06 (the excess of the $10 distribution over taxable income of $5.94) rather than the full $8.56 cost of the equity interest.[100]

(2) *Acceleration of net remaining phantom losses through sales of equity interests.* When an equity interest is sold, the seller generally recognizes gain or loss equal to the difference between the amount realized in the sale and his adjusted basis in the interest. To the extent that the seller has recognized a net amount of phantom income, such adjusted basis would be increased without a corresponding increase in value. Accordingly, to that extent, the gain that otherwise would be realized from the sale would be decreased, or the loss would be increased. Consequently, the sale should in effect cause the acceleration of phantom losses that would otherwise be recognized over time. However, if the sale produces a loss, this result may not be achieved for two reasons. First, for most investors other than certain banks and thrifts, any loss realized on a sale of an equity interest will be a capital loss that, in general, can be offset only against capital gain.[101] Further, a loss recognized upon the sale of a REMIC residual interest may be deferred under the special REMIC 'wash sale' rule discussed above.

(3) *Special rules for REMICs.* In the case of a conduit issuer that is a REMIC, any phantom income is taxable to the holders of the residual interests. However, in contrast to the rules for equity interests in owner trusts, there is no tax requirement that a REMIC residual interest have any minimum economic value. Also, because phantom income is not economic income, a residual interest could produce substantial phantom income without having any economic value. Accordingly, absent special rules, the tax on phantom income associated with residual interests could be avoided easily by reducing the economic values of those interests and transferring them (and their related tax liability) to investors that are tax-exempt, or that are not currently paying federal income tax (for example, because they have net operating loss carryovers) whether or not they would ordinarily invest in mortgage securities. In order to frustrate such tax avoidance, a specified portion of the income from a residual interest, referred to as an 'excess inclusion', is, with an exception discussed below for certain thrift institutions, subject to federal income taxation in all events. Thus, for example, an excess inclusion with respect to a residual interest (1) may not, except as described below, be offset by any unrelated losses or loss carryovers of an owner of such interest,[102] (2) will be treated as unrelated business taxable income, and thus subject to tax if such owner is a pension fund or other organization that is subject to tax only on its unrelated business taxable income, and (3) is not eligible for any reduction in the rate of withholding tax if such owner is a foreign investor, as further discussed in section 8.3.4.

In general terms, the excess inclusion with respect to a residual interest for a calendar quarter equals the excess of the income for that quarter from the holding of the residual interest over the income that would have accrued on that interest in that quarter if such interest had earned income at all times from its issuance through the end of such quarter at a constant, compounded rate equal to 120 per cent of a long-term US Treasury borrowing rate for the month in which the residual interest was issued.[103]

As an exception to the general rule described above, the Treasury has authority to issue regulations to treat all income from the holding of REMIC residual interests as an excess inclusion, if the residual interest is considered not to have 'significant value'. In addition, certain thrift institutions[104] are now exempted from the rule (discussed above) that prevents excess inclusions from being offset with unrelated losses. However, the Treasury has authority to issue regulations (which may be retroactive) that would subject thrifts to that rule where necessary or appropriate to prevent the avoidance of tax. The legislative history of TRA 1986 indicates that none of the foregoing regulations will apply to a REMIC if the aggregate value of the residual interest equals at least 2 per cent of the aggregate value of the residual interest and the regular interests.[105]

8.3.3 *Special Rules for Certain Institutional Investors*

Under section 7701(a)(19)(C), thrift institutions are required to hold a minimum percentage of their assets in certain investments, including residential real property loans, in order to qualify for special bad debt reserve deductions under section 593. Similarly, a real estate investment trust (REIT) will be eligible to deduct dividends paid to shareholders only if it holds a large percentage of its assets in the form of real property assets, including real property loans (see section 856(c)(3) and (5)). In general, pay-through bonds do not qualify as real property loans for these purposes, because they are not directly secured by real property (but only by other debt instruments that are so secured). Most pass-through certificates do so qualify to the extent the underlying mortgages are qualifying loans, because the holders of such certificates are treated for tax purposes as the owners of the underlying loans. A REIT that owns an equity interest in an owner trust is considered to own real property assets to the extent the assets underlying the trust are qualifying assets; arguably, the same should be true for thrifts but the matter is not entirely certain.

Both regular interests and residual interests in REMICs are qualifying assets for thrifts and REITs to the same extent that the assets of the REMIC are qualifying assets. However, if 95 per cent or more of the assets of the REMIC are qualifying assets, then the regular interests and the residual interests will be considered qualifying assets in their entirety.

Qualified pension plans, charitable institutions and certain other entities that are otherwise exempt from federal income taxation are nonetheless subject to tax on their unrelated business taxable income (UBTI). Although UBTI generally does not include interest income or gain from the sale of investment property, such income is included in UBTI to the extent that it is derived from property that is debt-financed. Because an equity interest in an owner trust is generally viewed for tax purposes as an interest in the mortgage collateral that is financed with the related bonds, it appears that substantially all of the income on such an interest would be subject to tax in the hands of such investors even if the equity interest itself is not debt-financed. In the case of a REMIC residual interest, under section 860E, any amount that is an 'excess inclusion' is deemed to be UBTI in the hands of a tax-exempt investor that is subject to tax on UBTI.[106]

The general rules of the Code relating to the accrual of discount and the amortizaton of premium on debt securities do not apply to life insurance companies. Under section 811(b) they are generally required to take discount and premium into account under the method which they regularly employ in maintaining their books, if such method is reasonable.

Under section 582(c), certain banks and thrift institutions are required to report gain or loss from the sale of an 'evidence of indebtedness' as ordinary income or loss. In general, mortgage-backed securities are considered evidences of indebtedness whether in the form of pass-through certificates or pay-through bonds. Both regular and residual interests in REMICs are considered evidences of indebtedness for this purpose.

8.3.4 *Special Rules for Foreign Investors*

Foreign investors not engaged in a trade or business within the United States are generally subject to a 30 per cent tax on US-source interest income, which is required to be withheld from interest payments. However, the tax does not apply to interest paid on obligations issued after 18 July 1984 that is 'portfolio interest'. Portfolio interest includes most interest paid on debt securities to investors unrelated to the issuer. The 30 per cent withholding tax is also subject to possible reduction or elimination through any applicable tax treaty. Interest paid on US mortgage-backed securities is typically considered to be derived from US sources and thus is subject to the 30 per cent tax when paid to foreign investors unless one of the exceptions mentioned above applies.

Portfolio interest is exempt from withholding tax only if paid on debt obligations issued after 18 July 1984. For this purpose, pay-through bonds and REMIC regular interests are considered debt instruments in their own right so that the issue date of the bonds or regular interests determines whether the portfolio interest exemption applies.

By contrast, a pass-through certificate is treated as an ownership interest in the underlying mortgages for federal income tax purposes. Accordingly, interest on a pass-through certificate qualifies for the portfolio interest exemption only to the extent that the mortgages backing the certificate were issued after 18 July 1984. Similar principles apply to equity interests in owner trusts and REMIC residual interests (except that income from such a residual interest that is treated as an 'excess inclusion' is always taxed at the full 30 per cent rate).

Except with respect to income from REMIC residual interests that is treated as an excess inclusion, interest on mortgage-backed securities that does not qualify for the portfolio interest exemption may qualify for a reduced rate or exemption from withholding if the investor is a resident of a country with which the United States has an income tax treaty.

The Foreign Investment in Real Property Tax Act of 1980 (FIRPTA) enacted section 897, which subjects non-US investors to US tax on gain from sales of certain US real property interests (including equity interests in 'real property holding corporations'). Section 1445 imposes a related requirement to withhold tax from the proceeds of sales. The FIRPTA rules do not apply to interests in real property that are solely creditor interests with no participation in the income, revenues or appreciation of the property. Thus, a foreign investor holding a mortgage-backed security will not be affected by this legislation if the mortgages underlying the security lack such participation features.

8.4 Taxation of Sponsors

8.4.1 *Introduction*

The discussion above concentrates on investors. This section looks at mortgage-backed securities from the perspective of a sponsor. With respect to any particular issue of mortgage-backed securities, the term 'sponsor' will be used herein to refer broadly to any person who owned an interest in the underlying mortgages before those securities were created, and who also owns at some time some or all of those securities or some other interest in the issuer of those securities. The tax treatment of a sponsor may be affected by numerous factors. Therefore, the discussion is intended only as a general summary of the most likely tax results in a number of common situations.

The federal income tax consequences to a sponsor of the issuance and sale of mortgage-backed securities will depend primarily on whether the transaction is treated as a financing or sale, and, if it is a sale, what proportion of the property held by the sponsor is considered to be sold. Pledging an asset as security for a loan is not ordinarily considered a taxable disposition of the asset. On the other hand, if the asset (or an interest therein) is sold, the seller would recognize gain or loss equal to the difference between the amount realized in the sale and his adjusted basis in the property sold. These fundamental tax principles produce different consequences for sponsors when applied to pass-through certificates, pay-through bonds and REMIC interests.

8.4.2 *Pass-Through Certificates*

If a sponsor transfers mortgages to a trust that is classified as a grantor trust in exchange for pass-through certificates, the exchange of mortgages for certificates is not considered a taxable disposition of the mortgages. However, when the sponsor sells some or all of those certificates, he is treated as selling an interest in the underlying mortgages and recognizes gain or loss equal to the difference between the amount realized in the sale and the portion of his adjusted basis in the mortgages that is allocated to the certificates sold.[107] In addition, if the interest in the mortgages retained by the sponsor represents rights to different percentages of principal and interest, so that the bond-stripping rules apply, then the sponsor may be required to recognize as ordinary income all market discount and interest on the mortgages that has accrued but not previously been included in income (including the portion that is allocable to the interest in the mortgages that is retained). However, the sponsor's adjusted basis in the mortgages and, hence, the basis allocated among the certificates, would be increased by the amount so included in income. Under the bond-stripping rules, the sponsor would be treated as if the sponsor had purchased the retained interest in the mortgages at a price equal to the sponsor's adjusted basis in such retained interest, and the difference between that price and the gross amount of payments to be received in respect of the retained interest would be treated as original-issue discount and taxed as it accrues.[108]

8.4.3 *Pay-Through Bonds*

Two steps may be involved in issuing pay-through bonds: (1) the issuance of bonds for cash and (2) if the issuer is not the original owner, the transfer of all or a portion of the mortgage collateral by a sponsor to the issuer in exchange for cash and/or other consideration. The issuance of the bonds is not considered a sale of the collateral and is not otherwise a taxable event. The tax treatment of the transfer of the mortgages to the issuer is quite complex, and would depend on at least three factors, the first two of which are related: (1) whether for tax purposes the transfer is recognized to be a sale, or is instead viewed as an exchange of mortgages for an equity interest in the issuer,[109] (2) the extent to which equity interests in the issuer are owned by the sponsor rather than unrelated investors, and (3) whether the issuer is a corporation or an owner trust and, if the latter, whether it is classified as a grantor trust or partnership.

In very general terms, if the issuer were an owner trust that is classified as a grantor trust, then the sponsor would recognize gain or loss as a result of the transfer of mortgages to the issuer only if equity interests in the issuer are owned by persons other than the sponsor, and then only to the extent that the sponsor would recognize gain or loss if the sponsor transferred directly to those other persons an interest in the mortgages corresponding to the equity interest that they own. If the issuer is an owner trust that is classified as a partnership, gain from a sale of the mortgages to the owner trust would be recognized, but loss would not be recognized, at least if the sponsor owns more than 50 per cent of the equity interests in the owner trust.[110] In general, no gain or loss would be recognized upon an exchange of mortgages for an equity interest.[111] If the issuer is a corporation, gain or loss from a sale of mortgages to the issuer by the sponsor would generally be recognized. However, if the sponsor is also a corporation and files a consolidated federal income tax return with the issuer, any such gain or loss would be deferred.[112] Moreover, even if the sponsor and the issuer do not file a consolidated return, loss would be deferred if the sponsor owns more than 50 per cent of the stock of the issuer.[113] If the mortgages are exchanged for stock (or stock and cash) upon formation of the issuer, loss would not be recognized in the exchange. Gain may be recognized, in an amount not exceeding the amount of cash received, but any such gain would be deferred to the same extent as gain from a sale.[114] The transferor may also recognize interest income up to the amount of accrued market discount on the mortgages not previously included in income.[115]

Regardless of whether the issuer is a corporation or owner trust or whether gain or loss was recognized upon transfer of the mortgages to the issuer, if the sponsor sells some or all of the equity interest in the issuer to unrelated investors, he will recognize gain or loss with respect to that sale equal to the difference between the amount realized and his adjusted basis in the portion of the equity interest that is sold.[116]

8.4.4 REMICs

A sponsor who transfers mortgages to a REMIC in exchange for regular or residual interests generally will not recognize gain or loss in the exchange.[117] However, the aggregate adjusted basis of the property transferred (increased by properly allocable costs of acquiring the REMIC interests)[118] will be allocated among the REMIC interests received in proportion to their respective fair-market values, and each time the sponsor sells an interest in the REMIC (whether a regular interest or a residual interest), he will recognize gain or loss equal to the excess of the amount realized over his adjusted basis in that interest.[119] The federal income tax consequences to the sponsor of a REMIC would be the same if, instead of transferring mortgages to the REMIC in exchange for interests therein, the sponsor contributed cash to the REMIC which used the cash to purchase the mortgages; the alternative transaction would be recharacterized for tax purposes as a purchase of the mortgages by the sponsor (if the mortgages were purchased by the REMIC from a person other than the sponsor), followed by their contribution to the REMIC.[120]

As the discussion above suggests, the major difference in tax consequences for a sponsor of pay-through bonds between making and not making a REMIC election relates to the portion of the sponsor's overall economic gain or loss (represented by the difference between the sum of the fair-market values of the bonds and equity interest in the issuer and the sponsor's basis in the mortgages) that is recognized at the time of the bond offering and upon sale of equity interests in the issuer. Suppose first that no election is made, and the sponsor exchanges the mortgages for all of the equity interest in the issuer plus the net proceeds of the bonds and subsequently sells all or a portion of the equity interest. In that event, the sponsor would not recognize any portion of such gain or loss at the time of the bond sale, but would recognize a portion of such gain or loss each time an equity interest is sold, corresponding to the portion of the equity interest that is sold. By contrast, where a REMIC election is made, the sponsor would recognize a portion of such gain or loss equal to the portion of *all* interests in the issuer (equity and bonds) that are sold, as those interests are sold. Thus, for example, if the bonds represent 95 per cent of the value of all REMIC interests, 95 per cent of such gain or loss would be recognized when the bonds are sold. The tax consequences for a sponsor of the creation and sale of pass-through certificates would be substantially the same whether or not a REMIC election is made.

REMIC securities are generally taxed as if they had been issued at their initial fair-market values, and not at a price equal to the sponsor's initial basis in those interests. Under section 860F(b), while the sponsor holds any REMIC interest, the difference between the issue price of that interest and its initial basis in the hands of the sponsor is required to be included in income, if the issue price is higher, or is allowed as a deduction, if the issue price is lower, (1) in the case of a regular interest, as if that difference were original-issue discount or bond premium, respectively, or (2) in the case of a residual interest, rateably over the anticipated period during which the REMIC will be in existence.[121]

Notes

1 The discussion below is current through 1 January 1991 and is, of course, subject to change through subsequent judicial decisions, legislation or administrative actions. An expanded version of the following discussion is available in J. Peaslee and D. Nirenberg, *Federal Income Taxation of Mortgage-Backed Securities* (Probus Publishing Company, 1989).

2 Thus, debt obligations that are secured by mortgages, but have payment terms unrelated to those of the mortgage collateral, are not addressed.

3 Pass-through certificates representing different proportionate interests in mortgage principal and interest are discussed below. See also note 24 below for a description of tax constraints imposed on the issuance by a single trust of multiple classes of pass-through certificates having different payment priorities.

4 However, when the pool includes mortgages with different interest rates and the fees are the same for all of the mortgages, the pass-through rate would be a weighted average of the interest rates (net of fees) on the mortgages. This structure is used more often in private transactions than in public offerings.

5 If the trust were classified as an association taxable as a corporation, it is likely that the income realized by the trust with respect to the mortgages, net of fees paid by the trust, would be subject to the corporate income tax. The balance of such income remaining after payment of the corporate tax would be treated as taxable dividends when distributed to certificate-holders.

6 The classification for tax purposes of an unincorporated entity such as a trust is not controlled by what it is called, but depends instead on its functional characteristics and activities. Under Treasury Regulation section 301.7701–4, entities that qualify as trusts under state law are generally classified as trusts for tax purposes if they are passive and merely hold property to protect and conserve it; by contrast, they are generally classified as associations taxable as corporations if they engage in a profit-making business. In particular, a typical investment trust of the type that issues pass-through certificates would be classified as an association if there was any significant power to vary the investment of the trust beneficiaries (for example, by reinvesting mortgage payments in other mortgages).

7 Except as otherwise noted, all section references herein are to the Internal Revenue Code of 1986 (the 'Code'). For federal income tax purposes, a trust is usually recognized to be a taxpayer and is subject to tax, at the rates applicable to individuals, on that portion of its income which it does not distribute currently to beneficiaries. Income distributed to beneficiaries is taxable to them. Certain trusts, however, are ignored for most federal income tax purposes under the so-called 'grantor trust' rules found in sections 671 through 679. These rules were devised in order to prevent the separate tax identity of a trust from being used to shift income to lower bracket taxpayers (for example, from wealthy parents to a family trust or to its beneficiaries) in cases where the grantor (the person creating the trust) retains an economic interest in, or significant rights of control over, the trust. The grantor-trust rules provide that if the grantor of a trust retains specified interests in the trust, including a right to income, then he is treated for tax purposes as the owner of the assets of the trust in which he has such interests and is required to include income from those assets in his own tax return. To that extent, the trust is ignored for tax purposes. While the holder of a pass-through certificate issued by a trust holding mortgages is not, strictly speaking, the grantor of the trust, the grantor-trust rules have

been seized upon by the Internal Revenue Service as a basis for disregarding the issuing trust and treating certificate-holders as tax owners of the mortgages, according to their interests.

8 Similarly, accrual-method holders would report income as it accrues on the mortgages, as distinguished from the certificates, although the difference between the two should not be substantial.

9 An individual certificate-holder's deductions for servicing and other expenses may be limited under section 67, which provides that an individual is allowed certain miscellaneous itemized deductions (including deductions for investment expenses) only to the extent that the aggregate amount of such deductions exceeds 2 per cent of the individual's adjusted gross income. The Revenue Reconciliation Act of 1990 would further limit itemized deductions for certain individuals. In addition, apparently, no deduction would be allowed in computing an individual's liability, if any, for the alternative minimum tax.

10 Revenue Ruling 70–544, 1970–2 C.B. 6, and Revenue Ruling 70–545, 1970–2, C.B. 7, both modified by Revenue Ruling 74–169, 1974–1 C.B. 147.

11 Revenue Ruling 81–203, 1981–2 C.B. 137; Revenue Ruling 80–96, 1980–1 C.B. 317; Revenue Ruling 74–300, 1974–1 C.B. 169; Revenue Ruling 74–221, 1974–1 C.B. 365; Revenue Ruling 72–376, 1972–2 C.B. 647; Revenue Ruling 71–399, 1971–2 C.B. 433.

12 Revenue Ruling 84–10, 1984–1 C.B. 155.

13 Revenue Ruling 77–349, 1977–2 C.B. 20.

14 See note 44 below and accompanying text in section 8.3.1.

15 See the discussion of special rules for certain institutional investors in section 8.3.3.

16 In general, these percentages must be set at the time of issuance of the certificates and may not subsequently change. Otherwise, the trust issuing the certificates would be considered an association taxable as a corporation under the 'Sears regulations' and would be subject to an entity-level tax. See note 24 below. Most tax counsel believe that creating a class of pass-through certificates that provides for a floating pass-through rate of interest (for example, based on an index of market interest rates) could run foul of the Sears regulations if the rate of interest on the underlying mortgages were fixed. On the other hand, if the underlying mortgages provide for interest at a floating rate, it may be permissible to allocate all interest up to a specified rate to one class of pass-through certificates and all remaining interest to another class without causing reclassification of the trust.

17 Alternatively, if the thrift could find a group of investors that have the same expectations that it has regarding prepayment rates, it could sell to those investors the strip of interest payments. This could be done

mechanically by transferring the mortgages to a trust in return for two classes of certificates which would be sold to the two investor groups. One class of certificates would be entitled to 100 per cent of the principal payments and 80 per cent of the interest payments on the mortgages; the other class would be entitled to 20 per cent of the interest payments.

18 Another example of a common pass-through arrangement that may be viewed as a sale of rights to different percentages of principal payments and interest payments is one in which the underlying mortgages have a range of stated interest rates and an 'excess servicing' fee is charged to reduce the interest that is passed through on the higher coupon mortgages. Such arrangements are discussed further below.

19 The reinvestment of reserve-fund assets by the trust could be viewed as a business activity that would be inconsistent with the required passivity of a grantor trust. See note 6 above. See also Internal Revenue Service General Counsel's Memorandum 39040 (30 September 1983), which revoked Internal Revenue Service General Counsel's Memorandum 38311 (18 March 1980), which had concluded that the limited reinvestment of certain reserve-fund assets would not cause a trust to be an association taxable as a corporation. However, the revocation appears to have been based primarily on other grounds.

In addition, as further discussed in note 24 below, under the Treasury's trust classification regulations, a trust having more than one class of ownership interest is taxable as an association unless the multiple-class nature of the trust is incidental to the purpose of facilitating direct investment in the assets of the trust. Treasury Regulations section 301.7701–4(c), Example (2), involves a trust holding mortgages that issues two classes of pass-through certificates. The classes are identical except that, in the event of a default on any of the mortgage loans, payments on one class are subordinated to payments on the other. The example states that the senior certificates were sold to investors and the subordinated certificates were retained by the pool sponsor. The example holds that the multiple-class nature of the trust is incidental to the purpose of facilitating direct investment in the mortgages because the arrangement is substantially equivalent to a single-class trust coupled with a guarantee, secured solely by the pass-through certificates retained by the sponsor of the trust, that is written by the sponsor in favour of the holders of the remaining certificates. Because the sponsor retained the subordinated certificates in the example, it has generally been assumed that a subordinated interest in a trust must be retained by the sponsor of the trust (or at least may not be freely traded) in order to fall within the example and avoid the risk of classification of the trust as an association taxable as a corporation. The Service recently issued a private letter ruling to this effect (Private Letter Ruling 8929030, 21 April 1989). As described below, the foregoing restrictions on maintaining a reserve fund in the trust and transferring subordinated interests would be avoided if the trust qualified as a REMIC and a REMIC election was made.

20 This analysis is supported by Treasury Regulations section 301.7701–4(c), Example (2), discussed above in note 19.

21 The term 'owner trust' is used to distinguish the trust from the indenture trust for the CMOs described below.

22 The collateral backing CMOs often takes the form of pass-through certificates guaranteed by the United States or a US-sponsored agency, although when the sponsor is a non-governmental person, the CMOs themselves are not obligations of, or guaranteed by, the United States or such an agency.

23 The reinvestment of mortgage payments and call rights are needed in order to conclude that the CMOs will be recognized to be indebtedness of the issuer for federal income tax purposes. See note 25 below.

24 With a limited exception, Treasury Regulations section 301.7701–4(c) classifies an investment trust as an association (or, in limited circumstances that would not apply to a typical mortgage pass-through trust, a partnership) if it has more than one class of ownership interest. These regulations were initially aimed in part at an issue of pass-through certificates sponsored by Sears Mortgage Securities Corporation which had a 'fast-pay/slow-pay' class structure similar to CMOs. For that reason, they are often referred to as the 'Sears regulations'. See Treasury Regulations section 301.7701–4(c), Example (1), which holds that a trust similar to the Sears trust will not be classified as a trust.

A trust that is used to create stripped pass-through certificates has more than one class of ownership interest. However, stripped pass-through certificates fall within an exception in the regulations which permits multiple classes of interest in a trust 'if the trust is formed to facilitate direct investment in the assets of the trust and the existence of multiple classes of ownership interest is incidental to that purpose'. Treasury Regulations section 301.7701–4(c), Example (4), holds that the exception would apply to a trust that has multiple classes of interest if those classes of interest are treated as stripped bonds or stripped coupons under section 1286. Section 1286 is discussed in the text in section 8.3.1 under the heading 'Treatment of discount and premium'. Stripping transactions involve a separation in the ownership of identified principal or interest payments on an obligation. Dividing a fixed-rate obligation into one ownership interest that bears interest at a floating rate and another that represents a right to interest at the fixed rate on the obligation minus what is paid on the first class, is sufficiently removed from the mere separation in ownership of identified payments so that it is not clear that section 1286 (and hence Example (4) in the regulations) would apply. Example (2) in the regulations applies the exception for incidental multiple-ownership classes to certain trusts that issue senior and subordinated classes of pass-through certificates. See note 19 above.

25 One reason for ensuring that there is significant surplus cash flow attributable to the factors listed in the text is to avoid the possible recharacterization of the bonds for tax purposes as additional ownership interests in the issuer. Such a recharacterization would result in the disallowance of deductions for interest on the bonds.

26 If an investor owned more than 50 per cent of the equity interest in a CMO issuer, it would be required, under generally accepted accounting principles, to include the CMOs and the related collateral as debt and assets, respectively, in its consolidated financial statements. If the CMO issuer were a corporation, the issuer could file a consolidated federal income tax return with a shareholder only if the shareholder was a domestic corporation that owned at least 80 per cent of the stock of the issuer, which is well above the threshold for financial statement consolidation. In the absence of tax consolidation, income of the issuer corporation could not be offset by shareholder losses, and earnings of the issuer would potentially be subject to a second layer of taxation when distributed to its shareholders (which might be reduced, but not eliminated, by the 70 or 80 per cent dividends received deduction in the case of shareholders that are themselves corporations).

27 Net income from a prohibited transaction is taxed at a rate of 100 per cent. Prohibited transactions, as defined in section 860F(a)(2), include, among other things, the disposition of a mortgage other than pursuant to certain specific exceptions and the receipt of income from a source other than qualified mortgages or permitted investments, as defined below. With limited exceptions, contributions of assets to a REMIC after the regular and residual interests have been issued are also subject to a 100 per cent tax.

28 The timing of principal payments may be contingent on mortgage prepayments or income from permitted investments (described below).

29 See Notice 87–41, 1987–1 C.B. 500, and Notice 87–67, 1987–2 C.B. 377. Each of the notices applies to REMIC regular interests issued on or after 15 June 1987. It is generally expected that the actual regulations will permit greater flexibility in setting interest rates.

30 See H.R. Rep. No. 841, 99th Cong., 2d Sess. (18 September 1986) (the 'Conference Report') at II-229; and Joint Committee on Taxation, General Explanation of the Tax Reform Act of 1986 (JCS–10–87) 4 May 1987 (which, following convention, will be referred to as the 'Blue Book') at 415.

31 Also, a subordinated regular interest may be freely traded. Conference

Report at II-228, footnote 7; Blue Book at 415, footnote 70. Compare note 19 above. It is not clear whether an interest can qualify as a regular interest if it is subordinated to a residual interest. However, it is generally anticipated that, when the issue is addressed by the Internal Revenue Service, such subordination will be allowed.

32 See Blue Book at 416 ('The Congress intended that an interest in a REMIC could qualify as a residual interest regardless of its value. Thus, for example, an interest need not entitle the holder to any distributions in order to qualify as a residual interest.') Notwithstanding the language in the Blue Book, many tax advisers believe it is advisable for residual interests to have at least a contingent right to some distribution from the REMIC in order to ensure that the residual interest is considered to be an interest in the REMIC.

33 The Conference Report at II-226 states that the phrase 'substantially all' should be interpreted to allow a REMIC to hold only a *de minimis* amount of other assets. The assets test is applied at the close of the third calendar month beginning after the inception of the REMIC and continuously thereafter until the REMIC liquidates.

34 In general, a 'qualified replacement mortgage' is a mortgage or REMIC regular interest that is received by the REMIC in substitution for another mortgage or regular interest within three months of inception of the REMIC for any reason, or within two years if the replaced mortgage or regular interest is 'defective'.

35 Conference Report at II-227, footnote 5; Blue Book at 413, footnote 67. Non-REMIC pay-through bonds would not be qualified mortgages. Blue Book at 413, footnote 67.

36 Notice 87–41, 1987–1 C.B. 500.

37 Section 860G(a)(7) requires that the amount of any reserve be promptly and appropriately reduced as payments on qualified mortgages are received. This requirement should not prevent the build-up of a reserve over time so long as at all times the size of the reserve does not exceed the size required to provide adequate default protection or to pay expenses, as evidenced, for example, by rating agency requirements.

38 More precisely, the rules for taxable mortgage pools described in the text will not apply to any entity in existence on 31 December 1991, unless there is a substantial transfer of cash or property to such entity (other than in payment of obligations held by such entity) after such date.

39 For example, this rule would prevent a special-purpose subsidiary that issues CMOs and meets the definition of a taxable mortgage pool from filing consolidated returns with its parent corporation even if the subsidiary would otherwise be permitted to file such consolidated returns.

40 This statement assumes that all of the mortgages underlying a single pass-through certificate have identical terms. Although this is rarely true

in fact, because all such mortgages are generally similar to one another, and information is not reported to investors on a mortgage-by-mortgage basis, an assumption of pool-wide uniformity of mortgages is usually made in practice. Cf. Internal Revenue Service Private Letter Ruling 8052046 (30 September 1980).

41 However, holders that are banks or thrift institutions always recognize ordinary income or loss from sales of debt obligations under section 582(c).

42 Even for a corporation it still may be necessary to know whether gain or loss is capital or ordinary, because capital losses generally can be deducted only to the extent of capital gains.

43 The exceptions are as follows: first, income from REMIC regular interests must always be reported under an accrual method even if the holder is otherwise a cash-method taxpayer; second, gain recognized by an investor upon sale of a REMIC regular interest that otherwise would be capital gain will be treated as ordinary income to the extent such gain does not exceed the excess of (1) the income that would have been reported by the investor if the investor had reported income as it accrued based on a yield to the investor equal to 110 per cent of the 'applicable federal rate' (generally, an average yield of US Treasury obligations of different ranges of maturities published monthly by the Internal Revenue Service) in effect for the month in which the interest was acquired by the investor, over (2) the ordinary income previously reported by the investor.

44 This distinction is based on a technical quirk in the Code. In order for gain to be capital gain, it must result from a 'sale or exchange' of a capital asset (see the definitions in section 1222). Under case law dating back to the early days of the tax law, gain from the extinguishment of a contractual claim, including gain realized upon retirement of a debt obligation, is not considered to result from a sale or exchange unless there is a Code provision which so states. Section 1271(a)(1) treats amounts received by the holder on retirement of a debt instrument as amounts received in exchange therefor, but this section does not apply to obligations of individuals (see section 1271(b)(1)). Since amounts received in retirement of an obligation of an individual are not received in a sale or exchange of the obligation, any resulting gain is ordinary income. On the other hand, if such an obligation is actually sold to a new holder, the sale or exchange requirement is satisfied and income from the sale can be capital gain.

45 Such an amendment was included in H.R. 3545 (the House version of the Revenue Act of 1987 passed by the House on 29 October 1987), but was dropped in the House–Senate conference.

46 Section 1273(a). Under a de minimis rule, if the discount as so defined is

218   JAMES M. PEASLEE AND DAVID Z. NIRENBERG

less than one-quarter of 1 per cent of the stated redemption price at maturity times the number of complete years to maturity, original-issue discount is considered to be zero. Proposed regulations applying the original-issue discount rules found in sections 1271 through 1275 were issued in 1986 (the 'Proposed Regulations'). The Proposed Regulations state that, in the case of an obligation that provides for more than one payment includible in its stated redemption price at maturity (an 'instalment obligation'), the *de minimis* rule will be applied based on the weighted average maturity of the obligation, which will be calculated by dividing (1) the sum of the products of the amount of each payment includible in the obligation's stated redemption price at maturity and the number of full years (rounding down for partial years) from the issue date to the date on which each such payment is due by (2) the sum of all such payments. See Proposed Regulations section 1.1273–1(a)(3)(ii). In the case of a debt obligation for which accruals of original-issue discount are calculated under the PAC method, described below, taking account of a reasonable prepayment assumption, the same assumption should be applied in determining such weighted average maturity.

The Proposed Regulations provide a simpler, elective *de minimis* rule for instalment obligations that call for principal payments to be made at a rate no faster than principal payments on a 'self-amortizing instalment obligation'. A holder of such an obligation is permitted to compute the *de minimis* amount as the product of one-sixth of 1 per cent of the stated redemption price at maturity and the number of full years (rounding down for a partial year) from the issue date to the final maturity date of the obligation. See Proposed Regulations section 1.1273–1(a)(3)(ii)(B). In general terms, a 'self-amortizing instalment obligation' is an instalment obligation that calls for equal payments of principal and interest at fixed periodic intervals of one year or less with no additional payments at maturity. See Proposed Regulations section 1.1273–1(b)(2)(iii). Accordingly, the typical fixed-rate residential mortgage would be a 'self-amortizing instalment obligation'.

47 In the case of an individual who holds a REMIC regular interest, Treasury Regulations may provide that in certain circumstances that holder's share of the REMIC's operating expenses must be included in that holder's gross income and allowed as a deduction, subject to the limitation of section 67. See section 8.3.2 below under the heading 'Special considerations applicable to REMICs'.

48 Floating-rate debt instruments are discussed in the second following paragraph in the text. For an illustration, see Proposed Regulations section 1.1273–1(a)(3)(iii), Example 4.

49 The reason for this result is as follows: original-issue discount is defined as the excess of the stated redemption price at maturity of an obligation

over its issue price. Section 1273(a)(2) defines the stated redemption price at maturity of an obligation to include all payments made on the obligation other than interest based on a fixed rate which is payable unconditionally at fixed periodic intervals of one year or less during the entire term of the obligation. Thus, to the extent that interest is paid in any particular period at a rate greater than the lowest rate at which interest is paid in any period over the entire life of the instrument, it is includible in the stated redemption price at maturity and thus in original-issue discount.

50 For example, suppose that a pay-through bond with a principal amount of $1,000 pays interest quarterly at a rate equal to 100 basis points over the value of LIBOR at the beginning of the quarter. If the value of LIBOR was 8 per cent on the issue date of the bond, then the bond would be taxed as if it provided for fixed interest at a rate of 9 per cent except that the interest income for each quarter, as so determined, would be increased or decreased by the difference between the actual rate of interest paid at the end of the quarter and interest at the assumed 9 per cent rate. The approach described in the text is based upon Proposed Regulations section 1.1275–5.

51 The constant-yield method was introduced into the tax law by the Tax Equity and Fiscal Responsibility Act of 1982 and first applied to corporate and governmental obligations issued after 1 July 1982. In the case of obligations issued on or prior to that date, original-issue discount was accrued under a straight-line method, which allocated the same portion of the discount to each year.

52 See J. Peaslee, 'Federal income tax treatment of mortgage-backed securities', in *The Handbook of Mortgage-Backed Securities*, ed. F. Fabozzi (Probus Publishing Company, 1985), at 591–8.

53 The new method is found in section 1272(a)(6), and applies, according to section 1272(a)(6)(C), to any regular interest in a REMIC, any qualified mortgage held by a REMIC and 'any other debt instrument if payments under such debt instrument may be accelerated by reason of prepayments of other obligations securing such debt instrument (or, to the extent provided in regulations, by reason of other events)'. Thus, the method would apply to any pay-through bond issued after the effective date of the section, which is 31 December 1986.

54 The method for determining the prepayment assumption will eventually be set forth in Treasury Regulations (see section 1272(a)(6)(B)(iii)). However, the Conference Report at II-238–II-239 states that the conferees intended that the regulations would provide that the prepayment assumption for any pay-through bonds will be the assumption used in pricing the bonds, provided that assumption is not unreasonable based on comparable transactions, if any exist. In the case of publicly offered

220   JAMES M. PEASLEE AND DAVID Z. NIRENBERG

instruments, a prepayment assumption will be treated as unreasonable
only in the presence of clear and convincing evidence. Unless regulations
otherwise provide, the use of a mortgage prepayment assumption based
on an industry standard (such as a percentage of 'PSA') would be
permitted. Typically, the prepayment assumption for a pool of mortgages would be expressed as an assumption that a specified percentage of
the pool principal balance at the beginning of a period will be prepaid in
that period. The specified percentage may change over the life of the
mortgages in the pool under certain circumstances.

55 Section 1272(a)(5) defines the term 'accrual period' as a six-month
period (or shorter period from the issue date of the bond) which ends on
a day in the calendar year corresponding to the maturity date of the bond
or the date six months before such maturity date. This definition is
subject to change through Treasury regulations, and an elaborate set of
rules for determining accrual periods (including the rule described in the
text) is found in the Proposed Regulations at section 1.1272–1(d). In the
case of a pay-through bond that provides for no payments for some
period followed by payments at regular intervals (such as an interest-
accrual class of CMOs), the Proposed Regulations define the accrual
periods in the same manner as described in the text, except that the dates
in each calendar year corresponding to the payment dates would be
substituted for actual payment dates with respect to the initial period
during which no payments are made.

56 Proposed Regulations section 1.1275–1(h).

57 See section 1272(a)(7); Proposed Regulations section 1.1272–1(g).

58 The stripped-bond rules also affect the computation of gain and loss by
the seller by requiring that the seller allocate the adjusted basis in the
obligation that is stripped between the stripped bonds that are sold and
those that are retained, in proportion to their respective fair-market
values. See section 1286(b). Thus, it is no longer possible, as it may have
been before 1982, to allocate basis solely to rights to principal with no
allocation being made to rights to interest payments regardless of their
value. The basis allocated to the stripped bonds that are sold is compared with the proceeds of the sale to determine the seller's gain or loss
from the sale. The seller is treated as having purchased the stripped
bonds which he retains at a price equal to the basis allocated thereto.
The difference between the purchase price and the face amount of the
stripped bonds is treated as original-issue discount under the rule of
section 1286(a) described above in the text.

As a result of TRA 1986, another consequence of stripping a debt
instrument having market discount is that it causes the owner to recognize income equal to the accrued but not yet recognized portion of such
discount. This rule applies only to debt instruments acquired after 22

October 1986 (the date of enactment of TRA 1986). It is possible but not certain that the rule is also limited to debt instruments issued after 18 July 1984 to which the TRA 1984 rules governing market discount apply. These rules are discussed below.

59 Section 1286(a) does not indicate how the respective fair-market values of stripped bonds purchased together should be determined where there is no market for the individual stripped bonds. Many tax advisers believe that an investor should assume that the fair-market value of each such stripped bond equals the present value of the expected payments thereon computed using a discount rate equal to the yield to maturity to the investor of all stripped bonds purchased together (that is, computed with reference to the aggregate purchase price and to all payments due on the stripped bonds). Any method that attempted to take account of the different maturities of the separate stripped bonds in determining their fair-market value would be very difficult to administer in practice.

60 As discussed above, in the case of a pay-through bond, the prepayment assumption is generally the assumption used in pricing the initial offering of the bonds. Because each purchase of a stripped bond is treated as a new issuance of a debt instrument, it is possible (although not certain) that the prepayment assumption for any holder of a stripped bond would be determined based on conditions at the time he purchased the stripped bond.

61 While it is common for a mortgage lender to charge the borrower 'points' in connection with the origination of a mortgage, such points are often paid out of the mortgagor's own funds and represent a prepayment of interest rather than original-issue discount. See section 461(g) (special rule allows a cash-basis mortgagor a deduction for prepaid interest paid in the form of points on a loan to finance a principal residence if the number of points does not exceed the number generally charged in the area in which the mortgage is originated). See also Proposed Regulations section 1.1273–2(f), which excludes points that are deductible under section 461(g)(2) from original-issue discount. However, the Internal Revenue Service has recently ruled that points paid in connection with a mortgage that is used to refinance an existing mortgage are not deductible under section 461(g), and consequently would be treated as discount. See Revenue Ruling 87–22, 1987–1 C.B. 146. Moreover, even if points were viewed as discount, they may be less than a *de minimis* amount (see note 46 above), so that they would be disregarded in determining whether the mortgages are subject to the original-issue discount rules of the Code. Under the special one-sixth of 1 per cent *de minimis* rule for self-amortizing instalment obligations, discount on a fixed-rate residential mortgage would be considered *de minimis* if it were less than 5 per cent of the stated redemption price at maturity in the case

222   JAMES M. PEASLEE AND DAVID Z. NIRENBERG

of a thirty-year mortgage, and less than 2.5 per cent in the case of a fifteen-year mortgage.

62 See section 1272(a)(2)(D).

63 See the discussion at note 50 above and accompanying text.

64 While regulations could be adopted extending the PAC method to individual mortgage loans that are used to back pass-through certificates, such a development is less likely in the case of pass-through certificates that are not subject to the stripped-bond rules than in the case of certificates subject to those rules. In any event, if the stripped-bond rules do not apply, any such regulations would apply at the earliest only to mortgage loans that were originated after 31 December 1986.

65 See note 44 and accompanying text.

66 But see the discussion of special rules for certain institutional investors in section 8.3.3 below.

67 TRA 1984 also offers investors a new election, in section 1278(b), to treat market discount as original-issue discount. Market discount obligations affected by the election are not subject to the income-conversion and loss-deferral rules described below.

68 Market discount is defined in section 1278(a)(2) as the excess of the stated redemption price at maturity of an obligation over its basis immediately after the acquisition by the taxpayer. However, in the case of an obligation issued at a discount, the stated redemption price at maturity is replaced by the revised issue price. This rule has the effect of excluding unaccrued original-issue discount from the definition of market discount. Also, under a *de minimis* rule, market discount is considered to be zero if it is less than one quarter of 1 per cent of the remaining stated redemption price at maturity multiplied by the number of complete years to maturity (after the taxpayer acquired the obligation). In the case of an obligation that provides for more than one payment that is includible in the stated redemption price at maturity, this *de minimis* rule would presumably be applied in the same manner as described in note 46 above.

69 See section 1276(d). These exceptions allow, among other things, certain transfers of obligations to a parent corporation from an 80 per cent owned corporate subsidiary, by a partner to a partnership or to a partner from a partnership, or in connection with a corporate reorganization, without triggering recognition of accrued market discount income. As a result of TRA 1986, accrued market discount is recognized upon a transfer of market discount bonds to a corporation in a transaction that is otherwise tax-free under section 351. See note 114 below. Apparently, a similar rule would apply to a transfer to a REMIC. See note 117 below.

70 See note 58 above.

71 The rule applies to obligations to which section 1276 applies that were

acquired by the holder after 22 October 1986 (the date of enactment of TRA 1986).

72 Under this method, accrued market discount is calculated by multiplying the market discount by a fraction, the numerator of which is the number of days the holder has held the obligation and the denominator of which is the total number of days after the holder acquired the obligation to and including the maturity date. See section 1276(b)(1).

73 See section 1276(b)(2).

74 See Conference Report at II-842.

75 In other words, the amount of market discount that accrues during any period would be the product of (1) the total remaining market discount and (2) a fraction the numerator of which is the original-issue discount for the period and the denominator of which is the total remaining original-issue discount at the beginning of the period.

76 Thus, the amount of market discount in any period would be the product of (1) the total remaining amount of market discount and (2) a fraction, the numerator of which is the amount of stated interest paid in the period and the denominator of which is the total amount of stated interest remaining to be paid on the debt instrument as of the beginning of the period. Presumably, if the instrument bears interest at a floating rate based on an index, a constant value for the index in the present and future periods would be assumed.

77 In a case of an obligation that was not issued with original-issue discount, the issuer would not ordinarily notify investors of the prepayment assumption that would apply under the PAC method and it is not clear how that assumption would be determined in practice.

78 For a description of these instruments, see note 53 above.

79 Non-governmental obligations that are merely guaranteed by the United States or a US-sponsored agency would not be considered obligations of a government for this purpose.

80 See Internal Revenue Service Private Letter Ruling 8724035 (16 March 1987).

81 Sections 1271(a) and (b). In the case of certain banks and thrifts, any loss attributable to bond premium would be an ordinary loss. See the discussion of special rules for certain institutional investors in section 8.3.3 below.

82 A REMIC is subject to tax with respect to prohibited transactions. See note 27 above.

83 In the case of holders of equity interests that are individuals, the deductibility of the issuer's operating expenses may be limited under section 67. See note 9 above.

84 See section 163(e); Treasury Regulations section 1.163–7(b). The *de minimis* rule is described in note 46 above.

85 However, the revised issue price would be calculated without regard to the *de minimis* rule. See note 84 above.

86 Section 448 generally requires a partnership to use an accrual method if it has any partner that is a corporation not taxable under Subchapter S.

87 See section 706(b).

88 If a partnership terminates, it is considered to distribute its assets to its partners, including the purchasers who are considered to contribute those assets to a new partnership. Under the partnership tax rules, one effect of a termination is to bring the new partnership's inside basis in its assets into conformity with the partners' bases in their partnership interests.

89 It is not clear whether the sale of a partnership interest in a partnership whose sole assets are debt instruments would be viewed as a sale of debt instruments for the purposes of section 582(c).

90 Such organizations are taxable on income that is 'debt-financed' within the meaning of section 514, and because substantially all of the cost of the assets of an owner trust would be financed with debt, substantially all of the income of an owner would be treated as debt-financed income.

91 Limitations on the deductibility of losses are discussed in the text below.

92 Under section 860F(b)(2), a REMIC's initial aggregate basis in its assets equals the aggregate fair-market value of those assets immediately after their transfer to the REMIC. It appears that such fair-market value would be deemed to equal the sum of the issue prices of the regular interests and the residual interests. The 'issue price' of an interest in a REMIC generally would equal its initial offering price to the public (excluding brokers and other middlemen) if the interest is publicly offered, the price paid by the first purchaser of the interest if the interest is sold privately and the interest's fair-market value if the interest is retained by the sponsor of the REMIC. See section 860G(a)(10) (definition of issue price); Conference Report at II-231–II-232.

93 There is no similar rule that treats premium mortgages as if they are newly issued, allowing the REMIC to amortize such premium under section 171 even if the mortgages were originated before 28 September 1985. See section 8.3.1 above under the heading 'Treatment of discount and premium'.

94 Conference Report at II-233, footnote 15.

95 See section 8.3.3 below.

96 Under section 1091 (without regard to section 860F(d)), loss arising from the sale of a security may be deferred if 'substantially identical' securities are purchased within the period beginning thirty days before and ending thirty days after the date of sale.

97 As discussed above, the taxable income allocable to the holder of a REMIC residual interest (and in certain circumstances the holder of an

equity interest in an owner trust that is classified as a partnership) is not necessarily adjusted to reflect the holder's adjusted basis in the interest. Thus, the deferred loss would not necessarily be recovered over the life of the acquired interest but may be recognized only upon the disposition of that interest (subject to further application of the special wash-sale rule if that interest is a REMIC residual interest).

98 The conduit issuer may also have reinvestment earnings that are used to pay bonds and make equity distributions. The effect of reinvestment earnings on phantom income is considered below in note 100.

99 For simplicity, it is assumed in the discussion below that income from the mortgages held by the conduit issuer is determined under a constant-yield method similar to the PAC method, based on the yield to maturity of the mortgages calculated as if they were issued at the time they were purchased by the conduit issuer at a price equal to their cost to the conduit issuer. Similarly, it is assumed that deductions on the bonds are determined under the PAC method.

100 A mismatch between the economic life of cash distributions and the period of cost recovery for tax purposes may also arise where the value of an equity interest is attributable in part to a right to receive earnings of the conduit issuer from the reinvestment of mortgage payments. Although the right to receive distributions of such earnings may be viewed as an asset from the perspective of the equity investor, future reinvestment earnings would not be recognized to be a separate asset of the conduit issuer for tax purposes. Accordingly, the portion of the cost of the equity interest that is attributable to reinvestment earnings generally would be treated as an additional amount paid for the mortgages held by the conduit issuer and would be recovered over the life of the mortgages (rather than over the life of the reinvestment earnings stream).

101 As noted above, a loss may be a capital loss even for banks and thrifts if the conduit issuer is an owner trust that is classified as a partnership. In the case of taxpayers other than corporations, capital losses may be used to offset up to $3,000 of ordinary income.

102 This result is accomplished by providing in section 860E(a)(1) that the taxable income of the holder of a residual interest for any taxable year shall not be less than the excess inclusion for such year. Apparently, it would be possible to offset the resulting tax with any available credits, since they would not affect taxable income.

103 More precisely, with respect to any holder of a REMIC residual interest, the excess inclusion for any calendar quarter is the excess, if any, of (1) the income of such holder for that calendar quarter from the residual interest, representing a share of the taxable income of the REMIC, over (2) the sum of the 'daily accruals' (as defined below) for all days during

the calendar quarter on which the holder holds such residual interest. For this purpose, the daily accruals with respect to a residual interest are determined by allocating to each day in the calendar quarter its rateable portion of the product of the 'adjusted issue price' (as defined below) of the residual interest at the beginning of the calendar quarter and 120 per cent of the 'federal long-term rate' in effect at the time the residual interest was issued. For this purpose, the 'adjusted issue price' of a residual interest at the beginning of any calendar quarter equals the issue price of the residual interest, increased by the amount of daily accruals for all prior quarters, and decreased (but not below zero) by the aggregate amount of payments made on the residual interest before the beginning of such quarter. The federal long-term rate is an average of current yields on Treasury securities with a remaining term of greater than nine years, computed and published monthly by the Internal Revenue Service.

A (hopefully) unintended result of the definition of excess inclusion is that the amount of income that is treated as phantom income increases as the amount of economic income increases above 120 per cent of the federal long-term rate. For example, suppose that the federal long-term rate is 10 per cent, that the yield on a residual interest is 20 per cent, and cash is distributed each year with respect to that interest equal to the economic income accruing in that year. Even if phantom income was virtually nonexistent (for example, because there was only one class of regular interests), income earned in excess of 12 per cent of the adjusted issue price would be treated as an excess inclusion and, when distributed, would reduce the adjusted issue price for purposes of calculating excess inclusion in later periods.

104 The special relief for thrift institutions is limited to those institutions that are eligible to calculate deductions for additions to bad debt reserves under section 593.

105 Conference Report at II-235. There is no other guidance in the legislative history as to the likely content of any such regulations. It is likely that the proportionate value of the residual interest would be tested only once on its issue date (or, perhaps, on the pricing date), although this is not certain.

106 Income from a residual interest that is not an 'excess inclusion', as well as income from pass-through certificates, pay-through bonds and REMIC regular interests, should not be considered UBTI, unless the security is itself debt-financed.

107 The sponsor would allocate the adjusted basis in the mortgages, in proportion to fair-market value, between the interest in the mortgages that is sold (represented by the certificates that are sold) and all retained ownership interests in the mortgages (represented by any certificates

that are not sold, and any interest in the mortgages not transferred to the trust, including any rights to mortgage payments that are denominated as servicing fees but treated for tax purposes as a retained ownership interest).

108 For further discussion of the bond-stripping rules, see section 8.3.1 above under the heading 'Treatment of discount and premium'.

109 A complete discussion of the circumstances under which a purported sale will be recharacterized for tax purposes as an equity contribution, or an equity contribution will be recharacterized as a sale, is beyond the scope of this chapter. However, the likelihood of recharacterization of a purported sale would clearly be high if the seller owns a substantial equity stake in the issuer and the stated consideration paid in the sale has a value less than the fair-market value of the mortgages. The discussion below of the tax consequences of sales, or exchanges of mortgages for equity interests, assumes that it has first been determined that the transaction in question will be characterized for tax purposes as a sale or an exchange, respectively.

110 If the sponsor is considered to own a greater than 50 per cent interest in the capital or profits of the partnership owner trust, then loss would be disallowed under section 707(b). If a sale of the mortgages to the owner trust occurs as part of a single transaction in which equity interests in the owner trust are sold to investors unrelated to the sponsor, then consideration should be given to the possible characterization of the transaction as a sale by the sponsor to those investors of a partial ownership interest in the mortgages corresponding to their equity interest in the owner trust, followed by the contribution by the sponsor and those investors of their respective interests in the mortgages to the owner trust in exchange for equity interests. Under that characterization, the sponsor would generally recognize gain or loss only with respect to the initial sale of a partial interest in the mortgages to those investors, which is the same result that would obtain if the owner trust were classified as a grantor trust.

111 See section 721.

112 Treasury Regulations section 1.1502–13. Any deferred gain or loss would be recognized by the sponsor as principal payments are received on the mortgages by the issuer, or when the issuer sells the mortgages outside of the group filing consolidated returns, or the sponsor or issuer leaves the group.

113 See section 267(b)(3).

114 Under section 351, gain or loss is not recognized upon a transfer of property to a corporation solely in exchange for stock if the transferors as a group control the corporation (generally, own at least 80 per cent of its stock) immediately following the transfer. However, if a transferor

receives cash or other property in addition to stock, then the transferor
will recognize gain (but not loss) in the same manner as if the property
had been sold, except that the recognized gain will be limited to the
amount of cash or other property received.

115 See note 69 above.

116 Such a sale may also trigger the recognition of gains or losses from sales
of mortgages to the issuer that were previously deferred, as described
above.

117 If the REMIC is a segregated pool of mortgages that is not a legal entity,
the sponsor would be deemed to exchange the mortgages for the interests in the REMIC. Market discount on any market discount bond that
has accrued and not yet been included in income would be recognized
upon transfer of the bond to a REMIC. The rule requiring recognition in
section 1276(a)(1) applies 'notwithstanding any other provision of this
subtitle' and there is no explicit exception for transfers to REMICs. See
notes 69 and 115 above.

118 See Blue Book at 417.

119 The amount realized will reflect the fair-market value of the mortgages
increased by any arbitrage profit realized in the transaction (that is, the
excess of the value of interests in the REMIC over the aggregate value of
the mortgages and other assets transferred).

120 Blue Book at 417; Conference Report at II-230, footnote 8.

121 See section 860F(b)(1).

9

Securities Regulation, Due Diligence and Disclosure – US and UK Aspects

GREGORY M. SHAW and DAVID C. BONSALL

Chapter Outline

9.1 Introduction

By the very nature of the financing techniques and instruments statement, asset securitization invariably involves specialized consideration of applicable securities investment laws. This chapter addresses these specialized concerns from the vantage point of US federal securities laws (see section 9.2) and of the UK Financial Services Act of 1986 (section 9.3). Subject-matter focus under these laws are regulatory, 'due diligence' and disclosure aspects.

9.2 US Securities Law Aspects Governing Asset-Backed Securities

This section examines US federal securities laws and regulations that govern asset-backed securities. The scope of this work does not permit exploration of state securities laws or even all federal securities laws but instead focuses on the most important federal securities laws that have general applicability to most asset-backed securities.

Of primary importance is the Securities Act of 1933 (the ''33 Act') as it relates to registration and disclosure requirements in public securities offerings and the participants' liability for incomplete or misleading disclosure. In addition, because the '33 Act provides a due-diligence defence for disclosure violations, the investigation necessary to bring the various participants in the offering within this defence is examined. Other federal securities laws, including the Securities Exchange Act of 1934 (the ''34 Act'), the Trust Indenture Act of 1939 (the ''39 Act'), and the Investment Company Act of 1940 (the ''40 Act'), are discussed because they also have significant impact on the issuance of asset-backed securities.

9.2.1 *The Securities Act of 1933*

Introduction   The Securities Act of 1933 has two purposes: (1), to ensure investor access to material, financial and other information concerning securities offered for public sale, and (2), to prohibit misrepresentations, omissions, deceit and other fraudulent acts and practices in the sale of securities.

Section 5 of the Act mandates that the sale of, or offer to sell, a security, in interstate commerce, must be preceded by a registration statement that has been filed with, and declared effective by, the Securities and Exchange Commission (SEC). In addition, after the registration statement is declared effective, any offer to sell must be preceded or accompanied by a prospectus disclosing all material information. Section 7 and related regulations and schedules specify the information to be included in the registration. Failure to comply with the requirements of the '33 Act is unlawful, may be criminal, allows the purchaser to rescind the sale and subjects a wide variety of participants in the offering to civil liability.[1] Sections 3 and 4, although not affecting the anti-fraud provisions of the Act, exempt certain transactions and instruments from the registration requirements of the Act.

Definition of a security The precise definition of a security for the purposes of the '33 Act is somewhat elusive. The Act defines a security as:[2]

> unless the context otherwise requires . . . any note, stock, treasury stock, bond, debenture, evidence of indebtedness, certificate of interest or participation in any profit-sharing agreement, collateral-trust certificate . . . investment contract . . . or any instrument commonly know as a 'security', or any certificate of interest or participation in . . . any of the foregoing.

Two tests have been developed by the courts in applying this definition. In *SEC* v. *W.J. Howey Co.*,[3] the court focused on the economic realities of the transaction and considered whether the instrument was an investment contract. Four factors are considered in this analysis:[4]

> [A]n investment contract for the purposes of the Securities Act means a contract, transaction or scheme whereby a person [a] invests his money [b] in a common enterprise and [c] is led to expect profits [d] solely from the effort of the promoter or third party. . . .

While this definition has been broadened over time to encompass the 'countless and variable schemes devised by those who seek to use the money of others on the promise of profits',[5] it still forms a useful analytical framework.

A second test for whether an instrument is a security was enunciated in *Landreth Timber Co.* v. *Landreth*,[6] in which the court held

232   GREGORY M. SHAW AND DAVID C. BONSALL

that an instrument is a security if, first, it 'bears a title traditionally associated with' securities, and second, it shares significant characteristics associated with instruments of that title. However, even if the instrument does not meet the *Landreth* test for a security, it may be classified as one under the *Howey* test.[7]

Thus, for example, a mortgage note is generally not considered a security because there is no common enterprise; the lender looks to the property only as security for his loan and not as an investment intended to yield a return based on the efforts of a third party. Nonetheless, the subsequent sale of the mortgage may be considered the sale of a security. The greater the purchaser's reliance on the credit, services, expertise and representations of the seller, the more likely is it that the instrument will constitute a security. In general, retention of servicing obligations, the provision of credit support, the selection of the receivables, all typical in an asset-backed securities transaction, count in favour of the instrument meeting the definition of an investment contract.[8] Consequently, nearly all asset-backed securities will meet the definition of a security for the purposes of the '33 Act.

However, while it is well accepted that asset-backed securities are securities, a less certain issue is whether a credit-support agreement for asset-backed securities is also a security. In general, a guarantee of a security is itself a security and must be separately registered under the '33 Act unless the guarantee is in the form of a bank-issued letter of credit (LOC) or an insurance policy, either of which is considered an exempt security.[9] Whether registration is required may be a function of the structure of the transaction.[10]

More specifically, in one typical asset-backed securities transaction, receivables are deposited in a trust together with a credit-support agreement guaranteeing payment on the receivables up to a specified amount. Investors then buy participation certificates in the trust or 'pass-through certificates' entitling them to payments on the receivables and under the credit-support agreement. In this case, investors are purchasing a direct interest in the credit-support agreement and, unless the credit-support agreement is an exempt LOC or insurance policy, it must be registered. In addition, the SEC apparently holds the view that, even if the credit-support agreement is exempt, separate disclosure with respect to the entity providing the credit-support agreement, including financial statements, is required if the credit support is 'material' to the pass-through certificates. As a rule of thumb, the SEC considers a guarantee of more than 20 per cent of a receivables pool to be 'material' for this purpose.

In a second typical structure, the transaction is structured so that the credit support is merely an asset of this structure and is not sold to investors. Under this structure, registration of the credit-support agreement may not be required. Thus, for example, where a special support agreement exists and debt obligations secured by the receivables and by the support agreement are issued, the support agreement is not generally treated as a separate security. Here again, disclosure, including financial statements, with respect to the issuer of the credit support will be required if the credit support agreement is 'material'.

Notwithstanding the classification of an instrument as a security, an exception to the registration requirement of the '33 Act may apply either because of the nature of the security or the manner in which it is sold.

Exemptions to the requirements of the '33 Act Sections 3 and 4 of the '33 Act provide exemptions from the registration and prospectus (but not the anti-fraud) requirements of the '33 Act. Section 3 is primarily directed to exempting certain securities while section 4 exempts certain transactions.

(1) *Exempt securities.* Subsections 3(a)(2)–(8), which have been amended from time to time, list particular classes of securities exempt from the registration requirements both at the initial offering stage and on subsequent resale. These exemptions generally cover the issuance of securities by entities that are already regulated by other state and federal laws and, thus, do not need the additional regulation of the '33 Act.

Section 3(a)(2) exempts, *inter alia*, securities issued by the United States government and its agencies, state and local governments, banks (but not bank holding companies), certain industrial development bonds, interests and participation in common trust funds maintained by banks as investment vehicles in which the bank holds the assets as a fiduciary and interests in collective trust funds maintained by banks for programmes qualified under section 401 of the Internal Revenue Code.

While section 3(a)(2) does not explicitly include securities representing beneficial ownership interest in exempt securities (that is, 'participation certificates'), the SEC has, on occasion, taken the position that under narrow circumstances, such securities are exempt.[11] An important factor in the determination is the similarity of the investment experience of a holder of the exempt security and a holder of the security representing a participation certificate in the exempt security. If rights accorded the holders of the participation certificates or payments made to the holders of the participation certificates differ in any significant respect from those experienced by a holder of the exempt security, then the participation certificates will not be exempt.

The section 3(a)(2) exemption for securities issued or guaranteed by the United States and federal, state and local authorities applies to recourse obligations issued or guaranteed by the Government National Mortgage Association (GNMA, sometimes called 'Ginnie Mae'), the Federal Home Loan Mortgage Corporation (FHLMC) and the Federal National Mortgage Association (FNMA).

The section 3(a)(2) exemption for banks applies only to securities that are recourse obligations of the bank. Pass-through certificates originated by a bank, where a bank deposits the receivables and services them but does not guarantee their payment, do not fall within the exemption. On the other hand, securities of any issuer, including pass-through certificates sold by a non-bank, which are fully guaranteed by a bank, through a letter of credit or otherwise, are exempt. Thus, for example, pass-through certificates sold by a finance company and representing interests in mobile home loans supported by a bank-issued LOC guaranteeing the entire payment obligation, will fall within this exemption.

Section 3(a)(5) exempts securities issued by state and federal thrift institutions. Unlike the section 3(a)(2) exemption, this exemption does not apply to securities which are only guaranteed by thrift institutions.

Section 3(a)(8) exempts insurance policies issued by a corporation subject to either state or federal insurance regulation. Here again, as in the case of thrifts, but unlike the section 3(a)(2) exemption, this exemption does not apply to securities which are only guaranteed by insurance policies even if fully guaranteed. The exemption does, however, apply to an insurance policy which is issued as a credit-support device for a security.

(2) *Exempt transactions.*   Section 4 exempts certain transactions from the registration requirements of section 5. Resales of securities issued

under an exempt transaction are not themselves exempt unless otherwise covered by an exemption.

Section 4(1) exempts transactions by 'any person other than an issuer, underwriter, or dealer'.[12] But for this exemption, every sale of a security, even one by an individual investor, would be subject to the registration requirements.

Transactions 'not involving any public offering' by an issuer, so-called 'private placements', are exempted by section 4(2).[13] Such securities are, however, considered 'restricted' securities for the purposes of Rule 144[14] and may not be traded freely. This restriction has a significant impact on the pricing of securities because the limited liquidity of securities considered 'restricted' has resulted in their being priced lower than otherwise equivalent publicly traded securities. The recently adopted Rule 144A will result in fewer restrictions on the trading of such securities and hence is expected to reduce the pricing differential between private and public offerings.

What constitutes a 'public offering' is a function of a number of factors including whether the offer is made on a limited basis to a selected number of persons and not pursuant to a general public solicitation; whether the persons to whom the securities are sold are sufficiently sophisticated so as to be able to make an informed decision absent a registration statement and prospectus; and access by purchasers to sufficient information of the type that would normally be contained in a registration statement.

Guidance on the standards for private placement is provided by SEC Regulation D, a non-exclusive safe-harbour provision comprised of Rules 501–8. Regulation D also specifies information which must be included in the private placement.[15] Section 504 exempts sales which, among other things, do not exceed $1,000,000 and which are regulated by state law. Section 505 exempts sales not exceeding $5,000,000, to less than thirty-five purchasers by an issuer that is not an investment company. Section 506 exempts sales to less than thirty-five non-accredited purchasers or an unlimited number of 'accredited investors' without regard to the dollar amount, provided certain other conditions are met.[16]

Institutional investors are the major purchasers of asset-backed securities and most institutional investors are accredited investors. Accordingly, under section 506, it is often possible to sell asset-backed securities to institutional investors without registration.

The owner of securities acquired in a private placement is limited in

236 GREGORY M. SHAW AND DAVID C. BONSALL

236 GREGORY M. SHAW AND DAVID C. BONSALL

the manner in which he can subsequently dispose of the securities. He can sell it (1) pursuant to a registered offering, (2) pursuant to a further private placement, (3) to the public in a transaction not involving a distribution as defined by Rule 144, or (4) to certain institutional investors in transactions that do not constitute public offerings pursuant to Rule 144A.[17]

Section 4(5), enacted in 1975 for the purpose of facilitating a secondary market in mortgages, exempts mortgage-related securities originated by savings and loan associations, savings banks and banks. However, the exemption afforded by this section is limited to, among other things, purchases for the purchaser's account only, of more than $250,000, in cash paid, within sixty days. In addition, the mortgagee must be either a commercial bank, a thrift, or approved by the Secretary of Housing and Urban Development (HUD). These limitations, along with several others, on the availability of the exemption of section 4(5), have limited the utility of the exemption.

The registration process Section 5 of the '33 Act, and related regulations, govern the procedure with which the registration process must comply. There are essentially three phases to the process. The first phase is the pre-filing period, which covers the period between the time there is an agreement or understanding to issue and sell securities, and the filing of the registration. During this period, there can be no offers to sell or buy by means of a prospectus or otherwise.[18] The next phase, the 'waiting period', is the time between the filing of the registration statement and its being declared effective. During this period, it is unlawful to 'sell such security . . . [by] any prospectus or otherwise', but offers are not prohibited.[19] Finally, after the registration is declared 'in effect', the securities may be sold.[20]

During the pre-filing period, the security cannot be offered or sold, prospective purchasers cannot be contacted, a prospectus cannot be used, and prospective underwriters cannot be identified. However, Rule 135 provides that during the pre-filing period a notice of a proposed offering which states that the offering will only be made by prospectus and contains no more than '(a) the name of the issuer, (b) the title, amount and basic terms of the securities . . . (c) the amount of the offering, if any, to be made by selling security holders, (d) the anticipated timing of the offer, and (e) a brief statement of the manner and purpose of the offering without naming the underwriters' may be used.[21] In addition, 'preliminary negotiations or agreements between an issuer . . . and any underwriter or among underwriters who are or are to be in privity of contract with an issuer' are permitted.[22] However, negotiations and agreements between the issuer and/or underwriter and the selling group are prohibited.

While sales are prohibited during the waiting period, offers to sell are permitted. Nonetheless, section 5(b)(1) limited such offers to either oral ones or ones pursuant to a statutory prospectus defined by section 10. During this period, underwriters commonly obtain so-called 'indications of interest' or non-binding 'circles' from prospective purchasers and this information is used to price the issue.

Any 'offer to sell' prior to effective registration, in addition to being unlawful, will entitle the purchaser to rescind the transaction, even if he receives the final prospectus after the effective date and accepts the offer on or after that date.[23] Consequently, great caution must be exercised in the pre-effective registration period to ensure that any publicity or communications do not constitute an offer to sell.

Once the registration is 'in effect' sales are permitted. However, such sales must be preceded or accompanied by a prospectus that meets the requirements of section 10(a). Other sales materials may also be used, provided they are accompanied, or preceded, by a prospectus.

Disclosure in the registration statement and prospectus   Both legal and business requirements govern the scope of disclosure in an asset-backed securities offering. The legal requirements are primarily those set by the '33 Act and the various regulations and schedules thereunder. The business requirement is to produce a selling document that sets forth sufficient details of the economics of the offering and the risks associated with the offering to enable a potential investor to judge the merits of the offering.

The person or entity responsible for the filing of the registration statement is a function of the structure of the transaction. Generally, asset-backed securities fall under one of two structures: (1) pass-through certificates, issued by a trust, representing the holder's undivided *pro rata* interest in a pool of receivables (including the right to receive principal and interest payments), deposited into the trust by an entity, which in most cases is the originator of the receivables (the 'depositor'), or (2) debt securities representing the obligation of a special-purpose corporation created by the depositor or a third party for the sole purpose of acquiring and financing the receivables. In both cases, the trust or the special-purpose corporation, the vehicle actually issuing the securities, is 'bankruptcy remote' from the depositor and, therefore, the creditors of the depositor have no claim to the assets in the issuing vehicle in the event of the depositor's bankruptcy and, conversely, the depositor is not directly liable on the securities except to the extent of any limited guarantee which the depositor may provide.

Under the '33 Act, for purposes of filing formalities and liability for false or misleading disclosure, the depositor in a pass-through transaction is considered the issuer.[24] In the case of a special-purpose corporation issuing debt securities, the special-purpose corporation is the 'issuer' under the '33 Act. In either case, only limited disclosure, and no financial statements, with respect to the depositor is required because the depositor is not obligated on the securities.

The primary disclosure in an asset-backed securities offering statement relates not to the issuing vehicle (which is normally a shell entity) or the depositor, but rather to the quality of the underlying asset and credit support held by the trust or special-purpose corporation. Moreover, the disclosure statements generally omit historic financial information on the issuing vehicle simply because the issuing vehicle has no prior financial history to be reported.

Notwithstanding these and other unique disclosure concerns in asset-backed securities, the general disclosure rules and regulations under the '33 Act are applicable.

Section 7 and Schedule A of the '33 Act specify information that must be disclosed in the registration statement. Generally, required information includes (1) the name of the issuer and underwriters, (2) the issuer's place of incorporation and principal business, (3) the names and addresses of the issuer's directors and certain officers, (4) other information related to the issuer's business, (5) the ownership and nature of the issuer's securities, and (6) financial statements of the issuer certified by independent public accountants. A form of prospectus must be included with the registration statement and usually forms the major part of the registration statement.

The scope of the disclosure is specified in detail by Regulation S-K. However, the SEC has developed a number of standard forms that specify, depending on the issuer and the nature of the offering, which information listed in Regulation S-K must be included in the registration statement. The most commonly used forms for asset-backed securities are Forms S-11, S-3 and S-1.

Form S-11, which is used for the registration of mortgage-backed securities, is specified for real estate investment trusts or other issuers whose primary business is acquiring or holding for investment, real estate, interests in real estate, or companies primarily engaged in real estate investment. Consequently, the S-11 disclosure is directed to the nature of the issuer's real estate investment practices and the nature of the real estate interests. In most mortgage-backed securities offerings, however, the issuing vehicle did not exist prior to the offering and much of the information required by Form S-11, such as that relating to the financial status, investment policies and history of the issuer, does not exist and is therefore omitted. Instead, the registration statement will describe the securities to be issued and any related agreements in detail and will otherwise focus on such matters as the loan underwriting and servicing policies of the depositor, historical mortgage delinquency, prepayment and loss experience and a description of any credit-support agreements and their provider.

Other asset-backed issuers generally use Form S-1, which, while specifying the most extensive disclosure of all the forms, has, in practice, and with the informal approval of the SEC, been limited to the same general scope of disclosure made in an S-11 mortgage-backed securities registration.

Outside of the asset-backed securities area, it has often been advantageous, where possible, to use Form S-3, which requires less extensive disclosure than either S-1 or S-11 and may allow the registrant to incorporate by reference information from both past and future fillings. In the area of asset-backed securities, Form S-3 has had only limited advantage over Form S-1 because disclosure with respect to the specific assets, which represent the bulk of the disclosure, must be included in either case. The principal advantage of Form S-3 in asset-backed securities offerings is that it permits the use of 'shelf registration' (discussed below). The availability of Form S-3 depends on both the registrant and transaction meeting certain requirements. For example, one condition is that the registrant, or its parent, has a class of securities registered pursuant to the '34 Act and has complied with certain filing requirements of the '34 Act for the past three years. In addition, there are transaction requirements for the use of Form S-3 which are a function of the type of security. For example, non-convertible debt or preferred securities must be 'investment grade securities', that is, ones rated as such by a recognized rating authority.

In contrast to the individualized registration for each offering under the standard registration procedure, Rule 415 permits, under certain circumstances, the option of 'shelf registration'. This procedure enables securities to be registered for offerings to be made on a continued or delayed basis without the need to file and have approved a registration statement for each offering, thus giving issuers immediate access to the market without the delay of the SEC approval process.

Shelf registration is available for certain asset-backed securities, including 'mortgage-related securities' and corporate debt issued by a corporation which qualifies for use of Form S-3. A mortgage-related security is defined in the Secondary Mortgage Market Enhancement Act of 1984 (SMMEA) as one which is rated in one of the two highest rating categories by at least one nationally recognized rating agency and either (1) represents ownership of notes (or certificates of interest or participation in such notes) 'directly secured by a first lien on a single parcel of real estate . . . upon which is located a dwelling or mixed residential and commercial structure' that were originated by one or more specified lenders, or (2) is secured by and provides for principal payments in relation to such notes. Thus, mortgage-backed securities backed by loans secured by mortgages on single-family homes or mixed residential properties and providing for pass-through payments qualify.[25] Pass-through certificates that do not represent an interest in mortgage receivables, however, do not qualify.

Liability for false or misleading disclosure and the due-diligence defence   A private right of action is provided by section 11 of the '33 Act, if, at the time the registration statement became effective, the offering material contained 'an untrue statement of a material fact or omitted to state a material fact required to be stated therein or necessary to make the statements therein not misleading'.[26] Any person acquiring a security registered under the registration statement (this includes both initial purchasers and anyone who purchased the security subsequently in the open market) has a cause of action under this section. The plaintiff need prove only that the statement was false or misleading. The plaintiff is not required to prove that the defendant knew that the statement was, or intended it to be, misleading. The plaintiff need not even show that he relied on the misstatement or omission or was even aware of it at the time he acquired the security.[27]

Liability extends to (1) every person who signed the registration statement (including the issuer); (2) every person who was a director (or functional equivalent of one) of the issuer, (3) every person who is or will become a director (or functional equivalent of one) of the issuer; (4) every 'expert' (for example, accountant or engineer) who has consented to be named as having prepared or certified any part of the registration statement or any statement or valuation used in the registration statement; and (5) every underwriter.

Notwithstanding the low threshold of liability, all the potential defendants, except the issuer, have, as a defence, that they exercised due diligence in compiling the registration statement. Thus, if the alleged misleading statement or omission was not made on the authority of an expert, the defendant will not be liable if he can show that he 'had, after reasonable investigation, reasonable ground to believe and did believe, at the time . . . the registration statement became effective, that the statements therein were true and that there was no omission to state a material fact required to be stated therein or necessary to make the statement therein not misleading . . .'.[28] The non-expert will additionally not be liable for omissions or misleading statements related to expert information if he 'had no reasonable grounds to believe, and did not believe, at the time the registration statement became effective that [the expertized material] did not fairly represent the statement of the expert'.[29] An expert, in addition to having the same defence of due diligence as the non-expert, may additionally avoid liability if the misleading part of the registration statement 'did not fairly represent his statement as an expert . . .'.[30] In all cases, the standard for reasonable investigation and grounds for belief is that 'required of a prudent man in the management of his own property'.[31]

Section 12 provides a private right of action for the purchaser of a security against anyone who violates section 5 or who sells, or offers to sell, a security by means of an oral statement or prospectus which is false or misleading. The plaintiff may recover the consideration paid for the security, with interest, upon tender of the security, or damages if he no longer owns the security. As under section 12, the defendant will not be liable if he can sustain the due-diligence defence.

Accordingly, both imperatives of good practice and the avoidance of civil and criminal liability require that all those potentially liable in the offering conduct a thorough investigation into all material aspects of the transaction.[32]

The scope of the due-diligence investigation is a direct function of the disclosure made in the registration statement. Because the most significant aspect of an asset-backed security is the quality of the underlying assets themselves, the primary focus of disclosure, and hence the due-diligence investigation, is on the assets. While the due-diligence investigation must be adapted to the specifics of each trans-action, the following general observation can be made.

In order to assess the quality of the receivables, a due-diligence investigation commonly may begin with an investigation of the manner in which the originator of the receivables issues credit. The object of the investigation is to gain an understanding of the credit policies as well as to verify that these policies are in fact followed at the various levels of the credit-solicitation and -issuing process. In many cases, there will be significant departures from standard procedures. This is particularly true when the issuance of credit is not highly centralized. Where such departures are found, it is important to ascertain their impact on the receivables portfolio.

For example, the manner in which the credit-card customers are selected and solicited is relevant to the assessment of the likelihood of delinquencies and losses. Reliance by the card issuer on mass mailings of 'pre-approved' applications to solicit customers is likely to result in significantly higher loss levels than reliance on review of individual credit applications using credit-scoring systems and credit-verification procedures. A review of collection and write-off policies and pro-cedures will provide further insight into the quality of the receivables portfolio. The age of a receivables portfolio is also important in asses-sing potential losses. Most credit-card issuers report a definite trend in losses on new portfolios, with low losses initially as credit-card holders 'charge up' their card, followed by a period of many losses as the worst credits in the portfolio default and with an eventual flattening out or even decline in losses, as the worst credits are eliminated from the portfolio. These and similar concerns must be investigated and disclosed.

Where the number of individual underlying assets is relatively small (for example, in a mortgage-backed security), an individualized and detailed review of each of the receivables is often undertaken. Thus, for example, in the case of mortgage loans, the mortgage file contain-ing all the mortgage-related papers (for example, appraisals, title insurance, credit reports and the mortgage note), or at least a file containing the most important papers, may be reviewed by the under-writer, the underwriter's counsel or an independent accountant. In addition, these files typically will be delivered to the trustee or custodian under the pooling and servicing agreement, who will have a limited time, usually thirty to sixty days, in which to examine the mortgages. In the event that a mortgage is found to be defective, the trustee or custodian can require the depositor to repurchase or replace the defective mortgage.

In contrast, where loan sizes are smaller and the number of receivables larger (for example, automotive loans and credit-card receivables), individual review of each loan account is often not practical. Consequently, it is common to review in detail only a representative random sample of the total pool. Additional problems are presented in securitization of revolving credit-card accounts because there is no 'loan file' containing evidence of each credit-card charge and payment, but only an electronic record of the account activity.

In nearly all cases, each receivable will be recorded in some form of computer database capable of generating a schedule of the receivable portfolio. Verification of the correspondence between the randomly selected entries in the database and the actual loan files is usually performed as a check of the accounting systems where possible. In addition, a detailed review of the receivable pool record-keeping system is performed by an independent accountant who typically issues an accountants' comfort letter which includes verification of account information with respect to the receivable portfolio.

Because the quality of the servicer is so important, an in-depth review of the capabilities of the loan-servicing systems is commonly undertaken.[33] The capability of the system to handle all matters affecting cash flow to security-holders including partial prepayments, late charges, insurance charges, rebates on prepayments, warranty repayments and any other matters likely to impact on the reliability and timing of reporting of payments is particularly important.

The due-diligence investigation by legal counsel to the underwriters will often include a review of significant agreements of the issuer, particularly as they may relate to the receivables and their servicing and verification of compliance under state and federal laws of the loan-solicitation, documentation and collection procedures.[34] Counsel will also review procedures used by the depositor to perfect its interest in any collateral securing the receivables and, because there is a pledge or sale of assets to the issuing entity, underwriter's counsel typically reviews the transfer documentation and reviews an opinion of depositor's counsel that the necessary actions have been taken to perfect the issuer's interest in the assets pursuant to state law.

9.2.2 The Securities Exchange Act of 1934

The Securities Exchange Act of 1934 (the ''34 Act'), as amended, through the imposition of periodic reporting requirements on the issuer (and officers, directors and certain large shareholders of issuers), carries forward the disclosure philosophy of the '33 Act to post-distribution trading of securities on national exchanges. In addition, through a series of amendments and judicial interpretations, the '34 Act's coverage has been extended to such additional areas as proxy solicitation and disclosure, market manipulation, fraud (including insider trading), and tender offers.

Notwithstanding the broad disclosure requirements imposed by the '34 Act, the SEC has discretion under section 12(h) of the '34 Act to grant exemptions to these requirements where such an exemption is 'not inconsistent with the public interest or the protection of investors'. Pursuant to this authority, the SEC has, on several occasions, exempted asset-backed securities issuers from the full reporting and disclosure requirements of the '34 Act.

As is the case under the '33 Act, some of the disclosure with respect to traditional corporate issuers is not relevant to an issuing vehicle for asset-backed securities. Instead, issuers are required to file periodic reports relating to the assets and covering such matters as loan balances, delinquencies, prepayments and material changes such as changes in servicing arrangements and draws under credit-support agreements.

Because the '34 Act has a number of substantive provisions that relate only to equity securities, a more problematic issue under the '34 Act has been whether pass-through certificates should be treated as debt or equity. In form, participation certificates are equity. However, because they entitle the holder to payment of a fixed amount plus interest, they are marketed and traded like debt securities. The SEC takes the position that pass-through certificates are equity securities but has nonetheless exempted them from a number of the restrictions that apply generally to equity securities. For example, the SEC has provided exemptions from section 16's reporting requirements and liability for short-swing profits by certain insiders and has limited the application of '34 Act rules relating to self-tenders.

9.2.3 *The Trust Indenture Act of 1939*

The Trust Indenture Act of 1939 (the "39 Act') is intended to supplement the '33 Act by regulation of the relationship between investors, issuers and indenture trustees in connection with the issuance of debt securities. The '39 Act's primary focus is on the regulation of the conduct and duties of trustees under debt indentures.[35] The indenture which sets forth these rights and duties is filed, along with the '33 Act registration, for non-exempt debt securities. The provisions of the '39 Act govern an indenture primarily to impose obligations on the trustee to act prudently on behalf of securityholders, particularly in the event of default. Such matters as eligibility and qualification of the trustee, the level of care to be exercised by the trustee, limitations on preferential collection of claims against the obligor by the trustee and reporting requirements for the trustee are covered by the '39 Act.

Most securities that are exempt from the registration requirement of the '33 Act are also exempt from the '39 Act. More surprisingly, the '39 Act exempts 'any certificate of interest or participation in two or more securities having substantially different rights and privileges'. Accordingly, pass-through certificates that represent an interest in a pool of dissimilar receivables are exempt, even though the receivables might be considered debt securities.[36]

Any person who makes a false statement in the indenture may be civilly liable to any purchaser of securities under the indenture who relied on such a misstatement unless the defendant can show that he acted in good faith and without knowledge of the misstatement. Wilful violations of the '39 Act are subject to criminal penalties.

9.2.4 *The Investment Company Act of 1940*

The Investment Company Act of 1940 (the "40 Act') imposes complex registration and post-registration regulatory requirements on companies engaged primarily in the business of investing and reinvesting in securities of other companies. In a registration required under the '40 Act, the issuer is required to disclose, among other things, detailed financial information similar to that required under the '33 Act, as well as its investment objectives and policies. In addition, through a complex set of regulations, the '40 Act imposes substantive restrictions on the conduct of investment companies covered by the

'40 Act. Most issuers of asset-backed securities, as they are normally structured, would be unable to comply with the substantive requirements of the '40 Act and, as a result, they must rely on an exemption from the '40 Act.

The '40 Act defines an investment company as, among other things, one which 'is engaged or proposes to engage in the business of investing, reinvesting, owning, holding, or trading in securities, and owns or proposes to acquire investment securities' exceeding 40 per cent of its total assets, excluding government securities.[37] In addition, the SEC takes the view that companies that merely 'own or hold' securities constitute investment companies under section 3(a)(3).

Further, the staff of the SEC has taken the position that the definition of investment securities, for purposes of the '40 Act's applicability, is even broader than the definition of securities under the '33 Act. For example, for the purposes of the '40 Act, mortgages (and many other common receivables not considered securities under the '33 Act) would be considered securities. Consequently, absent an exemption, all issuing vehicles for asset-backed securities would be investment companies because substantially all of their assets consist of receivables considered to be securities.

An issuer may be exempted from the requirements of the '40 Act either because of a specific exemption under the '40 Act or because the SEC has provided a discretionary exemption under section 6 of the '40 Act. Section 6, among other things, allows the SEC to exempt an investment company, which would otherwise fall within the requirement of the Act, when such an exemption is 'necessary and appropriate'.[38] The statutory exemptions most relevant to asset-backed securities are those under sections 3(c)(1), 3(c)(3) and 3(c)(5)(A) through (C).

Section 3(c)(1) exempts private offerings by an issuer whose outstanding securities, except for short-term (less than 270 days) debt securities, in total, are beneficially owned by less than 100 persons. Although this exemption has been used by asset-backed securities issuers, the limitation to less than 100 persons, which continues throughout the life of the issuer, has the effect of limiting the liquidity of the securities and has significantly limited the utility of the exemption.

Section 3(c)(3) exempts, among other entities, banks, insurance companies, savings and loans, common trust funds, or similar funds, maintained by a bank exclusively for the collective investment of moneys contributed to the bank in its capacity as a fiduciary. However, this exemption does not apply where a section 3(c)(3) entity merely establishes a subsidiary entity to issue obligations which are non-recourse obligations of the parent.

Sections 3(c)(5)(A) through (C) provide the exemptions relied on most frequently by issuers of asset-backed securities. These sections exempt:

> [a]ny person who is not engaged in the business of issuing redeemable securities, face-amount certificates . . . and who is primarily engaged in one or more of the following businesses: (A) Purchasing or otherwise acquiring notes, drafts, acceptances, open accounts receivable, and other obligations representing part or all of the sales price of merchandise, insurance, and services; (B) making loans to manufacturers, wholesalers, and retailers of, and to prospective purchasers of, specified merchandise, insurance and services; and (C) purchasing or otherwise acquiring mortgages and other liens on and interests in real estate.

The SEC interpretation of the 3(c)(5)(A) and (B) exemptions, which owe their existence to the lobbying efforts of the factoring industry, requires, as a threshold matter, that the issuer be engaged in the business of merchandise sales financing. Under this interpretation, it is not sufficient that the issuer owns loans secured by merchandise, insurance or services, but instead the loans must arise in connection with the sale of the merchandise, insurance or services. Accordingly, while subsections (A) and (B) have been applied to issuers which own a pool of credit-card receivables, the exemptions may only apply to credit-card receivables arising from the sale of goods or services and may not apply to receivables which arise from 'cash advances' to the cardholder.

Subsection (C) covers most issuers of mortgage-backed securities. The SEC, however, has taken the position that an issuer which owns securities, such as pass-through certificates, which themselves represent an interest in mortgages does not fall within this exemption. The theory behind this distinction is that an issuer which owns pass-through certificates, owns securities (not mortgages), even though the pass-through certificates may represent ownership of mortgages. The SEC has permitted an exception to this rule in the case of the 'whole-pool' GNMA, FNMA and FHLMC pass-through certificates. A 'whole-pool' pass-through certificate is a certificate that represents a 100 per cent participation interest in the underlying pool of mortgages. The SEC is currently considering a revised rule which would broaden this exception so that substantially all GNMA, FNMA and FHLMC pass-through certificates would qualify for the 3(c)(5)(C) exemption, whether or not they were 'whole-pool' certificates.

9.3 UK Securities Law Aspects Governing Asset-Backed Securities

9.3.1 Securities Regulation

The Financial Services Act 1986 Any analysis of securities regulation in the United Kingdom must necessarily start with the Financial Services Act 1986. This Act has generated considerable controversy and discussion on both sides of the Atlantic. The Act attempts to cover an enormous area, providing a statutory background against which the UK securities and related markets operate while retaining flexibility to deal with particular circumstances and sectors as well as accommodating developments which may occur. The Financial Services Act can certainly be regarded as a dynamic piece of legislation in every sense of the word – the Act, the supporting legislation and rules and everybody's thinking on the Act are continually developing in the light of experience. This is no less true in the field of mortgage securitization than in many of the other areas with which the Act is concerned.

(1) *Scope of the Act and the need for authorization.* The basic approach adopted by the Act is to prohibit the unauthorized carrying on of investment business in the United Kingdom. It is necessary, therefore, to analyse whether any aspect of the transaction involves 'investments', whether the particular activity involved constitutes 'investment business' and, as a result, whether authorization is required under the Act. If authorization is required but is not obtained, not only would a criminal offence be committed but there would be civil sanctions also. For example, a contract might be unenforceable and any money paid under it could have to be returned.

If one examines the typical structure involved in mortgage securitizations, one can see that they involve a sale by the originator of the mortgages to a special-purpose vehicle. The portfolio of mortgages over the residential properties of the borrowers are sold together with an assignment of various rights that the mortgage originator is holding as further or collateral security for the mortgage debt. Most mortgage securitizations to date have involved endowment mortgages where the mortgage borrower has taken out a life policy that is designed to repay the principal of the mortgage while he pays only interest during the twenty-five-year term of the mortgage. The mortgage originator takes a security interest in these endowment life policies and also has the benefit of other insurance protection if, for example, the house burns down. The special-purpose issuer issues its securities to investors in the Euromarkets and uses the proceeds of the issue to purchase the mortgages and associated rights. As security for the notes the issuer creates, in favour of a trustee for the noteholders, security interests over the property transferred to it. The issuer probably has no employees and therefore retains the mortgage originator as the administrator of the issuer's own business as well as of the mortgage portfolio.

(2) *Nature of investments and investment activities.* Any mortgage securitization will, therefore, involve mortgages, endowment life policies, other insurance policies, notes issued in the Euromarkets and different types of security interest. Potentially there are several types of investments which fall within the eleven categories of investment set out in Part I of Schedule 1 to the Act and several types of activity which, *prima facie*, fall within the five different paragraphs of Part II of Schedule 1 describing activities which can constitute investment business and therefore require authorization under the Act.

This section does not propose to discuss how crucial aspects were left unclear by the original drafting of the Act. Suffice to say that since the Act came into force in April 1988, the basic activity of mortgage lending as well as most of the arrangements made for generating mortgage business were excluded from the type of investment activities requiring authorization under the Act. However, it is still unclear whether a transfer by the mortgage originator to the issuer of its right as mortgagee in endowment life policies is a regulated investment activity. An endowment life policy is an investment within paragraph 10 of Part I. The mortgagee may also have a separate right in this investment which is itself an investment within paragraph 11. Transferring these investments to the issuer could be 'dealing in investments', which is a regulated investment activity. Fortunately, Part III of Schedule 1 provides various exclusions and it is likely that in most cases one (or more) of these exclusions will apply so that authorization will not be necessary for the mortgage originator or the issuer purely because of the transfer.

(3) *Collective investment scheme concerns.* Will the issuer require authorization because of its activity of issuing its own securities? In the public note issues so far, all the notes have been structured to be essentially full-recourse debt obligations of the issuer with the investor's right to payment being secured on all the assets of the issuer. This has important consequences both in the tax field, which is addressed elsewhere in this volume,[39] here, and in the context of the Act. It is now clear that the mere act of issuing these notes does not itself require authorization, although the notes are debentures which fall within one of the defined categories of investments[40] to which certain provisions of the Act apply. There had been concern that the nature of the security meant that noteholders were participants in a collective investment scheme that is subject to totally different regulations governing the operation and promotion of such schemes. These regulations would have made these issues very much more difficult, if not impossible.

However, as issuers and their advisers are continually devising new structures, it is necessary to examine the language of the relevant exemption (now in paragraph 35(b)(i) of Schedule 1) to see that it applies in the context of the particular transaction. The paragraph provides that it will not be a collective investment scheme if 'the arrangements under which the rights or interests of the participants are represented by investments falling within paragraph 2 of Schedule 1 to the Act which are issued by a single body corporate which is not an open-ended investment company'. Most issuers will not be open-ended investment companies as defined by the Act but the securities that they issue may not always fall within paragraph 2 of Schedule 1. One reason for this is that many mortgage securitizations involve the use of a permanent global note with no definitive notes ever being formally issued. Definitive notes are clearly within paragraph 2 but it is arguable that a global note may only be an investment within a different paragraph, namely paragraph 5. This will depend on its terms.

A further concern is that the rights of the actual investors might be said to be represented by their contractual arrangements with the two main clearance systems, Euroclear and CEDEL, and not by the investors in fact holding debentures which contain rights enforceable against the issuer. This concern is relevant not just to mortgage securitizations but to virtually all Euromarket issues. Nevertheless, the generally held view is that these concerns are only theoretical and the legislation was certainly not meant to apply to this type of transaction. It illustrates, though, the difficulty which the Act poses as its terms are so often unclear when analysed against particular circumstances.

(4) *Unsolicited calls.*   There are many other aspects of the Act that need to be considered, although they are common to all types of issues of securities, not just those involved in securitization. For example, the lead and co-managers of the issue will require to be authorized as they will definitely be involved in regulated investment activities, namely underwriting and arranging for the issue. While this will not be a concern to most investment and merchant banks operating in the Euromarkets, because they are already authorized, some of the managers may be based abroad and do not have authorization already. If they are not operating from any office or place of business in the United Kingdom, it may be possible for them to take advantage of the exemptions for overseas persons contained in Part IV of Schedule 1.

As a general point, all managers will need to take great care over the actual mechanics of obtaining the mandate and publicizing the issue. Whether a non-UK manager can take advantage of the overseas-persons exemption depends in part upon his not having broken section 56. That section provides that no one (whether or not authorized) shall in the course of or in consequence of an unsolicited call enter into an investment agreement with the person on whom the call is made. Therefore, the subscription agreement or the terms of a mandate letter could be unenforceable if any manager made an unsolicited call on the mortgage originator or on the issuer which was not permitted by the rules or regulations applicable to the person making the call. These rules and regulations are in fact fairly generous and this should not be a problem in practice. However, it is a point to bear in mind particularly if you are the lawyer rendering an opinion to the managers on the enforceability of the subscription agreement.

(5) *Restrictions on advertising.*   Another area that always needs to be carefully considered is the manner in which the issue is advertised. The basic restriction is contained in section 57. Subject to various

exceptions, no person other than an authorized person shall issue or cause to be issued an investment advertisement in the United Kingdom unless its contents have been approved by an authorized person. There will invariably be an information memorandum or other document outlining the terms of the notes and describing the mortgage portfolio. This will clearly be an investment advertisement within the meaning of the Act. The managers who are authorized persons should therefore issue the document and also approve it, given that the issuer or the mortgage originator could be said to be causing the document to be issued. The question of responsibility for information in that document will be discussed later.

There are various exceptions to section 57 including advertisements issued in circumstances specified by regulations made by the Secretary of State. As a result, the typical 'selling restriction' found in subscription agreements and in offering circulars specifies that no documents must be issued or passed on to persons other than those of a kind described in Article 9(3) of the Financial Services Act 1986 (Investment Advertisements) (Exemptions) Order 1988. Briefly, that Article specifies the sort of people who would be the professional investors to whom these types of securities are of interest.

Listing: London and Luxembourg exchanges   The restrictions on advertising just described apply to all the documents involved that constitute investment advertisements. This will include invitation telexes and may include other types of circulars. It may be, however, that the offering circular itself can be more widely distributed. This depends on whether the issue is listed. In order to achieve the widest range of investors it is likely that the securities will be listed and this is typically done on either the London stock exchange or the Luxembourg stock exchange.

(1) *London stock exchange.*   If the issue is to be listed on the London stock exchange, listing particulars are required under Part IV of the Financial Services Act. This involves the preparation of a document complying with the stock exchange's own regulations and requires the formal approval of the stock exchange before it can be freely distributed. The exchange has recently relaxed many of its general requirements and reduced its listing fees, which have been brought more in line with those of the Luxembourg stock exchange. However, it has also introduced additional requirements for asset-backed securi-

ties.[41] These are consistent with the best practice in securitizations which have occurred to date and are not an obstacle to transactions; indeed, recent trends have indicated a greater willingness to obtain London listings than in the past.

(2) *Luxembourg stock exchange.* To date, most issues have been listed on that exchange because of a tax advantage for UK-based investors. Following the Finance Act 1989, this tax advantage disappeared and more issues have been listed on the London stock exchange. Luxembourg-listed issues are not subject to Part IV of the Financial Services Act. Instead, the position is currently regulated by Part III of the Companies Act 1985, which lays down various form and content requirements which are fairly easy to comply with. The Companies Act also requires a prospectus to be delivered to the Registrar of Companies. There may not, in fact, be a 'prospectus' within the meaning of the Companies Act because of the mechanics by which securities are offered to investors in the Euromarkets. The document describing the issue, which may be called an information memorandum, offering circular or prospectus, typically does not itself contain any offer of the securities which it describes. The offer is in fact made in a formal allotment telex to investors including the co-managers. It is the allotment telex, therefore, which comprises the prospectus, although in practice the information memorandum is treated as being equivalent to the prospectus.

A prospectus that complies with the Companies Act and that has been registered can be widely distributed. It is to be hoped that the position will remain broadly the same when Part III of the Companies Act ceases to apply and is replaced by Part V of the Financial Services Act. This is designed to regulate all issues which are not listed on the London stock exchange, but it is currently unclear what this regime will be. There will be regulations exempting certain types of securities offerings from the form, content and registration requirements of a prospectus – the first draft of these regulations leaves a lot to be desired and extensive comments are being given to persuade the authorities to preserve the flexibility of the Euromarkets while adequately protecting individual investors.

General: allotments and Euro-commercial paper

(1) *Allotments.* One interesting consequence of the Euromarket mechanics for allotments of securities is that contained in section 82 of

the Companies Act. This provides that no allotment shall be made of a company's debentures in pursuance of a prospectus issued generally until the beginning of the third day after that on which the prospectus is first issued. That time is known as the time of the opening of the subscription lists. This legal requirement conflicts with the practice laid down by the International Primary Market Association (IPMA) in recommending that the lead manager allots securities within twenty-four hours of the launch of the issue. The IPMA requirement is usually satisfied by a telex indicating the allotment subject to signing of the subscription agreement and closing while the requirements of section 82 are met by sending a confirming telex to investors three days after the issue of the prospectus.

(2) *Euro-commercial paper.*   In contrast to most issues of long-term securities, the issue of Euro-commercial paper is not subject to the prospectus requirements of the Companies Act. By virtue of section 195 of the Financial Services Act, an exemption which was previously only available to non-UK issuers is extended to UK incorporated issuers of commercial paper whether or not it is denominated in sterling. As a result, provided the paper is only offered to persons whose ordinary business it is to buy or sell shares or debentures, the circular describing the notes should not constitute a prospectus for Companies Act purposes. This is important as the Inland Revenue continues to require, for the purposes of the MIRAS (mortgage interest relief at source) system, that the beneficial owner of the mortgage interest, that is, the issuer, is located in the United Kingdom.

9.3.2 *Due Diligence and Disclosure*

Responsibility for information   This is an important area that has often been accorded less importance in Euromarket practice than it receives in the offering of equity securities. The due-diligence process is often conducted in a fairly informal manner by the lead manager at a relatively late stage in the transaction and almost always after it has been launched into the market. This approach is perhaps understandable given the fact that creditors always rank ahead of shareholders in any liquidation but, in these asset-backed deals where the debt-to-equity ratio of the issuer is huge, it should perhaps be given greater significance. The responsibilities of those involved are quite extensive and encompass potentially both civil and criminal liability. Clearly the issuer itself is responsible for the information contained in the offering circular and a responsibility statement to this effect is required in the document by both the London and Luxembourg stock exchanges. The common form for this statement is as follows:

> The issuer is responsible for the information contained in this document. To the best of the knowledge and belief of the issuer (which has taken all reasonable care to ensure that such is the case), the information contained in this document is in accordance with the facts and does not omit anything likely to affect the import of such information. The issuer accepts responsibility accordingly.

As a matter of English law the directors of the issuer will also have responsibility and so indeed may the managers of the issue who are bringing it to the market.

Civil liability   The main heads of potential civil liability relate to action for misstatements, action for deceit and contractual liability under the subscription agreement. Actions for misstatements may be based in negligence under the rule in *Hedley Byrne & Co,* v. *Heller Partners*,[42] on fraudulent misstatements of fact (meaning that the statement is made either with knowledge of the falsity or not caring whether the statement is true or false), under the Misrepresentation Act 1967 and either under the Companies Act or under the Financial Services Act depending on whether the issue involves a Companies Act prospectus or listing particulars[43]. An action for deceit might be brought by an aggrieved investor to try and obtain greater damages than are likely to be available for negligent misstatements. However, such an action will need to prove fraud from the company or directors, the meaning of fraud being that which was described above.

More importantly and of more practical significance is the contractual liability which the issuer and the mortgage originator will have to the managers by virtue of the subscription agreement. This will contain detailed warranties relating to the assets being securitized as well as to the corporate position of the parties involved. Breach of the warranties will entitle the managers either to pull the issue or to sue for damages. The agreement will also contain indemnities to the managers against actions by investors based on misstatements in or omissions from the offering circular.

Criminal liability   There can also be potentially criminal liability
under the Theft Act 1968, under the Companies Act and under the
Financial Services Act. Of particular importance is section 47 of the
Financial Services Act. This effectively replaces the provisions of
section 13 of the Prevention of Fraud (Investments) Act 1958 relating
to the making of misleading, false or deceptive statements and it also
introduces a new statutory offence. Section 47(2) makes it an offence
to do 'any act', or engage in 'any course of conduct', which creates a
false or misleading impression as to the market in, or the price or value
of, any investments if done or engaged in so as to create that
impression and for the purpose of creating that impression unless the
person concerned reasonably believed that his act or conduct would
not create such an impression. Misstatements in or omissions from the
offering circular could give rise to liability under this section and,
incidentally, this is the section that has given most concern in the
context of stabilization practices of managers.

As can be seen, there are many heads of liability but the overriding
duty of those responsible for the offering circular must be to give the
necessary information to investors and their investments advisers to
make an informed assessment of the assets and liabilities, financial
position, profit and losses, and prospects of the issuer and of the rights
attaching to the securities, given the particular nature of the issuer and
of the securities. It is often extremely difficult in the course of a
transaction to determine whether one particular fact is relevant in the
overall context of the issue or is sufficiently fully described. A prag-
matic approach is rightly required although the legal background
must always be borne in mind.

9.4 Conclusion

Securities regulation, due diligence and disclosure (under both the US
and UK systems) are wide-ranging and potentially difficult areas.
They require great attention to detail and analysis of many statutory
provisions and common law principles. Nevertheless, these provide
only the context in which transactions can be done and by no means
prevent securities being offered attractively and widely to the professional investors who will be most interested in them.

Notes

1 See '33 Act, sections 5, 11 and 12.
2 '33 Act, section 2(1).
3 328 U.S. 293 (1946).
4 Ibid. at 298–9.
5 Ibid. at 299.
6 471 U.S. 681 (1985).
7 See *Developer's Mortgage Co.* v. *Trans Ohio Savings Bank*, 706 F.Supp. 570 (S.D. Ohio 1989).
8 The SEC has identified multiple factors characterizing a mortgage instrument as a security:

> Among the more common services and other attributes of the arrangements, offered in relation to the mortgages or deeds of trust, which have come to the attention of the Commission and which in the opinion of the Commission may give rise to the creation of 'investment contracts' within the meaning of the securities laws are:
>
> (a) Complete investigation and placing service.
> (b) Servicing collection, payments, foreclosures, etc.
> (c) Implied or express guarantee against loss at any time or providing a market for the underlying security.
> (d) Making advances of funds to protect the security of the investment.
> (e) Acceptance of small uniform or continuous investments.
> (f) Implied or actual guarantee of specified yield or return.
> (g) Continual reinvestment of funds.
> (h) Payment of interest prior to actual purchase of the mortgage or trust note.
> (i) Providing for fractional interests in mortgages or deeds of trust.
> (j) Circumstances which necessitate complete reliance upon the seller, *e.g.*, great distance between mortgaged property and investor.
> (k) Seller's selection of the mortgage or deed of trust for the investor.
>
> (Securities Act of 1933, Release No. 33–3892 (31 January 1958)

9 See section 9.2.1 under the heading 'Exemptions to the requirements of the '33 Act' below for a discussion of exempt securities.
10 See earlier chapters, particularly chapters 1, 2, 4 and 5, for more detailed discussion of US asset-backed securitization structures.
11 See, for example, *Newman and Associates, Inc.*, No Action Letter (pub.

avail. 9 November 1987); *Gem Savings Assoc.*, [1983 Transfer Binder] *Fed. Sec. L. Rep. No Action Sellers (CCH)*, para 77,528, at 78,697 (12 August 1983).

12 An 'issuer' is defined by section 2(4) as every person who issues or proposes to issue a security. An 'underwriter', defined by section 2(11), is one who has purchased a security from an issuer with a view to distribute the security.

13 Although section 4(2) provides an exception to the registration requirements, an issuer in a private placement is nonetheless obligated to provide the investor with all material information and is still subject to the antifraud provisions of the '33 and '34 Acts.

14 Rule 144 defines circumstances under which an owner of restricted securities, or a person selling restricted securities, may sell such securities to the public while being deemed not to be engaged in a 'distribution' and therefore not an 'underwriter'. In April 1990, the SEC adopted Rule 144A, which provides a safe harbour exemption from the registration requirements of the '33 Act for resales of restricted securities to 'qualified institutional buyers' as defined in the Rule.

15 See SEC Rule 502.

16 In the case of the 'non-accredited' investor, the seller must reasonably satisfy himself that his investor is one who either alone or with his representatives 'has knowledge and experience in financial and business matters that he is capable of evaluating the merits and risks of the prospective investment'.

Accredited investors, defined in section 501, include banks and other sophisticated investors meeting certain income and net worth standards. In March 1989, Regulation D was amended to, among other things, broaden the definition of 'accredited investors' to include state and federal employee benefit plans with assets exceeding $5,000,000.

17 See Securities Act Release No. 33–6806, 25 October 1988.

18 '33 Act, section 5(c).

19 See '33 Act, section 5(a)(1). The general term 'prospectus' (as opposed to a statutory prospectus defined in section 10) is broadly defined by section 2(10) to mean 'any prospectus, notice, circular, advertisement, letter, or communication, written or by radio or television, which offers any security for sale or confirms the sale of any security . . .'. However, a notice that contains only items specified in Rule 134 and includes the required designations is not a prospectus.

20 '33 Act, section 5(a).

21 SEC Rule 135(a)(1) and (2).

22 '33 Act, section 2(3).

23 *Diskin* v. *Lomasney & Co.*, 452 F.2d 871 (2d Cir. 1971).

24 '33 Act, section 2(4).

25 See *Sears Mortgage Securities Corp.*, No-Action Letter (pub. avail. 21 May 1985).
26 '33 Act, section 11.
27 However, if the security is acquired after an earnings statement for a twelve-month period beginning after the effective date of the registration statement has been made generally available to security-holders, then the plaintiff must prove reliance.
28 '33 Act, section 11(b)(3)(A).
29 '33 Act, section 11(b)(3)(C).
30 '33 Act, section 11(b)(3)(B).
31 '33 Act, section 11(c).
32 Although the '33 Act only covers registered securities, section 10(b) of the '34 Act and Rule 10b-5 promulgated thereunder proscribe the use of any manipulative or deceptive device in connection with the purchase or sale of any security, whether exempt from registration or not.
33 Recently, Bank of America was sued by several banks which had issued a letter of credit as support for a close to $1,000,000,000 pool of student loans, which, they alleged, Bank of America had improperly serviced. The loan-servicing agency retained by Bank of America to administer the loans is alleged to have lost control of a substantial portion of the loan was portfolio because of unreliable record-keeping procedures. The Department of Education, which had guaranteed the loans, also informed Bank of America that it would no longer honour its guarantee, because of the bank's failure to service the loans properly. See 52 BNA's *Banking Report* No. 17 at 1918 (24 April 1989).
34 In the case of credit-card receivables it is necessary to verify the legality, under applicable state and federal law, of the agreement between the card issuer and the card holder. A number of separate laws govern the relationship between the credit card-holder and issuer. These include general state consumer protection laws, the Federal Truth in Lending Act, the Equal Credit Opportunity Act, the Fair Billing Act, the Fair Credit Reporting Act and the Fair Debt Collection Practices Act.
35 An indenture is defined in section 303(7) as: 'any mortgage, deed of trust, trust or other indenture, or similar instrument or agreement . . . under which securities are outstanding or are to be issued, whether or not any property, real or personal, is, or is to be, pledged, mortgaged, assigned, or conveyed thereunder.'
36 '39 Act, section 304(a)(2).
37 '40 Act, section 3(a)(3).
38 '40 Act, section 6(c).
39 See chapter 7.
40 Namely, paragraph 2.

41 These are set out in section 7, Chapter 2 of The Stock Exchange's Yellow Book entitled 'Admission of Securities to Listing'.
42 1964 AC 465.
43 The disclosure obligations contained in Article 4 of the Listing Particulars Directive of 17 March 1980 (80/390/EEC) should not be overlooked if the securities are to be listed on an exchange in any member state.

10

The Impact of Loan Selling on the Profit and Loss Account and Balance Sheet

STEVE PARKINSON

Chapter Outline

10.1 Introduction

10.2 US Generally Accepted Accounting Principles (GAAP)

10.3 UK GAPP

10.1 Introduction

There are a considerable number of topics within the scope of this chapter. This chapter examines the general concepts that are relevant in both the US and the UK. In particular, it looks at issues relating to the consolidation of subsidiaries, and applies the relevant concepts to mortgage securitization. However, these concepts are mainly also relevant when looking at other types of asset-sale transactions.

It has been said earlier that, although many loan-sale transactions are quite simple, the issues that they involve are relatively complex. This is also true of the financial reporting issues. In general, as with the legal considerations, it is the degree of protection that can be built in for the seller that the auditor will be looking for. The crux of the problem is that we are likely to be taking a subjective view of who has the risks and rewards of ownership. Unfortunately for the seller, this leads to a degree of uncertainty in the financial reporting implications while they are planning their transactions, and the need to consult their auditors at an early stage.

In passing, as we shall see later, the US authorities have tried to solve this problem by taking a black and white approach, whereas the UK is, at present, taking a fuzzy grey approach.

In the past few years financing transactions and techniques have developed to enable companies in many industries to expand and take advantage of the relative boom conditions.

Since the October 1987 crash, attention has focused upon debt securities for both investors and those that require finance. However, the development of accounting standards has lagged well behind the transactions themselves particularly in the UK. This inability to respond to reality quickly is one of the things that led to the setting up by the UK accounting authorities of the Deering Committee. This committee recently reported its findings that responsive standard setting required a core full-time executive that would promulgate standard accounting practice. This executive would be overseen by a larger body that would represent companies, auditors and users. Among other things, they would monitor the speed and efficiency with which the executive acted. Therefore, it is possible that in the future we shall have a framework in place that will be able to cope effectively with complex transactions.

However, at present, we have the problem of a relatively rule-free environment in which to try to predict the financial reporting of new financing transactions, for example:

- convertible bonds with premium put options,
- deep discounted securities, and
- loan securitization.

As with many financial reporting issues, it is useful to look at the UK position in the context of what happens in the USA. US financial reporting standards are often considerably more developed than UK standards and give a useful pointer to the way standards may develop in the UK. The area of loan securitization is no exception.

10.2 US Generally Accepted Accounting Principles (GAAP)

The general US standard that is relevant is FAS No. 77, which deals with the transfer of receivables with recourse.

FAS No. 77
A sale of receivables occurs where:
- the transferor surrenders its control of the future economic benefits relating to the receivables
- obligations under the recourse provisions can be reasonably estimated
- the transferee cannot return the receivables except pursuant to the recourse provisions.

If a transfer can be recognized, the gain or loss will be recognized on sale.

If a servicing responsibility remains with the transferor, the sales price should be adjusted to allow for a normal servicing income receipt over the period of the loan servicing.

The theory behind this accounting method is the concept that: 'Every asset is an asset of some entity; moreover, no asset can simultaneously be an asset of more than one entity. . . . To have an asset, a business must control future economic benefit to the extent that it can benefit from the asset and generally deny or regulate access to that benefit by others.'

However, FAS No. 77 is supplemented by the much stricter FASB Technical Bulletin No. 85–2, which relates specifically to collateralized mortgage obligations (CMOs).

TB No. 85–2
Borrowings and collateral can be eliminated from the balance sheet if:
- future economic benefits are surrendered so that at most a nominal residual interest is retained
- there is no recourse to the seller for either principal or interest.

In short, TB No. 85–2 makes it very difficult to deal with CMOs off balance sheet. This is illustrated by the 1987 US financial statements of Salomon Inc., which showed over $4 billion of CMOs on their balance sheet. It is likely that some of these would be applicable to the

Exhibit 10.1

Salomon Inc.	1987 balance sheet	$m
Cash		561
Securities owned (at market value)		24,714
Commodities owned (at market value)		1,287
Securities purchased under agreements to recall		30,749
Loans and receivables		12,155
Assets securing CMOs		4,232
Other assets		1,049
		74,747
Securities sold under repurchase agreements		26,406
Short-term borrowings		8,749
Securities sold but not yet repurchased		19,068
Payables		11,532
CMOs		4,184
Long-term debt		1,282
Stockholders' equity		3,481
		74,747

Mortgage Corporation in the UK. It is interesting to note that, because these assets and liabilities are vested in companies that do not meet the legal definition of a subsidiary, they are off balance sheet in accounts prepared under UK GAAP. See exhibit 10.1.

The key issue in TB No. 85–2 relates to whether the loans can be considered to be fully sold, or whether there is more than a nominal residual interest in the loans that remain. In this regard, it seems that nominal is defined as less than 2 per cent of the value of the mortgage pool based on discounting any future net revenue streams. There are other requirements in TB No. 85–2 but, in general, this one is the most difficult to satisfy.

Of the other factors that need to be considered, the extent of recourse to the originator/sponsor will be relevant both in the US and, in the future, in the UK.

10.3 UK GAAP

At present in the UK it is relatively simple to deal with securitized loans off balance sheet as the loans can be sold to a company that is still part owned and even controlled, but because that vehicle company does not meet the Companies Act definition of a subsidiary it is off balance sheet. Matters of recourse and residual interests are simply not a problem. Therefore, an off-balance-sheet vehicle can be mechanically set up for any purpose as shown in figure 10.1.

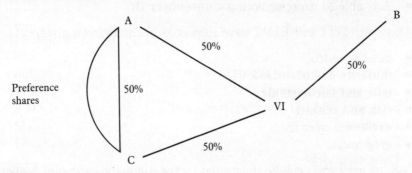

Figure 10.1 Traditional off-balance-sheet structures
Options for A to buy out B at cost plus IRR to B of 20%

The ownership of equity share capital is the key to the current definition of a subsidiary. Such structures are based on the fact that share capital can be regarded as equity for accounting purposes if the holders participate beyond a specified amount either in dividends (or other distributions of profit) or in capital on a winding up.

Traditional off-balance-sheet structures
Definition of equity share capital
Allocation of votes
e.g.

- Shares that rank with ordinary shareholders on a winding up are likely to be equity
- Each class of shareholder can appoint the same number of directors. However, one set of directors carries multiple votes.

However, the Department of Trade and Industry (DTI) has recently issued a proposal to change the definition of a subsidiary so that artificial sales are more likely to be retained on balance sheet. These proposals are running parallel with the Accounting Standards Committee's proposals in Exposure Draft 42.

The present UK company law definition of subsidiary:

- A holds 50 per cent of equity share capital of B, or
- A holds equity share capital and controls composition of a majority of the board.

New definition:

- A has an interest in B and
- A is able to exercise voting control over B.

Thus, the DTI and ED42 have impacted in the following respects:

- voting control
- minority-owned subsidiaries
- true and fair override
- risk and reward
- substance over form
- grey areas.

Such grey areas can be illustrated by the following example. A owns 50 per cent of the equity share capital of V, B owns the other 50 per cent and their shares rank *pari passu* in all respects. However, as shown below, there are put and call purchase options, A can obtain significant income from preference shares (maybe 100 per cent of profits depending on how coupon is set), and A has day-to-day management responsibility. B may have a significant portion of the debt and therefore this may be their main interest. However, their

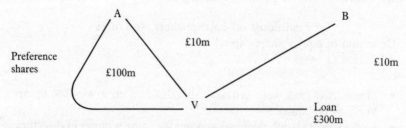

Figure 10.2 Grey areas in the new UK definition of 'subsidiary'

Options for A to buy out B at fair-market value
Day-to-day management with A, but B has veto on major transactions

equity holding gives the possibility of a substantial return on the £10 million investment, though the return on their overall investment is dampened by the large debt investment.

The importance of the off or on decision that is made can be indicated by table 10.1 if the above structure and funds are used for a company acquisition and goodwill on that transaction is written off to reserves.

Table 10.1 Off or on? – the difference

	A	Target	On	Off
Net assets other than net debt	60	150	210	170
Net debt	(10)	(20)	(450)	(120)
Shareholders' funds	50	130	(240)	50

Most loan securitization has been carried out without a retention of ownership, although there may be a retention of interest. As with the example above, these transactions tend to put securitization into the 'grey area' that is, at present, developing. The issues involved are also similar.

A recent example of a UK issue designed to meet the 'substance over form' criteria of proposed UK accounting rules, and Bank of England criteria required to remove debt from balance sheet ratios, was that by Exclusive Finance No. 1 plc (EF). The securities issued were backed by mortgages purchased from the TSB Group.

The key features that led to the mortgages being considered sold in substance as well as in form are as follows:

- the securities issued by EF are not guaranteed by TSB
- any surplus cash will be invested only in certain low-risk approved investments under the auspices of a third-party bank (Westdeutsche Landesbank Girozentrale). (I understand that this was done to satisfy the Bank of England. It would probably not be necessary to do this to satisfy accounting requirements.)
- EF is owned by a discretionary trust with the trustees being Eagle Star Trust Co. Ltd.
- Mortgages sold were backed by a high percentage of life assurance and buildings insurance
- Mortgage indemnity insurance, contingency insurance and mort-

gage pool insurance arranged so that the risks of default, or properties reducing in value, were minimized.

- Exposure to repayments is limited by the fact that the public debt is part repaid at six-monthly intervals based on the repayments of mortgage principal by the mortgagees.
- Late-payment and basis risk is reduced by having a facility arranged to ensure that the vehicle is in funds to pay its interest obligations to the public debt holders.

However, the TSB Group will obtain a servicing fee equal to 80 per cent of EF's profits and an origination fee, together with an interest-rate swap of the mortgage rate for the loan notes rate.

It is this that would be likely to lead to on-balance-sheet treatment in the USA if that were relevant. However, the provisions of the UK proposals, ED42, may well be more lenient.

The basic principles behind ED42 are that the risk and rewards of ownership should have substantially passed from the originator.

ED 42 provides for the elimination of risk, such as:

- bad-debt risk
- repayment delays
- basis risk
- reinvestment/surplus-cash risk
- administration risk.

Although the size of the residual interest that the TSB Group has in the above example will still be relevant, it is likely that the UK view would be to accept more than 2 per cent as being immaterial. The extent to which benefits have to be taken into account is, at present, being discussed by the ASC and we can expect further proposals on this subject prior to the issuance of the final standard.

Administration risk in the example lies with the originator, but as that is a relatively risk-free area it may not, in itself, be enough to keep the assets and liabilities on balance sheet.

As far as ownership and risk are concerned, it is relevant that TSB have no shareholding so, even under the new wider proposed legal definition, EF is not a subsidiary; and that the risk has been insured against so there are no guarantees by TSB.

Therefore, it seems possible that, under the present UK proposals, it will be considered that a sale has been made, so the liabilities will be off balance sheet and profit can be taken on that sale to the extent that it has been received in cash or can be estimated to be received with reasonable certainty.

Profit would therefore be:

Initial amount received on 'sale' of mortgages + origination fee less carrying value of mortgages + insurance and any other costs to minimize risk. From that point, annual income would be matched against any costs of achieving that income. To the extent that a loss can be foreseen, it should be taken up front.

The above leads us to conclude that accounting for a mortgage-backed securities transaction as a sale in the US is likely to be more difficult than in the UK. However, there is also likely to be debate as to which is more appropriate as world accounting standards are slowly harmonized. The US accounting standards could then prevail.

The same principles will apply to other types of loan sales such as sub-participations and novations. For instance, if a novation is properly carried out, the substance is that a new loan has been set up between the purchaser and borrower. The risk and reward of ownership have passed and a sale has taken place. With a sub-participation it will be necessary to look at whether the risk has been shifted, whether any recourse is measurable, the set-off risk, the appropriation risk, and so on.

In all these cases the issue is whether the risk and reward of ownership have really been sold, or whether they have been replaced by another set of risks and rewards. It is accounting for substance rather than accounting for legal form.

To conclude, the main issues, when looking at loan sales, are going to be those of substance over form, risk and reward, protection (or recourse), and the existence of reversing linked transactions. These are often going to be matters of subjective judgement, which initially may lead to some uncertainty.

11

Capital Adequacy Concerns: Basle Supervisors Committee, US and UK

DAVID BARBOUR, PROFESSOR JOSEPH J. NORTON and GRAHAM PENN

Chapter Outline

11.1 Introduction

The recent phenomenon of the rise of asset securitization must be seen in context of what has occurred and is occurring in international financial marketplaces. The past two decades have witnessed dramatic changes in international financial marketplaces, including significant international expansion and diversification of banking activities and operations, a relatively inflation-prone and unpredictable world economic environment, and the emergence of intense global competition among bank and non-bank financial intermediaries. Each of these phenomena has placed strains on the capital position of international and domestic banking institutions.[1] Attempts to meet these capital strains have led to substantial product innovation (for example, asset securitization), which, in turn, has raised regulatory concerns over new and different risks being assumed (on and off balance sheet) by such institutions and over the possible adverse impact upon the 'safety and soundness' of such institutions and the distortion of prudent capital bases.[2] The regulatory reaction (for example, in the guise of capital adequacy standards) in turn has led these institutions to implement increasingly broader and more sophisticated forms of securitization techniques in order to comply with or otherwise minimize these more stringent regulatory practices.

Further, world economic conditions have resulted generally in a deterioration of the asset quality of individual banking institutions – with a concomitant increase in loan loss reserves, write-offs, reductions in earnings and depletion in capital and in the rise in financially troubled institutions. Moreover, the increase in global competition has strained the financial and managerial resources of banking institutions and has undercut customary bank pricing and profit margins, thus exerting downward pressure on institutional earnings and capital bases.[3] In addition there has been a series of bank scandals or crises of international scope (including Franklin National Bank, Herstatt Bankhaus, the Secondary Banking Crisis and Johnson Mathey in the United Kingdom, Ambrosiano in Italy, and Continental Illinois in the United States),[4] each of which has served (along with the Third World debt crisis)[5] as specific catalysts for reform of regulatory practices in the prudential supervision area.

All of the above factors have translated into government apprehensions among the bank supervisors of the industrialized nations, which have kindled broad regulatory attention to the capital adequacy of banking institutions operating in the international area. Such concerns have rested largely on policy concerns for facilitating the 'safe and sound' development of an international banking system through the promotion of stability and transparency within such system, and through the insurance of competitive equality among international banking institutions. It is within this developing system that securitization practices are evolving in the United States, the United Kingdom and Continental Europe.[6]

This chapter discusses first the background leading to the issuance of the July 1988 Basle Supervisors Committee Report on capital adequacy standards, the subject-matter of the report, and (generally) the report's effect on national banking regulations.[7] Next, specific analysis is made of capital adequacy and other regulations in the United States affecting bank involvement in securitization. Then a comparable discussion is presented on United Kingdom laws and regulations affecting securitization practice of banks.

11.2 Prelude: Note on the Basle Supervisors Committee's Efforts

11.2.1 *The Initial Efforts*

In 1974, in the wake of significant international banking disruptions such as the failure of Bankhaus Herstatt in West Germany,[8] the governors of the central banks of the member countries of the 'Group of Ten' of the OECD[9] (plus the governor of the central bank of Switzerland) established, under the administrative auspices of the Bank for International Settlements (BIS) in Basle, Switzerland,[10] the Committee on Banking Regulations and Supervisory Practices ('Basle Supervisors Committee'). The membership of this committee has come to comprise the representatives of the central banks and other authorities with formal responsibility for the prudential supervision of banking institution from these eleven leading industrialized countries and from Luxembourg.[11] The committee, which operates without any extensive formal mandate or any constitution or bylaws, meets three or four times a year and serves as an informal forum for ongoing cooperation on bank prudential supervision matters.[12] The efforts of the committee, particularly its recent work in the bank capital adequacy area, have had a significant effect on bank regulation in the United States, the United Kingdom and elsewhere in the European Community relating to securitization transactions.

The Basle Supervisors Committee's primary aim is to encourage a gradual convergence of bank supervisory practices of the member regulatory institutions by enhancing the scope and effectiveness of supervisory techniques for international banking activities, by studying and making recommendations on specific areas of prudential concern in international banking, and by facilitating the exchange of information among bank supervisors so as to upgrade the quality of international bank supervision. Throughout its existence, the committee has sought to maintain a low profile (informal, and where possible, non-publicized).[13]

For present purposes, the key legal significance of the Basle Supervisors Committee has been its pronouncements and activities in the capital adequacy area. This legal significance manifests itself in its potential for law generation within the jurisdictions of its members. The committee has not only generated significant legal actions within its members' legal and supervisory systems, but it has helped move forward and shape the content of such national and regional (European Community) actions through the convergence process.[14]

With respect to capital adequacy, the committee (after a ten-year process) expressed its consensus view in 1988 that the principle of consolidated supervision should be applicable to this area of 'bank prudential supervision. In 1981, the member institutions of the committee were concerned increasingly with the continuing erosion of bank capital on a worldwide basis and commenced the preparation of a report to the G-10 central bank governors respecting bank capital adequacy in relation to the international business of banks. The committee was of the view that further erosion of bank capital ratios was undesirable and that, in principle, it was desirable to achieve a greater approximation in the levels of capital employed by major international banks. While realizing that it was not its role to attempt any formal legal harmonization of capital adequacy standards internationally, the committee did view its role as trying to achieve a 'greater convergence among its members with regard to national definitions of bank capital for supervisory purposes'.[15]

In June 1982, the Basle Supervisors Committee presented a paper to the central bank governors, who endorsed the committee's main conclusions, which were: 'that in the current and prospective environment further erosion of capital ratio should, on prudential grounds, be resisted; and that, in the absence of common standards of capital adequacy, supervisors should not allow the capital resources of their major banks to deteriorate from their present level, whatever those levels may be'.[16] The main thrust behind these conclusions was prudential concern for the fundamental safety and soundness of the major international banks and of the international financial system.

The Basle Supervisors Committee's 1982 report also set out an agenda for further work in the capital adequacy area. The committee would continue to work towards achieving a 'common view' among its member institutions regarding the main constituent elements of capital, with particular focus on the nature and role of subordinated debt instruments and 'hidden reserves'. Further, the committee would explore the viability of different ratios that relate balance-sheet items to capital, including risk–asset ratios, gearing ratios, and large loan exposure ratios. It was the hope of the committee eventually to evaluate the usefulness of these different ratios for different purposes and to make specific recommendations for the application of such ratios for prudential supervision purposes by its member institutions.[17]

For two years, the Basle Supervisors Committee continued its work on capital adequacy, but became increasingly conscious of the diversity of national systems capital measurements and the difficulties of devising meaningful and acceptable common standards. In addition, the committee began to focus on capital adequacy not only in terms of stability of the international financial system but also in competitive equality terms.[18]

The Basle Supervisors Committee was also particularly influenced by the enactment of the International Lending Supervision Act of

1983 (ILSA) in the United States and the subsequent concern of the US Treasury and the Federal Reserve Board to pursue these matters internationally within the Basle Supervisory Committee structure.[19] In fact, in 1984, the G-10 central bank governors approved further work towards a framework of 'functional equivalents' of capital measurement that might be devised to overcome national differences and to make possible development, in due course, of commonly agreed quantitative measures of capital adequacy.[20]

By the end of the summer of 1984, the Basle Supervisors Committee, in undertaking this task, linked its efforts closely with those of the European Community's Bank Advisory Committee, which was engaged in similar work in the context of European Community integration initiatives in the banking area. The reason for this linkage was that many of the members of the European Community were also members of the committee; therefore, divergent approaches by these two groups would only prove counterproductive. Thus, by the end of 1984, the Basle Supervisory Committee was concentrating its efforts on developing a common definition of capital and common capital adequacy assessment methods.[21]

At the end of 1986, the Basle Supervisors Committee had formulated a complex definition of capital based upon a six-tier system. The first tier comprised permanent shareholders' equity, retained earnings and disclosed reserves. The other tiers progressively added additional elements accepted as part of capital by some but not all of the member states of the committee. For example, tier two added undisclosed reserves; tier three, perpetual and certain other hybrid capital instruments; tier four, asset revaluation reserves; tier five, general provision; and tier six, subordinate debt. In addition, the committee attempted to evaluate the value of a simple gearing ratio vis-à-vis a risk–asset ratio. Although the committee had concluded that the risk–asset approach represented 'a more sensitive and reliable test of capital adequacy than the gearing approach', the framework being developed by the committee was to include both approaches in separate sets of calculations. With respect to the rating and off-balance-sheet items for the risk–asset test, the committee had segregated seven broad categories of assets with percentage ratios being 0, 20, 50 or 100 per cent.[22]

11.2.2 *An Intervening Catalyst: the US/UK Accord*

Although substantial progress was being made within the Basle
Supervisors Committee on formulating acceptable international capital adequacy standards, this progress apparently was not sufficient for
the US bank regulators, particularly for the Federal Reserve Board.
The Federal Reserve felt strongly that the US Congress had
established a firm mandate to work towards the convergence of international capital adequacy standards, and on a practical level the
Federal Reserve was becoming more perplexed and pressed in dealing
with foreign bank-acquisition applications in the United States (particularly with trying to cope with evaluating the capital bases of
Japanese banking institutions).[23] Accordingly, some time during 1986
(particularly the latter part thereof), private bilateral discussions
began and became intensified between the Federal Reserve Board and
also the staffs of the Comptroller and the FDIC on the one hand and
the Bank of England on the other hand. These discussions were
conducted outside the framework of the Basle Supervisors Committee.[24] One linkage making possible this collaboration was the fact that
in formulating its earlier 1986 risk-based capital proposals, the
Federal Reserve Board had considered and was familiar with the risk-
based capital approach of the Bank of England.[25] The Bank of England had developed this non-legal regulatory approach in 1980 and
had been utilizing it as an integral part of its prudential supervision
procedures.[26]

The fruit borne of this informal bilateral collaboration was an
'Agreed proposal of the United States federal banking supervisory
authorities and the Bank of England on primary capital and capital
adequacy assessment', released on 8 January 1987 ('US/UK Accord').
In legal terms, this Accord was a non-binding document in any international or domestic sense. While the banking authorities clearly had
authority to promulgate equivalent domestic regulations, there was no
legal basis, as such, to create a legally binding agreement among the
bank supervisory authorities of these nations. In fact, the Accord does
not purport to be a legal document at all: it is presented as a consultative paper 'to serve as a basis for consultation with the banking
industry and others in the United States and the United Kingdom'.
The Accord was also designed 'to promote the convergence of
supervisory policy and capital adequacy assessments among countries
with major banking centres'.[27]

Looked at strategically, the US/UK Accord appears conceived as a stimulus for prompt agreement on capital adequacy within the Basle Supervisors Committee (particularly, pressuring the hand of recalcitrant countries such as Japan). The fallback position was that the United States and the United Kingdom would proceed with international convergence on a bilateral basis (or, if Japanese agreement could be reached, with the three) in the event the Basle Supervisory Committee did not reach prompt agreement.

The US/UK Accord also had the effect of resolving, at least bilaterally, some of the difficult particulars involved in the convergence process addressed by the Basle Supervisors Committee membership: issues such as the definition of capital in light of the specific and variant financial, accounting and governmental practices among certain of the industrialized countries involved, and the risk-weight formula to be adopted. The bilateral agreement was to take effect in May 1987, after a period of comment in each country.[28]

The US/UK Accord led to the Federal Reserve Board revising its January 1986 risk-based proposal in the form of a new February 1987 capital adequacy proposal that substantially comported with the US/UK proposal.[29] However, the greatest significance of the bilateral Accord was that, whether rightly or wrongly, it added pressure on the Basle Supervisors Committee process and on individual members such as Japan, which resulted in the issuance of the Basle Committee's joint capital adequacy proposal in December 1987.[30] The US/UK Accord never was to be given effect.[31]

11.2.3 *The July 1988 Report*

In December of 1987, the Basle Supervisors Committee issued its 'Consultative Paper' on 'Proposals for international convergence of capital measurements and capital standards'.[32] This proposal set forth a common framework of capital adequacy measurement and a common minimum target capital standard to be achieved and maintained by banks operating internationally. In broad terms, there was general similarity between the December 1987 Basle Committee Proposal and the earlier 1986 US/UK Accord. The committee's Proposal made distinctions between core capital components and other supplemental capital elements; provided broad categories of weighted risk assets; provided an equivalent risk assessment of off-balance-sheet items; and recognized that the proposed risk-based capital standards were only one step in overall evaluations of a banking institution's capital adequacy and financial soundness.[33]

However, the December 1987 Basle Supervisors Committee's Proposal differed in a number of significant ways from the prior US/UK Accord. For example, although both proposals treat the capital structure on a two-tier basis, tier one would be comprised solely of common stockholders' equity (including retained earnings, and minority interest in the common equity accounts of consolidated subsidiaries). Allowance for loan and lease losses (that is, general loan loss reserves) would not be included in core capital: the Basle Proposal assigns general loan loss reserves to the tier-two supplemental capital elements, and phases in limitations on reevaluation reserves. Further, the Basle Proposal requires only a deduction of goodwill from capital, but other intangibles such as purchase mortgage servicing rights would not necessarily be deducted in calculating the risk-based capital ratio: the national authorities would be given discretion in the treatment of these other intangible items.[34]

Another significant difference between the two proposals is the role of subordinated debt, which was not included in the US/UK capital definition. However, under the Basle Proposal, term-subordinated debt, along with intermediate-term limited-life preferred stock, may be included in the supplemental capital tier up to an amount equal to 50 per cent of core capital.[35]

Also the risk-rating framework of the December 1987 Basle Proposal varies in a number of ways from the US/UK structure. Government securities with remaining maturities of ninety-one days or less would be assigned to the 0 per cent risk category rather than being placed in the 10 per cent category. All other US government and agency obligations would be assigned to the 10 per cent risk category; the weight of short-term bank claims is reduced from 25 to 20 per cent; the risk weight of securities issued by US government-sponsored agencies and general obligations of US local governments is reduced from 50 to 20 per cent; the risk rate for short-term commitments is reduced to 0 per cent; the weight for self-liquidating trade-related contingencies such as commercial letters of credit is reduced from 50 to 20 per cent; and portions of assets backed by the full faith and credit of domestic depository institutions is assigned a 20 per cent weight.[36] Further, the procedures for determining capital requirements or interest-rate swaps and foreign exchange rates are simplified and their respective capital requirements are reduced. Also, the assignment of claims on foreign banks to risk categories is based upon original rather than remaining maturity.[37]

The Basle Supervisors Committee's December 1987 Proposal established an explicit schedule for achieving a minimum level of capital to weighted risk assets by the end of the transition. By the end of 1990, a target risk-based ratio of 7.25 per cent (of which 3.25 percentage points must be in the form of common stockholders' equity, that is, must be in the form of core capital) was called for, and, by the end of 1992, a minimum standard of 8 per cent (of which at least 4 percentage points must be in the form of core capital) is required.[38]

After a six-month period of comment, the Basle Supervisors Committee promulgated its final risk-based capital adequacy report in July 1988.[39] The July 1988 report substantially paralleled the earlier December 1987 document, although there were several major changes. For example, non-cumulative perpetual preferred stock is to be included in the definition of tier-one core capital.[40] In addition, the committee indicated that if it could establish clear guidelines to distinguish general from specific reserves, then such general reserves would be includible within the supplemental tier-two capital category without limits; however, if such agreement is not reached, then the general reserves would be included in tier two on a limited basis as originally proposed.[41] The July revision also clarifies that term debt instruments must have a minimum original term of maturity of over five years.[42] Further, the July 1988 report assigns reduced risk rates to a defined group of OECD member nations and those that have concluded special lending arrangements with the International Monetary Fund under its General Arrangement to Borrow.[43] Also, the preferential 50 per cent risk rate for home mortgages on owner-occupied housing is extended to cover loans secured by mortgages on rental housing.[44]

In sum, the July 1988 Basle Committee's report on bank capital adequacy represents a comprehensive statement of the view of the committee, which has been subsequently endorsed by the central bank governors of the G-10 countries.[45]

11.2.4 *The Spin-Off Factor: Subsequent Law Generation*

While the Basle Supervisors Committee's July 1988 report is presented as a consultative paper, it has received the endorsement of the respective banks' supervisors of the member countries of the committee and has been formally endorsed by the G-10 central bank governors.[46] As such, at least on a political level, the respective government authorities of the member states have agreed that the principles of the report will be followed and implemented, albeit the means of implementation through legal or administrative mechanisms is left to the respective national authorities to choose. The report clearly envisages some form of subsequent adaptation by national authorities. In fact, national authorities have begun to act in reliance upon the other authorities so acting. In this sense, the July 1988 report can be seen, at least analogously, as a form of 'soft law' in that the formulators of the principles embodied in the July 1988 proposals intend these principles to be observed and to be implemented within their respective national jurisdictions (albeit, perhaps, through different legal and non-legal means).[47]

In countries such as the United States and Germany and within the European Community, the principles of the Basle Supervisors Committee's capital adequacy Proposal will be enacted through formal legal means. For example (as discussed below), the US banking agencies have already begun the process, at the time of this writing, for formulating new capital adequacy proposals derived from and consistent with the July 1988 Proposal.[48] Countries such as the United Kingdom (as also will be discussed below) will probably continue not to embody these provisions in any formal regulation, but the Bank of England has issued a public notice to the UK banking community as to its intent to implement the Basle Supervisors Committee's proposal.[49]

Thus, the Basle Supervisors Committee's July 1988 report is proving itself a major step in achieving the convergence of standards of national bank supervisors respecting capital adequacy. Clearly, the report has had a direct and pervasive impact upon the uniform capital adequacy regulations most recently adopted by the US federal banking authorities and the position taken by other banking authorities of the western industrialized world, including the Bank of England.[50]

11.3 US Bank Regulatory/Capital Concerns

As discussed in chapter 4 above, the issuance of asset-backed securities by commercial banks in the United States is subject to a fragmented state and federal bank regulatory system. The Office of the Comptroller of the Currency ('OCC' or 'Comptroller') is the primary regulator of national banks. State-chartered institutions are subject to primary regulation by state regulators. National banks and state banks that are members of the Federal Reserve System are also regulated by the Federal Reserve Board of Governors (FRB). The third federal bank regulator is the Federal Deposit Insurance Corporation (FDIC), which supervises FDIC-insured non-member banks (as well as managing the deposit insurance funds and being a receiver for insolvent institutions).[51]

This section endeavours to touch upon the commercial bank regulatory concerns in the capital adequacy area (thrift regulations are alluded to in chapter 4).

11.3.1 *The New Risk-Based Capital Standards*

In general The FRB has promulgated new risk-based capital adequacy guidelines for state-chartered, Federal Reserve System member banks and for bank holding companies,[52] and the OCC has adopted comparable capital guidelines for national banks.[53] The FDIC has also issued its 'Final statement' for state-chartered, non-member banks, which statement closely parallels the OCC and FRB guidelines.[54] In addition, as discussed in chapter 4, comprehensive risk-based capital adequacy rules for federal thrift institutions have also been adopted (although the thrift regulations are not discussed in this chapter).[55] Broad policy objectives underpinning these new capital adequacy standards for banking institutions include (1) the presentation of a meaningful risk profile of an institution's operations in light of its capital base; (2) the incorporation of off-balance-sheet (OBS) risks into this profile; (3) the provision for disincentives for banking institutions to shift resources from liquid, less risky assets to less liquid, riskier assets and activities; (4) the general strengthening of capital positions of banking institutions; and (5) the attainment of some level of international convergence of national treatment of bank capital adequacy.[56]

The FRB bank guidelines (used in this chapter for illustrative purposes) provide an extensive definition of 'capital' based on a two-tier concept:[57] deviations in the capital definition (particularly regarding the use of cumulative perpetual preferred stock and the treatment of goodwill) exist for bank holding companies.[58] Capital is required for varying percentages of an asset's face value, depending upon the assigned risk category. Effectively, the new standards create a risk analysis based on four risk categories derived from perceived credit risks. Further, a credit-conversion formula is utilized to factor in OBS activities (which have proliferated for banking institutions over the past decade).[59]

The new capital adequacy standards are to be put into effect over the next three years, with a total minimum capital-to-risk assets of 8 per cent required by the end of 1992, of which at least half (that is, 4 per cent) must comprise Tier 1, 'core' capital.[60] More specifically, the FRB guidelines became effective on 15 March 1989 with respect to the framework for calculating risk-based capital ratios, and the minimum supervisory ratios became effective on 31 December 1990;[61] the OCC's guidelines came into effect on 31 December 1990;[62] and the FDIC's 'Policy statement' was effective as of 20 April 1989 regarding the framework for calculating risk-based capital ratios, but with the interim minimum supervisory ratio having become effective on 31 December 1990.[63] These new capital adequacy standards are to coexist with a yet-to-be-announced minimum leverage ratio of 'core' capital to total assets.[64] The present minimum ratio of 6 per cent (total capital to adjusted total assets) will continue until then.[65]

The bank regulators recognize that the new guidelines are but one step in evaluating capital adequacy of banking institutions. Other types of risks (for example, interest-rate risks, transfer risks, market risks) are not factored directly into the new guidelines, but at some point in time need to be addressed by the regulators in a meaningful way. In addition, the focus upon capital adequacy is only one factor that can affect a banking institution's overall financial conditions: other important factors include liquidity, quality and level of earnings, investment or loan-portfolio concentrations, quality of loans and investments, the effectiveness of loan and investment policies, and management's overall ability to monitor and to control other financial and operating risks.[66]

The regulators are also concerned that, inasmuch as the new bank and bank holding company guidelines are geared to measuring credit risks only and provide a system of risks weighting, banking institutions may over-concentrate (that is, over-leverage) their assets into lower-risk weight categories. Accordingly, the bank regulators have concluded that some form of minimum leverage ratio needs to be maintained. The regulators intend to put forward, in the near future, an additional minimum leverage ratio, most probably based upon the ratio of Tier 1 ('core') capital-to-total assets. It has been indicated that this new minimum leverage ratio may be lower than the current standard of 6 per cent.[67]

The new guidelines are of general applicability to banking institutions. The FRB guidelines cover all banks and bank holding companies[68] that are subject to FRB supervision; the Comptroller's guidelines cover all national banks regardless of size; and the FDIC regulations embrace all state-chartered, non-member banks (regardless of size).

The new guidelines address four basic areas:

- a common definition of Tier 1, core capital and the provision of a 'menu' of items for Tier 2, supplementary capital;
- a general framework for assigning assets to broad risk categories, along with the provisions for calculating a risk-based capital ratio;
- with respect to the general framework provided, the requirements of banking institutions to maintain capital against OBS items, by assigning such items to the broad risk-based categories and by providing a conversion mechanism for such calculations; and
- required minimum levels of capital, including a prescribed time-table for obtaining a minimum ratio of total capital risk-based assets by the end of 1990 and a final higher ratio by no later than the end of 1992 and various transitional arrangements (for example, a phase-in period permitting banking institutions to include some supplementary capital items in Tier 1 capital on a temporary basis and providing time to align capital positions into full conformity with the risk-based capital definitions and minimum supervisory standards).[69]

It must be remembered that the development of the new domestic risk-based capital adequacy standards have been formulated in the context of an overriding concern for international prudential supervision of banking institutions through the forum of the Basle Committee, as discussed above. It is upon the Basle Committee's July 1988 report that the recent US capital adequacy standards for banks, bank holding companies and thrift institutions are closely based.[70]

Redefining capital   The new bank guidelines create two categories of capital: Tier 1 or 'core' capital and Tier 2 or 'supplementary' capital.

(1) *Tier 1*.   The emphasis of the guidelines is on Tier 1 capital. Tier 1

capital may comprise a banking institution's common stockholders' equity, non-cumulative perpetual preferred stock and related surplus, and minority interest in the equity accounts of consolidated subsidiaries. 'Common stockholders' equity' would include common stock, common stock surplus, undivided profits and capital reserves – adjusted for the cumulative effect of foreign currency translation and net of unrealized losses on non-current marketable equity securities. Perpetual preferred stock (that is, preferred stock having no maturity date, which cannot be redeemed at the option of the holder of the instrument and which has no other provisions that will require further redemption of the issue) is only includible in Tier 1 capital to the extent it is 'non-cumulative' (that is, paid dividends do not accumulate and therefore do not represent contingent claims on the issuer). However, perpetual preferred stock may be cumulative or non-cumulative under the bank holding company guidelines, but the total amount of all such stock cannot exceed 25 per cent of Tier 1 capital (including the preferred stock). Perpetual preferred stock excludes 'auction' preferred stock (that is, preferred stock having a floating interest rate adjusted periodically for changes in market interest rates and an issuer's current credit standing). Such 'auction' stock has been widely utilized in recent years by banking institutions.[71]

(2) *Tier 2*. Tier 2, 'supplementary' capital for banks would include cumulative perpetual preferred stock, intermediate-term preferred stock (that is, twenty years or more, subject to a 20 per cent downward discount for each of the stock's five years prior to maturity), convertible preferred stock and any related surplus (if the issuing bank has the option to defer payment of dividends on these instruments), hybrid capital instruments such as equity commitment notes (for banks, limited to those issued prior to 15 May 1985) and equity contract notes (that is, mandatory convertible securities), term-subordinated debt, general loan and lease loss reserves, and revaluation reserves on equity and real property holdings. Term-subordinated debt instruments and intermediate-term preferred stock with an original weighted average maturity of at least five years are includible as limited elements within Tier 2 capital, that is, such items are subject to a combined limit of 50 per cent of Tier 1 capital. 'General' reserves are those that are freely available to absorb future losses as distinguished from 'specific reserves' designated against identifiable impaired assets. General reserves would exclude specific reserves and

allocated transfer risk reserves, and would be limited to 1½ per cent of risk assets after 31 December 1990 and to 1¼ per cent of risk assets after 31 December 1991.[72]

(3) *Deductions.* The guidelines provide for certain deductions from capital. For example, all 'goodwill' is deducted from Tier 1 capital before the Tier 2 portion of the calculation is made, subject to various transition rules. Other intangible assets, such as mortgage servicing rights and core deposit premiums, will not be required to be deducted; and the FRB (unlike the OCC, with possible exception criteria, and FDIC) is not proposing a general policy of deducting automatically other intangible assets (all of which, nevertheless, will be closely monitored by the FRB). But goodwill of bank holding companies (but not banks) that was in existence prior to 17 March 1988 would be 'grandfathered' until the end of the transitional period in 1992. Further, goodwill arising from an acquisition of a failed bank would be permanently 'grandfathered' from the deduction requirements.[73]

Also, there would be deductions from the sum of Tier 1 'core' capital and Tier 2 supplementary capital for reciprocal holdings of 'core' capital in other banking institutions. Reciprocal holdings would include any intentional cross-holdings or formal or informal arrangements in which two or more banking institutions swap, exchange or otherwise hold each other's capital instruments.[74] However, such deductions would not be required for capital holdings in connection with so-called 'stake-out' transactions that comply with the FRB's *Policy Statement on Non-Voting Equity Investment.*[75] Deductions for investments in unconsolidated banking and finance subsidiaries would be made 50 per cent from Tier 1 'core' capital, and the remainder deducted from Tier 2 supplementary capital.[76] Further, there would be deductions for investments in 'risky' subsidiaries.[77]

Exhibit 11.1 (derived from the FRB guidelines) summarizes qualifying capital under the new capital adequacy guidelines.

Exhibit 11.1 Summary definition of qualifying capital for banks using the year-end 1992 standards

Components	Minimum requirements after transition period
Core capital (Tier 1)	Must equal or exceed 4% of weighted risk assets

Exhibit 11.1—*cont.*

Common stockholders' equity	No limit
Qualifying non-cumulative perpetual preferred stock	No limit; banks should avoid undue reliance on stock in Tier 1
Minority interest in equity accounts of consolidated subsidiaries	Banks should avoid using minority interest to introduce elements not otherwise qualifying for Tier 1 capital
Less: goodwill	
Supplementary capital (Tier 2)	Limited to 100% of Tier 1[a]
Allowance for loan and lease loss	Limited to 1.25% of weighted risk assets[a]
Perpetual preferred stock	No limit within Tier 2
Hybrid capital instruments and equity contract notes	No limit within Tier 2
Subordinated debt and intermediate-term preferred stock (original weighted average maturity of 5 years or more)	Subordinated debt and intermediate-term preferred stock are limited to 50% of Tier 1;[a] amortized for capital purposes as they approach maturity
Revaluation reserves (equity and building)	Not included: banks encouraged to disclose; may be evaluated on a case-by-case basis for international comparisons; and taken into account in making an overall assessment of capital
Deductions (from sum of Tier 1 and Tier 2)	
Investments in unconsolidated subsidiaries	

Reciprocal holdings of banking organizations' capital securities	
Other deductions (such as other subsidiaries or joint ventures) as determined by supervisory authority	On a case-by-case basis or as a matter of policy after formal rulemaking
Total capital (Tier 1 + Tier 2) less deductions	Must equal or exceed 8% of weighted risk assets

[a]Excess amounts permitted, but not includible as qualified capital.

Risk-weight categories The new bank guidelines established four risk-weight categories: 0 per cent, 20 per cent, 50 per cent and 100 per cent.

Exhibit 11.2 (derived from the FRB guidelines) summarizes the risk-weights and risk categories for banks.

Exhibit 11.2   Summary of risk-weights and risk categories for banks

Category 1: 0 per cent

1 Cash (domestic and foreign) held in the bank or in transit.
2 Balances due from Federal Reserve Bank (including Federal Reserve Bank stock) and central banks in other OECD countries.
3 Direct claims on, and the portions of claims that are unconditionally guaranteed by, the US Treasury and US government agencies and the central governments of other OECD countries, and local currency claims on, and the portions of local currency claims that are unconditionally guaranteed by, the central governments of non-OECD countries (including the central banks of non-OECD countries), to the extent that the bank has liabilities booked in that currency.
4 Gold bullion held in the bank's vaults or in another's vaults on an allocated basis, to the extent offset by gold bullion liabilities.

Exhibit 11.2—*cont.*

Category 2: 20 per cent

1 Cash items in the process of collection.
2 All claims (long- or short-term) on, and the portions of claims (long- or short-term) that are guaranteed by, US depository institutions and OECD banks.
3 Short-term claims (remaining maturity of one year or less) on, and the portions of short-term claims that are guaranteed by, non-OECD banks.
4 The portions of claims that are conditionally guaranteed by the central governments of OECD countries and US government agencies, and the portions of local currency claims that are conditionally guaranteed by the central governments of non-OECD countries, to the extent that the bank has liabilities booked in that currency.
5 Claims on, and the portions of claims that are guaranteed by, US government-sponsored agencies.
6 General obligation claims on, and the portions of claims that are guaranteed by the full faith and credit of, local governments and political subdivisions of the US and other OECD local governments.
7 Claims on, and the portions of claims that are guaranteed by, official multilateral lending institutions or regional development banks.
8 The portions of claims that are collateralized by securities issued or guaranteed by the US Treasury, the central governments of other OECD countries, US government agencies, US government-sponsored agencies, or by cash on deposit in the bank.
9 The portions of claims that are collateralized by securities issued by official multilateral lending institutions or regional development banks.
10 Certain privately issued securities representing indirect ownership of mortgage-backed US government agency or US government-sponsored agency securities.
11 Investment in shares of a fund whose portfolio is permitted to hold only securities that would qualify for the 0 or 20 per cent risk categories.

Category 3: 50 per cent

1 Loans fully secured by first liens on 1–4-family residential properties that have been made in accordance with prudent underwriting standards, that are performing in accordance with their original terms, and are not past due or in non-accrual status, and certain privately issued mortgage-backed securities representing indirect ownership of such loans. (Loans made for speculative purposes are excluded.)
2 Revenue bonds or similar claims that are obligations of US state or local governments, or other OECD local governments, but for which the government entity is committed to repay the debt only out of revenues from the facilities financed.
3 Credit equivalent amounts of interest rate and foreign exchange rate related contracts, except for those assigned to a lower risk category.

Category 4: 100 per cent

1 All other claims on private obligors.
2 Claims on, or guaranteed by, non-OECD foreign banks with a remaining maturity exceeding one year.
3 Claims on, or guaranteed by, non-OECD central governments that are not included in item 3 of Category 1 or item 4 of Category 2; all claims on non-OECD state or local governments.
4 Obligations issued by US state or local governments, or other OECD local governments (including industrial development authorities and similar entities), repayable solely by a private party or enterprise.
5 Premises, plant and equipment; other fixed assets; and other real estate owned.
6 Investments in any unconsolidated subsidiaries, joint ventures or associated companies – if not deducted from capital.
7 Instruments issued by other banking organizations that qualify as capital – if not deducted from capital.
8 Claims on commercial firms owned by a government.
9 All other assets, including any intangible assets that are not deducted from capital.

The FRB had originally proposed placing mortgage loans in the 100 per cent category, while the Basle Committee's recommendation was for them to be included in the 50 per cent category.[78] Under the final FRB guidelines, loans fully secured by mortgages on residential property that is or is intended to be occupied by the borrower or is rented are now included in the 50 per cent risk-rate category. However, such mortgage loans must be secured by first mortgages on one- to four-family residential properties; must include a conservative loan-to-value ratio; must not be ninety days or more pass due or on non-accrual status; and must be performing in accordance with the original terms of the loan.[79]

With respect to claims on foreign governments and foreign banks, the new guidelines make no differentiation between claims on US government securities and obligations of US banks and those respecting foreign governments and in banks in countries that are full members of the industrialized-nation bloc comprising the Organization for Economic Cooperation and Development (OECD) or that (like Saudi Arabia) have concluded special arrangements under the International Monetary Fund's General Arrangements to Borrow. Such domestic and such foreign government securities would fall within the 0 per cent category (regardless of maturity date), and claims on domestic and such foreign depository institutions would come under the 20 per cent category. Revenue and industrial development bonds (that is, non-general obligation bonds) would fall, however, within the 50 per cent category.[80]

Off-balance-sheet items   OBS exposures[81] would now be integrated into the base as to which capital is measured. For these OBS items there is a two-step conversion process. First, the face value of each OBS item is converted into an amount allowing it to be equated to an on-balance-sheet loan in terms of credit risk. This is the so-called instrument's 'credit equivalent'. The equivalent is arrived at by multiplying the nominal principal amount of the OBS instrument by a specific credit-conversion factor. Then, the credit equivalent is slotted into one of the four risk categories. Categorization is determined by analysing the type of the instrument, the obligor, the collateral or guaranty that is involved.[82]

Exhibit 11.3 (derived from the new FRB guidelines) indicates the credit-conversion factors for specific OBS items.

Exhibit 11.3   Credit-conversion factors for OBS items

100 per cent conversion factor

1 Direct credit substitutes (general guarantees of indebtedness and guarantee-type instruments, including standby letters of credit).
2 Risk participations in bankers' acceptances and participations in direct credit substitutes.
3 Sale and repurchase agreements.
4 Forward agreements (that is, contractual obligations) to purchase assets, including financing facilities with certain drawdown.

50 per cent conversion factor

1 Transaction-related contingencies (for example, bid bonds, performance bonds, warranties, and standby letters of credit related to a particular transaction).
2 Unused commitments with an original maturity exceeding one year.
3 Revolving underwriting facilities (RUFs), note issuance facilities (NIFs) and other similar arrangements.

20 per cent conversion factor

1 Short-term, self-liquidating trade-related contingencies, including commercial letters of credit.

0 per cent conversion factor

1 Unused commitments with an original maturity of one year or less.
2 Unused commitments which are unconditionally cancellable at any time, regardless of maturity.

The final risk-based calculation (including OBS items) is indicated in exhibit 11.4 (again derived from the new FRB guidelines).

Exhibit 11.4 Sample calculation of risk-based ratio for banks

Example of a bank with $6,000 in total capital and the following assets and off-balance-sheet items:

Balance sheet assets	
Cash	$ 5,000
US Treasuries	20,000
Balances at domestic banks	5,000
Loans secured by first liens on 1–4-family residential properties	5,000
Loans to private corporations	65,000
Total balance sheet assets	100,000

Off-balance-sheet items	
Standby letters of credit (SLCs) backing general obligation debt issues of US municipalities (GOs)	$ 10,000
long-term legally binding commitments to private corporations	20,000
Total off-balance-sheet items	30,000

This bank's total capital to total assets (average) ratio would be ($6,000/$100,000) = 6.00%

To compute the bank's weighted risk assets
1. Compute the Credit equivalent amount of each off-balance-sheet (OBS) item

OBS item	Face value		Conversion factor		Credit equivalent amount
SLCs backing municipal GOs	$10,000	×	1.00	=	$10,000

2. Multiply each balance sheet asset and the credit equivalent amount of each OBS item by the appropriate risk weight.

0% category

Cash	$ 5,000			
US Treasuries	20,000			
	25,000	×	0	= 0

20% category

Balances at domestic banks	5,000			
Credit equivalent amounts of SLCs backing GOs of US municipalities	10,000	×	0.20	= $ 3,000

50% category

Loans secured by first liens on 1–4-family residential properties	5,000	×	0.50	= 2,500

100% category

Loans to private corporations	65,000			
Credit equivalent amounts of long-term commitments to private corporations	10,000			
	75,000	×	1.00	= 75,000

Total risk-weighted assets 80,500

This bank's ratio of total risk assets (risk-based capital ratio) would be ($6,000/$80,500) = 7.45%

Required minimum levels of capital In determining the required levels of capital, there are certain basic limitations. First, Tier 2 'supplementary' capital cannot exceed the amount of Tier 1 'core' capital. Second, banking institutions must obtain an 8 per cent ratio of total capital-to-total risk-weighted assets and OBS items by the end of 1992. Accordingly, by the end of 1992, Tier 1 capital would have to be at least 4 per cent of total risk-adjusted assets and OBS items.[83]

Transitional rules apply for the periods of 1989 through 1990 and through 1991 to 1992. During 1989 through 1990, Tier 1 capital could be increased by Tier 2 capital to the extent of 25 per cent of all Tier 1 capital. In addition, as mentioned above, goodwill for bank holding companies would be grandfathered, and there would be no limitation on loan loss reserves in Tier 2 capital. During the period of 1991 to 1992, Tier 1 capital could be increased by Tier 2 capital to the extent of 10 per cent of all Tier capital; goodwill of bank holding companies would still be grandfathered; but loan loss reserves would be limited to 1.5 per cent of risk assets. In addition, for this period, a minimum total capital ratio of 7.25 per cent, of which 3.625 per cent must be Tier 1 capital, would be required.[84]

Exhibit 11.5 (derived from the new FRB guidelines) summarizes certain of the transitional arrangements for banking institutions under the new capital adequacy guidelines.

11.3.2 *The Practical Implications*

General impact Generally, the adoption of the new risk-based capital adequacy guidelines (in terms of concept, composition, measurement and institution applicability) has broad implications for a banking institution, its management, shareholders and depositors, and for domestic and international bank regulators and regulators of other financial intermediaries.

For a banking institution, regulatory bank capital requirements impose an inescapable strain and tension between the need for prudent risk management and the need to be competitive and to produce an acceptable level of return for investors. Most well-managed business enterprises will secure (from owner investments or retained earnings) an adequate level of capital to support infrastructure operations and expansion and to cover foreseeable growth and contingencies; management judgements on capital are normally reflected on a going-concern and foreseeable basis. But bank regulatory capital is based on absorption of unexpected losses, and if not on a worst-case, liquidation scenario, then on a sustained-bad-times projection. Larger than normal business amounts of required capital for banking institutions, in turn, amount to a regulatory tax that increases overall operational costs, costs of funds and regulatory reporting and compliance burdens. That levy may restrain dividend payments, competitive positions and growth capabilities, and may lead to an institution taking greater portfolio risks or 'untaxed' risks (for example, OBS activities) in pursuit of greater profits or divesting quality assets (that is, 'asset stripping' and 'asset securitization') to reduce the capital adequacy formula denominator for purposes of satisfying the required capital-to-assets percentages and to avoid having to raise additional capital funds.

Obviously, a capital-to-asset risk-based formula is intended, in part, to address the off-balance-sheet risk problem and trends toward selling off an institution's more liquid and less risky assets; but even this formula still leaves a banking institution in a probable uncompetitive position with competing non-bank financial intermediaries, which can lead to underpricing of competing products and, thus, to greater risks and lower profit possibilities for the banking institution.

Mandatory regulatory capital schemes, therefore, can leave banking institutions on the horns of a dilemma. To meet new and higher capital standards, the institution will have to do one or more of the following: go to the securities markets (which is probably only available to the very top creditworthy banks and which may still be adversely affected by the type of financial instruments includible in the permitted capital base); to revise its profit goals and attendant management policies for attempting to generate the needed earnings to be retained as capital; or to reduce its asset base (for example, through securitization) and to shift to more non-loan, fee-generating activities. Regulatory capital requirements not only place constraints on an institution's portfolio growth (as more assets means more capital and not simply more sources of available funds), but also place constraints on an institution's growth through acquisition policies, particularly if goodwill is to be deducted from acceptable capital and if the regulators (as under the new risk-based guidelines) indicate they will require higher levels of capital for growth and acquisition-oriented financial institutions.

Specific impact   In terms of specific impact on the general activities

Exhibit 11.5 Transitional arrangements for banks	Initial	Year-end 1990	Final arrangements year-end 1992
1. Minimum standard of total to weighted risk assets	None	7.25%	8.0%
2. Definition of Tier 1 capital	Common equity, qualifying non-cum, perpetual preferred stock, minority interest, plus supplementary elements[a] less goodwill	Common equity, qualifying non-cum, perpetual preferred stock, minority interest, plus supplementary elements[b] less goodwill,	Common equity, qualifying non-cum, perpetual preferred stock and minority interest less goodwill
3. Minimum standard of Tier capital to weighted risk assets	None	3.625%	4.0%
4. Minimum standard of stockholders' equity to weighted risk assets	None	3.25%	4.0%

5. Limitations on supplementary capital elements:			
(a) Allowance for loan and lease losses	No limit within Tier 2	1.5% of weighted risk assets	1.25% of weighted risk assets
(b) Qualifying perpetual preferred stock	No limit within Tier 2	No limit within Tier 2	No limit within Tier 2
(c) Hybrid capital instruments and equity contract notes	No limit within Tier 2	No limit within Tier 2	No limit within Tier 2
(d) Subordinated debt and intermediate term	Combined maximum of 50% of Tier 1	Combined maximum of 50% of Tier 1	Combined maximum of 50% of Tier 1
(e) Total qualifying Tier 2 capital	May not exceed Tier 1 capital	May not exceed Tier 1 capital	May not exceed Tier 1 capital
6. Definition of total	Tier 1 plus Tier 2 less: reciprocal holdings of banking organizations' capital instruments investments in unconsolidated subsidiaries	Tier 1 plus Tier 2 less: reciprocal holdings of banking organizations' capital instruments investments in unconsolidated subsidiaries	Tier 1 plus Tier 2 less: reciprocal holdings of banking organizations' capital instruments investments in unconsolidated subsidiaries

[a] Supplementary elements may be included in Tier 1 up to 25% of the sum of Tier 1 plus goodwill.
[b] Supplementary elements may be included in Tier 1 up to 10% of the sum of Tier 1 plus goodwill.

of banking institutions, the new risk-based guidelines will probably cause such institutions to consider:

- increasing mortgage loans (now in 50 per cent category);
- utilizing securitization to meet new requirements and taking advantage of low risk ratings of privately issued mortgage-backed securities, where the underlying pool of assets is comprised solely of mortgage-related securities issued by GNMA, FNMA or FHLMC (20 per cent category);
- building liquidity with short-term government obligations (0 per cent category);
- reducing standby letters of credit (now in 100 or 50 per cent category) and reducing or restructuring loan commitments (now also considered in OBS item conversion);
- evaluating and structuring more carefully acquisition transactions in event regulatory approval requires greater capital and goodwill is excludible as a capital item; and
- restructuring drastically pricing structures for products and services.

For bank depositors, interbank lenders and bank investors (existing and potential), a high capital ratio is often proffered as a badge for public confidence in the institution – an intangible factor or perception deemed needed to promote fund deposits, and equity and long-term debt placements and investments and to avoid liquidity runs. But a serious question exists whether the higher ratio can ever be fully adequate in a forced liquidation or insolvency situation. Moreover, bank depositors, many times, will be looking to a deposit protection scheme for primary protection against loss; interbank lenders will rely on the short-term nature of their loans and on their interbank management skills; and market investors will desire a reasonable return on investment for some inevitable investment risk-taking. Further, as the capital formula becomes more complicated and as more subjective regulatory judgements are required on such matters of risk assessment and capital adequacy, such parties will be in need of greater transparency for making sound deposit, lending or investment decisions.

For the bank regulator, reformulation of regulatory capital notions forces a rethinking and re-sorting of the policy justifications for prudential supervision regulations. Such reformulation considers the following: whether the large institutional and system costs of a mandatory capital scheme outweigh the benefits; what functional purposes do capital formulae serve for the regulators; and whether such tests are only for solvency evaluation purposes or are for broader purposes as institutional evaluation, bank management assessment and constraint, and enhancement of transparency for the regulators. More generally, the regulators will need to refine the use of capital adequacy as a financial institution restructuring tool.

In more mundane terms, use of a more sophisticated capital adequacy test imposes new and greater burdens on the regulators in implementing the test in a fair and meaningful manner. Better information-gathering, analytical assessment tools, trained staff and surveillance procedures will be needed. Also, the increased complexities of an asset-risk test exacerbate the potential for divergent treatment and use of the test. Because this divergence may give rise to competitive inequalities, the need arises for better cooperation, exchange of information, and convergence of capital and related prudential supervision policies with respect to the various national bank regulators.

In sum, mandatory regulatory capital requirements have significant external manifestations respecting numerous (and conceivably individualized and non-aligned) interests – including the banking institutions, its management, its investors, its depositors, its lenders and regulators from other jurisdictions. Furthermore, these requirements have significant internal implications for a particular bank regulator.

11.3.3 *The OCC's Policy for National Banks*

More specifically, the new capital adequacy standards for banks may have the following effects, as suggested in a recent analysis by the OCC staff:[85]

Risk-based capital standards should provide bank managers with a strong incentive to shrink bank size in order to lessen capital requirements.

The following are risk weightings (RW) that have some bearing on the securitization process (from 12 Code of Federal Regulations Part 3):

RW	Risk Based Capital
0%	Unconditionally guaranteed US governments, including non-collateralized GNMA pass-throughs.
20%	US government-sponsored agencies such as GNMA and

FHLMC; CMOs collateralized by US government-sponsored agencies including GNMAs, FNMAs, and FHLMC;
bank obligations such as CDs and deposit notes and 100
per cent bank-guaranteed securities.

50%   Residential REMs and CMOs collateralized by residential
REMs; revenue bonds.

100%   Other loans; asset-backed securities collateralized by
loans; corporate bonds, commercial paper, industrial
development bonds (IDBs), IOs, POs, Residuals.

Off-balance-sheet items will be converted to balance-sheet equivalents
and then risk-weighted according to the standard risk weights. Table
11.1 shows conversion factors that will have some bearing on the
securitization process.

Table 11.1 Conversion factors for off-balance-sheet items

Conversion (%)	RW (%)	Off-balance-sheet product
100	100–0	Loans sold with recourse; letters of credit; forward purchases
50	100	Unused home equity loan line (over one year)

The following are examples of how securitization can be used to
meet targeted ratios of risk-weighted assets to capital:

1 Higher-weighted assets can be sold as securities and the bank
shrunk:
   Example
   • Credit-card (CARDs) or automobile (CARs) loans with a 100
   per cent RW can be securitized and sold without recourse and
   the bank shrunk as source funds are paid out.

2 More likely, higher-weighted risk assets can be converted to lower-
weighted securities:
   Example
   • REMs with a 50 per cent RW can be converted to FNMAs or
   FHMLCs with a 20 per cent RW.
   • The federally sponsored mortgage agencies will be very accom-
   modating in arranging swaps.

3 Higher risk-weighted assets can be converted to securities, sold,
and the sale proceeds redeployed to lower-rated risk assets:

Example
- Commercial, credit-card and car loans with a 100 per cent RW or REMs with a 50 per cent RW can be converted to securities and sold.
- Funds can then be reinvested in lower-weighted Treasuries (0 per cent) or agencies (20 per cent) or medium-term deposit notes (20 per cent).

4   Banks with excess capital can certainly use this kind of redeployment of funds to expand their balance sheet by acquiring additional lower-weighted assets to improve their return on equity, provided they stay with the 0 per cent risk-based capital minimum.

Example
Sell: $1mm 100 per cent RW assets

Buy: $5mm in 20 per cent RW assets (capital weight same) but hopefully a significant increase in return on equity

Notably, the risk-based capital rules are separate from and in addition to the minimum leverage ratio imposed by 12 C.F.R. 3.

11.4 UK Bank Regulatory Concerns

11.4.1 *Introduction and Overview*

As indicated in 11.2 above, the Bank of England has moved to implement the Basle Supervisory Committee's July 1988 Report through means other than formal legal regulation.

The Bank of England moved quickly. In January 1988 it issued an explanatory paper entitled, 'Proposals for International Convergence of Capital Measurement and Capital Standards', even before the final Report of the Basle Supervisory Committee in July 1988 (entitled 'International Convergence of Capital Measurement and Capital Standards' (the 'Convergence Agreement')). Its historical approach to prudential supervision and its work on the development of the UK/US Accord had ensured the Bank of England was well placed to proceed with the implementation of the Convergence Agreement. The explanatory paper was followed in October 1988, after publication of the Convergence Agreement, with a further Notice (BSD 1988/3) entitled 'Implementation of the Basle Convergence Agreement in the United Kingdom' (the 'Implementation Notice').

The Implementation Notice makes it clear that the assessment of the capital adequacy of relevant credit institutions in the UK will closely follow the Convergence Agreement. It also explains how the Bank of England will exercise the various discretions given to national supervisory authorities under the Convergence Agreement, such as, for example, whether to include current year's earnings in the calculation of the capital base.

The development and implementation of capital adequacy standards as a means of supervising credit institutions is also being pursued within the European Community's Single Market Programme – a reflection of the degree of correspondence between the G-10 countries and the EC members. The European Parliament has passed two Directives: the Directive on Solvency Ratio for Credit Institutions, Council Directive No. 89/647/EEC (the 'Solvency Ratio Directive'), adopted on 18 December 1989 and the Directive on the Own Funds of Credit Institutions, Council Directive No. 89/299/EEC (the 'Own Funds Directive') adopted on 17 April 1989. Taken together the Solvency Ratio Directive and the Own Funds Directive embrace the concept of capital adequacy standards which is fundamental to the Convergence Agreement as the preferred basis for supervision for EC Members.

The Own Funds Directive provides a definition of capital, termed 'own funds', which is to be used by EC Member States in all law, regulation and administrative action implementing EC legislation, 'concerning the prudential supervision of an operative credit institution' (Article 1(1)). The Solvency Ratio Directive establishes a solvency ratio as the key indicator of capital adequacy to be used in the supervision of credit institutions. The ratio is a comparison of own funds with total risk-weighted assets and off-balance sheet items.

Strong attempts were made to ensure consistency between the EC approach and the Convergence Agreement and, subject to some minor differences, the Own Funds Directive and the Solvency Ratio Directive follow very closely the principles set out in the Convergence Agreement.

Since the Implementation Notice, there have been other regulatory developments in the UK that directly concern securitizations. Capital adequacy regulation requires that credit institutions maintain adequate 'core capital' to cover their risk-weighted assets such as mortgage, credit card and other loan portfolios. Assets with high risk weights, such as loans to companies in the non-bank private sector, require high core capital coverage. Securitization has developed as a technique to help institutions reduce the core capital coverage needed. It is used as a method of packaging assets in a structure to which credit enhancement techniques can be applied, thereby reducing the risk weighting. Securitization techniques are also used as a means of removing assets from the balance sheet altogether and thereby is outside the application of the risk weighting process.

The Bank of England became concerned about the effect on the integrity of the capital adequacy regulation of securitization techniques which employed elaborate and artificial corporate structures to take the assets off-balance sheet. To preserve the integrity of capital adequacy regulation the bank issued a Notice introducing controls on the divestment of loans in February 1989. This Notice, entitled 'Loan Transfer and Securitisation' (the 'Loan Sales Notice') (BSD 1989/1), provides standards and guidance as to when divestments will be effective to take an asset completely off-balance sheet and thereby eliminate the need for core capital coverage.

The ability to take an asset off-balance sheet has also been significantly circumscribed by recent developments in company law and accounting. Amendments to the Companies Act in 1989, which apply to institutions in respect of their financial years commencing after 23 December 1989, have made important extensions to the definition of a subsidiary. These amendments require that parent companies consolidate in their annual accounts companies with which they have a tenuous relationship. Also, Exposure Draft 49 of the Accounting Standards Committee proposes new accounting treatment for 'quasi-subsidiaries', which may include special purpose vehicle companies set up for securitizations, where the original lender/seller retains certain benefits or risks relating to the asset transferred to a quasi-subsidiary. Exposure Draft 49 also proposes that even where consolidation is not required under ED49, note disclosure is required to explain the lender's interest in the new lender and any income or benefits deriving from that new lender. ED49 is only *draft* at this stage. It adopts a cavalier approach to the reporting of transactions and arrangements by emphasising substance not fact and, for this reason, is likely to be controversial.

In the future, the effect of these amendments could be to restrict considerably the ability to use securitization as a means of taking certain assets totally off the balance sheet of lenders. However, securitization will still be valuable as a technique for creating a structure to which credit enhancement techniques can be applied, and so reduce the core capital coverage required under the Bank of England's capital adequacy standards. Moreover, securitization has a second, extremely important function – to obtain immediate funds for the original lender from a portfolio of 'longer term' assets. This benefit is not affected by regulatory controls on off-balance sheet financing techniques and will remain of prime importance to many lenders examining the quality of their balance sheets.

Each of these aspects of capital adequacy regulation in the United Kingdom, will be examined in more detail in the following sections.

11.4.2 *Implementation of the Basle Convergence Agreement in the United Kingdom*

The Bank of England historically has adopted a non-legal approach to supervision. Although, with the passage of the Banking Act 1987 the Bank's formal legal authority and power to supervise were strengthened in comparison with that of the United States and some other EC members, its *modus operandi* remains flexible and non-legalistic.

The Bank of England has implemented the Convergence Agreement consistently with its general supervisory style. Thus, the Explanatory Paper and the Implementing Notice have no direct legal force and are not delegated legislation. The Bank of England's extraordinarily broad powers to grant and revoke authorization on grounds relating to, *inter alia*, very broadly described prudential factors, provides strong encouragement for authorized institutions to comply with the principles and standards set out in these documents.

To enable it to supervise compliance with these capital adequacy standards, the Bank of England requires that institutions submit a Capital Adequacy Return. Again, this is not a legal requirement. However, the Bank of England has power under section 39 to obtain information and requires the production of documents or reports on any matter that relates to the performance of the Bank's functions under the Act by a formal legal request. This power effectively underpins the request to submit the Capital Adequacy Return.

The process of assessing capital adequacy detailed in the Convergence Agreement is closely paralleled by the Bank of England's Implementation Notice. There are some particular points to note.

Although the Convergence Agreement proposals are designed to be applied on a consolidated basis, the Bank of England will also (i.e. in addition to the consolidated basis) continue to assess capital adequacy on a consolidated or unconsolidated basis as appropriate, to ensure that there is a reasonable distribution of capital within a group. The principles of consolidation are set out in the Bank's Notice on Consolidated Supervision (BSD/1986/3 *and see* BSD/1989/2).

The Convergence Agreement specifies a minimum capital adequacy requirement of 8 per cent of the total of risk-weighted assets, including off-balance sheet amounts. However, the Bank of England has made it clear that for most institutions the actual figure for capital adequacy will be higher and that it will be assessed separately for each institution.

In the Annex to the Implementing Notice, criteria are set out for determining:

1 Capital (Schedule 1);
2 Risk weightings for on-balance sheet transactions (Schedule 2);
3 Risk weightings for off-balance sheet transactions (Schedule 3);
4 Risk weightings for interest and foreign exchange related transactions (Schedule 4).

Capital The Bank of England has continued the two-tier approach to the definition of capital used in the Convergence Agreement. Tier one capital (or 'core capital') consists of paid up equity share capital and disclosed reserves derived from post tax retained earnings. Tier one capital may include perpetual non-cumulative preference shares, provided that the Bank of England has given its prior approval to the terms of the issue. Tier one capital must not include goodwill and other intangible assets. Of concern to securitization projects is the Bank of England's position that mortgage servicing rights will be regarded as intangible assets unless it can be demonstrated that there is an active and liquid market in which they can be reliably traded. Such a market exists at present only for such rights traded in the United States market. Tier one capital must also be net of the current year's unpublished losses. At least 50 per cent of the capital base of an institution must consist of Tier one capital.

Tier two capital (or 'supplementary capital') includers undisclosed reserves, asset revaluation reserves, general provision/general loan loss reserves, certain hybrid debt capital instruments (e.g. preference shares and perpetual subordinated debt) and subordinated term debt. Tier two capital must not include more than 45 per cent of the increase in the market value of its long term holdings of equity securities, where they are available to meet losses. The 55 per cent discount factor is to take into account the volatility of such securities and the tax charge which might arise on the realization of gains.

The Bank of England requires that all provisions which are raised against identified losses or impairments in asset values must be excluded from the calculation of capital. In particular, provisions against problem country debt must be excluded. General provisions held against unidentified losses may be included in Tier two capital subject to limits.

In recognition of the difficulties encountered in defining reserves and provisions, the Convergence Agreement allows national authorities to phase down the amount of reserves and provisions that may qualify as capital during a transitional period and to permit a temporary and exceptional ceiling of 2 per cent. The Bank of England has implemented the transitional limits, that is, general provisions up to a maximum of 1.5 per cent of weighted-risk assets may be included until the end of 1992 and thereafter 1.25 per cent. However, the 2 per cent ceiling will not be permitted.

The Convergence Agreement gives national authorities a discretion as to whether holdings of bank and building society capital and capital instruments should be deducted from capital. The Bank of England has required that, (except to the extent that the Bank of England has agreed that these are held in a market-making capacity) they must be deduced from the total of Tier one and Tier two capital, as must investments in unconsolidated subsidiaries and associates. Trade investments, however, do not have to be deducted.

Risk weightings   The Bank of England has also implemented the risk weightings system used in the Convergence Agreement. The Agreement states that the preferred method of assessing the capital adequacy of banks is to relate capital to all the different categories of assets and off-balance sheet exposure, which are weighted according to broad categories of relative riskiness. Five bands of 'riskiness' have been used: 0 per cent, 10 per cent, 20 per cent, 50 per cent and 100 per cent.

The implementation Notice lists the assets falling within each of these bands. Risk weight categories for on-balance sheet assets are set out in Annex 1 to the Implementation Notice. The Bank of England has decided to apply a weight of 10 per cent to holdings of United

Kingdom Government Paper with a residual maturity of under one year, and a weight of 20 per cent if one year or over. A weight of 20 per cent is allocated to other public-sector bodies. The Bank of England has limited the 50 per cent weighting given under the Convergence Agreement to loans to owner-occupiers for residential house purchases that are fully secured by a mortgage. Thus it will only apply to lending to individuals and to Housing Associations registered with the Housing Corporation for the sole purpose of residential occupation that is fully secured by a first legal or equitable charge. The Bank of England has not imposed the additional requirements that such loans must not be 90 days or more past due and must be performing in accordance with the original terms of the loan, features of the US FRB guidelines (see p. 30). In the United Kingdom, mortgage-backed securities will attract a 50 per cent weighting if they are fully and specifically secured by mortgages which qualify for the 50 per cent weight or by other assets which qualify for a weight of less than 50 per cent.

The relevant risk/asset ratio is calculated by first multiplying the balance sheet value of each asset by its weighting, to give a risk-adjusted value. The Implementation Notice follows the Convergence Agreement by providing for off-balance sheet items to be converted to an equivalent on-balance sheet figure by multiplying the nominal principal amounts of items by the relevant applicable conversion factor (0 per cent, 20 per cent, 50 per cent or 100 per cent). Credit conversion factors for typical off-balance sheet items are set out in Annex 1 to the Implementation Notice. The resulting amount is then weighted according to the nature of the claim in the same way as for an on-balance sheet item. All risk-adjusted values are then totalled for a risk-weighted asset total which is compared with capital.

Special rules apply for determining the risk weightings of instruments relating to interest and foreign exchange transactions. For the assessment of credit risk on these items, the method used is to determine a replacement cost of marking contracts to market and adding on a factor to reflect the institution's potential exposure over the remaining life of the contract (although it is possible that for institutions which are not actively trading such instruments, or where they do not form a significant part of the institution's treasury operations, the Bank of England may be prepared to allow a credit risk assessment method based on original exposures rather than replacement cost). The Bank of England will apply a weight of 100 per cent to an institution's aggregate net short open foreign exchange position.

As a result of implementing the Convergence Agreement in the United Kingdom with minimal modifications, the Bank of England has also introduced one of the important weaknesses of the Convergence Agreement. Although the bands of risk weightings were devised to discriminate between counterparties on the basis of the perceived riskiness of that type of counterparty, the categorization of counterparties is very general and there is no distinction within categories between risky and non-risky. For some of the more general categories such as non-bank private sector companies this provides a very crude mechanism and fails to distinguish between a large profitable international conglomerate and, say, a small undercapitalized private venture.

11.4.3 *European Community Directives*

As indicated above, the combined effect of the two Directives (Own Funds and Solvency Ratio) is to establish a supervisory system based on capital adequacy standards which closely, but not exactly, follows that in the Convergence Agreement. Here we identify some areas where the Directives differ.

Technically, the Bank of England's Regulation applies to authorized institutions and the EC Directives apply to a broader category of credit institutions. However, by complementary regulation those credit institutions that are not authorized institutions under the Banking Act will be regulated under other United Kingdom laws so that the relevant coverage of the two regimes will be identical.

The nomenclature used in the Directives is different. The Directives refer not to Tier one and Tier two capital but just to 'own funds' which is composed of various elements which are added or subtracted. However, the effect of deductions and limits set out in Article 6 of the Own Funds Directive is to create a similar tiered structure. In effect, the 'supplementary capital' is limited to 100 per cent of the core capital as in the Convergence Agreement and as implemented by the Bank of England.

Unlike the Convergence Agreement, the Directives do not distinguish between disclosed and undisclosed reserves which may be included in capital (Article 6(1) of the Own Funds Directive). Under the Convergence Agreement special provisions – provisions ascribed to the impairment of particular assets and known liabilities – may not be included in the calculation of Tier two capital, while general reserves may be. The Own Funds Directive makes no such distinction – see Article 2(1) item 4.

As in the Convergence Agreement, assets and off-balance sheet items of a credit institution are weighted according to the degree of credit risk, primarily of the counterparty. So too does the Solvency Directive require a minimum standard of 8 per cent to be met by credit institutions.

In practice, any differences of approach between the Directives and the Convergence Agreement, as implemented in the United Kingdom, will be minimal because the Directives permit Member States to apply more stringent provisions than those set out in the Directive. The Bank of England has done so in the Implementation Notice and this must be complied with by institutions authorized under the Banking Act.

In the future it can be expected that differences between the two approaches will become irrelevant as the national supervisory authorities of Member States will, in exercising their discretions in implementing the Directives, look to the Convergence Agreement for a lead.

11.4.4 *Other UK Regulations with Capital Adequacy Implications*

Loan Sales Notice As mentioned earlier, with the development of sophisticated and somewhat artificial financing techniques to avoid reporting liabilities or assets in the balance sheet of institutions, such as have been used in some securitization projects, the Bank of England became concerned about the validity of the capital adequacy/risk asset ratio as a supervisory tool. By such techniques, institutions could escape core capital requirements without, in many cases, eliminating the actual risk associated with those assets.

The Bank of England issued the Loan Sales Notice to combat the practices underlying its concerns. The Notice applies to institutions authorized under the Banking Act and incorporated in the United Kingdom. It examines methods of transferring loans under English law and the ability of each method to eliminate risk for the transferor. It specifies how each method of transfer should be reported to the Bank for supervisory purposes.

As well as addressing the sale of single loans, it specifically covers the packing, securitization and sale of loan pools and the transfer of risk under sub-participation agreements. The terms of the Loan Sales Notice are broad enough to apply to sales of other forms of assets, and to the transfer of credit under contingent items such as letters of credit, acceptance credits and undrawn commitment.

The three methods of transfer available under English law are novation, legal assignment and equitable assignment. Novation involves a tripartite contract where all parties agree to the subordination of a new lender. It is the most complete transfer of risk. Under the Loan Sales Notice the loan will be excluded from the original lender/seller's risk asset ratio and included in the new lender/buyer's.

Legal assignment involves the transfer of rights but not liabilities from the lender to the new lender. The assignment is not valid until notice of the transfer is given to the borrower in accordance with section 13 of the Law of Property Act 1925. Moreover, until notice has been given, the new lender is vulnerable to new rights created over the subject matter of the contract in favour of the borrower and the date when notice is given governs priorities between competing assignees. In recognition of these and other difficulties with legal assignments, the Loan Sales Notice provides that transfer by legal assignment will be regarded as a complete transfer where notice has been given to the borrower, and the new lender has taken precautions to ensure that his rights under the transfer are not impaired by an intervening right.

An equitable assignment is a transfer of rights as between the lender and new lender, where notice has not been given to the borrower. The Loan Sales Notice provides that the Bank of England will regard such an assignment as a complete transfer of risk on certain conditions. The lender must recognize that he will remain the lender of record and be the focal point for pressure from the borrower to reschedule or renegotiate the terms of the loan or advance further funds. Therefore, it must monitor the volume of such loans to individual borrowers. The new lender must also monitor the risk of incurring additional liability because it is possible for the lender to create new rights in favour of the borrower. The new lender's priority may also be impaired where it has not given notice.

The Loan Sales Notice sets out a number of additional conditions which must be met before the Bank will recognize that a transfer is effective. For example, the transfer must not contravene the terms and conditions of the underlying loan agreement and the buyer/new lender must have no formal recourse to the seller/lender for losses. There are further conditions to be met where the lender/seller will act as the servicing agent of loan packaging schemes 'in order to ensure that its role is not seen as being more than acting as agent' (Loan Sales Notice para. 14). For example, the board of the new lender must be independent from that of the original lender, although the original lender may have one director representing it. Also, the name of the new lender must not include the name of the serving agent or imply any connection with it.

Companies Act amendments on subsidiary undertakings Recent amendments to the Companies Act introducing the concept of 'subsidiary undertaking' will bring more remotedly associated companies into an institution's group for accounting purposes and will, therefore, have important consequences for capital adequacy standards and securitizations.

Section 5 of the 1989 Companies Act inserts a new section 227 into the Companies Act of 1985. It imposes an obligation on a parent company to prepare annual; consolidated accounts of the parent company and its subsidiary undertakings. 'Subsidiary undertakings' is very widely defined, going beyond the present definition of a subsidiary based on either control of the Board or holdings of over 50 per cent of the nominal share capital. The new definition of 'subsidiary undertaking' (in section 258(2)) in addition looks to more substantive matters such as whether the parent has 'the right to exercise a dominant influence over the undertaking by virtue of provisions in the undertakings memorandum or articles or by virtue of a control contract' (258(2)(c)).

Under new sub-section 258(4) there will be a subsidiary undertaking if the parent has a participating interest and it 'actually exercises a dominant influence over it', or if 'it and the subsidiary undertaking are managed on a unified basis'. A participating interest, *inter alia*, shall be presumed where the parent holds 20 per cent or more of shares in an undertaking.

It is too early yet to definitively pronounce on the interpretation of new section 258(2)(c) but, as it appears to extend to an institution that need not be a member of a buyer/new lender nor need to control the board, it has the potential to catch special purpose vehicle companies of the type presently used in securitizations, requiring them to be consolidated in the original lender's accounts and be incorporated into an institution's capital adequacy ratio.

Accounting Standards Committee Exposure Draft 49 Changes to the accounting treatment of off-balance sheet assets may also require institutions to consolidate accounts of more remotely associated companies, or to note their interest in any benefits received from them. Similarly, this too would affect capital adequacy calculations.

ED49 is a Proposed Statement of Accounting Practice issued in May 1990 by the Accounting Standards Committee of the Institute of Chartered Accountants for England and Wales for public comment. It follows and revises ED42, entitled 'Accounting for Special Transactions' issued in March 1988. ED42 was directed specifically to the treatment of special purpose vehicles (used in securitizations as the new lenders/buyers) which the original lender/seller intended to take off its balance sheet. ED42 aimed to provide a framework for statutory accounting purposes which recognized the economic and commercial reality of off-balance sheet financing. ED49 revises ED42 in light of the new wider definition of subsidiary undertaking in the Companies Act and of other amendments to the reporting requirements contained in new section 227(6).

ED49 states the objective of achieving commercial reality in the method of accounting for transactions and arrangements. Consistently with this objective, ED49 proposes that assets and liabilities should be recognized where future economic benefit associated with the item will flow to or from the enterprise (and the item has a cost of value that can be measured). Moreover, ED49 proposes that an enterprise should consolidate the accounts of another enterprise where the risks and benefits of an asset will flow through to the first enterprise, notwithstanding that they are held by that other enterprise and notwithstanding that the two enterprises are not parent and subsidiary as defined by the Companies Act. ED49 names such other enterprises 'quasi-subsidiaries'. ED49 justifies this proposal on the basis that 'control of a resource generally comprises the ability to obtain the future economic benefits associated with the resource' (para. 47), and that 'the consolidation principle is founded on the belief that the assets under the control of the group and used in its operations, and the liabilities that finance them, should be incorporated in a single balance sheet so that, as far as practicable, the group balance sheet shows the resources which are controlled by the group (para. 43).

ED49 is related to the Companies Act through the true and fair view requirement for financial accounts. The 1989 Companies Act added a new qualification on the existing requirement that company accounts present a true and fair view (subsection 227(6)). Under the new provision if, in special circumstances, compliance with any of the provisions in Schedule 4A about contents and form of group accounts would not give a true and fair view of the state of affairs, the directors must depart from any of the provisions to the extent necessary to give a true and fair view.

ED49 provides that the existence of a quasi-subsidiary will often constitute special circumstances, requiring them to be treated in group accounts in the same way as a legally deferred subsidiary.

In the Application Notes to ED49 there is further specific discussion of securitizations. The notes also provide that even where there is no quasi-subsidiary, minimum note disclosure should be made to explain the original lender's interest in the income as coming from the new lender (para. D.14).

As explained above, any requirement to consolidate a company's accounts will bring assets onto an institution's balance sheet, to be included in the calculations of its risk/asset ratio. Even the noting of an asset will make it an off-balance asset and similarly, have implications for risk asset ratio and capital adequacy level.

Because of its emphasis on the substance and commercial effect of transactions, ED49 is innovative and controversial. It is not yet known whether, and if so when, it may be implemented as a Standard Statement of Accounting Practice. If it is published as an SSAP, it will be followed by members of the Institute of Chartered Accountants, have the broadest impact in the accounting profession and, hence, for institutions and enterprises generally.

Notes

1 See generally R. M. Pecchioli (for OECD), *The Internationalization of Banking: The Policy Issues* (1983).
2 See generally Study Group established by the Central Banks of the Group of Ten Countries (Sam Y. Cross, Chair), *Recent Innovations in International Banking* (1986).
3 See generally R. M. Pecchioli (for OECD), *Prudential Supervision in Banking* (1987).
4 For discussion of these and certain other banking crises affecting prudential supervision developments for international banking activities, see R. Dale, *The Regulation of International Banking* (1984), pp. 156–7.
5 On the Third World debt crisis, see, *inter alia*, J. J. Norton (ed.), *Prospects for International Lending and Reschedulings* (1988).
6 For discussion of the policy, practical and legal significance of the capital adequacy issue, see Norton, 'Capital adequacy standards: a legitimate

regulatory concern for prudential supervision of banking activities', 49
Ohio St. L.J. 1267 (Spec. Symposium Winter 1989), on which portions of
this chapter are based.

7 The formal name of the committee is the 'Basle Committee on Banking
Regulations and Supervisory Practices', the formation and purposes of
which are briefly discussed in section 11.2 below.

8 See note 4 above.

9 The OECD stands for the Organization for Economic Cooperation and
Development, an international consultative organization which presently
comprises twenty-four of the principal Western industrialized countries
and which undertakes research and affords a forum for high-level economic discussions for its members. See, *inter alia*, R. W. Edwards Jr,
International Monetary Collaboration (1985), pp. 66ff.

The G-10 Group came into existence in 1974 as a consequence of the
establishment in 1962 of the General Agreement to Borrow (GAB) pursuant to a decision of the Executive Board of the International Monetary
Fund (IMF). The Group was informally established with the support of
the IMF, OECD and the Bank for International Settlements (BIS), by the
finance ministers of Belgium, Canada, France, Germany, Italy, Japan,
The Netherlands, Sweden, United Kingdom and United States for the
primary purpose of intergovernmental consulting regarding implementation of calls upon the lines of credit extended to the IMF under the GAB
– the scope of such consultation being broadened over the years.

Subsequently, Switzerland has become an active member of the Group,
rendering the 'G-10' designation a misnomer. The G-10 Group operates
through the respective finance ministers on the highest level, but also on
specific subject-matters through various *ad hoc* committees (for example,
in banking through a committee of the central bank governors of its
member states meeting ten times a year at the BIS, with these governors
and the finance ministers and staffs from the IMF, BIS and OECD also
meeting several times a year within Working Party No. 3 of the OECD's
Economic Policy (Committee). For further discussion of GAB and G-10,
see J. Gold, *Legal and Institutional Aspects of the International Monetary
System: Selected Essays* (1984), vol. II, ch. 6.

10 On the BIS, see generally, BIS (50th Anniversary publication, 1930–80),
The Bank for International Settlements and the Basle Meetings (1980).

11 The institutions represented on the Basle Supervisors Committee are:
Belgium – National Bank of Belgium, Banking Commission; Canada –
Bank of Canada, Office of the Inspector General of Banks; France – Bank
of France, Banking Commission; Germany – Deutsche Bundesbank,
Federal Banking Supervisory Office; Italy – Bank of Italy; Japan – Bank
of Japan, Ministry of Finance; Luxembourg – Luxembourg Monetary
Institute; Netherlands – the Netherlands Bank; Sweden – Sveriges
Riksbank, Royal Swedish Banking Inspectorate; Switzerland – Swiss

National Bank, Swiss Federal Banking Commission; United Kingdom – Bank of England; United States – Federal Reserve Board, Federal Reserve Bank of New York, Office of the Comptroller of the Currency, Federal Deposit Insurance Corporation; Secretariat – Bank for International Settlements.

12 Reference to the founding mandate for the committee from the governors of the central banks of the G-10 countries is a press communiqué of the G-10 central bank governors of 12 February 1975 issued through the BIS. Since 1982, the Secretariat of the committee has endeavoured to prepare an annual *Report on International Developments in Banking Supervision*, which summarizes the work of the committee.

13 See discussion of the role of the committee by W. P. Cooke, the Chair of the committee, in *Basle Supervisors Committee* (Committee document for external distribution) (21 June 1984).

14 See section 11.2.4 below.

15 See Basle Supervisors Committee, *Report on International Developments in Banking Supervision 1981* (1982), p. 7.

16 See Basle Supervisors Committee, *Report on International Developments in Banking Supervision 1982* (1983), p. 3.

17 Ibid., p. 4.

18 See Basle Supervisors Committee, *Report on International Developments in Banking Supervision 1984*, at 8–15 (1985).

19 See Pub. L. No. 98–181, Title IX, 975 Stat. 1278 (30 November 1983). For legislative history of the Act, see *U.S. Code and Adm. News*, 1768, at 1913ff. (1983). For further discussion of ILSA, see, *inter alia*, Bench and Sables, 'International lending supervision', 11 *N.C.J. Int'l L. & Com. Reg.* 427 (1986); and Lichtenstein, 'The US response to the international debt crises: the International Lending Supervision Act of 1983', *Va. J. of Int'l L.* 401 (1985).

20 See Basle Supervisors Committee, International Developments, p. 9.

21 Ibid., pp. 10–12.

22 See Basle Supervisors Committee, *Report No. 5 on International Developments in Banking Supervision*, pp. 10–27.

23 For example, see discussion in Holland, 'Foreign bank capital and the United States Federal Reserve Board', 20 *Int'l Law* 786 (1986).

24 On the historical backdrop to the US/UK Accord, see Bardos, 'The risk-based capital agreement: a further step towards policy convergence', *Fed. Res. Bd. of N.Y. Q. Rev.* 26, at 27–8 (Winter 1987–8).

25 See 51 *Fed. Reg.* 3,976 (31 January 1986).

26 See Bank of England, *Measurement of Capital* (September 1980).

27 For copy of the Accord, see, *inter alia*, *BIS Rev.* No. 43 (3 March 1987); *Bank of England Q. Bull.* (February 1987); and 52 *Fed. Reg.* 5,135 (19 February, 1987).

28 For further discussion of accord see, *inter alia*, Statement by Paul A.

Volcker, Chairman, Board of Governors of the Federal Reserve System, before the Subcommittee on General Oversight and Investigations of the Committee on Banking, Finance and Urban Affairs, US House of Representatives, 30 April 1987, 73 *Fed. Res. Bull.* 435 (1987); Murray-Jones and Spencer, 'The US/UK proposal on capital adequacy', *Int'l Fin. L. Rev.* 27 (September 1987); and Mintz, 'International banking: United States–United Kingdom capital adequacy agreement', 28 *Harv. Int'l L.J.* 498 (1987).

29 See 52 *Fed. Reg.* 5,119 (19 February 1987).

30 See Basle Supervisors Committee (Consultative Paper), *Proposals for international convergence of capital measurements and capital standards* (December 1987).

31 For critique of Accord, see 'Dr Lusser assesses various aspects of international cooperation in the field of monetary policy', *BIS Rev.* No. 64, at 6 (1 April 1987).

32 See note 30 above.

33 For discussion of the December 1987 Basle Committee Proposal see Comptroller of the Currency, Federal Reserve Board and FDIC, 'Joint inter-agency preamble on risk-based capital proposal', 52 *Fed. Reg.* 8550 (15 March 1988).

34 See Basle Supervisors Committee, *Proposals*, Part I and Annex I.

35 Ibid., para. 20.

36 Ibid., Part II and Annex 2.

37 Ibid., para. 42 and Annex 3.

38 Ibid., Parts III and IV.

39 See Basle Supervisors Committee, *International Convergence of Capital Measurement and Capital Standards* (July 1988).

40 Ibid., para. 12.

41 Ibid., paras 18–21.

42 Ibid., para. 23.

43 Ibid., paras 33–7.

44 Ibid., para. 41.

45 For discussion of the July 1988 Basle Committee Report, see, *inter alia*, Federal Reserve Board, 'Staff summary and recommendations on risk-based capital plan', a copy of which is at 51 *BNA Bank. Rep.* 232 (8 August 1988).

46 See Basle Supervisors Committee, *International Convergence of Capital Measurement*, para. 1.

47 Cf. discussions of 'soft law' by Baade, 'The legal effects of codes of conduct for multinational enterprises', 22 *German Ybk Int'l L.* 11 (1979); Gold, 'Strengthening the soft international law of exchange arrangements', 77 *Am. J. Int. L.* 444 (1983); and Seidl-Hohenveldern, 'International economic "soft law"', 163 *Recueil des Cours (Hague)*, Part II 169 (1979). In fact, one author (albeit with minimal supporting authority)

characterizes the committee's actions as a form of 'international administrative law' (see Coing, 'Das Basler Concordat von 1975 – ein Bertrag zur Entwicklung des internationales Verwaltungsrechts', in *Festschrift für Frank Vischer* 1233 (1983)). The author is presently preparing a detailed article discussing this and related issues of legal significance of the Basle Supervisors Committee's actions.

48 For example, see 'Regulators negotiate over capital rules, final action not expected soon', 51 *BNA Bank. Rep.* 422 (12 September 1988).

49 For example, see Bank of England (Banking Supervision Division Explanatory Paper No. 1/88), *Proposals for International Convergence of Capital Measurement and Capital Standards* (January 1988). See discussion in section 11.4 below.

50 See discussion in section 11.3 below.

51 See generally J. J. Norton and S. C. Whitley, *Banking Law Manual* (1989), ch. 3.

52 See 54 *Fed. Reg.* 4,185 (27 January 1989). Bank holding companies with less than $150 million in consolidated assets would generally be exempt from the new guidelines' risk-based ratios provided they are not engaged in non-bank activities involving significant leverage or have significant amounts of debt outstanding to members of the general public; although, in such excluded instances, any subsidiary bank would be required to maintain a total capital-to-total-assets ratio of 7 per cent. Further the new guidelines permit the FRB to exclude certain non-bank subsidiaries from the new consolidated capital analysis provided the FRB is satisfied that there exist strong 'firewalls', adequate non-bank capital and other protections thought necessary by the FRB to safeguard the health of affiliated banks. See 54 *Fed. Reg.*, at 4,195 and 4,197.

53 See 54 *Fed. Reg.* 4,167 (27 January 1989).

54 See 54 *Fed. Reg.* 11,500 (21 March 1989).

55 See 53 *Fed. Reg.* 51,800 (23 December 1988).

56 See generally 'Supplementary Information' to the new guidelines prepared by the FRB (54 *Fed. Reg.*, at 4,1986–97), by the OCC (54 *Fed. Reg.*, at 4,168–77), by the FDIC (54 *Fed. Reg.*, at 11,500–9), and by the FHLBB (53 *Fed. Reg.*, at 51,800–16). See also, Norton, 'Capital adequacy standards'. In particular, Norton contains a detailed discussion of domestic and international policies underlying the standards, including various 'safety and soundness', competitive equality and transparency considerations.

57 See, for example, the FRB's newly adopted Appendix A ('FRB's Appendix A') to 12 C.F.R. Part 208, Section II, 54 *Fed. Reg.* 4,185, at 4,198–201.

58 See discussions in section 11.3.1 below under the heading 'Risk-weight categories'.

59 See, for example, FRB's discussion of risk-weight categories and conver-

318 DAVID BARBOUR *ET AL.*

sion factors for OBS items in 'Supplementary Information', Part III to
new guidelines, 54 *Fed. Reg.*, at 4,189–93.
60 For example, 'FRB's Appendix A', Part IV.
61 See 54 *Fed. Reg.* 4,186, at 4,186.
62 See newly adopted OCC's Appendix A (Subsection 1(b)(2)) to 12 C.F.R.
Part 3, at 54 *Fed. Reg.*, 4,177.
63 See 54 *Fed. Reg.* 11,500, at 11,500.
64 See discussion in 'Supplementary Information' (Part IV.A.) to FRB's
new guidelines, 54 *Fed. Reg.*, at 4,193.
65 See, for example, 1985 FRB capital adequacy guidelines, 50 *Fed. Reg.*
16,057 (15 May 1985).
66 54 *Fed. Reg.*, at 4,187.
67 See OCC's remarks at 54 *Fed. Reg.*, at 4,170.
68 See exceptions referred to in note 52 above.
69 For early FRB examination experience with risk-based capital notions,
see Federal Reserve Board Form FR 363 (1956), 'Form for Analyzing
Bank Capital', a copy of which is contained in Appendix I to Vojta, *Bank
Capital Adequacy* (1973), and Federal Reserve Board Form FR 363 (Form
ABC) (Dec. 3/72), 'Form for analyzing bank capital', a copy of which is
contained in Vojta, *Bank Capital Adequacy*, app. II. Generally on historical development of US capital adequacy standards, see Norton, 'Capital
adequacy standards'.
70 A copy of the July 1988 report can be found in *BNA Banking Rep.* No. 4,
at 143 (25 July 1988).
71 See 'FRB's Appendix A', Part II, A.1.
72 See, for example, 'FRB's Appendix A', Part II, A.2, and 54 *Fed. Reg.*, at
4,210.
73 'FRB's Appendix A', Part II, B.1. On treatment of goodwill for bank
holding companies, see 54 *Fed. Reg.*, at 4,212.
74 See, for example, 'FRB's Appendix A', Part II, B.2 and 3.
75 See 12 C.F.R. Part 225–143.
76 See, for example, 'FRB's Appendix A', Part II, B.3.
77 Ibid., Part II, B.2.
78 See 53 *Fed. Reg.* 8,550, at 8,559 (15 March 1988).
79 See, for example, 'FRB's Appendix A', Part III, C. 3.
80 Ibid., Part III, C. 1 and 2.
81 For discussion of off-balance-sheet risks, see Comm. on Banking Reg.
and Supervisory Prac., *The Management of Bank's Off-Balance Sheet
Exposures: A Supervisory Perspective* (March 1986) ('Cross Report').
82 See, for example, 'FRB's Appendix A', Part III, D.
83 See 43 *Fed. Reg.*, at 4,209.
84 Ibid.
85 The following text is derived from OCC, Investment Securities Division,
Conceptual Overview of Securitization of Bank Assets (draft, 25 April 1989).

12

Transplanting US Structures to the UK

MITCHELL S. DUPLER, BARBARA A. NUNEMAKER,
ROBERT PALACHE and ANDREW WILSON

This chapter is a transcript of a panel discussion held on 13 July 1989
at the Seminar on Asset Sales and Securitization, Centre for Commercial Law Studies, Queen Mary College, University of London.

MODERATOR: This afternoon we raise two general issues projecting
into the future. One is whether and to what extent US
structures and techniques can be transplanted or
otherwise can influence the development of securitization within the United Kingdom. This is what this
panel will be talking about. On the panel we are very
fortunate to have distinguished members. Robert
Palache of Clifford-Chance will chair this panel. Barbara Nunemaker is a senior vice-president of Standard
& Poor's. Mitch Dupler of Cleary Gottlieb will also be
a panel member, along with Andrew Wilson from
Goldman Sachs. Our panel will speculate on whether
and to what extent US structures and techniques may
be transplanted into the UK or may otherwise
influence the development of securitization.

PALACHE: My first inquiry is: how likely is it that there might be
developed in the UK a securitization market in receivables other than mortgages? To date, we have seen this
movement to a very limited extent. There was one
transaction in which trade receivables of Union Car-

bide and its affiliates were repackaged into rated commercial paper. That transaction relied upon a letter of credit from Credit Suisse to provide the rating. How do you see taking it further beyond the mortgage stage?

WILSON: Goldman thinks there is a lot of possibility in the UK. We are working on structuring one such transaction now. Without a good knowledge of the way the market works in the US it would be very hard to try to develop structures in the UK; but it is impossible to adapt blindly US structures in the UK. We have come across a number of legal, tax and accounting questions, particularly questions under the Companies Act, on what constitutes a sale and questions on the UK stamp tax. Problems with accounting treatment and problems with internal information assistance. One of the problems is that many companies do not have assets that readily can be securitized and they do not have accurate tracking systems. It is hard to secure the information comparable to what we have in the US.

PALACHE: Yes. I think one of the problems that we will have will be consumer-protection legislation. The British legislation provides considerable protection to borrowers of consumer type activities of less than $15,000.

NUNEMAKER: Standard & Poor's has certainly thought about this problem. We have been told that there are ways around these problems; however, we are not far enough down the line to have the answers. The other problem is whether you do car loans or car leases. There is a significant problem as at the end of the lease you have the right to buy it out and you have to account for that residual value. Most companies in the UK use leases; automobile leases are much more predominant than car loans. The real problem to me is less the Consumer Credit Act than taking the leases.

PALACHE: The structure that Barbara mentions is really for company cars where the receivable is owned by a company. Of course if you have a transaction like that you are outside of the Consumer Credit Act completely. It has to be a loan to an individual. I think that the main problem that the Consumer Credit Act will raise for people trying to take consumer loans into the securitization field is that the legislation is so 'pro-borrower' that it is easy to find yourself losing all your rights. Also, the quality of servicing has to be looked at even more closely because there are provisions in the Act that say that if you do not execute the documentation in the right form, if you do not behave during the 'cooling off' period in the correct way, or if you try and enforce your claim other than through the courts, the whole thing can be made unenforceable without a court order. In one circumstance it is possible for the creditor to be required to pay over to the borrower everything he has recovered. I think all of that would require greater scrutiny of the servicing.

NUNEMAKER: But who has the economic incentive to do this? The big clearing banks are reasonably well capitalized and do not need to do this very badly. These banks are the ones that have the individual loans. The specialized finance companies and the auto companies may have an interest in securitizing, but there are fewer of those. There are a number of specialized finance companies but there is not a big car producer lending business here, the way there is with GMAC or Volvo or any of those other non-UK producers. Actually, some of the fleet leasers and the companies and banks that do fleet leasing seem to me to be the prime customers. I think these parties may very well be among the first to securitize auto receivables.

PALACHE: What we have seen in other transactions done in the UK probably involve specialist insurers particularly involved in transactions by upgrading them. To what extent do you see an institution like that having a role in non-mortgage securitization?

WILSON: Well, it is difficult to have that sort of credit enhancement in the US.

PALACHE: The surety takes away all the need for the investor to look at the underlying receivable.

WILSON: That is right.

PALACHE: Do you think their requirements will be so stringent and expensive that they might chase the market away?

WILSON: Goldman has not gotten there yet so it is very hard to say.

NUNEMAKER: It has a lot to do with how credit-conscious the market is. The reason many companies have not been here sooner and have not done better is because this market is not nearly as rating sensitive as the US market (e.g. as between AAA/AA). So they may be 'investment grade or better' sensitive. But the real value of an insurer is getting it from BBB to AA or BBB to A; however, this does not mean much to a Eurobond investor yet. The challenge is getting to that point of sensitivity. While it certainly means more than it did four years ago, it is still at the margin that it is important. Frankly, Standard & Poor's gets more calls on why we rate these monolines AAA than any other rating inquiry we get, because they are fairly thinly capitalized. They are, in fact, well capitalized for their risk if you analyse them. I am just thinking of the DeBartolo or the Stop and Shop deals. You know the investors in the Eurobond market that say those two transactions (both involved commercial property insured by a monoline insurer) looked at the bond insurer but they all looked through to the commercial property and they felt safer with the commercial property than they did with the monoline insurance. Now, that was four years ago and two years ago. Things have changed and they are over here marketing and trying to make themselves better known and all the rest. But until you can get people sensitized to the differences in pricing between those ratings and the value of the rating adding the monoline to a commercial property transaction, English investors, who know commercial property pretty well, do not think it makes a whole lot of sense.

WILSON: It is probably pretty important to consider the way things actually work. Barbara, this is more of what rating agencies and the monoline insurers insist upon, but to get the others to play the deal you need to walk in their door with a deal that would otherwise be rated A by being supported by letters of credit or other enhancements. From a legal perspective once you get an FSA or some other credit enhancer in the transaction it changes your perspective on disclosure. Do you need to disclose quite as much of the underlying assets as you needed to if there was no surety bond wrapped around the whole picture?

It is also dependent upon the degree to which there is recourse. It is a little bit unclear in the UK at this stage how much recourse they would have.

PALACHE: That is right. It remains very uncertain and we have entered a period of uncertainty in the UK as to what 'off balance sheet' means, and how one achieves it is still in a state of uncertainty because we have the companies still going through the problem. I think if one looks carefully at the foreign heads of consolidation as they go into countries, it is certainly true that a fourth are a function of continued share ownership and if you get rid of share ownership four of those five heads of consolidation are going to walk out straightaway. The fifth head is the one that I think the legislature has funded to make sure that they did not create any trap for themselves, especially in terms of having the right to direct the operating and financial policies of the company. The next job for the market is to develop a way of being able to select auditors. The servicing contract does not give the originator that backbone or right. There is also the new accounting standard which has similar rules about so-called control over subsidiaries. A greater problem is the question of the retention of risk and benefit because the standard does look at the question of retention of risk and says that if you retain a significant risk you are going to have a problem. How do you see the auditors viewing the retention of half a per cent first losses? It still will be a problem?

DUPLER: It is very hard to say.

WILSON: None of these problems are solved by FASB 77. They have some retention of risk. There are ways to do it, we think.

DUPLER: The analogy I think is useful is in the US regulatory accounting context. For a long time, 'significant risk' has been the standard for national banks getting things off their balance sheets and for a long time the Comptroller had given informal advice. Depending on whom you called and what day you called, you got a different percentage answer. A lot of people acted on the assumption that that was perhaps 5 per cent. Some people acted on the assumption that that was perhaps 10 per cent, and about two months ago the Comptroller issued new guidelines for filing bank call reports, which clarify that 'significant risk' is any risk greater than the expected loss. It would not do the rating agent much good at all.

NUNEMAKER: Four times the expected loss and we are talking reasonable.

PALACHE: I think that that does indicate that those American institutions have perhaps been providing recourse most happily in the United States. They are probably going to have to stop doing that buying insurance in third parties. Certainly over here I think there has been a recognition that you cannot really provide any recourse at all because the British banks are not allowed to do so by the Bank of England rules on off balance sheets. They are allowed to lend long-term subordinated to companies but it is a deduction from capital so it is a waste of space as far as anybody is concerned.

NUNEMAKER: There is a bigger issue there though. The bigger issue is whether the insurance companies are ever going to have to learn to play like the banks, because you have got insurance regulation in this country which is not very onerous or very disabling. So basically people abiding by Bank of England guidelines and FDIC guidelines send all that banking business to the insurance companies who gladly pick it up. So increasingly the insurance companies and the banks are in the same business really and yet the insurance companies do not have capital guidelines. You know they have their actuaries telling them how much to reserve but that is a very qualitative area and they can go out and do this business until someday they end up in the kind of trouble some of the US banks are in.

WILSON: Do underwriting agencies look at that in assessing people like these monoline insurers and other insurers?

NUNEMAKER: Well, I do not worry about it quite as much in the US, although I know less about US insurance companies than I do in the UK; I think the New York state regulators are fairly severe and that is the only insurance regulator system I know at all. But it is certainly not, to put it in English terms, a 'level playing field' in the world of international insurance. And eventually there has got to be some kind of Basle paper for insurance companies. If the banks are smart that is what they would be pushing for.

PALACHE: Yes, the Basle paper really brings us on to the topic of capital weighting and asset-backed securities and how that is going to affect the investor base. As we have seen, the Basle paper came out and said mortgages can attract 50 per cent weighting because they are so terribly risky. The Bank of England translated that into meaning that mortgage-backed securities and mortgage self-participation is going to attract 50 per cent weightings. Has anybody sort of seen some problems in being able to comply with the rules on 50 per cent weighting of mortgage-backed securities? Have you seen any appetite for anybody to try and make sure that it does attract that weighting?

WILSON: I think Germany.

NUNEMAKER: In Japan, as well. They cannot buy mortgage-backed securities full stop, because those are securities in their banking system. The weird thing is they can buy debt of companies but they cannot buy assets. So, no they cannot buy grantor-trust certificates but they can buy TMC securities, because they say they are buying corporate debt of The Mortgage Corporation. Is that not amazing?

DUPLER: Except that their rules can be analyzed by analogy to the US Glass–Steagall Act. It is pretty well settled under Glass–Steagall one can certainly buy all of those things that you were mentioning – either under the rationale that certain provisions in our Glass–Steagall Act make it clear you can or by arguing that while maybe it looks like a security it is the functional equivalent of the underlying loan. There is a line of case law and regulatory determinations in the US that make it very clear that banks can buy those things notwithstanding the fact that you put it in a package that calls itself a security.

NUNEMAKER: That does not stop them from buying them. They just hold them in their London subsidiaries.

PALACHE: There is certainly a critical appetite out there for securities at 50 per cent weighting. One of the things the Bank of England said in the notice they issued on this topic was that you go 50 per cent weighting if you have fully and specifically secure mortgages or against assets which have a weighting of less than 50 per cent. And there was really a bit of a trap here because people focused fairly quickly on the fact that they, of course, have prepayments in the form of cash lying around and if they reinvest that cash in corporate commercial paper, of course, it means that some of the principal security of the security is not in the form of mortgages nor is it in the form of assets attracting a weighting of less than 50 per cent; corporate commercial paper is 100 per cent. So you need to watch out and make sure that if you think an instrument does attract 50 per cent weighting make sure that this cash is invested in such a way that it can only go into government debt or bank deposits.

NUNEMAKER: There is good news and there is bad news. The bad news is we had one building society with a rated commercial paper programme outstanding done through a special-purpose vehicle. It was fairly expensive to do, I am told. And it turns out with the new Building Society Commission rules, it is cheaper for them to consolidate those assets than to run them as an off-balance-sheet company; so they have consolidated a subsidiary and not taken it off balance sheet. Thus, that rating has been withdrawn, so the only building society securitization in this country was withdrawn, in case you need an example. But the other side is securitization will be a very effective tool for the mid- to small-size building societies that do not have the capital base to expand their assets at the rate at which they would like. And we have already seen that. Most of the Big Three say they could not be bothered as they have all the deposits they need – more money than they know what to do with. With the middle-sized, some are pro and some are con. But of the small-sized, almost all have set up either third-party servicing companies to capitalize on their expertise in the administration side, whether or not it is their own book they are securitizing; or, they are doing their own mortgages and they can get them off balance sheet – there are at least two building societies actively pursuing this.

DUPLER: Is there much general interest and discussion about it?

NUNEMAKER: Yes, but you have got the Big Three and even the Big Six that have more deposits than they know what to do with.

PALACHE: I think it will prove to be a fairly difficult and expensive exercise for those that decide to put their toe in the water. Maybe if they are to be encouraged it will have to be by continuing reductions in the pricing in the market generally. Andrew Wilson, how do you see investors in this case?

WILSON: To go back to the point we were just discussing – one of the problems in the UK market has been building societies have not securitized in a manner to involve a secondary market. I think it has had detrimental effect on the volume of security or outstanding mortgages that has been securitized.

NUNEMAKER: Is there the trading in the secondary market that existed two years after that started?

WILSON: One would expect this to develop more quickly.

NUNEMAKER: You would.

WILSON: There has not been a lot of activity.

PALACHE: One of things about building societies (I suppose as investors) is that they are required to treat mortgage-backed securities in a particular way. Building societies actually divide them into different classes and they have to maintain certain minimum amounts of their assets in 'class one' to their mortgages. Mortgage-backed securities on the other hand are 'class three' assets and you are only allowed a certain percentage of your assets in the form of 'class three' assets. The result being, of course, that building society mortgages are being packaged and they immediately convert themselves. But they trade from class one to class three assets. But, again, the building society cannot hold the securities in the volume that it can hold mortgages and this clearly is going to create some market inefficiencies. The Commission cannot do anything about it because they have said that that will require legislation with power to amend and nobody at Parliament has got the intellectual stamina to be able to cope with anything like that.

I am surprised to hear you say that building societies are keen investors. I think there remain some uncertainties of the capital adequacy treatment of the instruments of the building societies being 'class three' assets. On the face of the Commission's current recommendations, 'class three' assets generally attract a very high capital weighting. Something between 7 and 20 per cent depending upon which category. Whereas a mortgage attracts a weighting between 1 and 4 per cent in a more precise nature. The Commission has formally indicated how it is likely to come about the capital weighting applied to mortgage-backed securities; that is, it will look through the security and look at the underlying mortgage. And if that comes about, the position will be very clear. For the moment there seems to be a bit of uncertainty. There is nothing firmly in writing to that effect.

NUNEMAKER: Is commercial property 'class three' or is that 'class two'?

PALACHE: Commercial property is class two.

NUNEMAKER: There are also limits on that and that is one of the areas we are seeing a lot of investors.

PALACHE: From building societies.

NUNEMAKER: Though we don't have criteria in place for UK commercial property at this stage, we are working on it. I have recently heard, since there are such strict limitations on the amount of the 'class two' and 'class three' assets but there is a lot of opportunity in that area, they would like to securitize because then they can do much more than their balance sheet will take – in a way that would be hard to securitize packages of mortgage-backed. I mean you could.

PALACHE: Yes, there is a certain logic to that. I think the other area where perhaps they will get entrusted is with respect to those having formed special servicing companies to set up transactions under which they could have their own off-balance-sheet vehicle and start chucking in the mortgages which they have originated on behalf of their customers. So there is no bounty for anybody at all. It is just the building society's own pet servicing company. It can increase its assets on to management by being able to offer an off-balance-sheet structure to their customers as well.

What else do we want to talk about?

DUPLER: Before we leave that classification point that you were mentioning from the perspective of building societies, the US had similar problems from the perspective of thrifts and the legislation in 1984 and 1986 was in part designed to make clear that mortgage-backed securities were interests in real property for various tax and regulatory purposes. The legislature made clear that they qualified for what we call, in our hopelessly inarticulate way, the 'thriftness test', which requires that to be a thrift you need to have a certain portion of your assets invested in assets like loans on real estate and the legislation helped clear that up in 1984. So I think the problem may be the absence of that sort of legislation to get rid of some of those roadblocks to a liquid market in which all the people who really ought to be planning to purchase can fully participate. The legislation in 1984 certainly helped a great deal in the United States.

PALACHE: This is the Secondary Mortgage Marketing Enhancement Act. The British Parliament passing a piece of legislation for something like that is inconceivable.

I think not too long ago, the Americans first came over and started talking about mortgage-backed securities. Naturally from your own domestic environment you tend to use the language of the domestic environment and when Americans start talking in their own terminology, even the most hardened UK players' eyes glaze over.

NUNEMAKER: They just start throwing legal terms at you. The thing to think about, and I do not know that any of us here are experts on it, is where else this is going.

PALACHE: Well, we have seen one transaction done in New Zealand recently which is where we had a deal by Bankers Trust. This involved a portfolio of New Zealand mortgages originated by a New Zealand building society, which was repackaged into a US dollar-fixed bond using an FSA financial insurance wrap-around guarantee. That was interesting, I think, because we are prepared to analyse the credit risk of a country which is about as far away from anywhere as anybody can get to. It is not one with which they were particularly familiar and yet they were prepared to get to grips with it. I think in the end the building societies were very happy with the results and with the authority financing that they got. Now whether that will continue, whether we will really see France begin this insurance, or whether the US market is next – these questions remain to be answered.

NUNEMAKER: Let us put it this way. Anybody who is a government-owned bank does not have a choice. You make a bill, it will be a success.

WILSON: Opinion is actually more divided than that.

PALACHE: The Bank of France does not know its full position yet.

NUNEMAKER: No, I do not think the economics are there at the moment. But I think the long-term economics will be there.

PALACHE: In France?

NUNEMAKER: Yes, they are not there at the moment.

PALACHE: I have heard that the economics might stack up only because the French banks are under-capitalized and they have a need to sell off assets. Does that sit with your understanding?

WILSON: That is true. On the other hand the problem of the mortgages is very different.

NUNEMAKER: The price competition is pretty big these days here too. You have got a US-style product. You have got a fixed-rate amortizing product and you've got a US-style structure. You are not issuing debt. And you know nobody much wants to do it in the current cost structure. I mean, it is not an unfamiliar instrument is what I am saying with the US parallels. It is not like a kind of mortgage you have ever seen before. The competition to get market share in consumer financing is going to be very severe.

DUPLER: The minute that turns around . . . ?

PALACHE: Economic logic, I suppose – that it actually will turn around.

NUNEMAKER: But you are talking about a country that has had regulated interests and credit controls until 1986. You know they are just getting used to a little bit of deregulation.

WILSON: You were mentioning the requirement in France that there be a ratings report before one can list. I am a little concerned about the possibility of a 'Catch 22' that the market opportunity is there, the investment bankers are ready to go. They are on the phone to the lawyers to get ready the documents, but one finds there is no rating report yet. How do you think things will sort out when one has the capital market on the one hand and someone looking through the mortgage loan files and you can not get listed until you are given the rating?

NUNEMAKER: I think we are less likely to be the real source of trouble. I think basically you will have something in the pipeline. You will have it packed up and ready to go if it works. If this market works there will be a blank set of documents just waiting to be printed off when the market is right or that they will go in because of what the government authority is asking. These guys are incredible, in that you go in and discuss the day you start thinking about it, what you are structuring, how it works, give them all your files, let them study from start to finish and so that when it actually comes to the authority that approves it they are already going to know the deal inside and out. That is why they say their approval process can be quick. What they expect is to have all the information about what it would look like and then you use the pricing opportunity to say all right turn it on and they give you their approval. In principle.

WILSON: It is disturbing that the authorities tend to give you sort of winks and nods. They look at it and tell you whether they think it is a good thing for the market or not.

NUNEMAKER: But there is an enormous political pressure on them right now. I am not an expert on this subject, but they have gotten so much bad press in the last nine months over the different bad takeover battles, mishandling of the stock market, the mishandling of money market funds, that they are under pressure to look as clean and as scrupulous and as investor friendly as possible and I think they have gone overboard on this.

DUPLER: The difficulty from the real economic perspective reminds me of the difficulty you have in the US with the SEC where if you are not able to take advantage of the accelerated procedures then you really need to go through four to six weeks of SEC registration. On each deal it sounds as if this could work out to be even more protracted and that will tend to stifle liquidity in the market and make it impossible to bring the right deal to market at the right moment.

PALACHE: It all sounds quite ridiculous. I think it has worked out reasonably well. We have not had much interference from the Bank of England and they were kind enough to withdraw the five-year minimum requirement at exactly the right time for Goldman's recent deal. I want to talk a moment about that. About market appetite.

WILSON: Yes. We have recently completed an offering for CMS No. 1, a special-purpose company established by Canadian Shell as a securitization vehicle. It was the first collateralized mortgage obligation or CMO deal done in the UK markets. In CMO deals people cash-flow and create different securities with different maturities to appeal to different markets. And basically, you try to give the investors a menu and let them choose whichever they think is the best value. By tailoring it for specific classes of investors. In this case we had three tranches of senior securities. In the UK markets we find – theoretically in the US people know which securities are needed – it should work the same way but people tend to look at the securities and try to make guesses as to what they think is the best deal. And they look at it and say I really need the fast pay but on the other hand I think the slow pay is priced more favourably for me so I will take that. And there is a lot of horse-trading, second-guessing. But it was very successful, a lot of interest. We talked about the problems in the US structures. The problems there were relatively simple. There really were very few problems.

NUNEMAKER: Why was not it done sooner in the UK? The five-year rule was dropped in April and that was the first transaction.

WILSON: That is a good question. We know that there were others . . .

DUPLER: What is the five-year rule?

PALACHE: There used to be a rule that the Bank of England was required to give its consent to issues of sterling-denominated securities exceeding £3 million and they made it very clear that they would not give such consent to Eurobond issues which have any repayments occurring or likely to occur during the first five years. Now, they applied this rule when the mortgage-backed securities market first developed. They did object originally when the first proposals came up on the grounds that the fast payments were extremely likely to have an average life much under five years. They certainly objected to it on those grounds. Then they had a total repeat of the market as you know and they have recalled the five-year requirement and they have abolished the controlled borrowing order. So you do not need Bank of England consent for an issue any more. And it does not mean that you could do a six-month bond issue if you want to.

WILSON: Initially there was some confusion: which is the simplest kind of structure? All principal that comes in goes first to retire the debt. In the UK the main thing is uncapped plain-rate mortgage. It is ideally suited for this kind of securitization. You do not have the interest-rate problems, you do not have the SEC.

PALACHE: One of the advantages I suppose, if you can call it an advantage, is 'UK simplicity'. It is a relatively straightforward product that has been offered to investors. Do they distinguish between different servicers?

WILSON: Sophisticated ones. There is some tendency among less sophisticated investors not to differentiate.

NUNEMAKER: You opened yourself up to this one if you say they are all simple and relatively homogeneous.

PALACHE: I think we better explain to our audience what we are talking about. It is a programme for issuing mortgage-backed securities which basically involves TMC group companies – The Mortgage Corporation – to enter into normal documents for a mortgage-backed security with effective shelf listing on the London stock exchange £3 billion. They have done a single issue so far of £250 million. That was a very straightforward single-class issue. They will do subsequent issues over time not to the £3 billion limit, using these documents basically, and they will never have to write a mortgage agreement again. They will just lock everything into this structure. It will bring down issuing costs quite considerably. One of the problems with these deals has been the paper intensity of it even if you are repeating a transaction you have already done. You have still got to go through all the hoops and cradles and bits of paper again. That goes away with this structure. Anyway that is interesting and that is advantageous. The plus to the deal is the decision that was made to restrict the participants in the programme to five dealers who would all have the job of getting a reasonably considerably sized flood of paper in relation to each issue. This was perceived as comparing very favourably to a market perspective with the traditional bond-issue structure where you have one weak manager who takes 90 per cent of the paper and leaves the remainder for the others. And with this structure and the prospective loss, the dealers will be much keener to deal aggressively with the issue in terms of pricing because of that fact. And in a way it can be seen almost as a sterling medium-note programme. It has got those characteristics with the potential for continuous offering for a relatively restrictive dealer group, relatively restrictive control as to where the secondary market is going to be. I think saving really costs for the country.

WILSON: But clearly it is not possible to standardize the amounts.

NUNEMAKER: But that is it. If Robert Palache is right and every one looks like every other one. But, we are still a little sceptical, Robert. If somebody else comes up with a new product they will obviously want to stick this one in as well. There are provisions to do that, but everybody always say their deal looked just like the last one and it never does.

WILSON: They really do not.

NUNEMAKER: They swear they do. They swear they are using the same documents. It is just there is not a single word left on the old documents by the time they are done blacklining it. In principle all we will have to do on paper is size the pool each time basically and in terms of liquidity. And they will have to go out and find liquidity cover depending on what they want to use for that, but they can do a senior, they can do an insured transaction, they can do a lot of different things. And if it holds that the documents do not have to be altered each time it saves us an enormous amount of time. Yes, you have got a reduced fee.

DUPLER: You mentioned a few moments ago that it should be possible to do lots of different structures off of UK mortgages. In the States adjustable-rate mortgages have been very difficult to use in CMOs. Is it the cap feature that is causing the problem?

WILSON: Caps of course. The interest rates do not move. Any time you have this kind of structure where you have unlimited floater, it works very well. Particularly in the UK, where you have the possibility for the administrator to raise interest rates.

DUPLER: In some US deals with fifteen to seventeen classes, typically one has various 'IO' interest only and 'PO' principal only classes and other strange principal types of classes. Could you do that in the UK?

WILSON: Because you do not have the same kind of principal review, the characteristics are very different.

NUNEMAKER: They are not amortizing mortgages.

WILSON: If you are amortizing mortgages, very, very complicated. On the one hand they make it possible to devise all these structures. The structures are really an attempt to make it more efficient. In the UK you really do not need to do that. You have the mortgage rates so closely related to the security which appeals to a hard class of investors. And as to the type of CMO that we produce I do not think we had some debate as to whether it would be two or three. At this point we do not think there is much of a market for it.

DUPLER: In ballpark terms, if one were to compare it to the speed at which US mortgages prepay, how quickly are the UK mortgages prepaid? How often does the average British person move or pay off his mortgage?

WILSON: It is an interesting question and there seems to be a lot of debate in the securitization community as to whether the historical experience is really relevant. It is very hard to say. The mortgage historic experience is that they have been paid faster than the US in general. But the historic experience is not bad. People look at building society statistics for six years ago

	sometimes and it has no relation to the current market.
NUNEMAKER:	It is also very related to the house-pricing industry, which I presume it is in the States. But you can see dramatic changes in the average life if you do a slice over a different three-month period. If you took the last six months the average life would have gone up dramatically. I am guessing that is not a qualitative basis. Where if you took the previous year or eighteen months where house prices were moving up dramatically and everybody was cashing in the average life would have shortened. It happens very quickly.
DUPLER:	I am sure it happens in the United States as well. I am not an investment banker but I know the assumed speeds at which CMOs in the United States price. They are published in disclosure documents for tax reasons and can fluctuate by say 10 to 20 per cent from one month to the next and all that is is an assumed speed. There is no guarantee that what the disclosure documents say will actually happen.
WILSON:	In determining the assumed speed people do look at these.
NUNEMAKER:	I get the feeling that in the UK mortgage-backed security market the incorporation and substitution provision has taken another turn. Are we going to see people unable to substitute?
WILSON:	I do not think so. Some of the current bills are still being set up.
PALACHE:	That's right.
WILSON:	Investors to date have not seemed overly concerned.
PALACHE:	What about the prospect of more fixed-rate issues backed by conventional mortgages?
WILSON:	It is an interesting question. It is very hard to say.
NUNEMAKER:	They do not have many that are fixed rate for term. They have them fixed rate for three years and fixed rate for four.
PALACHE:	To be able to take out the fixed-rate element.
NUNEMAKER:	There is one in the market now.
WILSON:	There is interest in it. The economics are very tricky.
NUNEMAKER:	And have slowed down the market because you tend to

do a fixed-rate bond for a very clear fixed life – five to seven years – and most of the mortgages are twenty to twenty-five, even though they may have an average life of five to seven. You need a commitment to buy out by an equally rated counterparty, and that is fairly expensive.

PALACHE: That is right. The two deals that have been done so far in the market have both involved Household Mortgage Corporation. Two five-year fixed-rate sterling issues. They did a swap for a AAA rated. Which does suggest there is not that huge a market out there. I wonder that too. I do not know the answer. That is their problem and their affair. I suspect the answer is that it was probably OK because the shareholder was not the majority shareholder. He was just one of the joint venturers.

DUPLER: We created a series of securities in the United States which were issued with certain classes with 'puts'. It was $2,500,000,000 of it in the fall but the accountants' Emerging Issues Task Force decided that that would do some harm to your balance sheets.

WILSON: Substitution is one of the interesting things – it is easier to do in the UK. One of the chief legal differences in the structuring of it is the distinction between a passive trustee in the United States and the equally passive trustee in England. But a trustee in England is willing to delegate a lot of the discretion.

NUNEMAKER: If you substitute mortgages in and out of the vehicle, are you effectively a lending institution and not a special-purpose vehicle for tax purposes?

PALACHE: I do not see that as a problem because the restrictions that we have in banking home in on the acceptance of deposits not on lending. I mean any of us can actually lend money.

NUNEMAKER: I do not think it is a problem area.

PALACHE: What about using the foreign currency market to provide any opportunities?

WILSON: Here again swaps can be expensive. I mean, to sell sterling or to use sterling to back securities will upset the UK. To do say Eurodollar bonds back, so far the economics have not worked; and, for the asset securitization markets the current thinking is that it is more or less impossible to sell securities backed by assets outside the UK. It is certainly so unless you have a very active UK market. There has to be a valid domestic market before you can hope to sell abroad.

PALACHE: There has been one transaction done involving the UK mortgage-backed note which was acquired by a US commercial paper and acquired an A1-plus rating. And in that transaction the advantage I think to the issuing entity was that they get what I was told was a AA rating. A AA rating was necessary because that is the minimum equivalent of an A1-plus rating. And a series of short contracts used to hedge the sterling problem. The sterling-backed securities got a one-month rollover, which is unique. But in the context of converting it into US CP commercial paper, it works very well, because thirty-day US CP has a market, I gather.

NUNEMAKER: There are an awful lot of investors in Europe where the dollar is the deep market in Euro-commercial paper, that do not want dollars but they only do that on an opportunity basis.

PALACHE: Well, I think we have probably exhausted ourselves.

13

Securitization of Financial Assets Under French Law

ROBERT BORDEAUX-GROULT

13.1 Introduction

This chapter analyses the new French legislation providing for the creation of securities representing interests in pools of financial assets such as consumer loans. The basic legislation, Law No. 88–1201 (23 December 1988) (the 'Act'), has been supplemented by an implementing decree, Decree No. 89–158 (9 March 1989) (the 'Decree'). English translations of both the Act and the Decree are appended to this chapter.

These basic enactments have now been supplemented by a series of further regulatory measures. Rules for approval of issuers and listing of their securities are now set forth in a regulation and an implementing instruction of the French stock exchange commission, the *Commission des Opérations de Bourse (COB)*.[1] The banking regulatory commission, the *Comité de la Réglementation Bancaire* (CRB), has adopted regulations on accounting for dispositions of assets in connection with securitization[2] and regulations modifying the risk-coverage ratios applicable to French banks to take account of securitization.[3] The tax administration has issued a release concerning the tax treatment of securitization transactions,[4] and the Ministry of Finance has designated authorized rating agencies.[5]

The purposes of the Act as they appear from the ample legislative history are, first, to permit banks to improve their capital ratios by disposing of certain assets and, second, to reduce the differential between interest rates on consumer credit and on other forms of credit by reducing the costs of intermediation between credit markets. The Act is intended to facilitate the development of a market in securities backed by various forms of loans, especially mortgage loans. Several provisions of French law have made this process of 'securitization' difficult in the past. In particular, the Civil Code makes the transfer of consumer loans impractical, and French banking law restricts the ownership of loans to credit institutions which are subject to capital ratios.

The Act eliminates these and other obstacles for transactions that fall within its provisions. It does not rule out securitization by other means where that is feasible.

This chapter discusses the nature of the special-purpose issuing vehicle created under the Act, the assets eligible for securitization, the transfer and servicing of loans under the Act, the nature of the securities to be issued, certain regulatory considerations and certain tax considerations.

13.2 The Fund

The new legislation authorizes the creation of a limited-purpose investment vehicle called a *fonds commun de créances* (hereinafter, a 'Fund'). The Fund is patterned on the *fonds commun de placement* (FCP), a form of investment vehicle that is in turn modelled on the unit investment trust. In the simplest terms, a Fund owns a pool of receivables (*créances*) and issues certificates (*parts*) to investors.

A Fund does not have legal personality, and accordingly it is not subject to companies law or insolvency laws. Instead Article 34, paragraph 1 of the Act describes a Fund as a 'co-proprietorship' (*copropriété*) among the holders of certificates; this term is borrowed from the legislation governing FCPs, but without many of the specific provisions that apply to FCPs. The precise meaning of the term under French law is not entirely clear, but the intention in adopting it was to ensure that holders of the certificates would have a direct claim on the underlying receivables and any collateral securing the receivables, rather than holding indebtedness of an entity that in turn owns receivables. For the most part, the rights of the certificate-holders are left to be defined by the charter (*règlement*) governing the Fund. With limited exceptions regarding removal of statutory auditors, certificate-holders have none of the usual rights of either shareholders or bond-holders under French law.

The purchase of receivables and the issuance of securities constitute the exclusive purpose of a Fund. Article 34 of the Act sets forth a number of further restrictions on its operations, including the following:

- It may only acquire assets once (except for limited powers of reinvestment described under 'Eligible Assets' below).
- It may only issue certificates once.
- It may not sell its receivables, except that under Article 6 of the Decree it may sell them all, in preparation to liquidate, after their value falls below 10 per cent of their initial value.
- It may not pledge its receivables.
- It may not borrow.

These limitations may rule out certain features that have been used in the US market to ensure that the assets purchased by a special-purpose vehicle meet certain underwriting standards and standards of legal regularity. A Fund can receive a warranty from the seller of the loans, but the remedies for breach will be limited because of the prohibition on subsequent sales or purchases of loans. In particular, it does not appear that the seller could replace a defective loan.

13.3 Eligible Assets

There are few limitations on the types of assets that may constitute the pool of receivables held by a Fund:

- They must be purchased from a French credit institution or the *Caisse des Dépôts et Consignations*. Act, Article 34, paragraph 1.
- They must have an original term to maturity of over two years. Decree, Article 8.
- They must not, at the time they are sold to the Fund, be classified as *immobilisées*, *douteuses* or *litigieuses* (Decree, Article 8); these terms designate categories in which French banks place problem loans. According to public statements of the Ministry of Finance, the intention of this provision was to exclude any delinquent loan, but the precise criteria used to classify problem loans vary in practice from one institution to another.
- They must arise from the lending of money (*opérations de crédit*). Decree, Article 8.
- All the receivables in a given Fund must represent transactions 'of the same nature'. Decree, Article 8. The apparent intention is to ensure that a single Fund does not combine broadly different categories of loans, such as automobile and housing loans. It remains, however, possible that French authorities would rely on this language to require some degree of homogeneity as to other characteristics of the receivables, such as original term to maturity, remaining term, underwriting criteria, interest rates or principal amounts.

The Fund mechanism is not limited to consumer loans; a Fund could also hold commercial loans. For commercial loans, however, simplified transfer procedures already existed under prior law, and some of the features of securitization may be achieved without resorting to the provisions of the Act.

The investment powers of a Fund remain to be clarified. As noted above, a Fund may not acquire any further receivables (*créances*) after its initial constitution. By way of exception to the prohibition, a Fund is expressly authorized to invest amounts temporarily, pending their distribution, in limited categories of debt instruments: French Treasury bills (*bons du Trésor*), certain mutual funds (SICAVs and FCPs), and debt instruments traded on a regulated exchange (Act, Article 34, paragraph 3; Decree, Article 4). The resulting powers, if the legislation is taken literally, present a number of problems: the prohibition on acquiring *créances* could be read to prohibit a Fund from depositing money in a bank; funds may only be invested temporarily, which presents a problem if reserve funds are built up (see section 13.6 below); and the legislation does not clearly limit the Fund's power to make investments other than in *créances*. Presumably investment powers will be defined in each Fund's charter and will be the object of scrutiny at the time it is approved.

13.4 Management and Servicing

A Fund must be co-founded by a management company and a depository. The management company must be a French company devoted solely to the management of Funds under the Act, with capital of at least 1,500,000 French francs. Concerning the management company's duties and powers, the Act only states that it is responsible for management of the Fund and for its legal representation before the courts; any detail is left to be defined in the charter of the Fund. The legislation does not contemplate replacement of the management company, and it is not clear under what circumstances and in what manner that would be possible. The government has, however, stated in response to a parliamentary question that a management company could be replaced, at least where its authorization has been withdrawn by the Ministry of Finance.

The depository must be a French credit institution or otherwise approved by the Ministry of Finance, must hold the assets of the Fund (specifically including the receivables and liquid assets) and must monitor the activity of the management company. Otherwise its responsibilities, too, are left to be defined in the Fund's charter.

Article 48 of the Act arguably authorizes the depository to petition a court for removal of the officers of the management company.

In addition to a management company and depository, each Fund must have a statutory auditor. The Act contains detailed provisions, and incorporates others by reference from French companies law, on the appointment, duties and removal of the statutory auditor.

Article 36 of the Act provides that the institution selling loans to the Fund will continue to 'ensure their collection', under contract with the Fund's management company. This provision was designed to ensure that borrowers would continue to deal only with the originating institution, by requiring the latter to remain as the servicer. Accordingly, servicing responsibility may be transferred to a new institution only if the debtor consents in writing at the time of the transfer. These provisions will make it impractical to replace the servicer for breach of the servicing agreement.

The Act itself does not address whether the depository, the management company and the seller/servicer of the receivables may be affiliated companies. Article 4 of the COB Regulation, however, limits the influence of the seller/servicer over the management company: neither the seller/servicer, nor any company controlled by it or under common control with it, may own one-third or more of the shares of the management company. Under French companies law this limitation will prevent the seller/servicer from exercising significant power over the management company. On the other hand, it is clear that the depository may be an affiliate of either the management company or the seller/servicer.

13.5 Transfer of Loans to the Fund

General rules of French law provide several different methods for transfer of a receivable, each of which presents significant disadvantages of timing and cost in the context of securitization. As an exception to these general rules, Article 34 of the Act provides that the transfer of a loan to a Fund is made by means of a *bordereau* or assignment, which may cover a number of loans. This technique is adapted from the provisions that govern factoring of commercial loans under a 1981 law. The assignment is valid against third parties from the moment it is delivered, and it results without any further action in the transfer of any collateral securing the loan. The Act also requires that the debtor be notified by letter, although it appears that this is not a condition to perfection of the transfer.

Because these simplified procedures do not require compliance with the rules that, under general French law, ensure notice to third parties, they could give rise to practical problems concerning competing claimants to a loan or to the collateral securing the loan. The applicable legal rules will depend on the legal nature of the specific receivables and collateral involved, but several different types of questions are likely to arise.

In the first place, the Act does not prevent claims arising prior to the transfer of receivables to the Fund, or indeed defences valid against the lender, from being asserted against the Fund. Measures of 'due diligence' will have to be devised to counter this possibility, and this will be especially important because of the difficulty of replacing defective loans, as described above in section 13.2.

In the second place, although the Act provides that a transfer to the Fund is immediately valid against third parties as to a receivable and its collateral, the possibility that claims to the loan or the collateral could arise after they are transferred to the Fund will have to be studied for particular types of loans and collateral. Such risks can be avoided for some types if the depository has custody of the documents that would be required to effect a subsequent transfer, but for other types (including real property mortgages or loans executed before a notary) this will not be possible. Thus the requirement of the legislation (Act, Article 40, paragraph III; Decree, Article 3) that the depository of the Fund's assets hold 'the receivables' transferred to the Fund will be difficult to apply in practice. With respect to collateral, Article 2 of the Decree requires that the assignment contain an express undertaking of the seller to take any measures requested by the Fund for the recording, modification or enforcement of security. It may prove prudent, as to both receivables and collateral, for the depository to take further measures from the outset to prevent competing claims of bona-fide transferees from arising. In the specific case of real property mortgages, the Act does not squarely address the question whether public filing is required to perfect the Fund's ownership, but commentary suggests that it is.

13.6 The Certificates

The legislation specifies little about the nature of the certificates. The legislative history and the comments of officials of the Ministry of Finance make it clear that the legislation is intended to permit the widest possible range of financial engineering. This apparent freedom will undoubtedly be constrained somewhat by administrative practice in the review and approval of proposed Funds. The following points summarize features of the certificates that are specified by the legislation, or that can be inferred from the legislative history, the regulations adopted so far and other sources.

13.6.1 Legal Characterization

Article 34 of the Act specifies that the certificates are securities (*valeurs mobilières*). Certain further features follow from this characterization: they are negotiable; they can be listed on a stock exchange; they must be issued in series; and their form and transfer will be governed by the provisions of French law requiring all securities to be in book-entry form unless they are issued outside France.

In other respects, however, the legal nature of the certificates does not fit neatly into pre-existing categories under French law. For example, Article 1 of the Act itself contains a general definition of the term *valeurs mobilières* (heretofore undefined in French law), intended to be used in construing investment limitations on SICAVs and FCPs; the definition does not include the certificates issued by a Fund. Although it appears from the legislative history and other sources that this was not intended to limit investment in Fund certificates by SICAVs and FCPs, the confusion is symptomatic. In addition, the French tax treatment of the certificates (see section 13.8 below) is generally based on the treatment of debt instruments, although in light of the legal character of the Fund itself (see section 13.2 above) the certificates are clearly not debt instruments. This kind of uncertainty may make it difficult to classify earnings and capital gains or losses for purposes of tax treaties and the tax legislation of other jurisdictions, and it may also make it difficult to classify the certificates for purposes of legal investment restrictions applicable to particular categories of non-French investors.

13.6.2 *Basic Financial Characteristics*

It appears from the legislative history, and from press accounts, that French officials expect the certificates to be structured as though they were debt securities, with a par value representing a claim for principal, and a contractual right to interest on the par value of the claim from time to time. Unless more restrictive policies are developed in administrative practice, it would appear that:

- Certificates can be issued at a discount or a premium to their initial par value (principal amount).
- Principal can be subject to amortization, on a fixed schedule or depending on the performance of the pool of receivables. The certificates may not, however, provide for redemption at the option of the holder.
- Under Article 5 of the Decree, the 'minimum amount' of a certificate may not be less than 10,000 French francs. This provision is intended to reduce the retail appeal of certificates, and it presumably refers to the initial par value. It may present interpretative problems for some types of certificates (those issued at a discount or a premium, for example, or those representing interest only or principal only).
- Certificates can bear interest at fixed or floating rates, or not at all; the tax provisions of the Act contemplate the possibility of 'deep-discount' or 'zero-coupon' certificates.
- The Act does not rule out certificates denominated in a currency other than French francs (or in ECU).
- Listing on a French stock exchange is required, under Article II of the COB Regulation, for certificates that are offered to the public and that have an initial par value of less than 1,000,000 French francs. Conversely, it is not permitted for privately placed certificates. (See section 13.7 below.)

The legislation does not specify the relationship between the flow of interest and principal payments on the pool of receivables and the flow of payments to the holders of certificates. In view of the clear legislative intent to permit maximum flexibility, it is safe to assume that there are no particular requirements other than a case-by-case evaluation of the sufficiency of the aggregate cash flow from the receivables to service the certificates. Moreover, Article 34 of the Act specifies that the certificates of a single Fund may give rise to 'different rights to principal and interest of the receivables', so that a single Fund might issue multiple classes of certificates, with different payment characteristics. For example, a single Fund could: (1) issue two or more classes of certificates, with principal to be repaid sequentially on each class ('fast-pay/slow-pay' certificates); (2) issue a class of certificates whose holders receive only the amount (or some fraction) of the interest earned on the pool of underlying receivables, while the other class or classes receive the amount of principal repaid with respect to the pool ('stripped' certificates); or (3) issue classes of certificates that are subordinated or preferred (see Decree, Article 9).

The cash flow from the receivables may also exceed that needed to service the certificates, so that the Fund builds up cash in what US practice calls 'reserve funds'. In particular, Article 34 of the Act specifically envisages the existence of residual funds following liquidation (a *boni de liquidation*), and provides that the originating bank may be entitled to receive them. It does not, however, specify whether this interest can be transferred or whether any other party may own it.

13.6.3 *Credit Enhancement*

Under Article 37 of the Act, as implemented by Article 9 of the Decree, holders of certificates must be protected against the risk of defaults on the receivables in the pool by means of one or more of three specific measures:

- The Fund may obtain a guarantee from a French bank or insurance company.
- The Fund may issue a subordinated class of certificates that bears the risk of defaults. Such certificates may not, however, be held by individuals or by FCPs or SICAVs.
- The Fund may hold 'an amount of receivables that exceeds the amount of the certificates issued'. The legislative history suggests that this provision should be read to include holding receivables (1) whose principal amount exceeds the principal amount of the certificates or (2) whose cash flow exceeds the cash flow on the certificates. In such a situation, referred to as *surdimensionnement*, the value of receivables held by a Fund would presumably exceed the aggregate subscription price of its certificates. The balance (beyond any amount needed to provide for administration of the Fund) would constitute a liquidation interest (a *boni de liquidation*) retained by the originator.

The prohibition on acquiring receivables after constitution of the Fund will rule out any undertaking by the seller of the receivables to replace loans that are in default or otherwise defective. This technique of credit enhancement will thus be unavailable.

The institution selling receivables to the Fund will be an obvious candidate to provide credit enhancement, whether by means of over-collateralization, by retaining a subordinated class of certificates or by issuing a guarantee. The retention of risk by the selling institution raises the question whether the transfer of receivables to the Fund can be treated as a sale, or whether instead the seller must retain the assets on its balance sheet at least for purposes of bank regulatory account-ing. In the latter case, the stated objective of permitting French credit institutions to dispose of assets in order to improve their capital ratios could only be achieved if outside providers of credit enhancement, such as pool insurers, could be found at economical prices. CRB Regulation No. 89–07 addresses this problem by providing that any transfer of receivables to a Fund is treated as a sale, regardless of over-collateralization or the retention of a subordinated interest in the Fund. This treatment is a derogation from the general rules for the classification of true sales, codified for the first time in the same regulation.

CRB Regulation No. 89–07 also provides that subordinated certifi-cates of a Fund, or the liquidation rights of an over-collateralizing seller, should be valued net of the risk of loss, as determined initially by the rating agency that evaluates the receivables and the certificates (see section 13.7 below) and as revalued at the close of every account-ing period.

13.6.4 *Treatment Under Risk-Based Capital Requirements*

In France as elsewhere in Europe (see chapters 11 and 14), the risk-based capital requirements developed under the aegis of the Bank for International Settlements (BIS) have not yet been officially implemen-ted, pending adoption of a European directive on the subject. French international banks have, however, been informally required to monitor their capital levels using an adapted version of the BIS requirements. There has not so far been any indication of the treat-ment to be accorded to Fund certificates when the BIS requirements and the European directive are fully implemented.

For several years, however, all French credit institutions have been subject to a risk-coverage ratio requiring them to maintain a minimum ratio of 5 per cent between amounts representing capital and the sum of weighted risks. For this purpose, CRB Regulation No. 89–08 specifies the consequences of various aspects of securitization. Ordinary certificates held by credit institutions are given the same risk weighting as the underlying receivables, except that where another credit institution guarantees the certificates they are weighted at only 20 per cent, like bank securities and other interbank assets. A guarantee granted on Fund certificates is weighted at 100 per cent, as is any subordinated certificate of a Fund or the liquidation interest of an over-collateralizing seller of receivables to a Fund.

As noted above, a credit institution is permitted to treat a transfer of receivables to a Fund as a sale, even if it continues to provide credit enhancement. The credit enhancement itself will be counted as a risk, but still this treatment will in many cases be more generous than under bank accounting rules in some other countries, notably in the United States. It remains to be seen whether this approach, designed to foster securitization, will withstand comparative scrutiny in the implementation process for the BIS risk-based capital standards.

13.7 Approval, Offering and Reporting

13.7.1 *Approval, Offering and Placement in General*

The creation or liquidation of a Fund requires approval of the COB, acting after consultation with the *Banque de France*. The COB is also specifically charged with approving the charter of any Fund and the nomination of its statutory auditors. In addition, the COB, which generally oversees French securities markets and attends particularly to the protection of investors, can be expected to play, through its power to approve Funds, an active role in the regulation of securitization. While it has set forth certain requirements in the COB Instruction, further requirements will surely be developed by administrative practice in approving Funds.

As a condition to approval of any Fund, the COB must receive a report on the certificates and the pool of receivables from a rating agency approved for this purpose by the Ministry of Finance. Three rating agencies have been approved to date: Agence d'évaluation financière (ADEF), Moody's France and Standard & Poor's France.

352 ROBERT BORDEAUX-GROULT

Article 35 of the Act and Article 7 of the Decree describe the scope of the rating agency's report in some detail.

The Act also imposes certain limitations on the placement of certificates, applicable to all Funds. In particular:

- A copy of the rating agency evaluation must be sent to every subscriber in the primary placement of certificates.
- *Démarchage* is not permitted in connection with certificates. The term *démarchage* (roughly translated as 'solicitation') refers to a range of selling practices, rather vaguely defined and interpreted under present law, that involve the solicitation of prospective purchasers in their homes, in public or in their places of employment. The same restriction applies to certain FCPs.
- If a SICAV or FCP is related, in ways specified in Article 26 of the Act, to the seller of the receivables held by a Fund, the SICAV or FCP may not hold more than 50 per cent by value of the certificates issued by the Fund.

Otherwise, the only limitations on investors eligible to purchase certificates are those described below that apply to privately placed certificates. Thus, notwithstanding the view, frequently expressed in the parliamentary debates and by the Ministry of Finance, that certificates should not be attractive to retail or individual investors, for the most part the limitations on placement and trading will be those applicable to securities generally.

13.7.2 *Public Offering and Private Placement*

Other provisions governing approval of Funds, offering of certificates and continuing information requirements differ depending on whether the certificates are to be offered to the public or privately placed. It is possible for a single Fund to issue both types of certificates.

Privately placed certificates can be approved upon presentation of a simplified application and prospectus, and they are subject to less stringent continuing information requirements. In order for certificates to qualify for this treatment, certificates must meet the following requirements:

- They must not be listed.
- They must be in registered book-entry form. The register is to be maintained by the management company.

- They may not be held by individuals or by SICAVs.
- The number of holders may not exceed twenty-five.
- Although the COB Regulation does not so specify, presumably they must be placed without reliance on methods that, under French law, are indicia of a public offering.

The approval of certificates to be publicly offered, in contrast, requires that a more complete application be submitted to the COB, including an offering prospectus to be approved by the COB and provided to subscribers. The COB Instruction contains detailed provisions for the contents of the application and the prospectus. The offering itself must be made with a firm underwriting commitment with a placement period not to exceed thirty days. The COB Instruction also prescribes certain mechanics of closing the issuance of certificates, which vary depending on the form of the underwriting commitment. The certificates must be listed on a French exchange, unless their initial par value is 1,000,000 French francs or more.

13.7.3 *Information Requirements*

Within three months following the end of each fiscal year, the management company must prepare the financial statements of the Fund, which must be audited by the statutory auditors of the Fund, and a management report. The COB Instruction sets forth specific information that must be included in the management report. For example, the report must analyse the Fund's prepayment experience, default rates and weighted average life, and describe any events that may require the Fund to call on its credit enhancement. The management report and financial statements must be made available to holders of certificates on request and to the public at the premises of the depository.

Each Fund is also required to publish additional information semi-annually, within two months after the end of the fiscal half-year. The information required is less extensive for Funds that have outstanding only privately placed certificates. In addition, if a Fund has publicly offered certificates with initial par values under 1,000,000 French francs, it must publish monthly information on prepayment experience, default rates, weighted average life and other matters concerning its receivables.

13.8 Tax Matters

13.8.1 *The Seller of Receivables to the Fund*

The gain or loss realized upon sale of receivables to a Fund is treated as ordinary income or loss. Where the seller provides credit enhancement by delivering receivables with a value in excess of the face amount of the certificates (*surdimensionnement*), it will generally receive proceeds worth less than the receivables, with the difference consisting of a liquidation interest in the Fund. Gain or loss on such a transaction for tax purposes will be determined taking account of the face amount of the liquidation interest, and the liquidation interest may not be depreciated for tax purposes until defaults on the Fund's receivables become likely. The seller will thus recognize, at the moment of transfer, any gains on the excess receivables transferred to the Fund. On the other hand, upon liquidation of the Fund, the seller would not be subject to tax on previously recognized gains.

Where the seller retains subordinated certificates, they are valued, for tax purposes, at their purchase price in accordance with ordinary rules concerning taxation of securities. The use of subordinated certificates would thus avoid the accelerated recognition of gain associated with *surdimensionnement*.

The Tax Release is silent on the deductibility of provisions for possible losses created at the time the Fund is organized. It seems prudent to assume that these are not deductible until defaults become likely.

The sale of receivables is not subject to mandatory transfer tax. It is exempt from value added tax, and the parties may not opt for subjection to value added tax.

13.8.2 *The Fund*

The Fund itself is not subject to corporate income tax, and registration duties and value added tax do not apply to its transactions. In particular, the issuance of certificates is exempt from registration duty; the transfer of certificates is exempt from registration duty or stamp duty (*impôt de bourse*); and fees paid to the management company, the servicer and the depository are exempt from value added tax. While the servicer may not opt for subjection to value added tax with respect to its fees, both the management company and the depository may do so.

13.8.3 *Holders of Certificates*

The Act and the Tax Release use the term 'earnings from certificates' (*les produits des parts*) without defining it. Presumably earnings from certificates include amounts characterized as interest or redemption premium and the recovery of any original-issue discount. The Act and the Tax Release appear to look to the way amounts are characterized with respect to the certificates, and not with respect to the underlying receivables. Thus amounts paid to investors as the repayment of principal on their certificates would not be taxed (subject to the rules on recovery of original-issue discount), and amounts paid as interest or premium would be taxed, regardless of the relative proportions of interest and principal received by the Fund in the same period on the underlying receivables. Earnings of the Fund are taxable only upon distribution to certificate-holders.

Entities subject to French corporate income tax treat earnings from certificates, and any gain on the distribution of a liquidation interest, as ordinary income. Capital gains and losses on disposition of certificates are ordinary income or loss if the certificates have been held for two years or less, and are treated as long-term capital gains or losses, taxable at a reduced rate, if they have been held for over two years.

For individuals subject to French income tax, earnings on certificates are taxable as ordinary income, and may be included (under a system called the *abattement*) in a yearly amount of tax-free income from securities investments. The holder may also choose to be subject to withholding on earnings from certificates, which frees the payments from any further taxation. The rate of this withholding (called *prélèvement libératoire*) was reduced to 15 per cent on 1 January 1990. Capital gains and losses are also ordinary income or loss, except that with respect to certificates with an original term to maturity in excess of five years they are eligible for tax exemption or taxation at a special reduced rate. For individuals, recovery of original-issue discount and capitalized interest income may be subject to special recognition rules if the original term to maturity is in excess of five years.

Earnings of non-resident holders are exempt from French tax, provided that the holder establishes to the satisfaction of the paying agent that it is not a resident of France or the French franc zone. Otherwise, earnings are subject to withholding (*prélèvement*) at a rate that will be reduced to 15 per cent beginning 1 January 1990. Holders that benefit from a tax treaty with France may also use treaty procedures (which are generally more cumbersome) to escape withholding. It will in principle be possible for an issue of certificates made outside of France to qualify for an exemption from withholding under the provisions applicable to Eurobonds. Capital gains derived by non-resident holders should not be subject to any French tax.

Liquidation interests held by non-residents will be subject to withholding at the rate of 45 per cent, which was reduced to 35 per cent on 1 January 1990. Tax treaties will generally permit this rate to be reduced, and in some cases to be eliminated.

Notes

1 COB Regulation No. 89–01 (the 'COB Regulation') and the related Instruction (the 'COB Instruction').
2 CRB Regulation No. 89–07 of 26 July 1989.
3 CRB Regulation No. 89–08 of 26 July 1989, modifying CRB Regulation No. 85–08 of 28 June 1985.
4 Instruction of the *Direction Générale des Impôts* of 17 October 1989 (the 'Tax Release').
5 *Arrêté* of 31 July 1989.

Appendix 1
Law No. 88–1201 of 23 December 1988
Concerning Collective Investment
Vehicles and Funds of Pooled Receivables
Chapter VII
Fund of Pooled Receivables

Article 34 A fund of pooled receivables shall be a coproprietorship (*copropriété*) having as its sole object the acquisition of receivables held by financial institutions or the *Caisse des dépôts et consignations* and the resale, on one occasion, of units representing such receivables.

The fund shall not have an independent legal identity. The provisions of the Civil Code concerning certain jointly held property (*indivision*), as well as the provisions of Articles 1871 to 1873 of said Code, shall not apply to a fund.

Translation: Cleary, Gottlieb, Steen & Hamilton.

It may not acquire receivables after the issuance of units, except for receivables the acquisition of which corresponds to the temporary placement of available funds prior to distribution under conditions set by decree. The fund may not borrow.

The units may give rise to different rights with respect to principal and interest.

The units shall be securities. They cannot be redeemed by the fund at the request of the holders. The minimum amount of a unit issued by a fund of pooled receivables shall be established by decree. It shall not be less than 10,000 francs.

The fund may not transfer the receivables that it acquires, except in the event of liquidation in accordance with conditions established and set forth by decree. It may not grant security interests in the receivables that it holds.

Transfer of the receivables shall be effected by the delivery of an assignment (*bordereau*), the terms of which shall be fixed by decree. The transfer shall take effect between the parties and with respect to third parties as of the date borne by the assignment at the time of its delivery. Any collateral security for the receivables shall be automatically transferred at the time of delivery of the assignment.

The debtor shall be informed by regular mail.

The transfer agreement may provide that the transferor shall receive all or part of the profit realized upon any liquidation of the fund.

In all cases where a specific legislative or regulatory provision requires the indication of the last name, first name and address of the owner of the instrument, as well as for all transactions entered into on behalf of the co-owners, designation of the fund may be validly substituted for that of the co-owners.

Article 35   The approval of the *Commission des opérations de bourse* envisioned by Article 40 shall be subject, as provided by decree, to the submission of a document describing the units that the Fund proposes to issue and the receivables that it proposes to acquire and evaluating the risks that the latter present. This document shall be prepared by an entity approved pursuant to an *arrêté* of the minister responsible for the economy after notice to the *Commission des opérations de bourse*. It shall then be distributed to subscribers of the units.

Funds may not be the subject of solicitation.

Article 36   The transferring institution shall continue to ensure collection of the transferred receivables in accordance with the terms set forth in an agreement with the management company of the fund.

Collection may be entrusted to a person other than the transferring institution if agreed by the debtor in writing at the time of the transfer of responsibility for collection.

Article 37   A fund shall be established upon the joint initiative of a company responsible for the fund's management and a legal entity which will be the depository of the fund's assets. This company and this legal entity shall establish the rules of the fund, which must be approved by the *Commission des opérations de bourse* after consultation with the *Banque de France*.

A decree shall fix the nature and characteristics of the receivables that may be acquired by funds and the conditions under which they will be obligated to cover the risks of default of the debtors of the receivables transferred to them or to obtain guarantees against these risks from an entity approved for this purpose by the minister responsible for the economy.

The charter shall set forth terms governing the allocation of the liquidation interest.

Article 38   In the first modified paragraph of Article 5A of *ordonnance* 67–833 of 29 September 1967 cited above, the words 'or funds of pooled receivables' shall be inserted following the words 'stock exchange companies, management companies and depositories of mutual funds'.

Article 39   Managers, in law or fact, of a fund that undertakes a placement of securities without approval or that continues its activity after withdrawal of approval shall be punished by a fine of 100,000 to 5,000,000 francs and from six months' to two years' imprisonment.

Article 40   I   The creation or liquidation of a fund of pooled receivables shall be subject to the approval of the *Commission des opérations de bourse* after consultation with the *Banque de France*.

II   The company envisaged by Article 37 that is responsible for management shall be a commercial enterprise, the exclusive purpose of which is the management of funds of pooled receivables. It shall represent the fund *vis-à-vis* third parties in all judicial proceedings whether as plaintiff or defendant.

III   The legal entity envisaged by Article 37 that is the depository of the assets of a fund shall be a credit institution or other entity approved by the minister responsible for the economy. It must have its principal place of business in France. It shall be the depository of the receivables acquired by the fund and of liquid assets. It shall ensure the regularity of the decisions of the management company.

IV   The holders of the units shall be liable for the debts of the fund only to the extent of the fund's assets and in amounts proportional to their holdings.

V   The charter of the fund shall set forth the length of the fiscal year, which may not exceed twelve months. The first fiscal year, however, may have a longer duration, not exceeding eighteen months.

Within six weeks following the end of each half fiscal year, the management company must take, for each of the funds that it manages, an inventory of the assets under the control of the depository.

VI   The statutory auditor (*commissaire aux comptes*) of the fund shall be appointed for a term of six fiscal years by the board of directors, manager or supervisory board of the management company after the approval of the *Commission des opérations de bourse.*

The provisions of Articles 218 to 222; 230; 231; 233, second and third paragraphs; 234 and 235 of Law No. 66–537 of 24 July 1966 cited above shall be applicable to the statutory auditor.

The statutory auditor shall inform the management of the management company, as well as the *Commission des opérations de bourse*, of any irregularity or inaccuracy that he discovers during the course of his duties.

Holders of units of the fund shall have the rights granted to shareholders by Articles 225 to 227 of Law No. 66–537 of 24 July 1966 cited above.

Article 41   Within six months following the discharge of the last receivable, the management company shall proceed to liquidate the fund.

[Article 42 omitted.]

Appendix 2
Decree No. 89–158 of 9 March 1989
Interpreting Articles 26 and 34 to 42
of Law No. 88–1201 of 23 December 1988
Concerning Funds of Pooled Receivables

Article 1   The percentage envisaged by Article 26 of the above-cited law shall be 5 per cent of the value of the units issued by the fund, as indicated in the last semi-annual report described in paragraph V of Article 40 of the above-cited law.

Within three weeks of the end of each semi-annual period, SICAVs and management companies of FCPs shall inform the management company of a pooled receivables fund of the number of units they hold.

The management company of a pooled receivables fund shall disclose the percentage of units held by collective investment vehicles in the semi-annual report described in paragraph V of Article 40 of the above-cited law.

Article 2   The assignment (*bordereau*) envisaged by Article 34 of the above-cited law shall contain the following elements:

(1)   the title 'Transfer of Receivables';
(2)   a statement that the transfer is subject to the provisions of Law No. 88–

Translation: Cleary, Gottlieb, Steen & Hamilton

1201 of 23 December 1988 concerning collective investment vehicles and funds of pooled receivables;

(3) the name of the transferee;

(4) the name and characteristics of the transferred receivables, the identity of the debtors, the amount of the receivables, their date of final maturity. If the transfer is made by a computer procedure permitting identification of the receivables, the assignment shall indicate, in addition to the elements mentioned in (1), (2) and (3) above, the method by which the receivables are identified, the number of receivables and their aggregate amount;

(5) a statement that the transfer obligates the transferor, at the request of the transferee, to take all actions necessary for the recording, identification, enforcement, release or foreclosure of the collateral security.

Article 3   The depository is responsible for the safekeeping of the documents representing receivables transferred to the fund.

Article 4   The available funds mentioned in the third paragraph of Article 34 of the above-cited law may be invested in:

• Treasury bonds;
• shares of SICAVs or interests in FCPs, except FCPs governed by Articles 22 and 23 of the above-cited law;
• securities traded on a regulated market, except units of pooled receivable funds and equity securities (or securities exchangeable for or convertible into equity securities).

The charter of the fund shall specifically include rules governing the use of such available funds.

Article 5   The minimum amount of a unit of a fund of pooled receivables shall be FF10,000.

Article 6   If the amount of the assets of a fund falls below 10 per cent of the amount of the initial issue, the receivables held by the fund may be transferred, in whole and in a single transaction, in accordance with the terms set forth in Article 2 of this decree.

Article 7   The document described in Article 35 of the above-cited law shall be prepared prior to the issuance of units by a fund of pooled receivables. This document is required regardless of the nature or the characteristics of the receivables transferred. It shall indicate *inter alia* the characteristics of the receivables transferred and of the units issued. It shall also indicate the nature and the scope of the guarantees applicable to the issued units.

Article 8   A fund of pooled receivables may only acquire receivables that have an initial term of at least two years and that are not classified as *immobilisées, douteuses* or *litigieuses*. The receivables acquired shall be representative of similar credit operations.

Article 9   The fund of pooled receivables shall ensure against the risk of default by the debtors of receivables transferred to it by:

- obtaining a guarantee from a financial institution or an insurance company, which may not defer payment of sums due to the fund;
- issuing special units that bear the risk of default on the receivables. These units may not be purchased by collective investment vehicles or individuals;
- transferring an amount of receivables to the fund in excess of the amount of units issued.

The charter of the fund shall specifically describe the ways in which the fund will protect itself against the risk of default by debtors of transferred receivables.

When granting approval of funds, the *Commission des opérations de bourse* shall take into account the guarantees which ensure the payment of sums due to the holders of units.

Article 10   The Minister of Economy, Finance and Budget shall be responsible for ensuring compliance with this decree, which shall be published in the *Journal officiel* of the French Republic.

14

'1992' and the Future of Securitization in Western Europe

PROFESSOR EDWARD P. M. GARDENER

Chapter Outline

14.1 Introduction

14.2 '1992' and European Capital
    14.2.1 Trends in European Securities Markets
    14.2.2 The Impact of '1992'
    14.2.3 Regulatory Influences
    14.2.4 Post-'1992' Scenario

14.3 Securitization Developments
    14.3.1 The Nature of Securitization
    14.3.2 An Economic Perspective of Securitization
    14.3.3 Domestic Commercial Paper in Europe
    14.3.4 Mortgage-Backed Securitization

14.4 The Future

14.1 Introduction

This chapter considers broadly the impact of '1992' on securitization developments in western Europe. The economic consequences of '1992' on the financial services sectors of the European Community (EC) have been the subject of considerable analysis and controversy. Completing the internal market is the immediate focus of attention following the '1992' proposals, but this emphasis on the 'structural deregulation' and 'European' aspects of '1992' are only a part – albeit a vital part – of the developing scenario in European securities markets and related business. In order to set these in context, the first part of the chapter considers some of the wider trends in European capital markets and the impact of '1992' on the European securities industry. This provides a kind of overview of European capital markets. Attention will also be focused on the general regulatory pressures that may influence or stimulate the evolution of securitization. The second main part of the chapter focuses more specifically on securitization developments in western Europe.

14.2 '1992' and European Capital

14.2.1 Trends in European Securities Markets

Experiences in the United States have emphasized that the sophistication of domestic capital markets has an important bearing on the success of issuers and investment bankers in expanding the market for the securities that are produced through securitization. This does not necessarily imply a supply-leading approach towards the development of securitization. Growth in capital-market sophistication and activity is also associated with a more performance-oriented investment culture, thereby intensifying competition and increasing the propensity towards spectrum-filling in the market for securities. US empirical experience has suggested, at the very least, strong associative relationships between these factors and the growth of securitization.

The stock exchange in London is the largest stock exchange by market capitalization in Europe; table 14.1 summarizes the comparative sizes of European stock exchanges at the end of 1988. The United Kingdom stock market has also been one of the most rapidly changing capital markets in the world. One expert puts these changes into context:[1]

In US terms it is as if Glass–Steagall had been abolished, May Day took place, the SEC were set up, primary dealerships set up in the government bond market, NASDAQ was introduced, most securities houses were sold to foreign banks, the NYSE merged into an international exchange and the trading floor abolished – all in the space of three years.

Table 14.1   Stock market capitalization

Exchange	Market value at 31 December 1988 ($ millions)[a]	
	Equity shares of domestic companies	Bonds and debentures
Amsterdam	103,644.0	131,409.8
Basle	136,337.1	n.a.
Barcelona	83,554.6	64,006.8
Brussels	58,786.0	98,679.8
Copenhagen	26,878.1	159,004.9
Geneva	126,963.4	n.a.
German Fed. Rep.	250,867.0	n.a.
Helsinki	30,549.2	n.a.
Italy	135,416.6	n.a.
London	711,527.1	558,389.8
Luxembourg	46,146.3	677,475.6
Madrid	90,904.0	67,431.8
Oslo	15,755.8	32,255.4
Paris	222,892.6	364,979.9
Stockholm	99,723.9	n.a.
Vienna	10,030.3	59,918.3
Zurich	140,359.0	144,614.4
Tokyo	3,789,033.0	1,135,813.7
New York	2,366,106.0	1,561,031.0

Source: Tables 1B and 6C of Fédération International des Bourses de Valeurs, *Activités et Statistiques, Rapport 1988*
[a]Translated at year-end rates.

As in the United States, the UK system has become more strongly 'market oriented'. This Anglo-Saxon model is being increasingly adopted in Continental Europe, especially in countries like France and The Netherlands. Continental capital markets have traditionally been 'bank oriented' (like that of West Germany) or state controlled (as with the French equity market until recently).

Major European stock exchanges, like other important stock exchanges across the globe, have been subject *inter alia* to three fundamental market trends: the concomitant rise of globalization, securitization and risk-management products and services.[2] Globalization has made markets less fragmented; the swaps mechanism has been especially important in this respect. The completion of the

European internal market is a European globalization process, but the globalization of the world's capital markets has taken place largely independently of European initiatives and the actions of individual countries. Securitization has created a more liquid marketplace; market-based intermediation has been increasingly substituted for institution-based intermediation. Another environmental character-istic of the so-called financial revolution has been the evolution of more active risk management associated with the rise of futures and options exchanges.

The rapid growth of international securities markets has in its turn stimulated far-reaching changes in European stock exchanges.[3] The demise of exchange controls in the late 1970s and the rapid develop-ment of communications technology increasingly led fund managers to internationalize their portfolios. Across Europe exchanges are modernizing their traditional systems and installing new technology in order to handle the growth in equity trading. Table 14.2 depicts the character of stock-market performance experienced in Europe up to early 1987.

Privatization initiatives in some countries and the growth of the international equities market – so-called Euroequities – have increased significantly the importance of international equity flows in Europe. Better-known markets, like those in Switzerland, West Germany and The Netherlands, were foremost in experiencing this surge of new activity by fund managers. France has experienced enormous inflows since 1985 and so have countries like Italy and Spain. Many countries have begun to deregulate their exchanges in order to match interna-tional trends and investor expectations, and also to improve the alloca-tive efficiency of their own markets. These reforms have been especially marked in France and have been labelled 'France's financial revolution'.

Most European stock exchanges are out-performing the London stock exchange. Recent survey evidence[4] suggests that buoyant mergers and acquisitions activity have allowed many European exchanges to exceed their pre-crash peaks. Recent statistics of new-issues activity confirm the general, upward trend in European stock exchanges. Equity markets in Europe are expected to experience growth in capitalization and turnover of 10–15 per cent a year over the next few years.[5] Eurobond-market growth has probably peaked and domestic bond markets in Europe will continue to be dominated by large issues by governments with budget deficits. A recent detailed

Table 14.2   European stock-market performance

Market	Sept. 1982 low to Dec. 1982 (%)	Calendar 1984 (%)	Calendar 1985 (%)	Calendar 1986 (%)	Sept. 1982 low to end 1986 (%)
Belgium	+12.1	+16.3	+36.4	+39.1	+147.4
Denmark	+17.9	−21.9	+41.5	−18.9	+5.7
France	+6.8	+16.4	+45.7	+49.7	+171.1
Germany	+18.2	+8.3	+76.1	+4.9	+136.5
Italy	+12.0	+19.2	+100.3	+58.1	+322.8
Netherlands	+17.1	+18.0	+40.6	+8.8	+111.4
Norway	+5.4	+29.1	+37.1	−9.1	+69.6
Spain	+1.2	+40.7	+35.3	+108.3	+301.3
Sweden (From 16.9.80)	+157.2	−6.3	+28.3	+41.5	+337.5
Switzerland	+21.6	+0.5	+52.5	+0.2	+86.7
UK	+24.5	+25.3	+19.7	+22.3	+128.4
World comparisons					
Japan	+17.0	+16.0	+13.6	+39.7	+115.4
US	+34.7	−4.3	+28.4	+22.3	+102.4

Source: Ben Davies, 'Reveille for Europe's exchanges', *Euromoney Supplement*, August 1987, p. 4

study on the future of European capital markets concluded that, of the European exchanges, only London will play a significant role in the international equities market.[6] The major problem for Continental European exchanges is that they are fragmented, small by world standards and divided on national lines.

14.2.2 The Impact of '1992'

The development of capital markets results from the complex interplay of a number of factors. The behaviour of capital-market participants – institutional investors and intermediaries – is important. Trends in exchanges and financial instruments are other significant factors. In this respect technology has been one of the fundamental causes of change. Revell[7] suggests that very few of the major recent developments in securities exchanges and related business could have taken place without the aid of technological developments. Demand from issuers and investors plays an important, developmental role in capital markets. Regulation and taxes are other important factors.

A widely publicized study of the impact of '1992' on the European financial services sectors was presented in the so-called Cecchini Report.[8] The analysis within this study hypothesized economic gains on the assumption that the process embodied in the law of one price obtains after the EC internal market is completed. Potential falls in financial product prices in different EC countries were measured against a set of suggested benchmark prices for each sector. Table 14.3 summarizes the results of this exercise for selected securities-market products. Details of the respective products and a comparison of the securities-sector results with the banking and insurance sectors studied by Cecchini are also summarized in Table 14.3.

These hypothesized reductions in the costs of financial services provide an interesting picture of one aspect of competitive conditions in European capital markets. On the basis of these data, the biggest single drop in price is hypothesized for institutional gilts transactions in Belgium: this is indicative of a corresponding big surge in competition within this market segment in Belgium after the internal market is completed. However, this kind of quantification exercise is extremely difficult to validate and it is invariably suspect because of the assumptions that have to be made. The Commission of the European Communities strongly emphasized these limitations, and related ones imposed by the tight timescale of the project. A more recent study[9] has been critical of some of the methodological assumptions of the analysis that underpins the table 14.3 results.

Another view has been that '1992' by itself is likely to have a limited or marginal effect on capital markets in Europe.[10] The argument runs that wider international or global trends dominate specific European or individual country initiatives. This is true up to a point, but it is a highly simplified view for two reasons. One is that '1992' is in reality an important milestone in a longer-term and more fundamental process. Stock-market deregulation in Europe has been part of a wider economic policy process that has evolved in Europe since the late 1970s. This is reflected in the growing acceptance by governments in their economic policies of free-market philosophies and reduced state interference. We saw earlier that in financial systems it involves a growing acceptance of the so-called Anglo-Saxon model of allocative efficiency. Another reason why this view is simplistic is that '1992' is likely to have many secondary effects on financial sectors and the behaviour of market participants.

14.2.3 *Regulatory Influences*

In considering the post-'1992' situation in Europe it is important to isolate two important and concomitant regulatory trends.[11] The first is structural deregulation: the allowing of financial institutions and markets to compete more freely. London's 'Big Bang', France's recent financial reforms and Europe's 'Horizon 1992' objective of completing the internal market are examples of this kind of deregulation. The underlying economic objective is an attempt to capture the hypothesized economic gains from allowing the market a greater role in resource allocation.

In capital markets and financial systems generally this kind of deregulation represents a growing adoption of the so-called Anglo-Saxon model of financial systems. This model emphasizes the role of free-market forces rather than any kind of directed or government-controlled system of resource allocation. Many Continental European countries, such as France, have increasingly accorded structural deregulation a much higher priority in their own domestic financial systems. Wider globalization pressures and questions of reciprocity have sometimes dictated particular deregulation moves. Some countries, for example, have allowed foreign banks into their domestic systems in the belief (or implied threat) that their own banks would otherwise be precluded from entering markets in other countries. One of the noteworthy characteristics of western governments during the past decade, and more, has been their remarkable policy commitment towards structural deregulation. 'Europe 1992' is the latest example of this kind of commitment.

Structural deregulation may have an important bearing on the future of asset securitization in Europe. The process is characterized by intensified competition, pressures on funding costs and the breaking down of historically segmented financial institution sectors. New forms of competition and new competitors increasingly encroach upon the territory of established institutions. A good case study of the securitization implications of these kinds of developments is offered by the UK building-society sector. Deregulation allowed new players into the UK mortgage market and enabled new financial structures to be launched. In this respect the development of the UK secondary

Table 14.3 Estimate of potential falls in financial product prices as a result of completing the internal market

	B	D	E	F	I	L	NL	UK[d]
1 Percentage differences in prices of financial products[a] compared with the average of the four lowest observations[b]								
Securities[a]								
Private equity	36	7	65	−13	−3	7	114	123
Private gilts	14	90	217	21	−63	27	161	36
Institutional equity	26	69	153	−5	47	68	26	−47
Institutional gilts	284	−4	60	57	92	−36	21	(4)
2 Theoretical, potential price reductions[b]								
Banking	15	33	34	25	18	16	10	18
Insurance	31	10	32	24	51	37	1	4
Securities	52	11	44	23	33	9	18	12
Total	23	25	34	24	29	17	9	13
3 Indicative price reductions[c]								
All financial services								
Range	6–16	5–15	16–26	7–17	9–19	3–13	0–9	2–12
Centre of range	11	10	21	12	14	8	4	7

[a] The financial products are defined as follows:

Brokerage services

1 Private equity transactions: commission costs of cash bargain of 1,440 ECU.
2 Private gilt transactions: commission costs of cash bargain of 14,000 ECU.
3 Institutional equity transactions: commission costs of cash bargain of 288,000 ECU.
4 Institutional gilt transactions: commission costs of cash bargain of 7.2 million ECU.

[b] The figures in part 1 of the table show the extent to which financial product prices, in each country, are above a low reference level. Each of these price differences implies a theoretical potential price fall from existing price levels to the low reference level. Part 2 sets down the weighted averages of the theoretical potential price falls for each sub-sector.

[c] Indicative price falls are based upon a scaling down of the theoretical potential price reductions, taking into account roughly the extent to which perfectly competitive and integrated conditions will not be attained, plus other information for each financial services sub-sector, such as gross margins and administrative costs as a proportion of total costs.

[d] The country abbreviations are as follows: B Belgium, D Federal Republic of Germany, E Spain, F France, I Italy, L Luxembourg, NL Netherlands, UK United Kingdom.

Source: Commission of the European Communities, Directorate-General for Economic and Financial Affairs, *The Economics of 1992* (Commission of the European Communities), No. 35, Brussels, March 1988).

mortgage market has been prompted by different economic forces to those of the US secondary mortgage market. UK experiences may be a good role model for some of the likely European-specific experiences with mortgage and other asset securitization after '1992'.

The other important regulatory influence after 'structural deregulation' is 'supervisory re-regulation', or 'prudential re-regulation'. The strong growth of supervision and investor protection regulations seems almost paradoxical but an economic rationale may be developed. Supervisory re-regulation may be viewed as an economic attempt to keep the new, deregulated system a safe and viable marketplace that can develop without periodic contagion risks materializing. For present purposes, however, we need only observe that supervisory re-regulation is a positive economic fact; we do not need in this analysis to consider its wider, normative dimensions. A core element in supervisory re-regulation is capital adequacy.

Capital adequacy rules generally operate through balance sheet ratios that relate capital, defined by supervisors, to various kinds of assets, typically 'weighted' nowadays by numerical coefficients that reflect their relative credit or counterparty risk. (The regulators of securities houses focus more on flow concepts of capital adequacy that relate profits to various kinds of position risk.) Capital adequacy rules of this kind set a kind of implicit profit target for banks. In this respect they also act as a mechanism that impacts on the pricing of risks.[12] There has been considerable empirical evidence that capital adequacy regulation has a strong impact on securitization trends. The growth of the US commercial-paper market in the 1970s, the post-1982 securitization trends in international financial markets and the post-1987 growth of asset securitizations by US banks were all prompted to a significant extent by capital adequacy regulation.

'Europe 1992' is associated also with a renewed surge of capital adequacy supervision. The new Bank for International Settlements (BIS) rules on capital adequacy published in July 1988 are already putting pressures on some European banks. The new mortgage securitization system in France of 23 December 1988 has been stimulated partly by the pressures on French banks to meet the BIS capital adequacy rules. Faced with difficulties in raising new capital, the securitization of pools of assets is an alternative or complementary method of meeting the new constraints. The EC is also developing new capital adequacy rules for '1992' which will parallel closely the BIS rules.

Capital adequacy will undoubtedly help to stimulate securitization in some EC countries, especially where banks may face difficulties in meeting the new '1992' rules. These pressures will not only come from the economic need by banks to raise new risk capital; the attitudes of supervisors to the credit quality (explicated via the corresponding risk-asset weighting) of the securities produced through the securitization process are also significant. Supervisory attitudes will also be important in defining off-balance-sheet positions and deciding on the rules and nature of securitizations. Like structural deregulation, supervisory re-regulation is likely to have a positive impact on securitization and related capital-market developments in Europe.

14.2.4 Post-'1992' Scenario

The post-'1992' scenario for securities markets and related business appears to be one of significantly increased capital-market activity. The post-'1992' environment will permit access to financial markets and activities by a widening range of competitors. Many believe that 'Europe 1992' may rival London's Big Bang in its impact on investment banking.[13] It is likely that these effects will flow not only from the financial sectors themselves but also from other sectors using an increased volume and variety of financial services.

The demand to raise capital will increase as companies restructure in order to take advantage of the new environment. Following London's Big Bang, the approach of '1992' has focused corporate thinking in Europe on new alliances. Mergers and other kinds of linkups are already buoyant as the market for corporate control continues to become more active and liquid in Continental Europe; it would appear clear that merger and acquisition business is growing rapidly. A dramatic, visionary signal to many of the potential for a more united Europe was the recent activity of the Italian entrepreneur Benedetti, whose unsuccessful attempt to take control of Société Générale de Belgique was prophetic of a possible post-'1992' corporate scenario.

Alongside increased new-issue activity, the demand for other securities business products and services will certainly grow. Corporate financial advice and investment management services, together with brokerage and trading activities, are all likely to increase as the internal market is completed. Traditional distinctions between bank and bond-market finance will probably continue to erode in several market segments. All of these developments will enhance the growing maturity of European capital markets. Although the European exchanges still have a long way to go before they can compete strongly with London, New York or Tokyo in areas like equities, European banks have been highly competitive for some time in new issues and related business. These banks were quick to use the new techniques that developed in the Euromarkets in the early 1980s.

The EC has accorded a high priority to liberalizing capital movements. Countries like West Germany, The Netherlands, Belgium, Luxembourg, Denmark and the United Kingdom have had little or no restriction on capital movements for some time; during the first three months of 1989 Austria, France and Sweden also liberalized their foreign exchange controls. These liberalization developments in Europe have been accelerated by international globalization trends in capital markets, the worldwide movement towards increased structural deregulation and marked progress within the European Monetary System. On 24 June 1988, an EC directive was adopted that will eliminate all restrictions on capital movements within the Community. The 'single passport' for investment firms (like that of banks) is part of the European scenario that implies a more integrated and deeper European capital market developing after '1992'.

Continued structural deregulation will link increasingly the European stock exchanges and other major centres. It seems unlikely that 'Europe 1992' and other developments imply the demise of the Euromarket. What is more likely is that national capital markets in Europe will develop to comprise part of a wider, global capital market that will encompass the Euromarket. Securities business opportunities and activities will be enhanced through the ability of fund managers, governments and other market participants to access an increasing variety of financial alternatives.

Despite the suggestions by many students that '1992' will produce a more integrated, homogeneous market, the '1992' proposals contain nothing by themselves that can achieve such an aim. Trade liberalization of the kind promulgated in the '1992' proposals will mainly affect supply; demand is the product of other characteristics that are unlikely to be affected by '1992'. A recent study[14] argues that there are three main ways that the '1992' EC objectives are likely to affect the structure of European markets: first, companies that export to other EC states are likely to find their costs reduced compared to their domestic competitors; secondly, existing market segmentation strategies may be weakened through completion of the internal market; finally, new competitors are likely to be brought into previously unattractive or closed markets.

As we have suggested, all of these developments are likely to increase the volume, depth and variety of securities business in Europe. The attempts by Continental exchanges to prevent London attracting an even bigger share of the total capitalization of European exchanges will attract higher volumes and enhance the expertise of domestic intermediaries. Another indicator of the continuing innovation and expansion of European exchanges has been the development of new futures and options exchanges like MATIF (France) and SOFFEX (Switzerland). It is within this developing and buoyant environment that we have to consider further the prospects of securitization developments in Europe after '1992'.

14.3 Securitization Developments

14.3.1 *The Nature of Securitization*

The generalized growth of securitization in the Euromarkets is well documented. The comparative decline of syndicated credits and the corresponding growth of Eurobonds, floating-rate notes (FRNs) and Euronote facilities (including Euro-commercial paper) since 1982 have been dramatic.[15] The 'liquefaction of the Euromarkets' is a phrase that has been coined to describe this process. Since 1985 the syndicated credits market has experienced a revival associated partly with the development of multiple-option facilities (MOFs) and increased mergers and acquisitions activity. Table 14.4 summarizes recent trends in international financial markets.

European banks and other capital-market institutions are active and successful players in the Euromarkets and many successful US domestic securitization techniques have been 'transplanted' in various ways by US banks into the Euromarkets. However, there are still important differences between different capital markets, their respective techniques and the corresponding attitudes of issuers, investors and other participants. Commercial paper (CP) is one example;[16] the slowness of Europe compared to the United States in taking up medium-term notes (MTNs) is another.[17] Important domestic mortgage markets in Europe tend to operate (unlike in the United States)

Table 14.4   Gross new activity by market sector ($ billions)

	1985	1986	1987	1988	% change 1987–8
Fixed-rate bonds[a]	108.6	173.7	163.6	202.3	+24
Straights	95.2	144.8	117.0	160.3	+37
Equity Related	11.6	26.7	43.3	42.0	−3
FRNs	55.9	47.8	12.0	23.0	+92
Euronote facilities	50.7	70.8	72.9	75.8	+4
Syndicated credits	18.9	29.8	88.7	102.0	+15
Total	234.1	322.1	337.2	403.1	+20

[a]The differences between fixed-rate bonds and the respective (subsets) straights and equity-related issues in each column are accounted for by miscellaneous items like oil-related and gold warrant bonds.
Source: Bank of England Quarterly Bulletin (various)

on the basis of flexible-rate mortgages. Domestic financial systems in Europe are typically very different from the US system in both their structure and regulatory environment. These comparative differences should serve as a warning that securitization in Europe is not simply a matter of translating US experiences and techniques without a careful regard to the unique characteristics of particular systems. In order to appreciate the development of securitization and its future prospects we need to consider the fundamental nature of securitization.

At its most basic level, securitization involves transforming bank loans into negotiable securities; loans are pooled and repackaged into securities, which are then sold on to investors. In practice securitization may take many forms and a wide array of transmutations have already emerged. In a broad sense, securitization is credit intermediation that entails the buying and selling of securities at some stage of the process. A narrower definition is that it facilitates the repackaging of generally illiquid balance-sheet assets into securities that may be sold in capital markets.

In a recent study,[18] the authors define securitization as follows:

> the process which takes place when a lending institution's assets are removed in one way or another from the balance sheet of that lending institution and are funded instead by investors who purchase a negotiable financial instrument evidencing the indebtedness, without recourse (or in some cases with limited recourse) to the original lender.

This definition covers CP, mortgage-backed securities, car loans and credit receivables, commercial property and export credits. It does not extend to banker's acceptances, because banks retain a contingent liability when their name is on an acceptance.

It is possible to identify three main forms of securitization: sale and trading of bank loans; the issue of securities that are effectively substitutes for bank loans; and issuance of asset-backed securities. Although banks have always had a need to sell or trade loans, recent securitization trends have prompted the evolution of more structured or developed approaches in the London market; loan participations may be sold by assignment, novation or sub-participation.[19] The second 'displacement' kind of securitization is exemplified in table 14.4, which shows the replacement of bank loans by financial-market instruments like bonds and Euronote facilities. The third kind of securitization covers the secondary-mortgage and similar markets.

These different definitions and views of securitization indicate some of the special features and complexities of the market for securitized assets. One of the most useful, generic views of securitization is that it is a process or vehicle for matching up savers or borrowers, either wholly or partly, through financial markets. 'Open market' credits (through financial markets) are used to replace 'closed market' credits via banks and other financial institutions. It is this generic view that emphasizes securitization as market-based intermediation (of credit) as opposed to institution-based intermediation.[20]

Securitization and the associated strong growth in securities-markets transactions have been among the most important recent trends within the financial sector. The two major, or basic, forms of securitization in the United States have been CP (which was the first form of securitized loan) and mortgage securitization; as has been discussed by Paul Spellman in chapter 5, US techniques are moving well beyond these traditional markets. We will focus shortly on European experiences with these basic kinds of securitization and the respective post-'1992' scenarios. It will be useful first to consider briefly the underlying economics of securitization.

14.3.2 *An Economic Perspective of Securitization*

The shift of credit flows into capital markets (depicted in table 14.4) and the rise of CP and secondary-mortgage markets beg a fundamental question. Why should market-based intermediation be apparently more efficient than institution-based intermediation? A related question is why this comparative efficiency has now shifted in favour of financial markets. Globalization, technology and trends like deregulation have increased the depth and efficiency of capital markets. As a result, liquidity – a fundamental 'economic good' produced by capital markets – has increased. The competing 'bank good' is a bundle of services that focuses on the control and monitoring services associated with credit extension.

It appears that the premium for liquidity (through capital-market financing) has exceeded the comparative benefits of the corresponding and competing bank services. Nevertheless, this is only part of the story. Banks, for example, may still perform useful economic services in an era characterized by widespread securitization: for example, they may act as 'delegated monitors' of open-market credits for some kinds of (non-rated) credits. Banks themselves may wish to securitize their own assets for portfolio management purposes. In practice, a particular kind of securitization should not be viewed in isolation from other capital-market facilities that are often engineered and delivered by banks. For example, the swap innovation has been important in attracting high-grade European companies to the use of US CP: they are able to use the swaps mechanism to convert the facility into a more desirable form of funding. Another example is the use of options in some kinds of mortgage-backed facilities.

Despite these practical complexities, it is useful to consider some basic principles. The first set of principles is concerned with the broader economic forces that have stimulated modern securitization trends. In an earlier section we discussed broadly the influence of deregulation and capital adequacy on securitization trends. Against this background we can identify four elemental forces that bear on the development of securitization:

- increased financial risk and a deterioration in banks' perceived credit standing;
- increased bank capital requirements and a concomitant rise in the cost of bank capital;
- increased competition and growth in the development and efficiency of financial markets;
- reduced utility to borrowers of the bank/lender relationship.

Several of these forces have already been mentioned and they are often highly interrelated.

Increased financial risk is reflected in environmental characteristics like the rise in volatility of interest and exchange rates and the Third World debt crisis. These, and periodic bank failures and crises, have helped to reduce the market's perceived credit-rating of major banks. One result has been a tightening up of supervisory capital requirements; another has been a rise in market-determined required rates of return (cost of capital) on bank stocks. The cost of bank (institution-based) intermediation has correspondingly increased.

Resultant securitization trends – which may be initiated by the banks themselves in search of short-term profits – leave banks with a growing, potential adverse-selection problem. They are increasingly left with the poorer credit risks as the prime credits are able to access directly the cheaper and more liquid capital markets. These 'domino-like' effects have taken place in an environment of increased competition and a strong growth in the efficiency and depth of financial markets. Rating agencies are increasingly able to monitor open-market credit risks. The market is becoming more efficient in translating credit risk and other relevant information into appropriate risk premiums.

These developments enhance the liquidity and reduce the costs associated with financial-markets transactions. The traditional economic advantage for banks of their access to private information in the lending process is eroded. The flexibility of many of the new financial instruments allows them to incorporate economically many of the characteristics of the traditional bank/lender relationship: liquidity, for example, may be assured for borrowers through the use of instruments like note-issuance facilities (NIFs). An issuer may have the same kind of contract with its investment bank as that between a commercial bank and a lender.

Commercial bankers, however, emphasize the dangers of modern, transactional banking. They often point out that the open market may not be reliable as a source of funds in a crisis; banks are able to lend at all times on the basis of their own liquidity resources. But it is not our purpose to debate these issues. Securitization in general, and asset securitization in particular, are now important facts of financial life. New theories of banking are being developed in recognition of these important developments.[21]

It is a fundamental requirement of any economics of securitization that it should explain securitization through the identification of its corresponding 'value added'. Lenders will securitize their assets so long as the resultant benefits exceed the costs. The major benefits to the lender are flexibility and improved income. Balance sheet management may be improved through securitization: interest-rate risk exposures, for example, can often be more closely matched. Securitized assets may be funded more cheaply than the funding available to the originating institution if the latter has a reduced credit rating. This is achieved through pooling assets and 'credit enhancing' these pools. Assets may be securitized as a funding source in order to release capital and provide scope for more originating business. It is these kinds of benefits that have to be weighed against the corresponding costs.

The liquefaction process that is embodied in securitization adds value. At the same time, banks are able to decompose their financial intermediation, that is institution-based intermediation, into its more basic activities like origination, servicing, funding and guaranteeing. This decomposition process allows banks to specialize more in those activities in which they have a comparative advantage. It is this feature of securitization that could help to improve the efficiency of banking systems. At the same time, if economies of scale exist in bank deposit-taking or lending, securitization may facilitate the generation of the necessary volume of business.

Securitization may add value in a number of ways and we have discussed some of the most important of these. The multi-faceted nature of securitization suggests that the importance of particular securitization attributes will vary in different systems and under various economic conditions. Balance sheet flexibility, the need for risk-based capital, improved quality of income, enhanced liquidity and access to AAA/AAA or AA/AA funds sources are among the most important of these attributes. Another characteristic attribute of securitization might be the wider strategic implications that favour a particular kind of financial institution moving into securitization. Insurance companies, for example, may use the facility to cross-sell insurance products into the special-purpose vehicle (SPV) created in an asset securitization.

14.3.3 Domestic Commercial Paper in Europe

It is against this background that we may examine two basic kinds of securitization in a European context. A useful starting point is to look at the growth of domestic CP markets in Europe (ECPs). CP can

Table 14.5 Domestic CP markets in 1988

	Outstandings[a]		Estimated number of programmes
	Local currency (bn)	US$ (bn)	
US	$420.0	420.0	1,700
Japan	Yen 4,000.0	29.7	180
Canada	C$20.1	15.4	200
France	PF£60.0	10.5	100
Australia	A$8.7	6.2	142
Italy	L6,500.0	5.2	250
Sweden	Skr28.0	4.8	200
UK	£3.0	5.0	107
Spain	Pta410.0	3.3	n.a.
Norway	Nkr19.4	3.1	30
Finland	Fmk9.9	2.5	100
Hong Kong	HK$14.0	0.6	27
Netherlands	Dfl150.0	0.9	31
New Zealand	NZ$0.5	0.3	12
Turkey	TL53.0	0.5	11

[a]Dates when figures reported are different for each country. Some data estimated because official data unavailable.
Source: Supplement to Euromoney Corporate Finance (October 1988), p. 35

figure as part of an SPV in an asset securitization, but the growth of CP markets may have a wider significance for present purposes. More specifically, we shall chart the development of CP markets as a kind of 'economic barometer' of wider securitization developments (CP being a fundamental kind of securitization) and the growth of 'spectrum filling' in securities and related financial innovations within European financial systems.

Table 14.5 depicts the comparative sizes of domestic CP markets in 1988.[22] The growth of these markets has been stimulated since the middle of the 1980s by pressures to deregulate and modernize the respective stock exchanges. Nevertheless, it is debatable whether some of these markets are really CP markets; in Italy, for example, the market comprises mainly tradable intercorporate loans. All of these markets, except for Spain, have grown rapidly.

New domestic European CP markets emerged throughout the 1980s in Spain (1982), Sweden (1983), France (1985) and Finland (1986). A CP market started in The Netherlands in January 1986, but its impact has been small; the demand for guilder CP has been restricted because Dutch companies actively place intercompany loans. The sterling CP market was launched on 20 May 1986, but it has not matched its initial growth expectations. Two noteworthy omissions in Table 14.5 are Germany and Switzerland; regulations and taxes in both countries are preventing the creation of formal domestic short-term money markets in securitized loans.

Although the European domestic CP markets have grown, except for that of Spain, they have attracted few foreign investors. Only the UK, Japanese and Spanish CP investors have attracted overseas issuers in any significant way. These markets are still small and relatively immature. Excluding Japan, the total outstandings in all the world's domestic CP markets would barely match the total of ECP outstanding. The latter in its turn is much smaller than the giant US CP market. An important factor in the development of domestic CP markets is the growing involvement of rating agencies. The traditional lack of rating is an important factor that distinguishes European CP markets from the US CP and (to a lesser extent) the ECP markets.

'1992' will accelerate Europe down the learning curve with CP and other forms of securitization. Nevertheless, the recent increased provisioning of major banks against Third World debt may be the start of a recovery in the credit rating of banks compared to major corporations. This may improve the value added of banking services in shorter-term finance provision. In this respect some authors[23] are cautious about forecasting future developments in CP markets:

> the next bear market and slowing down of economic growth may well topple some of the giants of the corporate world. Should this occur, then the appetite of investors for corporate paper may well be significantly diminished. After all, the Penn Central crash changed the US commercial paper for years to follow.

This speculative note reminds us of the need for care in forecasting. Nevertheless, the general prognosis for European CP markets in the context of 1992 is a positive one of steady growth. Increased capital-market development and integration, together with an accelerating movement towards regulatory and tax harmonization in Europe, will be positive stimulants for the development of domestic CP markets.

PROFESSOR EDWARD P. M. GARDENER

14.3.4 *Mortgage-Backed Securitization*

The second major form of securitization has been mortgage securitization. In the United States the development of this market dates back to at least the 1950s. Its growth has been fuelled by the interest-rate volatility that began to characterize the US financial environment from the late 1950s, and the growing support of agencies like the Government National Mortgage Association (Ginnie Mae) and the Federal Home Loan Mortgage Corporation (Freddie Mac). An important milestone occurred in 1970 when the 'Ginnie Mae' 'pass-through' was developed, a mortgage-backed security collateralized by single-family Federal Housing Administration (FHA) and Veterans Administration (VA) mortgage loans. The main developments in secondary mortgages in Europe have taken place so far in the United Kingdom and France. Unlike in the United States, the UK and French mortgage markets have not been characterized by the inefficiencies of the US primary-mortgage market.

France has long had a kind of secondary-mortgage market through the Caisse de Refinancement Hypothécaire (CRH), but this is not a true securitization. Mortgage loans under the French Napoleonic Code are not negotiable instruments and, therefore, not transferable to investors. As discussed at length in chapter 13 of this volume, on 23 December 1988, however, a legal framework was established that created common claims funds (CCF).[24] Securitization is based on the transfer of ownership of claims by the transferring institution to the CCF, thereby removing them from the institution's balance sheet. The French government has pushed ahead with securitization (*titrisation*) in order to help the larger French banks to meet the new Basle capital adequacy rules by selling off pools of assets.

The CCF may issue several categories of securities. Detailed rules have been laid down in areas such as the demarcation of the powers of each party. It is recognized that a real separation between the producer of loans and the investor is necessary in order to ensure that securitization develops in a proper market. Because of fears by the monetary authorities about the potential for banks rapidly expanding their short-term lending to households, there is a prohibition for the moment against securitizing claims with an initial term of less than two years. Present yield relationships in France suggest that the return for securitizing mortgages using the CCF would not be sufficient. An important, potential impact of '1992', however, will be the ability of financial institutions to 'trade without establishment'. This, together with the evolving market conditions, may provide the needed stimulus for the development of true securitization in France.

Asset securitization has developed more rapidly in the United Kingdom. Deregulation and growing competition have fragmented the UK domestic mortgage market, and this has allowed new players to enter the market. A good illustration of this kind of fragmentation for present purposes was the emergence of specialist mortgage vehicles. An early example (January 1985) was the issue of MINI (Mortgage Intermediary Note Issuer (Number 1) Amsterdam BV), a securities issue backed by UK residential mortgages to acquire 1,200 mortgages from BankAmerica Finance International. The driving force in the development of this market came from the companies who wished to share in the lucrative UK mortgage market but who lacked their own retail outlets.[25] During the period from late 1985 through to early 1986, a number of specialist mortgage-funding vehicles were created; these included the National Home Loans Corporation and the House Mortgage Corporation. A common feature of all these vehicles was their funding of mortgage portfolios by wholesale borrowing: reverse yield relationships (between retail and wholesale deposits) facilitated the use of wholesale funding vehicles. By November 1988 the public sterling mortgage-backed market had an outstanding volume of £4.1 billion.

It is a noteworthy feature that these UK developments have centred on new lenders. The future of this kind of asset securitization in the United Kingdom is likely to hinge ultimately on the active participation of the building societies and the banks. The decision by TSB to launch a £135 million deal and, more recently, Barclays, are noteworthy in this context. The attitude of the Bank of England is also important. There appears to be significant barriers to entry for many UK institutions into the field of securitization: legal costs, underwriting fees, upfront structuring fees and the costs of manpower and systems are often cited. Other problems for potential investors have been the uncertain final maturities of the new mortgage-backed structures and concern about liquidity.

Some observers believe that it will be important to attract US investors in developing mortgage-backed securitization in the United Kingdom. The increasing acceptance of sterling as a global investment currency is important in this respect, but its volatility and that of sterling interest rates remain a problem. The swap market may provide at least a partial solution to this problem, but widening the investor base is a fundamental need if the UK market is to develop. But it is unlikely that these positive possibilities will have a large effect by themselves on the development of UK mortgage securitization. The basic challenge to the market must lie in attracting the big originators, especially the building societies, into the market.

Deregulation trends – of which '1992' is the latest and one of the most important to date – are potentially important in this respect. The 1986 Building Societies Act in the United Kingdom has given the societies greater freedom by allowing them to move into new kinds of activity, including unsecured lending. Capital adequacy and profitability have become much more important to societies in this new environment. The capital adequacy, risk–asset rules of the UK societies assign a lower capital backing to mortgage lending than to other kinds of loans. Despite the propensity this induces to stimulate more securitization of non-mortgage (higher-risk) assets by the societies, many believe that the growth of the market will be steady but unspectacular. Nevertheless, the new environment for UK societies may help foster a concomitant movement towards securitizing small personal loans and other receivables.

14.4 The Future

The impact of '1992' on the future of securitization should be positive but not dramatic if the recent deregulatory experiences of countries like the United Kingdom are any guide. It is clearly unrealistic to expect immediate and direct effects on asset securitization from the '1992' proposals themselves. It is also unrealistic to seek close replications of US securitization experiences in Europe; the US structural and regulatory forces that have stimulated domestic asset securitization have been markedly different from those in Europe.

The general prognosis is one of steady progress for asset securitization after '1992' as European capital markets and institutions continue to evolve. The wider, likely effects of '1992' on European corporate restructurings and the market for corporate control will broaden the European investor base, increase the sophistication of all participants and attract more international investors. Privatization is likely to remain another important fillip to the increasing maturity and sophistication of European capital markets. A more performance-oriented investment culture in Europe and the increasing internationalization of portfolio management will also help to boost capital-market performance in Europe. These potential, environmental developments post-'1992' need no further elaboration.

In this environment, we may draw attention to four particular areas in which '1992' may impact more directly on asset securitization:

- harmonized regulatory and tax rules in Europe,
- increased competition and liberalization,
- capital adequacy rulings, and
- 'single-passport principle'.

The generalized movement towards the harmonization of financial-sector regulations and tax systems throughout Europe will help to eliminate some of the more artificial barriers to asset securitization that still exist in countries like Germany and Switzerland. Increased competition and liberalization associated with '1992' will weaken further the institutional barriers that have assigned particular kinds of institution to specific areas of activity; specifically, this may reduce margins and increase the pressure on institutions' funding costs. Stricter capital adequacy rules could reinforce these pressures; they are likely to reduce the marginal returns from conventional on-balance-sheet financing. The 'single-passport principle' for banks and securities houses will help reduce the corresponding costs of operating in different European countries. All of these reinforcing trends should help to shift the balance of attraction towards increased asset securitization in Europe. It is at this point, coupled with the post-'1992' environmental developments we have discussed, that increasing value added is likely to emerge from asset securitization in western Europe.

Notes

1 Julian Walmesley, *The New Financial Instruments: An Investor's Guide* (1988).
2 See I. Cooper, in Chartered Institute of Bankers, *New Financial Instruments* (1988).
3 See Edward P. M. Gardener and Philip Molyneux, *Changes in European Banking* (Allen & Unwin, 1990).
4 See Terry Wilkinson, 'European bourses beat London', *Independent*, 31 December 1988.

5 See Arthur Andersen & Co., *European Capital Markets: A Strategic Forecast* (Arthur Andersen & Co. Special Report No. 1161, January 1989).
6 Ibid.
7 Edward P. M. Gardener and Jack Revell, *Securitisation: History, Forms and Risks*, Institute of European Finance Research Monographs in Banking and Finance, No. 5 (Institute of European Finance, Bangor, 1988), p. 22.
8 Commission of the European Communities: Directorate-General for Economic and Financial Affairs, *The Economics of 1992* (Commission of the European Communities, No. 35, Brussels, March 1988).
9 Centre for Business Strategy, *1992: Myths and Realities* (London Business School, 1989).
10 See, for example, Kathryn Gordon, '1992 – Big Bang or little whimpers', *Banking World*, October 1987.
11 See Edward P. M. Gardener and Philip Molyneux, *Structure and Regulation of UK Financial Markets*, Institute of European Finance Research Monographs in Banking and Finance, No. 6 (Institute of European Finance, Bangor, 1988).
12 See Edward P. M. Gardener, *The Capital Adequacy Problem in Modern Banking*, Institute of European Finance Research Papers in Banking and Finance, RP 89/2 (Institute of European Finance, Bangor, 1989), p. 3.
13 Gardener and Molyneux, *Changes in European Banking*.
14 Centre for Business Strategy, *1992*.
15 See table 1 in Edward P. M. Gardener, *A Strategic Perspective of Bank Financial Conglomerates in London After the Crash*, Institute of European Finance Research Papers in Banking and Finance, RP 88/22 (Institute of European Finance, Bangor, 1988).
16 See also Paul Feeney, *Loan Securitisation: Euronote and Eurocommercial Paper Markets*, Institute of European Finance Research Monographs in Banking and Finance, No. 1 (Institute of European Finance, Bangor, 1986).
17 See Simon Brady, 'Europe may learn to love the MTN', *Euromoney*, January 1989, pp. 75–82.
18 John Henderson and Jonathan Scott, *Securitisation* (Woodhead Faulkner, 1988).
19 See Jeffrey Barratt, 'Selling loan assets – some guidelines and some problems', *Butterworths Journal of International Banking and Financial Law*, June 1988, pp. 367–74.
20 This latter process is financial intermediation in the sense described by John G. Gurley and Edward S. Shaw in *Money in a Theory of Finance* (The Brookings Institution, January 1960).
21 See, for example, Kareken, 'The emergence and regulation of contingent commitment banking', 11 *Journal of Banking and Finance* 359–77 (1987).

22 See 'Commercial paper on display', *Euromoney Corporate Finance Supplement*, October 1988, 35–8 at 35.
23 Barratt, 'Selling loan assets'.
24 See François Henrot, 'France introduces securitisation', *Housing Finance International*, May 1989, 32–4; and, particularly, chapter 13 of this volume.
25 See Barratt, 'Selling loan assets', p. 46.

15

LDC Debt-Reduction Techniques: Debt/Equity and Debt Collateralization Transactions – Legal and Accounting Implications for US Banks

ANDREW C. QUALE JR

15.1 Introduction

In spite of intense efforts on the part of developing nations, commercial banks, multilateral financial institutions and the United States and other governments over the past seven years, the international debt crisis persists with few signs of amelioration. Since the crisis erupted in 1982, total external indebtedness of the developing countries has increased from $831 billion to an estimated $1,320 billion in 1988.[1] The total external debt of the highly indebted countries (Argentina, Bolivia, Brazil, Chile, Colombia, Costa Rica, Côte d'Ivoire, Ecuador, Jamaica, Mexico, Morocco, Nigeria, Peru, the Philippines, Uruguay, Venezuela and Yugoslavia) amounted to $529 billion at the end of 1988.[2] Per-capita income of the highly indebted developing countries has fallen dramatically during the 1980s, as much as 5 per cent per year in some cases, in spite of six years of economic expansion in the industrial countries.[3] Net financial transfers to the highly indebted countries, that is, the excess of new

Unless otherwise indicated, this chapter speaks as of 30 March 1990. The author is grateful to his colleague, Robert M. Plehn, for his fine assistance in its preparation. Another version of this chapter appeared in the Inter-American Law Review, vol. 21:2, 1989–90.

loans over debt service payments, have been estimated at a negative $11 billion in 1987.[4] In light of these statistics, it is not surprising that social and political turmoil in these countries is increasing, as evidenced by the riots in Caracas in February 1989 and in Argentina in May 1989.

Ironically, although experiencing a period of sustained domestic economic growth, the United States has become in recent years the world's largest debtor nation. At the end of 1987, the net international investment position of the United States was a negative $400 billion, as compared to a positive $260 billion for Japan and $165 billion for Germany, and, by the end of 1988, the United States' debt to the rest of the world had swelled an additional 40 per cent to $532.5 billion.[5] Some of the capital flowing into the United States is coming, of course, from the developing nations. For the first time in fifty years, foreigners earned more in 1987 on their investments in the United States than Americans earned on their investments abroad. In brief, the Third World has sunk deeper into debt, per-capita income has declined and developing countries that should be importing capital to fuel their economic growth are exporting it to the developed nations.

Fortunately, US commercial banks have during this same period substantially increased their capital and dramatically increased their loan-loss reserves, so that they are now in a much better position to absorb any losses that may result from their LDC loans. As a result, after years of tedious debt reschedulings and forced new money exercises, the commercial banks have now moved beyond the 'muddling through' stage and have begun actively to manage and reduce their debt portfolios.

Instead of passively holding on to their debt for what could be for ever, banks have begun aggressively to pursue the various following alternatives in the management of such debt:

- *selling* debt in the secondary market, at increasingly greater discounts;
- *swapping* debt of one sovereign nation for that of another in order to concentrate their debt in those countries with which they feel most comfortable;
- *converting* debt into equity investments in the debtor nations; and
- *exchanging* debt for securitized and/or collateralized debentures or other debt instruments.

Because of their relatively weaker capital positions and greater desire to maintain a long-term financing role in the debtor nations, the money-centre banks have generally been less willing and able than regional banks to sell or trade their LDC debt. Straight debt sales or debt swaps, both of which will result in substantial losses to a bank, are thus less attractive to money-centre banks than to regional and foreign banks. By contrast, conversion of debt to equity interests may be more attractive to money-centre banks than to regional banks because such conversions usually involve less of an accounting loss, require a long-term interest or commitment to the developing countries and necessitate an ongoing presence in such developing countries which most regional and foreign banks lack. Thus, in terms of their goals, the banks tend to fall into two categories. One group of banks seeks to cash out its loan position and take whatever losses may result, while the other is more inclined to convert some of its debt into equity or other debt instruments that may provide a more profitable and flexible long-term investment than existing debt and may not involve a substantial and immediate accounting loss.

The primary goal of the debtor nations is to reduce the amount of principal and/or the rate of interest payable on their debt so that their remaining debt can be serviced under reasonably normal circumstances without undue adverse effect on economic growth. The amount of reduction of principal and/or interest necessary to accomplish this objective will vary greatly depending upon the particular circumstances of each country. No *single* scheme for debt relief, if available to banks on a voluntary basis, is sufficient to enable the debtor nations to meet their interest obligations comfortably. Nonetheless, significant debt relief can be accomplished through a combination of debt/equity conversions, debt-forgiveness arrangements similar to the recent Mexican debt exchange offer (the 'Mexican debt exchange'), debt buy-backs, and reductions in the rate of interest payable on the countries' debt.

The quickest and most efficient way to achieve meaningful debt reduction is to enable the debtor nations to capture to the fullest extent possible the discount at which their debt is selling in the secondary market. Such discount ranges from 96 per cent for Peru, down to about 40 to 45 per cent for Chile and Colombia, the better credit risks in Latin America today.[6] If banks are willing (as many have been) to sell their LDC debt at the substantial discounts prevailing in the secondary market, debtor nations should be encouraged to acquire their own debt, thereby cancelling and eliminating the accompanying debt-service obligations. Debt/equity conversions and exchanges similar to the Mexican debt exchange are also designed in part to enable debtor nations to capture some of this discount for their own benefit.

The new US debt policy announced by Secretary of the Treasury Nicholas Brady on 10 March 1989 recognized publicly for the first time the US government's belief that debt reduction (that is, forgiveness of part of the principal on the LDC debt) is essential to the solution of the debt problem.[7] To implement such debt-reduction proposal, Secretary Brady encouraged the debtor nations and their creditor banks to undertake several types of transactions:

• debt buy-backs;
• exchanges of old debt for new longer-term collateralized debt instruments; and
• debt/equity conversions.

To facilitate such transactions, Secretary Brady called on commercial banks to waive the sharing and mandatory prepayment provisions and negative pledge clauses of existing loan agreements. Sharing and mandatory prepayment provisions prohibit debtors from treating one creditor in preference to other creditors. Such provisions may limit the debtors' ability to negotiate debt-reduction transactions with individual creditors and thus the structuring of such transactions may be more difficult. Negative pledge clauses generally limit the debtors' freedom to grant collateral security in respect of existing or new loans. These clauses may limit the debtor nations' ability to obtain new money from lenders through loans (if such loans cannot be obtained on an unsecured basis) and may also limit the debtor nations' ability to exchange portions of old debt for new debt which is secured by collateral. Representatives of the commercial banks have apparently advised the US Treasury Department of their reluctance to waive such important protective clauses under their loan agreements. The US Treasury has subsequently indicated that debt-reduction techniques of the type contemplated under the Brady Plan can be implemented without the necessity of obtaining waivers of such clauses.

Secretary Brady also proposed that the World Bank and International Monetary Fund (IMF) dedicate a portion of their policy-based loans to replenish reserves used by the debtor nations to buy back their debt and to finance the purchase of collateral to secure new collateralized debt instruments issued in exchange for old debt. Secretary Brady also suggested that the World Bank and IMF could provide additional financial support to collateralize a portion of the interest payments (such as twelve months of interest payments on a rolling-forward basis) on new debt issued in debt-reduction transactions.

Both the World Bank and the IMF have responded positively to Secretary Brady's proposal. The IMF's Executive Board has decided that approximately 25 per cent of a country's access to IMF resources, under an extended or standby arrangement, can be set aside to support operations involving principal reduction such as debt buy-backs or exchanges.[8] In addition, the IMF may approve on a case-by-case basis additional funding, up to 40 per cent of a member's quota, for interest support in connection with debt or debt-service-reduction operations where such support would be decisive in facilitating further cost-effective operations and in catalysing other resources, including where feasible the debtor country's own efforts to contribute resources in support of the operations.[9] Such approvals have already been given to Costa Rica, the Philippines and Mexico. The World Bank has decided to allow certain countries, on a case-by-case basis, to use up to 25 per cent of their three-year economic adjustment loans for the purpose of reducing payments of principal and interest on such debt.[10] However, it should be noted that both the IMF and the World Bank have expressed resistance to proposals that they directly guarantee new instruments created as the result of debt-reduction schemes.

The commercial banks have not responded as positively to the Brady Plan as had been hoped. However, some progress has been made. After months of bitter negotiations between Mexico and its commercial bank lenders, a debt reduction agreement was signed by these parties on 5 February 1990. This accord (the 'Brady Mexican Debt Accord'), the first major agreement under the Brady Plan, reduces Mexico's $48.5 billion medium-term commercial debt by approximately seven billion dollars of principal. It also saves Mexico about $1.4 billion in annual interest payments and brings in $1.2 billion in annual new loans during 1990–92. The debt package provides for debt reduction through two different options whereby bank creditors can exchange existing debt for new thirty-year bonds. Under one option, new bonds will be issued in exchange for existing debt at a thirty-five discount and will pay an interest rate of Libor plus $\frac{13}{16}$ per cent. Under a second option, new bonds will be issued in exchange for existing debt at face value but the new bonds will bear interest at a lower, fixed annual interest rate of 6.25 per cent. For banks choosing to accept reduced principal or interest, the bonds are collateralized by US Treasury zeros. Special funds from the World Bank, the IMF, the government of Japan, as well as a commitment from Mexico, will guarantee the payment of the principal of the new bonds plus eighteen months of interest. These measures will improve the credit quality of the bonds. As of February 1990 bank creditors holding approximately 41 per cent of the debt (or about $19.9 billion) which submitted bids for the new bonds opted for the discount bonds, while bank creditors holding 49 per cent of the debt (or about $23.8 billion) opted for the par value bonds.

In addition, Venezuela recently reached a preliminary agreement with its bank creditors regarding the basic terms of a debt reduction proposal. The proposal covers approximately twenty billion in outstanding loans and offers bank creditors numerous debt reduction options. The first option allows banks to exchange their existing debt for new thirty-year bonds at a 30 per cent discount. The bonds will bear interest at Libor plus $\frac{13}{16}$. The second option allows bank creditors to exchange their existing debt for new thirty-year bonds with an equivalent face value but which would bear interest at a lower, fixed annual rate of 6.75 per cent. Principal payments under both types of bonds would be collateralized by US Treasury zero-coupon obligations. Fourteen months of interest payments would be secured by a cash collateral account established by the Venezuelan Government. Under both options the Venezuelan Government would guarantee to make additional payments to the bondholders after six years if oil prices rise beyond a designated level. Such guarantees of additional payments would be issued in the form of certificates and would trade separately from the debt reduction bonds. Under a third option. Venezuela would offer to buy back existing debt at a discount to be set by the Venezuelan Government. Such discount is expected to be approximately 60 to 65 per cent.

The agreement also contains a temporary interest reduction option under which bank creditors would receive a seventeen-year bond bearing interest at a rate of 5 per cent in the first two years, 6 per cent in the second two years and 7 per cent in the fifth year. For the remaining twelve-year life of the bonds, the interest rate on the bonds would be Libor plus $\frac{7}{8}$ per cent. A collateral account sufficient to cover interest payments for twelve months would be provided by the

Venezuelan Government during the five-year interest reduction period. All of the above programmes will be enhanced by funds provided by the IMF, the World Bank, the Republic of Venezuela and other official sources.

The Philippines has also reached a debt reduction accord with its bank creditors. Under the agreement, the Philippines will buy back at a 50 per cent discount $1.3 billion of the $1.8 billion bank debt which was tendered to it. In addition, under the plan the Philippines will receive approximately $600 million in new money.

Finally, Costa Rica is close to consummating a debt reduction scheme with its bank creditors. Under the proposed Costa Rican transaction, bank creditors will be asked to offer up to 60 per cent of their outstanding debt for repurchase by the Costa Rican Government at a price of approximately $.16 on the dollar. The banks would receive a twenty-year 6.25 per cent par bond for the remaining 40 per cent of their respective debt. Such bonds would allow Costa Rica a ten-year grace period on interest. Twelve to eighteen months of the interest but none of the principal would be collateralized. In addition, Costa Rica would make a 20 per cent down payment on its interest arrears and would offer fifteen-year bonds paying interest of Libor plus $\frac{13}{16}$ per cent for the remaining amount of its interest arrears. Three years of interest payments on such bonds would be collateralized. The proposal also provides for an option for banks which offer less than 60 per cent of their outstanding debt pursuant to the transaction. In such a scenario, the banks would receive twenty-five year 6.25 per cent par bonds which would not be collateralized and which would allow Costa Rica a fifteen-year grace period on interest payments. Costa Rica would offer the same terms as above with respect to its interest arrears in such a scenario, except that none of the interest on the interest arrears bonds would be collateralized.

Despite some success, commercial banks and debtor nations have found it difficult to reach a consensus on the level of discount. This may be due in part to their failure to develop structured transactions that maximize the advantages which may be available under applicable tax and accounting regulations. It may also be attributed to the inherent difficulty of the creditor banks to reach an agreement through their steering committees on a single colution which is acceptable to all creditors. A more practical solution would be to permit the market place to develop a number of separate solutions which may be better tailored to meet the needs of different groups of creditors. This

chapter will analyse, *inter alia*, some of the legal and accounting implications of two of the more innovative approaches to reducing the LDC
debt, debt/equity conversions and debt exchanges involving new collateralized bonds. The author hopes that this analysis will assist the
debtor nations and their creditors in developing mutually beneficial
approaches to achieving substantial debt reduction.

15.2 Debt/Equity Conversions

15.2.1 *The Structure of a Debt/Equity Conversion*

The simplest, most straightforward debt/equity conversion occurs
when a creditor of a company exchanges or converts the debt that is
owed to it by such company for an equity interest in the same company. Such conversions are not common since they require that the
creditor itself have an interest in acquiring equity in its debtor. Such
interest is likely to exist only where a foreign parent of a local subsidiary seeks to capitalize the loans which it has made to the subsidiary.

Debt/equity conversions are more likely to occur as a two- or three-
part transaction. First, a foreign bank creditor holding public sector
debt sells such debt to the central bank of the debtor country for local
currency equivalent in amount to the face value of the external debt,
or at some preestablished discount. The bank creditor then takes such
local currency and uses it to acquire an equity interest in a company in
the debtor country. This is essentially what Bankers Trust did when it
converted approximately $60 million of Chilean public sector debt
(consisting partly of debt that Bankers Trust held in portfolio and
partly of debt that it purchased from other lenders) into shares of a
Chilean pension fund and an affiliated insurance company. Chase
Manhattan also undertook a debt/equity transaction pursuant to
which it obtained a non-voting equity stake in Autolatina, a Brazilian
car manufacturer operated as a joint venture between Volkswagen and
Ford. Chase swapped $200 million of Brazilian bank debt previously
acquired on the secondary market for other purposes in exchange for
its equity share in Autolatina.

Some bank lenders may not be interested in converting the debt
they hold into equity and, indeed, may be prevented from doing so by
applicable banking regulations. A three-step transaction involving a
multinational corporation may instead be effected. The foreign bank

lender initially sells public sector (or possibly even private sector) debt to a multinational company, usually at a significant discount depending upon the particular country involved. The multinational corporation then exchanges, usually with the debtor nation's central bank, such dollar-denominated debt for local currency equal in amount to the face value of the debt exchanged or at some fixed or auction-determined discount. Finally, the multinational company invests the local currency in a domestic company, which may well be its own subsidiary.

15.2.2 *United States Banking Laws and Regulations Affecting Debt/Equity Conversions*

The basic framework The acquisition of an equity interest in a foreign company through a debt/equity conversion or otherwise by a US banking organization may be subject to the Federal Reserve Act (FRA),[11] the Bank Holding Company Act (BHCA),[12] and Regulations K[13] and Y[14] of the Board of Governors of the Federal Reserve System (the 'Board'). Pursuant to section 25 of the FRA, a member bank may invest directly in Edge Act Corporations[15] and Agreement Corporations.[16] Since a member bank generally may not own directly other types of foreign equity investments, the acquisition of stock by a US banking organization must usually be effected through a bank holding company (BHC) or through an Edge Act Corporation.

Section 4(c)(13) of the BHCA permits BHCs to acquire shares of any foreign company that:

> does no business in the United States except as an incident to its international or foreign business, if the Board by regulation or order determines that, under the circumstances and subject to the conditions set forth in the regulation or order, the exemption would not be substantially at variance with the purposes of the BHCA and would be in the public interest.[17]

Section 25(a) of the FRA provides for the establishment of Edge Act Corporations and authorizes them to engage in activities overseas which the Board considers to be usual in connection with the business of banking in foreign countries.[18] Edge Act Corporations may also, with the consent of and subject to the regulations of the Board, own shares of any foreign company provided that such company is 'not engaged in the general business of buying or selling goods . . . in the

United States and [is] not transacting any business in the United States except such as in the judgement of the Board . . . may be incidental to its international or foreign business'.[19]

The Board has set forth extensive regulations implementing the foregoing provisions of the FRA and the BHCA in Regulation K.[20] Since Regulation K will govern most debt/equity conversions, the pertinent provisions of Regulation K will be described in detail below.

In addition to section 4(c)(13), several other provisions of the BHCA may be relevant to the acquisition of an equity interest in a foreign company. Section 4(c)(6) of the BHCA permits a BHC to hold not more than 5 per cent of the outstanding voting stock of *any* company, irrespective of the nature of its business and where it engages in such business.[21] Additionally, section 4(c)(7) of the BHCA permits a BHC to hold shares (without any percentage limitation) of an investment company, provided that such company is engaged only in the business of investing in securities and that it does not hold more than 5 per cent of the outstanding voting stock of any company.[22]

Finally, a US banking organization may acquire an equity interest in a company without limitation as to the nature of the business of such company or the percentage amount of voting stock being acquired if such acquisition is necessary to prevent a loss on a 'debt previously contracted'. Such 'dpc' exceptions to the general limits on the acquisition by banking organizations of equity interests in companies are found in the National Banking Act,[23] the FRA in respect of Edge Act Corporations,[24] the BHCA,[25] Regulations K[26] and Y[27] and various state banking laws.

Regulation K   On 18 February 1988, the Board announced a major liberalization of Regulation K designed to facilitate equity investments by US banks in foreign countries through the use of debt/equity conversions.[28] This amendment expanded the scope of an August 1987 amendment to Regulation K[29] which permitted banks, through debt/equity swaps, to own up to 100 per cent of non-financial companies acquired from the government of a heavily indebted developing country. But the prior liberalization, which permitted banks, in effect, to buy privatized companies, had been criticized widely as being of limited use and perhaps even misguided in its ultimate effect. The new amendment extends the authority, already generally available to banks under Regulation K, to make certain equity investments through debt/equity conversions.

(1) *General equity investment authority*. Regulation K sets forth the Board's long-standing policy that foreign investments made by BHCs, member banks and Edge Act and Agreement Corporations (which are collectively defined in Regulation K, and will be referred to hereinafter as 'investors') pursuant to the BHCA and the Edge Act should be limited primarily to organizations whose activities are 'confined to those of a banking or financial nature and those that are necessary to carry on such activities'.

'Permissible activities'. Regulation K sets forth a list of those activities that are considered 'usual in connection with the transaction of banking or other financial operations abroad' and which are considered to be 'permissible activities'. These include:

1 commercial and other banking activities;
2 commercial and consumer finance;
3 lease financing;
4 providing investment, financial or economic advisory services;
5 data processing;
6 managing a mutual fund which does not exercise managerial control over the firms in which it invests;
7 management consulting;
8 underwriting or distributing securities outside the United States; and
9 activities which the Board has determined to be closely related to banking under section 4(c)(8) of the BHCA.

In addition to these listed permissible activities, the Board, upon application by an investor, may approve other activities if the Board finds them to be banking or financial in nature, or finds that other financial institutions in the foreign country in question engage in such activities, and determines that for competitive reasons investors should also be permitted to engage in such activities.

Eligible investment levels or categories. An investor may acquire up to 100 per cent of the voting stock of a foreign company provided that 95 per cent or more of its activities are listed permissible activities or have been specifically determined to be permissible by the Board. An investor may also acquire lesser amounts of voting stock in a company even though it engages to a significant extent in non-permissible activities. More specifically, an investor may make investments in the following types of companies to the extent indicated:

- acquire more than 50 per cent of the voting stock of a foreign entity or acquire control of such entity (a 'subsidiary' investment), provided that at least 95 per cent of such entity's assets or revenues relate to permissible activities that are enumerated in Regulation K or have been determined by the Board to be permissible;
- acquire 20 per cent or more of the voting stock of a foreign entity but not a controlling interest (a 'joint venture' investment), provided that at least 90 per cent of the assets or revenues of such company relate to permissible activities;
- acquire less than 20 per cent of a foreign entity (a 'portfolio investment') irrespective of what activities the company engages in, provided that the aggregate amount of all such portfolio investments by the investor does not exceed the investor's capital plus surplus.

Requirement of divestiture. An investor will be required to divest an investment (unless the Board authorizes retention) if the company in which the investment is made (a) engages in the general business of selling goods, wares, merchandise or commodities in the United States; (b) engages directly or indirectly in other business in the United States that would not be permitted to an Edge Act Corporation; or (c) engages in impermissible activities to an extent not permitted by the regulations. Thus, in addition to making sure that the company in which an investor seeks to invest fits within one of the eligible investment categories, an investor must also make sure that such company's activities in the United States are narrowly circumscribed.

Even if a foreign company's activities in the United States exceed such limits so that investment in such company would not be permitted under Regulation K, nonetheless an investor can always hold up to 5 per cent of the voting stock of such company pursuant to section 4(c)(6) of the BHCA regardless of its activities.

Notice and consent requirements. Depending upon the magnitude and nature of the proposed investment, an investor's acquisition will be subject to the Board's general consent procedure or to its prior-notice, or specific-consent, procedure.

Assuming that an investor's proposed investment fits within one of the subsidiary, joint-venture or portfolio-investment categories described above, no prior notice need be given to the Board of the proposed investment if the investment in such entity does not exceed the lesser of $15 million or 5 per cent of the bank's capital plus surplus.

An investment which fits within one of the three investment categories, but exceeds the level permitted for general consent, may be made pursuant to the prior-notice procedure. Under this procedure, the investor must give the Board forty-five days' prior notice of its intention to make such investment, during which time the Board may object to the investment.

An investor must seek the specific consent of the Board to an acquisition if its proposed acquisition does not come within the general-consent or prior-notice provisions. Such consent is essentially required where the investor seeks to acquire more than a portfolio investment in a company whose activities are not included within the Board's list of permissible activities.

(2) *The February 1988 amendment.* The February 1988 amendment liberalized the authority of BHCs to make equity investments in developing countries through debt/equity conversions by: (a) increasing the amount of equity ownership a BHC may have in a *non-financial* company; (b) permitting the BHC to provide loans, in addition to equity, to such company; (c) extending the time period during which the equity investment may be retained by the BHC; and (d) liberalizing the general-consent procedure.

Permissible equity investments. In addition to investments permitted under other provisions of Regulation K, a BHC may now make the following equity investments through a debt-equity conversion:

- up to 100 per cent of the shares of any foreign company, which shares are acquired from the government of the country or its agencies or instrumentalities (that is, a privatization of a public sector company); and
- up to 40 per cent of the shares of any private sector company, provided that:
  (a) a BHC may acquire more than 25 per cent of the voting shares of such company only if another shareholder or control group of shareholders not affiliated with the BHC owns a larger block of voting shares of such company; and
  (b) the BHC may not have a greater representation on the board of directors or management committees of the foreign company than is proportional to the shares it holds in such company.

By permitting a BHC to own up to 25 (and under certain circumstances up to 40) per cent of the voting shares of the foreign company, the Board enabled BHCs to have not merely portfolio, but 'operational', investments in private sector non-financial companies. The Board believes that BHCs will be able to have an important voice in the management of the companies through proportionate, non-controlling representation on their boards of directors. A BHC should be able to protect its investment in a non-financial company, the Board feels, without having the sole operational control over the company which a BHC is ill-equipped to exercise. Also, holding 20 per cent or more of the shares of non-financial companies will allow BHCs to use consolidation or equity accounting, rather than cost accounting, in respect of such investments.

Permissible debt financing. If a BHC acquires 20 per cent or more of the voting shares of a non-financial private sector company, it will not be permitted to extend loans or other forms of financing to such company in excess of 50 per cent of the total loans or extensions of credit to such company.

Permissible holding period. BHCs will be permitted to retain investments made pursuant to debt/equity conversions for a period of two years beyond the end of any period established by the host country restricting the repatriation of such investment, but in no event for more than fifteen years. This holding period will apply to investments in both public and private sector companies. Its imposition reflects the Board's view that investments of 20 per cent or more in the voting stock of non-financial companies are intended to be temporary, and upholds the Board's general objective of maintaining the separation between banking and commerce. The divestment requirement at the end of the holding period is not applicable, however, to investments otherwise permissible under Regulation K, even if such investments resulted from debt/equity conversions.

General consent procedures. The Board grants a general consent to investments made pursuant to the February 1988 amendment if the total amount invested does not exceed the greater of $15 million or 1 per cent of the equity of the BHC. Prior notice to, or the specific consent of, the Board is required, however, if a country's debt/equity conversion programme requires the BHC to invest new money after converting debt obligations to equity, if the amount of such new money exceeds $15 million or if the investment is to be made through an insured bank or its subsidiary.

Investments to be held through the holding company. Debt-for-equity investments in non-financial companies are required to be held through a BHC and not directly by a bank or a subsidiary of a bank. The Board thus sought to protect banks from the potential risks of investments in commercial and industrial companies, and to make it clear that the federal safety net does not apply to non-banking activities. The Board is willing, however, to grant exceptions to this general requirement on a case-by-case basis if it can be demonstrated that there is a special reason (for example, local legal requirements) why a bank, rather than a BHC, must hold the investment in the non-financial company.

Private sector debt not eligible for debt/equity conversion. Despite comment urging the contrary, the Board has limited application of the liberalized investment rules to equity investments made through the conversion of *sovereign* debt, thus excluding the swapping of private sector debt. In support of its position, the Board noted that a bank can already convert private sector debt to an equity investment through the use of the 'debt previously contracted' exception, whereas, according to the Board, sovereign debt is not eligible for such conversion.

Some observations on the February 1988 amendment. Although the February 1988 amendment provides a useful liberalization of Regulation K, the ability of banks to undertake debt/equity conversions has not been significantly enhanced. BHCs may now own up to 25 per cent of the voting stock of a non-financial company (or up to 40 per cent if another stockholder holds a larger block), whereas previously they were limited to less than 20 per cent. The power to acquire this relatively small additional amount of voting stock has, however, been coupled with limitations on the permissible holding period of the investment, the amount of debt financing that may also be provided, the manner in which the investment may be held and the type of debt that is eligible for conversion.

The Board in its August 1987 amendment permitted BHCs to acquire 100 per cent of a public sector company pursuant to a debt/equity conversion. Since public sector companies are likely to have been less well managed than private sector companies, the acquisition of a 100 per cent interest in a private sector company would present less commercial risk to a BHC than a public sector company and should, *a fortiori*, also be permitted. Such treatment would be consistent with the purpose of the 'debt previously contracted' exception described below, namely, to enable a bank to exchange debt for an equity interest, without limit as to the percentage of voting stock, if the bank believes such exchange is a reasonable step toward collecting on its loan. The 'dpc' exception is a very limited but well-established departure from the general principle of the separation of banking and commerce. The Board would, therefore, have ample precedent for permitting BHCs to acquire up to 100 per cent of private, as well as public, sector companies.

Other legal bases for holding an equity investment in foreign companies Assuming that an investor cannot make an investment under the eligible investment categories of the newly amended Regulation K, there are nonetheless several alternative legal bases on which an investor may rely to acquire equity in a foreign company. The most flexible of these is the 'dpc' exception, which permits an investor to acquire an equity investment in exchange for a 'debt previously contracted'. Of more limited use to an investor are two exceptions to the general prohibitions of the BHCA that permit an investor to acquire directly, or indirectly through an investment company, up to 5 per cent of the voting stock of a company.

(1) *The 'debt previously contracted' exception.* The 'dpc' exception permits a banking organization to acquire up to 100 per cent of the voting stock of a company in exchange for a 'debt previously contracted'. 'Dpc' exceptions to limitations otherwise imposed by the banking laws are found in Regulation K, the BHCA, Regulation Y, the FRA and in state law.

Regulation K. Pursuant to the 'dpc' exception set forth in section 211.5(e) of Regulation K, equity interests acquired in exchange for 'debts previously contracted' are not subject to the limitations of Regulation K provided that:

• such equity is acquired in order to 'prevent a loss on a debt previously contracted in good faith'; and
• such equity interests are disposed of no later than two years after their acquisition, unless the Board authorizes retention for a longer period.

The 'dpc' exceptions set forth in the BHCA and Regulation Y are very similar to that of Regulation K except that they permit the Board to authorize the retention by the BHC of conversion-generated shares for a maximum period of five years, whereas Regulation K contains no such absolute limit.

By means of the 'dpc' exception, an investor may acquire an unlimited amount of the voting stock in a foreign company irrespective of whether such company engages in non-'permissible' activities. Thus, an investor could acquire voting stock in a company engaged to a substantial extent in non-'permissible' activities such as manufacturing, mining or tourism.

Whether the 'dpc' exception is available will depend upon the facts of the particular case. Generally speaking, this provision has been used to permit the conversion of debt into equity of the *same* debtor or into equity which served as collateral for the debt in question, although Regulation K does not on its face preclude a conversion into equity of a third party.

Some members of the staff of the Board, however, have apparently taken a somewhat restrictive view of the 'dpc' exception, suggesting that it may not be used to permit the acquisition of equity in exchange for debt of a sovereign nation. Their reasoning appears to be twofold. First, the 'dpc' exception should be limited to debtors that are bankrupt or have been declared in default. Although some debtor nations may be in arrears on their obligations, they have not been declared in default and, therefore, their situation is considered to be not so serious as to justify 'dpc' treatment. Second, there is concern as to how the remainder of a banking organization's portfolio of debt of a particular country should be treated if some of such debt has been converted to equity 'in order to prevent a loss'.

The language of Regulation K, however, does not necessarily compel such a restrictive interpretation. If a banking organization were to sell a particular loan in the secondary market or swap it for debt of another Third World debtor it would incur a loss which, depending on the discount at which such debt is selling, may be substantial, irrespective of whether the debtor was bankrupt or had been declared in default. Moreover, if it were to incur a loss on such transaction, it would not necessarily be required to write down the rest of its portfolio of such debt. Thus, by effecting a conversion of debt to an equity investment, a banking organization not only might be able to 'prevent a loss', but would also not necessarily have to write down any remaining debt of the same debtor held in its portfolio.

The National Banking Act. Even if the Board will not permit a BHC to undertake a debt/equity conversion pursuant to the 'dpc' exception, the bank itself may be able to effect such a transaction directly. Ordinarily debt/equity conversions will be effected either at the holding-company level, that is, by the BHC itself, or by a non-bank subsidiary of the BHC. If, however, the debt is held by the bank and is converted by it, then the applicable laws and regulations will instead be, in the case of a national bank, the National Banking Act and the regulations of the Office of the Comptroller of the Currency (OCC) and, in the case of a state bank, state laws and regulations. The OCC has interpreted the 'incidental powers' clause of the National Banking Act as permitting the exchange of debt for equity if the bank believes in good faith that such exchange is a reasonable and appropriate step toward collecting a bank's loans.[30] The OCC has also relied on the powers of a national bank to hold real property received in satisfaction of a debt previously contracted in cases where the equity in question was in a real estate holding company.[31] The OCC is apparently prepared to give considerable weight to a bank's determination that the exchange of debt for equity is reasonably necessary to salvage the bank's assets.

The OCC's interpretation of the National Banking Act as permitting 'dpc' transactions is elaborated upon in two recent no-objection letters issued in 1987 and 1988[32] involving, in the first instance, an investment in a Mexican holding company whose sole asset is a Mexican hotel and, in the second instance, an investment in a Chilean insurance company.

If a 'dpc' transaction is undertaken by a national bank pursuant to its inherent powers under the National Banking Act, neither approval nor a no-objection letter is required to be obtained from the OCC. Nonetheless, the interpretations set forth in the above-described no-objection letters will provide useful guidance to banks making an equity investment in reliance on such powers.

New York State banking law. Under New York law, a bank 'may invest in, and have and exercise all rights of ownership with respect to, so much of the capital stock of any other corporation as may be specifically authorized by the laws of [New York] or by resolution of the banking board upon a three-fifths vote of all its members'.[33] Additionally, 'a bank or trust company may acquire stock in settlement or reduction, or a loan, or advance or credit or in exchange for an investment previously made in good faith and in the ordinary course of business, where such acquisition of stock is necessary in order to minimize or avoid loss in connection with any such loan, advance or credit or investment previously made in good faith'.[34] The New York State Banking Department takes a flexible attitude in permitting the acquisition of stock for a debt previously contracted. If the bank reasonably believes the acquisition of equity in exchange for debt is necessary in order to minimize or avoid a loss in connection with a loan, and the transaction is not a subterfuge, the Banking Department will not object.

(2) *Section 4(c)(6) of the BHCA.* Assuming a banking organization cannot effect a debt/equity conversion in reliance on Regulation K because the target company is engaged in more than incidental business activities in the United States or in reliance on the 'dpc' exception, it still will be permitted to acquire up to 5 per cent of the voting stock of any company pursuant to section 4(c)(6) of the BHCA. This exception is self-executing and, accordingly, no prior notice to, or consent by, the Board is required. The exception is available irrespective of the nature of the business in which the company is engaged or the extent of its activities in the United States. Such investments, however, are required to be passive and should not involve active participation by the investor in the management of the company.

(3) *Effecting debt/equity conversions through investment companies.* Section 4(c)(7) of the BHCA permits a BHC to hold up to 100 per cent of the shares of an investment company which is not engaged in any business other than investing in securities, provided that such securities do not represent more than 5 per cent of the outstanding voting stock of any company. No comparable provision is contained in Regulation K and the Board has not been called upon to determine what rules would pertain to the acquisition by an investor of shares in an investment company which invested solely in foreign equity securities.

Since a BHC may acquire up to 25 (and under certain circumstances up to 40) per cent of the voting shares of a non-financial company, presumably a BHC could acquire shares in an investment company which, in turn, could hold at least such percentage amount of voting stock of a company. Query whether a BHC could hold up to 25 (or 40) per cent of the shares of an investment company which, in turn, could hold any amount of the voting stock of a company. The Board's reaction to such a proposal and variations thereof may depend, in part, on the extent to which the BHC has excessive operational control over the company in which the investment company is investing or whether, through the use of the investment company vehicle, the BHC is, indirectly, investing in the target company with one or more substantial joint-venture partners which can bring managerial and/or technical expertise to the investment.

15.2.3 *US Accounting Treatment of Debt/Equity Conversions*

Debt-for-equity swaps With Regulation K having been partially liberalized, perhaps the most significant US regulatory obstacle to debt/equity conversion is US accounting treatment. The proper accounting treatment for a debt/equity conversion has been the subject of considerable uncertainty and controversy. Recently, however, the Accounting Standards Executive Committee of the American Institute of Certified Public Accountants (AICPA) and the AICPA Banking Committee have reached substantial agreement on the appropriate treatment and have released AcSEC Practice Bulletin No. 4 dealing with 'Accounting for foreign debt/equity swaps'.[35]

Under the AcSEC Bulletin, a debt/equity swap will be treated as an exchange transaction of a monetary asset for a non-monetary asset, which latter asset is to be reflected at its 'fair value' on the books of the bank or BHC as of the date the transaction is agreed to by both parties.

What is 'fair value'? The Bulletin states that to determine 'fair value' one should consider the fair value of the consideration given up, that is, the old debt, as well as the fair value of the assets received, that is, the equity investment, especially if the value of the consideration given up is not readily determinable or may not be a good indicator of the value received. The AICPA notes that since the secondary market for debt of financially troubled countries is thin, that market may not be the best indicator of the value of the equity investment received. Therefore, the AICPA committees concluded that, to determine the fair value of the equity received in a debt/equity conversion, *both* the secondary-market price of the debt given up and the fair value of the equity investment received should be considered. The following factors should be considered according to the AICPA in determining current fair value:

- similar transactions for cash;

- estimated cash flows from the equity investment received;
- market value, if any, of similar equity investments; and
- restrictions, if any, affecting payment of dividends, the sale of the investment or the repatriation of capital.

If the fair value of the equity investment received is less than the book value of the debt, the resultant loss should be recognized and charged to the allowance for loan losses and should include any discounts from the official exchange rate that are imposed as a transaction fee. All other fees relating to the debt/equity conversion should be charged to expense, rather than capitalized.

Will the recognition of a loss in a debt/equity conversion contaminate the remainder of a bank's loan portfolio with respect to that debtor or country? The Bulletin does not require that the remainder of the bank's debt be written down to the same value. The AICPA notes, however, that in accordance with Generally Accepted Accounting Principles (GAAP), a financial institution's loan portfolio should be carried at amortized historical cost less both loan write-offs and the allowance for loan losses, provided that the institution has the ability and intent to hold the loans until their maturity. Thus, the bank need not mark down such debt to its 'fair value' simply because of a debt/equity conversion. Loan write-offs and loan-loss allowances are to be taken based on management's judgement regarding the ultimate collectability of the loans in the normal course of business. The recognition of a loss on a debt/equity conversion should be one of the factors considered by management in its periodic assessment of the adequacy of its allowance for loan losses. If, however, management demonstrates its intention to dispose of loans *prior* to maturity, the loan should be carried at cost or fair value, whichever is lower. Thus, the recognition of a loss on a debt/equity conversion will not require a bank to write down the remainder of its loans to the same borrower, but the occurrence of such recognition should be taken into account by the bank in determining the adequacy of its allowance for loan losses.

In practice, will this proposed treatment require more than an insignificant write-down of the value of the equity asset received? If the 'fair value' of such equity must take into account the secondary-market value of the debt given up, as well as the US dollar value of a local-currency-denominated equity interest which is not readily convertible into hard currency, it is possible that more than an insignificant loss will result. Thus, for an equity investment in Mexico acquired in exchange for debt selling at approximately 40 per cent of par, the loss might well be 25 to 45 per cent. If such is the case, some banks may be discouraged from undertaking debt/equity conversions until such time as their reserves are adequate to absorb such losses. Even then, they may prefer to hold on to such debt or, alternatively, to sell it, realize the loss and no longer have to worry about their exposure to the developing country in question.

Debt-for-debt swaps The market among banks for debt-for-debt swaps was severely dampened by the AICPA's 'Notice to practitioners' of May 1985[36] and the OCC *Banking Circular* 200,[37] both of which provided that a swap of loans to different debtors represented an exchange of monetary assets that should be accounted for at fair value. The OCC's *Circular* went even further and stated that, for loan swaps involving loans to debtors of foreign countries which are currently experiencing financial difficulties, '[i]t is *presumed* the estimated fair value would be less than the respective fair value of the loans and other consideration [given up]. Assuming the general presumption is not overcome, this would result in a loss on the swap.' (Emphasis added.)

Now that many banks have established substantial reserves for their Third World debt and have indicated a willingness to realize losses in dealing with such debt, it can be expected that there will be more debt-for-debt swapping. If, however, the loss realized in the swap of debt is quite similar to that which would be realized if the debt were simply sold for cash, banks may prefer to sell, rather than swap, their debt if they are prepared to realize the loss.

15.3 Some Suggestions for Structuring Equity Investments

In order to avoid some of the limitations placed upon US banks by Regulation K and the BHCA on acquiring voting stock of non-financial entities, and to avoid the restrictions imposed by certain debtor nations on foreign investment generally, investors may need to consider some creative structuring techniques.

Additionally, since the equity investments into which banks will be converting their debt will be subject not only to the vagaries of the profitability of such investments, but also to the risk of devaluation of the local currency, banks quite naturally will want to protect themselves as much as possible from both these risks. To reduce these risks, a bank might concentrate on investments that have a high foreign exchange earning capability, such as the manufacture of exports and tourist resorts, or might obtain insurance, if available, from the Overseas Private Investment Corporation (OPIC) and the Multilateral Investment Guaranty Agency (MIGA) (especially for inconvertibility risks) in appropriate cases.

Such risks, as well as the limitations on acquiring voting stock imposed by Regulation K and the BHCA, may be alleviated by using a non-voting preferred stock that has attributes similar to those of debt and adopting one or more of the following 'bells and whistles':

- The dividends on the preferred stock could be cumulative and mandatorily payable as soon as the venture has sufficient profits.
- A sinking-fund arrangement could be established into which funds would be deposited for subsequent use in paying dividends on, and ultimately redeeming, the preferred stock.
- The issuer of the preferred stock could be an entity within an affiliated group which would be structured so that, even if the overall venture were not profitable, the particular entity issuing the preferred stock could be the beneficiary of contractual arrangements which would assure it sufficient profitability to service the dividends due on such stock.
- To protect against the devaluation of the local currency, it might be possible to adjust or index the dividend and redemption payments so as to reflect inflation or changes in exchange rates. Alternatively, the preferred stock could have a bonus dividend which would compensate for losses due to devaluation.

Whether any of such arrangements will work in a particular country will depend upon local laws, the regulations applicable to debt/equity conversions, and regulations affecting remittances of foreign exchange in respect of dividends.

Because BHCs are generally limited by US regulations to owning up to 25 (and under certain circumstances up to 40) per cent of a company's voting stock (assuming the investments are not banking or financial in nature or are not necessary to prevent a loss on a debt previously contracted, in which case more voting stock may be acquired), they are logical minority partners for US and other industrial companies which desire to establish or expand an operation in one of the debtor countries. By selling a minority equity interest to a bank, an industrial company can obtain outside financing in local currency (which at times may otherwise be difficult) at a relatively reasonable cost. By so doing, they can also share the equity risks of investment with a minority partner with which they feel comfortable. The banks, on the other hand, will also feel comfortable being a minority partner of an industrial company which will have operational control over the business and with which they may well have an existing customer relationship in the United States.

15.4 LDC Debt Securitization and Collateralization Schemes: The Mexican Debt Exchange and Similar Debt-Reduction Proposals

Proposals to turn part of the LDC debt into securities that would be tradable on a securities exchange, rather than merely in the informal secondary market for LDC debt, have been fantasized about by investment and commercial bankers, and their lawyers and accountants, for several years. Such schemes have frequently included credit-enhancement devices, such as guarantees by multilateral financial institutions or collateral consisting of US Treasury obligations. The goal has been to create a new instrument which, fulfilling the alchemist's dream, has a value in the marketplace exceeding the cost or value of its constituent components. The Mexican debt exchange, although not the only such scheme to see the light of day, is certainly the most ambitious and noteworthy to date and will be analysed below. Other debt-exchange proposals have been developed which have avoided some of the problems that were encountered in the Mexican debt exchange and are described below. Most of these proposals are of a private nature and have not yet become part of the public domain and, therefore, are not appropriate for discussion in this chapter. Nonetheless, some of the tax and accounting considerations that may be relevant to these proposals will be discussed in the following sections.

15.4.1 *The Basic Outline of the Mexican Debt Exchange*

Pursuant to an 'Invitation for bids',[38] Mexico, on 18 January 1988, offered to exchange a new issue of Mexican Collateralized Floating Rate Bonds Due 2008 ('bonds'), denominated in US dollars, paying interest at a floating rate and maturing in twenty years, in exchange for certain existing obligations of Mexico outstanding under its 'Restructure and new money' agreements. The bonds were to be secured, as to their principal only and not as to interest, by non-interest-bearing US Treasury obligations ('Zeroes') which were to be purchased by Mexico using its own reserves. The Zeroes were to be pledged to holders of the bonds and have a maturity date and principal amount payable at maturity to match the maturity date and principal amount of the bonds. In the event of a default under the bonds, a bondholder would not have access to the Zeroes until the final originally scheduled maturity date, at which time the proceeds of the Zeroes would be available to pay the principal of the bonds at maturity.

Banks desiring to exchange their existing debt for bonds were invited to submit bids on a voluntary basis to the exchange agent, Morgan Guaranty Trust Company of New York. In its bids, each bank was asked to specify the principal amount of eligible existing Mexican debt obligations (the 'eligible debt') that the bank was willing to tender and the principal dollar amount of bonds that the bank would accept in exchange for such eligible debt. For example, a bank could state in its bid that it was willing to tender $10 million of eligible debt and would accept in exchange therefor bonds with a principal dollar amount of $7 million, thereby indicating its willingness to accept a discount of the principal amount of its eligible debt equal to 30 per cent.

To enhance their attractiveness to the banks and, ultimately, to third parties, the bonds had the following features:

1 the bonds would pay interest at a margin of $1\frac{5}{8}$ per cent above LIBOR, which was double the margin of $\frac{13}{16}$ per cent currently being paid by Mexico on the eligible debt;
2 the bonds would be listed on the Luxembourg stock exchange;
3 the bonds, according to Mexico, would not be subject to future restructurings or reschedulings which might otherwise apply to its eligible debt; and,
4 also according to Mexico, neither the bonds nor the eligible debt given in exchange would be considered part of any base amount for purposes of future requests by Mexico for new money.

15.4.2 *Consents and Waivers*

In order to issue the bonds, it was deemed necessary for Mexico to obtain a waiver of the negative pledge provisions under its outstanding credit agreements and, in the case of one credit agreement that did not permit an exchange offer, even if unsecured, the waiver of mandatory prepayment and sharing provisions. In addition, it was necessary for Mexico to collateralize certain outstanding publicly held bond issues since it was not practicable to obtain a waiver of the negative pledge provisions relating to such issues.

15.4.3 *The Results of the Bid*

Mexico and Morgan Guaranty had publicly stated that they expected that up to $20 billion of eligible debt would be tendered and, projecting that the banks would tender at a 40 to 50 per cent discount, the total amount of new bonds issued was predicted to be as high as $10 billion. The results of the auction were much less dramatic. Over $6 billion of eligible debt were tendered, but Mexico accepted only those obligations tendered at an exchange ratio of 74.99 per cent or less, with the result that Mexico accepted $3.67 billion of debt to be exchanged for $2.56 billion of bonds. Thus, the average exchange ratio of the accepted bids was 69.77 per cent. Upon completion of the exchange, Mexico had succeeded in reducing its outstanding indebtedness by $1.1 billion, an amount substantially lower than the reduction of $10 billion originally envisaged. Although the results seemed disappointing in light of such expectations, the transaction justifiably deserves to be considered a moderate success, not only because it did achieve a reduction of Mexico's debt of $1.1 billion, but also because it showed that debt securitization and collateralization schemes can play a significant role in the management and reduction of LDC debt.

15.4.4 *Accounting Treatment of the Mexican Debt Exchange*

Perhaps the two most important issues confronting the banks in evaluating the Mexican debt exchange were the accounting treatment of the exchange and the value that the marketplace would put on the bonds. Three principal accounting issues were raised by the exchange.

Accounting treatment of the exchange itself Price Waterhouse

rendered an opinion to Morgan Guaranty on the appropriate accounting treatment for the transaction, concluding that the exchange of
eligible debt for the bonds should be treated as an exchange of monetary assets.[39] As a result, a bank would recognize an accounting loss or
gain equal to the difference between the carrying value of the eligible
debt on its books prior to the exchange and the 'fair value' of the
bonds received in exchange. Such loss should generally be recorded as
a charge to the allowance for loan losses. The amount of the loss was
affected not only by the discount factor at which a bank exchanged its
eligible debt for the bonds, but also by the amount by which the fair
value of the bonds received exceeded the face value of such bonds.

'Fair value' normally is equal to market value if a broad-based,
active market exists. Since it might take some time for such a market
for the bonds to develop, banks might need to use other appropriate
valuation techniques, such as discounted cash-flow analysis, to
determine fair value.

Some accountants have argued that the Mexican debt exchange
could be treated not as an exchange of monetary assets with the bonds
being booked at 'fair value', but rather as part of a troubled-debt
restructuring pursuant to Statement of Financial Accounting
Standards No. 15, 'Accounting by debtors and creditors for troubled
restructurings' (FAS No. 15).[40] As described below, if the exchange of
bonds for eligible debt were considered a restructuring of the eligible
debt, FAS No. 15 would not require a bank to write down the value of
its restructured loan unless the amount of the loan on its books
exceeded the total future cash receipts, including both principal and
interest, to be received by the bank pursuant to the restructured terms
of the debt. Since the total payments of principal plus interest over the
twenty-year life of the bonds would clearly exceed the recorded value
of the eligible debt on the books of the banks prior to the exchange, no
loss would be required to be recognized.

**Accounting treatment of debt tendered but not accepted by
Mexico**   Under GAAP, a bank should carry a loan it has the intent
and ability to hold to maturity at its historical cost less the allowance
for loan losses. If, however, management clearly demonstrates its
intent to dispose of a loan or a group of loans prior to maturity, then
such loans should be carried at cost or market, whichever is lower.
Because Price Waterhouse viewed the Mexican debt exchange as a
unique opportunity, it concluded that if management does not have a

present intention to dispose of the eligible debt other than through the tender offer, the mere act of tendering eligible debt which is not accepted by Mexico does not necessarily constitute a clear intention to dispose of such loans prior to maturity.

The staff of the Securities and Exchange Commission, however, took a contrary view in its Staff Accounting Bulletin No. 75 ('SAB No. 75'), which set forth the SEC staff's views regarding certain accounting-disclosure issues applicable to the Mexican debt exchange. SAB No. 75 states:

> The tender of the existing loans is an event that must be given account-ing recognition either (i) by writing the loans down to the price at which the bank has agreed to accept bonds in the tender (tender price) or (ii) by increasing, as necessary, the allowance for loan losses to an amount sufficient to result in a net carrying value of the loans tendered that equals the tender price.

Treatment of debt not tendered to Mexico Price Waterhouse opined that, even though a bank exchanges part of its eligible debt for bonds and recognizes a loss on the exchange, the accounting treatment of the bank's untendered eligible debt should not change solely by reason of the fact that a portion of the bank's eligible debt were exchanged, so long as the bank has the ability and intent to hold such remaining loans to maturity. The SEC staff in SAB No. 75 did point out, however, that pursuant to Statement of Financial Accounting Standards No. 5, 'Accounting for contingencies', management has a continuing responsibility to assess the adequacy of the allowance for loan losses relative to untendered Mexican debt to ensure that such allowance is adequate to provide for losses due to ultimate collect-ability, including anticipated losses from the sale, swap or other exchange of loans.

15.4.5 *Securities Laws Aspects*

The bonds were issued in registered definitive form. They were not registered under US securities laws, but were sold to US persons pursuant to a private placement, with appropriate legends and restric-tions on transfer. Bonds issued outside the United States to purchasers that were not US persons were required, for a period of ninety days after issuance, not to be sold in the United States or to US persons.

The bonds to be issued to non-US persons were initially represented by a single, temporary global bond. Individual bonds were to be issued to non-US persons ninety days after the closing date for the transaction upon appropriate anti-flowback certifications by such persons.

15.4.6 *FAS No. 15*

As noted above, the Mexican debt exchange could have been structured as a 'troubled restructuring' pursuant to FAS No. 15, thereby avoiding the necessity of the banks' recognizing a current accounting loss. FAS No. 15 might also be used to reduce the accounting loss on other debt-reduction transactions. Under FAS No. 15, if a bank restructures a debt owed to it by a debtor, the bank does not have to account for a loss at the time the exchange occurs as long as the total future cash receipts, including principal and interest, to be received by the bank under the terms of the new debt are at least equal to the amount of the loan recorded on the bank's books. The bank must write down a loss at the time of the exchange only if the total aggregate amount to be received under the terms of the new debt is less than the recorded book value of the old debt.

Thus FAS No. 15 can provide an accounting incentive for commercial banks to enter into debt restructurings with debtor nations since it effectively allows them to defer the losses associated with a restructuring. For example, assume a bank exchanges debt of a debtor nation for which it has a book value of 100 for new debt with a par value of 65, a term of six years and bears interest of 10 per cent per year. Such exchange could be treated as a FAS No. 15 restructuring and the bank would incur *no* accounting loss on the exchange since the total sum of principal and interest payments would exceed the original book value of the loan.

Some US banks, however, are hesitant to take advantage of the benefits offered by FAS No. 15. The banks fear that although they may not have to write down currently the loss resulting from the debt rescheduling, the use of FAS No. 15 in conjunction with reschedulings may provide a negative signal to the market. In addition, FAS No. 15 has been criticized by some accountants on the ground that the present value of the new asset received in exchange for the old has decreased and, therefore, the creditor should be forced to realize currently the loss, rather than defer it as FAS No. 15 allows.

15.4.7 *US Tax Treatment of Debt-Reduction Transactions*

Generally under the 1986 Tax Reform Act, with the repeal of Internal Revenue Code section 166(c), voluntary loan-loss reserves are no longer deductible.[41] The commercial banks may only take a deduction for the losses associated with their loans upon the actual realization of the loss, that is, when the debt has actually been exchanged or sold for a loss. Whether or not the current tax law provides an incentive or deterrence for banks to enter into debt-reduction schemes is unclear. Some bankers have argued that if loan-loss reserves were deductible, banks would more readily accept the devaluation of assets that usually accompanies debt-reduction deals. Other bankers have argued however, that because the current tax law only allows a deduction upon the actual sale or exchange of debt, the law provides an incentive for banks actually to consummate a debt-reduction transaction.

On 22 May 1989, the Internal Revenue Service issued Notice 89–58 dealing with the allocation and apportionment of loan losses suffered by US banks.[42] This notice has raised great opposition from US banks. Notice 89–58 states in effect that with respect to loan losses, US banks must apportion their losses with respect to such loans between US- and foreign-source interest income according to the tax book value asset method described in section 1.861–9T(g) of the Internal Revenue Regulations (that is, a bank must apportion its losses with respect to such loans between foreign and US income according to the ratio of its foreign assets (loans) to its overall assets (loans)). The effect of this notice is that now that foreign loan losses are linked to foreign income in a strictly proportional method, the tax credits which the banks can effectively use as the result of paying foreign taxes on their foreign-source interest income may be substantially reduced. Under section 901 of the Internal Revenue Code, when a US bank pays a foreign tax on its foreign-source income, it receives a tax credit to be applied against its US income tax.[43] If the tax rate of the foreign country is higher than the US tax rate, as is often the case, then the greater the amount of taxes that are paid in the foreign country by the banks and are applied as tax credits for US income tax purposes the lower will be the banks' overall tax burden. The banks can only use tax credits, however, up to an amount equal to their foreign-source income divided by their total income multiplied by their US taxes for that year.[44] Before the issuance of Notice 89–58, US banks were allocating substantial amounts of their foreign loan losses to US-source income such that their foreign-source income was higher and thus the cap on their tax credits for US income tax purposes was also higher. As a result of Notice 89–58, US banks are now restricted in their ability to allocate loan losses to US-source income and thus are limited in their ability to use increased foreign tax credits. This limitation thus may have the effect of removing an incentive for US banks to enter into debt-reduction schemes because large amounts of the losses resulting from such schemes will be forced to be allocated to foreign sources. Thus, not only will the banks realize a significant financial loss as a result of entering into debt-reduction schemes but, due to Notice 89–58, the US banks may also lose a substantial part of the tax benefits associated with the utilization of foreign tax credits.

15.4.8 *Some Observations on the Mexican Debt Exchange and Suggestions for Similar Transactions*

The Mexican debt exchange deserves genuine recognition for blazing a new trail in the quest for solutions to the debt crisis. A number of criticisms and comments have, however, been put forth which should be taken into consideration and evaluated in structuring other debt-reduction transactions:

- The fact that Mexico itself had to purchase with its own reserves the Zeroes to collateralize the bonds renders the scheme impracticable for most developing countries, which have limited reserves. The requirement by the SEC in SAB No. 75 that eligible debt tendered but not accepted by Mexico be written down to the tender price, or that sufficient loan-loss reserves be maintained to reflect a carrying value of such debt equal to the tender price, discouraged some banks from participating in the tender. It is possible to structure debt-reduction transactions to avoid the adverse accounting consequences of such a tender.
- The transaction could have been structured to qualify as a FAS No. 15 troubled-debt restructuring, thereby avoiding the immediate financial accounting loss suffered by banks that participated in the exchange.
- Mexico was unrealistic in anticipating that banks would tender their eligible debt at a discount which, when combined with the market discount of the bonds when issued, would result in an overall discount in excess of that at which the eligible debt was trading in the secondary market.

- The interest payable on the bonds was purely Mexican credit risk, depressing the anticipated market price at which the bonds would trade. Some credit enhancement, such as a one-year rolling-forward guaranty or collateral arrangement as has been suggested by Secretary Brady, might be desirable to support Mexico's interest obligation.

With the financial and credit-enhancement support that will apparently be forthcoming from the World Bank and the IMF, it is expected that new debt securitization and collateralization schemes will be developed based in part on credit support from such institutions. In addition, by taking advantage of FAS No. 15 and by carefully structuring debt-reduction transactions, both the banks and the debtor nations should be able to reach agreement on mutually beneficial transactions.

15.5 Conclusion

As a result of having substantially increased their capital and loan-loss reserves during recent years, the commercial bank creditors are in a much better position to absorb the losses inherent in their LDC loan portfolios and, therefore, to manage aggressively such portfolios. Thus, the banks are much freer to engage in debt/equity conversions and debt securitization and collateralization schemes similar to the Mexican debt exchange.

The Brady Plan has provided further encouragement to such schemes as a means to effect substantial LDC debt reduction. Although the World Bank, the IMF and Japan have pledged direct financial assistance to help finance debt-reduction schemes, as of the end of June 1989, the creditor banks' steering committee and the Mexican government had failed to reach agreement on a debt-reduction programme, although the substantial gap between their negotiating positions was narrowing.

The degree of flexibility and objectives of the banks in dealing with their LDC debt portfolios differ greatly. Perhaps it is unwise and impractical to seek an essentially single, common approach for all the banks to substantial debt reduction. Instead, if the bank steering committees and the debtor nations cannot reach prompt agreement on an overall approach, perhaps such committees should let the market match specific transactions or schemes to deal with the particular needs of certain banks and certain debtor nations. The development of innovative debt-reduction schemes will require a careful blending and balancing of the regulatory, accounting and tax environments affecting the creditor banks, on the one hand, with the cash-flow and political and economic limitations of the debtor nations.

The recent liberalization by the Federal Reserve Board of Regulation K has alleviated to a certain extent one of the regulatory hurdles to debt/equity conversions. Although debt/equity programmes have been curtailed recently in a number of countries, debt/equity conversions can be a powerful tool not only in reducing the LDC debt burden, as Chile has demonstrated, but also in serving as an engine of growth in encouraging new capital investment. Similarly, debt securitization and collateralization schemes can be quite effective in reducing the LDC debt burden while at the same time giving the banks, especially those seeking an exit vehicle from LDC lending, flexibility in determining whether to retain or liquidate their LDC debt.

These techniques and others currently being developed cannot, singly, be viewed as a 'solution' to the LDC debt problem. However, taken together they can, if not unduly restricted by government regulations, accounting rules and loan agreement provisions, produce a significant reduction in the debt burden to a level that the principal debtor nations should be able to manage comfortably. It is hoped that, with the support of the US government, as demonstrated by the Brady Plan, other OECD governments, the World Bank and the IMF, the LDC nations will be able to achieve with the commercial banks substantial debt reduction through debt/equity conversions, debt securitization and collateralization schemes and other innovative transactions.

Notes

1 World Bank, *World Bank Debt Tables, 1988–1989* (1989).
2 Ibid.
3 *World Bank Atlas* (1988).
4 See, Dep't Treas., *First Report to the Congress Concerning World Bank Strategy and Lending Programs in Debtor Countries* (March 1989), p. 18.
5 Mossberg, 'New "one worlders" are conservatives', *Wall St. J.*, 3 April 1989, at A1, col. 5; Wessel, 'U.S. debt to rest of world increased 40% to $532.5 billion last year', *Wall St. J.*, 30 June 1989, at A2, col. 3.
6 Dep't Treas., *Interim Report to the Congress Concerning International Dis-*

cussions on an International Debt Management Authority (March 1989), p. 13.

7 Remarks by Secretary of the Treasury Nicholas F. Brady to the Brookings Institution and the Bretton Woods Committee Conference on Third World Debt, 10 March 1989.

8 'Executive board adopts guidelines for role of fund in debt strategy', *IMF Survey*, 29 May 1989, p. 172.

9 Ibid.

10 *Wall St. J.*, 2 June 1989, at A12, col. 6.

11 12 U.S.C. sections 611–31 (1980 & Supp. 1988).

12 12 U.S.C. sections 1841–50 (1980 & Supp. 1988).

13 12 C.F.R. sections 211.1–211.45 (1988).

14 12 C.F.R. sections 225.1–225.43 (1988).

15 12 U.S.C. section 615(c) (1980).

16 Ibid. at section 601.

17 Ibid. section 1843.

18 Ibid. sections 611–31 (1980 & Supp. 1988).

19 Ibid. section 615(c).

20 12 C.F.R. section 211.5.

21 12 U.S.C. section 1843(c)(6) (1980 & Supp. 1988).

22 Ibid. section 1843(c)(7).

23 Ibid. sections 21ff.

24 Ibid. section 615(c).

25 12 C.F.R. section 1843(c)(2) (1980 & Supp. 1988).

26 12 C.F.R. section 211.5(e).

27 Ibid. section 225.12(b).

28 12 C.F.R. section 211.5(f), 3 *Fed. Banking L. Rep. (CCH)*, para. 31,451 (4 March 1988).

29 12 C.F.R. section 211.5(f) (1988), amended by 12 C.F.R. section 211.5(f), 3 *Fed. Banking L. Rep. (CCH)*, para. 31,451 (1988).

30 12 U.S.C. section 24 (Seventh) (1980 & Supp. 1988).

31 12 U.S.C. section 29.

32 No-Objection Letter No. 87–10, dated 27 November 1987, from Peter Lieberman, Assistant Director, Legal Advisory Services Division of the Office of the Comptroller, reprinted in *Fed. Banking L. Rep. (CCH)*, para. 84,039, and No-Objection Letter No. 88–7, dated 20 May 1988, also from Peter Lieberman, reprinted in *Fed. Banking L. Rep. (CCH)*, para. 84,047.

33 N.Y. Banking Law section 97(5) (*McKinney Supp.* 1989).

34 Ibid.

35 Accounting Standards Executive Committee of the American Institute of Certified Public Accountants, *Practice Bulletin No. 4* (May 1988).

36 American Institute of Certified Public Accountants, *Notice to Practitioners* (May 1985).

37 'Accounting for loan swaps', Comptroller of the Currency, *Banking Circular* 200, 4 *Fed. Banking L. Rep. (CCH)*, para. 51,145 (22 May 1985).

38 Invitation from Gustavo Petrocelli, Minister of Finance and Public Credit of the United Mexican States, to the Banks Party to Mexico's Public Sector Restructure and New Restructure Agreements and 1983 and 1984 New Money Agreements, to Exchange Existing Indebtedness for United Mexican States Collateralized Floating Rate Bonds Due 2008 (18 January 1988).

39 Ibid., app. III, Letter from Price Waterhouse.

40 Financial Accounting Standards Board, *Accounting Standards Original Pronouncements*, p. 169.

41 See 26 U.S.C.A. section 166 (1988).

42 Notice 89–58, I.R.B. 1989–20.

43 26 U.S.C. section 901 (1988).

44 26 U.S.C. section 904(a) (1988).

Index

Index compiled by Robert Spicer